Freedom and culture in Western society

What does freedom mean? Does everyone in Western liberal democracies enjoy maximum freedom? Has freedom become a dogma, the meaning and justification of which has been forgotten? Critically examining the conceptions of freedom of some of the leading contemporary philosophers from Isaiah Berlin to Charles Taylor, Hans Blokland explores the value and significance that freedom has acquired in our political consciousness. He looks specifically at:

- Positive and Negative Freedom
- Emancipation and Paternalism
- Freedom and Cultural Politics

On a theoretical level, Hans Blokland shows that it is possible to have a reasonable discussion on the meaning of contested concepts such as freedom and autonomy. Crucially, he investigates how political communities could enlarge the capacity of their citizens to master their own lives, without unacceptable interference in their private realm. Because the ability to participate in culture is regarded as one of the important conditions for individual freedom, in this context particular attention is devoted to the legitimation, as well as the opportunities and bounds, of a cultural policy. In this manner the book not only addresses the question what we can *know* about values like freedom and autonomy, but also of what we can *do* to foster their realisation.

First published in Dutch, this book was awarded the Pieter de la Court prize by the Royal Netherlands Academy of Arts and Sciences and the Political Science prize by the Netherlands Political Science Association. It has been extensively updated to include material from the United States, Great Britain, France and Sweden as well as from The Netherlands.

Hans Blokland works as a Fellow of the Royal Netherlands Academy of Arts and Sciences at Erasmus University, Rotterdam.

ROUTLEDGE STUDIES IN SOCIAL AND POLITICAL THOUGHT

Freedom and culture in Western society

Hans Blokland

Translated by Michael O'Loughlin

London and New York

First published as *Wegen naar vrijheid: Autonomie, emancipatie en cultuur in de westerse wereld* in 1991 by BOOM of Amsterdam.

First published in English in 1997
by Routledge
11 New Fetter Lane, London EC4P 4EE

Simultaneously published in the USA and Canada
by Routledge
29 West 35th Street, New York, NY 10001

© 1991, 1995 BOOM of Amsterdam.
English language translation © 1997 Routledge

Typeset in Times by Routledge
Printed and bound in Great Britain by T. J. International, Padstow,
Cornwall

British Library Cataloguing in Publication Data
A catalogue record for this book is available from the British Library

Library of Congress Cataloging in Publication Data
A catalogue record for this book has been requested

ISBN 0–415–15000–0

It may be that, without the pressure of social forces, political ideas are stillborn: what is certain is that these forces, unless they clothe themselves in ideas, remain blind and undirected.

(Isaiah Berlin)

A nation is not civilized because a handful of its members are successful in acquiring large sums of money and in persuading their fellows that a catastrophe will occur if they do not acquire it. . . . What matters to a society is less what it owns than what it is and how it uses its possessions. It is civilized in so far as its conduct is guided by a just appreciation of spiritual ends, in so far as it uses its material resources to promote the dignity and refinement of the individual human beings who compose it.

(Richard Tawney)

As our traditional objectives are gradually fulfilled, and society becomes more social-democratic with the passing of the old injustices, we shall turn our attention increasingly to other, and in the long run more important, spheres – of personal freedom, happiness, and cultural endeavour: the cultivation of leisure, beauty, grace, gaiety, excitement, and of all the proper pursuits, whether elevated, vulgar, or eccentric, which contribute to the varied fabric of a full private and family life.

We do not want to enter the age of abundance, only to find that we have lost the values which might teach us how to enjoy it.

(Anthony Crosland)

CONTENTS

Preface

Everyone knows what freedom means. Until you ask him or her what this meaning is. In Western liberal democracies everyone also knows that the citizens in these political systems enjoy maximum freedom, until you ask them to justify this conviction. Freedom has become a dogma. This value forms the basis of our civilization and of our political consciousness, but often we have forgotten its meaning and justification. Also, in our world it is considered so evident that citizens are free that enlargement of their freedom is seen as superfluous. We regard a policy to this end as a threat to, rather than as a stimulus of, this value.

In this book, the significance and value which the concept of freedom could have in our society is analysed. Also studied is how political communities could enlarge the capacity of their citizens to be masters of their own lives, without unacceptable interference in their private realm. Because being able to participate in culture is regarded as one of the important conditions for individual freedom, in this context particular attention is devoted to the opportunities and boundaries of a cultural policy.

In books the discussions are generally on various theoretical levels. So too in this book. On the most concrete level, its thesis is that in present-day Western liberal democracies there is great social inequality in the ability to acquire and exercise freedom and that the opportunities offered by these political systems for developing this value, are insufficiently exploited.

On a higher theoretical level, the book tries to demonstrate that it is possible (although we will never arrive at an 'objective' or 'universal' conclusion) to have a reasonable and rational discussion on normative issues in which 'essentially contested concepts' like freedom, autonomy, emancipation, paternalism or cultural participation play a pivotal role. Hence, a central purpose of the book is to counter relativism, a relativism which, under the influence of behaviourism and postmodernism, has become exceptionally strong in contemporary social and political science and in our society.

The book does not only deal with the question of what we can *know* about the meaning of concepts like freedom or autonomy, but also of what we can *do*. In this case, it is not just trying to develop a plausible conception of freedom, the practical question is also addressed of how political communities could enlarge the capacity of their citizens to be masters of their own lives. In this manner it is attempted to bridge the gap between social and political philosophy on the one hand, and empirical social and political science on the other. Generally, both disciplinary streams hardly ever meet. As a consequence, the results are often either normative theories without practical meaning or empirical theories without depth and direction.

This book already has a long history. I started to write in the summer of 1987 and completed a first manuscript in the autumn of 1990. This was published by EBURON under the title *Vrijheid Autonomie Emancipatie: Een Politiekfilosofische en Cultuurpolitieke Beschouwing* (Freedom Autonomy Emancipation: A Politico–Philosophical and Cultural Analysis). For this I received my doctorate in early 1991 at the Erasmus University in Rotterdam. My mentor was professor J. M. M. de Valk. He is the first whom I would like to thank here for the moral and intellectual support which I received from him during these years.

I was also surprised by the positive reception accorded my book by the media and my colleagues, from whom, after all, I had distanced myself somewhat. It was awarded the Pieter de la Court prize by the Royal Netherlands Academy of the Arts and Sciences and the political science prize 1992 by the Netherlands Political Science Association. However, most important in this context was that the Netherlands National Science Foundation and the Trustfunds of the Erasmus University awarded a subsidy to make an English translation of the thesis.

For this translation, I decided to rewrite and expand the book on a number of important points. The literature had to be updated and I wanted to supplement the empirical data, which originally applied mainly to the Dutch situation, with material from the United States, Great Britain, France and Sweden. The book has ultimately been completely revised and because of the many changes and adjustments it was decided to publish it under a new title.

In the revision, too, I have been supported by a number of people. I want to mention two by name here. In the first place, thanks are due to the late Professor Mark van de Vall, with whom I was able to collaborate in the last years of his life. His boundless passion for the science, as well as his great capacity for friendship, contributed enormously to the success of this undertaking, and secured for years my faith in the possibility of an academic *community*. In the second place, I thank Talja Potters, who checked the text of large sections of the book and has also contributed in many other ways, which cannot be adequately described in this context, toward its completion. I dedicate this book to her and to Mark.

Hans Blokland
Rotterdam, December 1995

1   General introduction

CULTURAL PARTICIPATION IN WESTERN LIBERAL DEMOCRACIES

In our Western world, freedom is also unequally divided. Certainly, in general everyone has a constitutionally protected personal realm within which he can go his own way undisturbed by others. But the material and non-material conditions for everyone to do something with this freedom are not equal. Not all citizens of the former 'Free West' have the opportunity to develop their capacities fully and be really masters of their own life.

Over the last century, attempts to change this situation have concentrated on the material level. And not without success: prosperity has grown enormously and mutual differences have become smaller, even if in recent decades in countries like the United States, Great Britain and the Netherlands that levelling has been again reversed. The cultural aspects of individual freedom, certainly just as essential, have received less attention. After the Second World War, for the first time various Western social institutions, political parties and authorities seriously set themselves the goal of levelling somewhat the great social inequality in the capacity to participate in culture. However, to date, the cultural dissemination policy to this end has not turned out to be very successful. This applies to the dissemination of art, literature, knowledge – of everything which makes a culture into civilization and, as shall be argued, freedom into autonomy.

Empirical research, which will be extensively examined in Chapter 7, points out again and again that cultural participation is declining in absolute figures, or at best is remaining at the same level. It would also appear that people from the lower classes are turning away from culture. Increasingly, it is the higher, better educated and salaried strata which profit from the existing art subsidies. Of current visitors to theatres, concert halls and museums, two-thirds to three-quarters have followed a higher professional or university education. Research also shows that the average time spent on reading books, journals and newspapers during the last four decades has declined sharply, and that reading has also increasingly become an almost exclusive activity of an economic and cultural elite.

People with a relatively low educational level born after 1950, thus after the introduction and expansion of television, have largely abandoned the written word.

This inequality in being able to participate in culture is not an accident. Although nowadays most people have had a better education than their parents, social educational inequality has hardly declined. Children from higher milieux still have a considerably better and longer education than children from lower socio-economic classes and therefore get more opportunities to participate in culture. This inequality is not exclusive either. Research shows that a social 'dichotomy' within a number of Western societies has become more than a theoretical possibility. For example, paid work is increasingly carried out by a small group of people in the prime of life, between thirty and fifty years old. This privileged group have better incomes, have had higher educations, therefore come mainly from the same social milieu, make the most use of all kinds of cultural facilities and subsidies, are most often members of political parties, action groups and pressure groups and therefore exercise the strongest political influence, and they are people who still read and visit museums, concerts and theatrical performances.

In brief, it is difficult to maintain that in Western liberal democracies, since the end of the Second World War, for example, there has been or continues to be a levelling in the field of the cultural aspects of individual freedom. Even growing differences are imaginable.

POSITIVE AND NEGATIVE FREEDOM

Although the material and non-material aspects of freedom are related, the division of knowledge and culture cannot be seen separately from the distribution of work, incomes and power, this books deals primarily with the cultural dimension of individual freedom. The reason for this, as has already been remarked, is that it has received relatively little attention in politics or in scientific discussion.

A central question in the following chapters will be how governments or other institutions can make a cultural–political contribution to the development of individual freedom. This latter pursuit is not without problems. The most important question is how a balance can be found between what, in political science, are called 'negative' and 'positive' freedom. This could be dubbed an *emancipation dilemma*, a dilemma because it is a matter of two significant, but also partly conflicting, values which cannot be simultaneously fully realized and which will inevitably have to be weighed up against each other.[1]

Negative freedom can be defined as the area within which one can, undisturbed by others, do that or be that which lies within one's capacity. The greater this private realm, the bigger the negative freedom. The judgement that the government has no reason to interfere in the area of culture, that the citizens are old enough and wise enough to determine for themselves what is beautiful or ugly, good or bad, or that the government can only intervene in someone's private realm if the people involved cause damage to others, is mainly based on the negative conception of freedom.

People who, on the other hand, are of the opinion that the state does indeed have a task in the field of culture, generally appeal to the positive conception of freedom. *Positive freedom* or *autonomy* is a much more comprehensive and more fundamental value than its negative counterpart. It refers to people's capacity to independently give direction to their lives, or be masters of their own existence. The greater this capacity, the greater the positive freedom. Isaiah Berlin, who will be extensively discussed later, states that this conception of freedom arises from the desire to be able to choose for oneself and to be able to justify the choices made by referring to one's own ideas and goals – the desire therefore to be *somebody* and not just anybody, someone who is responsible for his deeds and not some object deprived of will, plaything of external forces and powers.

Negative and positive freedoms are partly complementary, partly overlapping values. One can only be master of one's own life if one is not coerced by others to do something one does not actually want to do. Positive freedom is broader because it also includes a notion of 'self-realization'. People must first have developed themselves to some extent if they want to take their own lives in their hands, independently of others. They must, for example, develop their judgement skills if they want to be in a position to make real choices: they must learn to distinguish alternatives, to evaluate and to choose. In order to make an autonomous choice one must, in addition, be aware of the possibilities of choice. Someone who has all his life been confronted with only 'popular' music has no real choice between Mozart and Springsteen.

The idea of autonomy or positive freedom is closely related to the humanistic ideal of culture, the ideal of personal development. The enlightened or autonomous person is seen here as a broadly developed personality, who is not swayed by prejudice, ignorance or habit, but consciously and with careful consideration steers his life, has resolutely taken his own fate in his hands. Both liberals and socialists, social democrats or radicals share this cultural ideal, partly based on the Enlightenment. However, there are differences of opinion on the answer to the question of how society must be organized in order to be able to realize this ideal. These differences of insight are to a high degree the result of a deviating image of man. More than socialists, liberals think that the individual is independently capable of developing his talents. In general, liberals regard the social environment as a potential threat rather than a stimulus to this development, and they therefore emphasize the negative freedom of the individual. Thus the concept of freedom is ultimately intended as a barrier against the people, against the community and the state, and is therefore anti-social in character.

The positive conception of freedom has been mainly formulated in socialist circles. Socialists have a more social image of man and assume to a higher degree that individuals can only develop in interaction with others. The development of intelligence is an illustration: the boundaries of what is possible are genetically determined, but these are rather far apart. The degree to which the potential present is developed is ultimately dependent on the stimuli received from the environment.

There is therefore an important difference between positive and negative freedom, which is relevant for cultural policy. It could be stated that negative freedom relates to the question of whether one can make possible choices undisturbed by others, while positive freedom is also concerned with the question of whether people really have anything to choose, whether they thus possess real choice alternatives and are competent to make a reasoned choice. Related to this is the fact that, in contrast to its positive counterpart, no one is needed for negative freedom. One preferably enjoys one's privacy on an uninhabited island. However, according to the advocates of positive freedom, one can only become autonomous with the help of others, in a culture.

THE EMANCIPATION DILEMMA

We will return to the idea of social cultural dissemination. Its goal is not to impose a specific ethical or aesthetic preference on people. The goal is to create the situation in which they themselves can make real choices, choices thus on the basis of a reasonably developed capacity for argued choice and a reasonable knowledge of the available alternatives. This capacity and this knowledge can only be acquired through learning. The acquisition of culture, and with it of positive freedom, is therefore closely connected to enculturation, education and socialization. A society and its political frameworks can play an important role in this.

It is obvious that this learning process, which is indispensable for the development of individual autonomy, is at loggerheads with the equally significant negative freedom of the individual. While it is true to say that, to a high degree, a person only develops due to the education or stimuli which they receive from their environment, this development first becomes valuable if they are also allowed the freedom to do something with it. The inevitable balance between positive and negative freedom, which will have to be made by every serious socio-political theory, can be regarded as the *first dimension* of the emancipation dilemma. This dimension concerns not only children, of whom it can be assumed they have not yet developed any fixed personal preferences of their own and that their capacity for judgement leaves much to be desired, it also refers to adults (in so far as these can be identified) who do not look to their own initiative for alternatives which, if they were familiar with them, they would possibly highly esteem.

Cultural critics who want to bring about change in the current cultural preferences, seen as objectionable or not optimal, run up against the concomitant problem, which can be seen as the *second dimension* of the emancipation dilemma. If the first dimension refers mainly to an individuality with personal preferences which have yet to be formed, with the second dimension, which can only be distinguished analytically from the first, it is a matter of already existing preferences. The relevant problem is shared by numerous socialists, Christian Democrats and social liberals, who in Anglo-Saxon countries are often designated 'radicals' and in the countries of the European continent generally as 'progressives'. The critics concerned emphasize that the values, objectives, desires and preferences of the individual are to an important degree a product of the social interaction with his environment. The authenticity, and thus the status, of the individual preferences can therefore be placed somewhat in perspective. It can be supposed that the individual has developed preferences which, while they are perceived personally as valuable and original, are in fact a casual, if not objectionable, product of the existing social structures and are not optimal: there are wishes and accompanying gratifications which the individual would prefer to current preferences, if familiar with these alternatives. That the latter is not the case, can have two causes. First, the parties concerned can possess too little of the volition required for autonomy to look for alternative truths, to research whether what has been assumed up to now is indeed true, good or beautiful. Second, and perhaps partly explanatory of this, the existing social structures and processes can make it impossible, to a greater or lesser degree, for the people concerned to come in contact with alternatives. These can also lead them to the conviction that their present preferences are the only ones imaginable. Certainly, if one is not in agreement with these cultural preferences, it is an obvious step to want to change the mechanism of socialization which is operative in every culture. The will for this has always been present in radicals or progressives (and equally in conservative circles). For example, within socialism and schools such as the Frankfurter Schule there has always been an aversion to mass culture, a culture which is seen mainly as the product of the culture industry and which is mainly prominent through its flatness and uniformity.

Because progressives are generally inspired by democracy and egalitarianism, they must wrestle with a dilemma with regard to the regrettable preferences (cf. Benton 1982). This consists of the following: on the one hand, on the basis of the democratic principles subscribed to, they want to respect the existing individual preferences, while, on the other hand, they consider these objectionable, due to content or for reasons of the way in which they have been created, and want to change them. On the one hand, therefore, they assume on the basis of the negative conception that people should be treated as responsible beings, who are capable of making autonomous choices or developing preferences, and should not be patronized in this. However, on the other hand, they refuse to take completely the existing preferences as starting point, as this has the drawback that one is uncritical with regard to the manner in which these have come into being and one can never create the situation which, if they were familiar with it, the people concerned would prefer to the existing one. The question is, once again, how can this preferable situation be shaped without limiting unacceptably the negative freedom of the individual.

To resume: if one wants to disseminate culture and, at the same time, wants to take negative freedom seriously, then it is not possible to implement changes without the permission of those who are affected. However, it will not be easy to obtain this agreement due to the existing cultural preferences. If no changes are enforced, this means in practice accepting the continuing existence of a social system and the cultural preferences and needs produced by it, which are hard to square with the ideals of development cherished. It is, therefore, one thing or the other. If one wants to completely respect the sovereignty of people's cultural preferences, then it will be necessary to temper ambitions with regard to the self-development or cultural emancipation of large parts of the population. If, on the other hand, we want to make the development of the many possible, then it will have to be accepted, as Benton has remarked (see Chapter 5) that this cannot always be self-development.

The task of getting out of this dilemma as unscathed as possible can be regarded as one of the most important cultural–political problems. In this book, an attempt is made to contribute a solution to this. The development of a conception of autonomy will be made, which makes it possible to break out of the dilemma described above in a manner acceptable to the parties concerned. A central question in what follows will therefore be how government, in particular, by implementing a cultural policy, can contribute to enlarging the positive freedom of the individual, without his negative freedom being unacceptably limited.

Before we start on all this, however, some attention will first be devoted to the nature, possibilities and sense of a political scientific analysis of concepts like freedom and autonomy. Considering the scepticism which has developed in our age in this field, this would not appear to be a superfluous exercise. Also, the objective of this study can be more precisely defined.

ESSENTIALLY CONTESTED CONCEPTS

Terms like 'freedom', 'autonomy', 'emancipation', 'democracy' and 'paternalism' form what the American philosopher W. B. Gallie has entitled essentially-contested concepts (1956: 169). The meaning of these concepts can be endlessly discussed because they are always defined in the context of a particular *Weltanschauung*. If this view is changed then these concepts also acquire other meanings. *Weltanschauungen* are inevitably based on a number of metaphysical, epistemological and ethical assumptions which are always contestable. The debate about their 'correct' meaning, therefore, always remains open just like the debate on and between the various world views.[2]

The idea that concepts can never be given uncontested contents, is naturally also contestable in itself. According to Gray, it is an expression of 'the pluralist, morally and politically polyarchic character of contemporary Western liberal society' (Gray 1977: 337). People with a monist philosophy, who are of the opinion that there is a recognizable order in the cosmos, will not want to subscribe to the thesis concerned. The process of rationalization is taking place within our Western culture, notwithstanding, and unlike what Gray suggests, these people are probably still in the majority. Many amongst us, usually unconsciously, assume that each word has only one correct meaning. Richard Rorty writes that they believe 'in an order beyond time and change which both determines the point of human existence and establishes a hierarchy of responsibilities'. The intellectuals who do not share this belief are according to him 'far outnumbered (even in the lucky, rich, literate democracies) by people who believe that there *must* be one. Most non-intellectuals are still committed either to some form of religious faith or to some form of Enlightenment rationalism' (Rorty 1989: xv). We will see, therefore, that numerous authors, with a vehemence only explicable by such a belief, have been looking for the last word on – the only correct meaning of – freedom.

Despite the essentially contested character of socio-political concepts, it is unnecessary, and certainly also undesirable, to conclude that every debate on their content is meaningless or inevitably without issue. It is not the case that every meaning forms an incomparable product of a completely autonomous, completely closed ideology or philosophy, which has no similarity at all to other visions of reality. If this were indeed the case, then there could be no debate at all. What could the participants talk about to each other? In this context, Gray rightly notes that 'unless divergent theories or world views have something in common, their constituent concepts cannot be "contested", even though their proponents are in conflict. References to definitional "contests" have a point only if there is something which is not treated as "contestable"' (Gray 1977: 342, cf. Rorty 1989: 40 ff.). Extreme interpretations of the 'contestability thesis' are therefore self-contradictory, as in that case there would be no more criteria even to identify the relevant concepts and disputes.

TASK AND METHOD OF POLITICAL SCIENCE

By going somewhat deeper into the methodology of political science, the possibilities and the meaning of the debate on terms like freedom and autonomy can be made clearer. Political scientists have two tasks. In the first place, they attempt to make the presumptions of political thinking explicit and to evaluate them. In the second place, they attempt to develop general theories or models in which our values, objectives and empirical knowledge are consistently organized or reorganized. Political science includes both empirical and normative political theory. These two areas of theory can be epistemologically distinguished with regard to the questions on which they concentrate: the questions about 'being' and 'belonging' differ analytically, at least within Western thought. The epistemological status of the answers, however, show strong correspondences. Behaviouristic political scientists, who only want to concern themselves, with 'empirical' questions, and believe they do so, are insufficiently aware of how implicit principles in the meta-physical, epistemological and ethical field limit their perception, description and explanation of political reality. They are therefore not practitioners of political science, who through their distance, objectivity and systematic approach distinguish themselves from their philosophical opponents, gener-ally held to be woolly, confused and irresponsibly engaged. They are just bad political scientists.

Because political science is always practised within the framework of a particular philosophy or paradigm, it is inevitably politically involved (cf. Bernstein 1976; Bluhm 1978; Taylor 1967, 1971). Thus, every political sci-entist is also a politician. However, not every politician is also a political scientist. The latter is distinguished by the capacity and willingness to make his principles explicit and to rationalize them, and by the awareness of how these direct his perception and explanation of reality. He is characterized, in short, by what William Connolly called his 'theoretical self-conscious-ness'. This self-awareness can be acquired through a confrontation, sup-ported by scientific theory, of his own thinking, bound as it is to time and place, with that of others.[3] Knowledge of the history of political thought and of the theory of science is indispensable for this. Nowadays, this knowledge, as a consequence of the hard distinction made by the posi-tivists between, on the one hand, empirical political theory or science and, on the other, normative political theory or philosophy, is still only expected from political philosophers. Unjustly so; every serious practitioner of polit-ical science is also a political philosopher, just as every political philoso-pher – if their theories are to have any reality value and therefore not float like soap bubbles above reality – must also practice political science (see Chapter 2).

Through its attempts to make the starting points of our thinking explicit, and to evaluate them, political science is by nature a critical science. It raises for discussion the values, ideas, attitudes which are taken as a matter of course by people because that is how they were taught; it has always been like this. In this discussion or evaluation, the thought is checked for internal consistency and empirical support. A social image of man, for example, is difficult to combine with an atomistic vision of society. And images of man, on which every political theory is based, gain in 'actual' plausibility when they chime with psychological and sociological insights gained in a particu-lar acceptable paradigm. (Of course it is not a matter of bridging the logical gap between values and facts, but of the 'actual' gap.)

If one wants to reach a consensus when disputing the inner consistency of someone's ideas, then one will attempt to make it plausible that A and B are related, and that the opponent, because they subscribe to A, must also sub-scribe to B. A precondition for the carrying on of a meaningful discussion which is ended with a joint conclusion is therefore that there are one or more shared principles which can serve as a starting point, as a basis. John Rawls writes about this in his *A Theory of Justice*, in a chapter on the justification of moral theories in general:

> Being designed to reconcile by reason, justification proceeds from what all parties to the discussion hold in common. Ideally, to justify a conception of justice to someone is to give him a proof of its principles from premises that we both accept, these principles having in turn consequences that match our considered judgements. Thus mere proof is not justification. A proof simply displays logical relations between propositions. But proof becomes justification once the starting points are mutually recognized.
>
> (Rawls 1971: 580–1; cf. Rawls 1987)

A precondition for a fertile debate is therefore also that the participants want to have a logically consistent view of reality. If they do not meet this (Kantian) condition, then every discussion is naturally useless in advance.

This brings us to the epistemological basis of a political theory. Rawls' ideas can be a starting point here. According to him, the development of a political theory plausible within a particular culture, boils down to the organization or reorganization in the most consistent manner possible of the ideas and intuitions, usually incoherent and ill-considered, which are found in this civilization. We do this by going 'back and forth' as it were between, on the one hand, the existing feelings and judgements and, on the other hand, the abstract, consistent theory which is to be formulated. The first ideas are the starting point: one attempts to deduce the theory from this in the most acceptable manner. In doing so, it is attempted to have the coherence between the existing judgements and theory as great as possible. The immediate plausibility of the latter is, after all, the strongest. From the abstract theory, it is then argued back to the concrete approaches. It can now appear that some of these cannot be resolved in a single theory. It is then necessary to either adjust the theory or, if this is not possible, to reject one or more of the original judgements. By going back and forth in this manner, we can ultimately achieve what Rawls calls *reflective equilibrium* (1971: 20),[4] a balance which incidentally is not necessarily stable, in which our general theoretical principles coincide with our, until then, unexamined convictions.

The plausibility of a political theory is now not only dependent on its coherence with the original convictions, convictions which naturally cannot claim absolute validity or indisputability, but also on the consistency of the entire theoretical construction which is based on this. A justification, writes Rawls, 'rests upon its entire conception and how it fits in with and organizes our considered judgements in reflective equilibrium . . . justification is a matter of the mutual support of many considerations, of everything fitting together into one coherent view' (Rawls 1971: 579; cf. Rorty

1989: 67 ff.). The empirical support which can be found for the theory can thus be included among those considerations – something which Rawls does not do explicitly (but, naturally, always implicitly).

To resume, the conception of freedom to be developed in this book will depend on three factors for its plausibility. In *the first place*, on its empirical support: a conception which, for example, requires of people that they arrive at a particular action or idea completely independent of and uninfluenced by others has little reality value. This, in view of our knowledge of the actual functioning of people, knowledge which is valid within a number of psychological paradigms regarded as plausible in our present culture.[5] In *the second place*, on its internal consistency: it cannot argue, on the one hand, that individuals should be left completely alone and on the other, be based on the knowledge that people first develop their individuality in interaction with others. In *the third place*, its plausibility is determined by its coherence with already existing moral intuitions and ideas. The feeling or the notion that it is essential that people be left a personal realm in which they can go their own way undisturbed by others, is widespread and deeply felt, and for this reason conceptions which do not do justice to this lose credibility.

In what follows, it will become clear that in our culture there is no lack of shared intuitions and knowledge which can serve as a basis for a fertile debate about freedom. In Western political and social theory, there is a greater agreement on the meaning of the content of this concept than the sometimes vehement debates would lead us to suspect. In line with the tasks set here for political science, a second objective of this book therefore is to make explicit and critically evaluate the most important assumptions of contemporary Western thinking about freedom, and the formulation of the most consistent synthesis possible of our convictions and knowledge in this field. (The study of the way in which, for example, the state could, by implementing a cultural policy, contribute to the enlargement of the positive freedom of the individual, without his negative freedom being unacceptably limited in the process, was already mentioned as a first, more specific objective.)

STRUCTURE OF THE DISCOURSE

The starting point of the discussion in the following chapter is formed by the two concepts of freedom which were developed by Isaiah Berlin in his lecture *Two concepts of liberty*. This was chosen for a number of reasons. First, because of the central place which Berlin has occupied in the debate on freedom since 1958, the year of his speech. Wellnigh all authors comment on his position directly or indirectly and this can serve therefore as something on which to hang the argument. Second, because the majority of the questions which are relevant for the objective set here have been looked at in the discussion set forth by Berlin. With the help of this discussion, therefore, it is possible to make a justified selection from the great quantity of literature available. Third, it is Berlin, above all, who has warned against the ways in which arguments for positive freedom, in theory and practice, can end in totalitarianism. Precisely because it will be defended here that positive freedom should have a more central place in our hierarchy of values than is currently the case, Berlin's standpoint is an attractive point of departure. The incorporation of his acute and largely justified critique of, and warning against, certain interpretations of this conception of freedom can only make our own position stronger. Fourth, and finally, Berlin is a suitable point of departure as his metaphysical, epistemological and, to a large extent, his ethical principles too are representative of the mainstream of the Western intellectual tradition and are also shared by this writer. Thanks to these common principles, there is a sturdy basis for a fertile debate and for an alternative concept of freedom equally acceptable within the Western tradition of thought.

In the third chapter, we will be examining the positive concept of freedom. Berlin, in his treatment of this concept, has mainly exposed its less desirable sides. He emphasizes what he considers to be the possibility offered by this theory for justifying totalitarianism. It requires no commentary that, in doing so, he has invited much criticism from the advocates of the positive conception. Partly on the basis of this critique in this chapter, it will be attempted to further develop the positive conception, only summarily described by Berlin. This will be done, in so far as this is possible, from the viewpoint of the individual. The question will therefore be: which demands can be made from this individual or his situation before he can be called 'free' in the positive sense?

In the fourth chapter, attention will be turned to the question of how someone's positive freedom can be impeded or promoted by his social environment, and how realistic the chance of a totalitarian result is with the latter. The critique of the social models which are one-sidedly based on the negative conception of freedom, will be treated by going deeper into the thinking of a number of theoreticians, representative of the positive conception. Some overlap is therefore unavoidable, but, on the other hand, the coherence between the various parts of a concept of freedom will become more visible and it will avoid taking standpoints from their context.

In conformity with the earlier commentary on essentially contested concepts, the latter is a general principle for this book. As every conception is indissolubly linked to a particular *Weltanschauung*, this view, if justice is to be done to the concept concerned, must be involved in its presentation and analysis. It is better therefore to go deeper into a limited number of standpoints, than to take from a large quantity of conceptions that one which is apparently a support of one's own position.

In Chapter 4, the spotlight is chiefly on the social context of individual autonomy and a first dimension of the emancipation dilemma. In the fifth chapter, the second dimension of this dilemma is primarily examined. The question here will therefore be how the existing socialization and preference structure can be broken up without the negative freedom of the individual being unacceptably restricted. In particular, the possible role of paternalism will be discussed here.

In the sixth chapter, an attempt will be made to arrive at a synthesis of the insights earlier acquired, and also to make a connection on a theoretical level between promoting individual autonomy and the social or 'vertical' dissemination of culture.

Finally, in Chapter 7, the cultural policy implemented in five Western countries since the end of the Second World War will be examined more concretely. These are the United States, Great Britain, France, Sweden and the Netherlands. The most important questions here are: first, how participation in cultural activities is socially disseminated; second, how it is attempted in practice to promote cultural participation and with it the development of individual autonomy; third, to what extent this goal has been realized; and, fourth, how the policy can if necessary be improved.

2 Isaiah Berlin on positive and negative freedom

INTRODUCTION

Isaiah Berlin was born on 6 June 1909, the son of a Jewish timber merchant in Riga, capital of Latvia. In 1915, he left with his parents for St Petersburg, where he was to witness both Russian revolutions. From there, the family, characterized by Berlin as 'bourgeois liberal' emigrated to England in 1919. His father was an anglophile, which explains his choice of destination. In England, he attended St Paul's School in London and Corpus Christi College in Oxford. He was to spend the greater part of his academic career attached to the University of Oxford, as professor of social and political theory (1957–67), chairman of Wolfson College (1966–75) and Fellow of All Souls College (1932–8 and 1960 to the present). Berlin, who was knighted in 1957, was also chairman of the British Academy (1974–8). He is mainly known for his work in the history of ideas and political theory, but has also been active in the fields of theory of knowledge and science, literature (especially Russian) and musicology.[1]

A thread running through Berlin's work is his crusade against the widespread monistic conviction that there is only one correct answer to every question and that all correct answers can be arranged in a harmonious manner into a single knowable rational system. Opposed to this belief, which according to Berlin has led to inertia, intolerance and cruelty, he suggests that there are many values, each of which is worth emulating in itself yet which are conflicting, so that inevitably they must be weighed up against each other. In his history of ideas, which can be characterized as a sort of phenomenology of Western consciousness, he studies in particular how this idea of pluralism has developed since the end of the eighteenth century. The philosophers Giambattista Vico (1668–1744) and Johann Gottfried Herder (1744–1803), and above all the Russian writer Alexander Herzen (1812–70) are his heroes in this history.

It could be said that Berlin's thinking has been formed by three traditions: a Russian one, a British one and a Jewish one (cf. Hausheer 1983: 50–1). The most important thing he retained from his Russian youth is perhaps the awareness of the power of ideas. Of all the powers which have formed the modern era, this one seems to Berlin to be of primary importance. Anyone who has studied the history of the nineteenth and twentieth centuries, will realize that this applies to Russia in particular. If, therefore, one wants to understand and, if possible, guide in positive directions the strongest motives behind the history of individuals, groups and civilizations, it will be necessary to analyse and evaluate the concepts and categories which are at the bottom of human thinking and action.

The second formative tradition, that of careful British Empiricism, compensates perhaps for the first, characterized by passions and emotions (cf. Brodsky 1989). Despite his Russian origins, Berlin, as is often the case with emigrés, seems more British than the British themselves. In an interview in the Dutch newspaper *NRC-Handelsblad* of 21 October 1983, he said: 'I owe all my ideas to Great Britain. The idea of tolerance, the striving for a decent society, the awareness that human beings are imperfect, the deep faith in empirical methods, the conviction that the only source of knowledge about the world comes from experience and perception, all that comes from England.'

The last tradition is the Jewish one (cf. Jahanbegloo 1992: 85–90; 99–106). To this, he owes perhaps the awareness that people have a deep need to belong to an abiding community with its own cultural identity. Herder, unjustly seen as the father of nationalism, was the first to realize this according to Berlin (1973, 1976). Berlin and Herder therefore see the rationalist, cosmopolitan or universalist ideas of Enlightenment thinkers, and their accompanying rejection of *Gemeinschaftlichen* notions of tradition, convention and culture as being incorrect. Nevertheless, Berlin considers himself 'fundamentally' also as 'a liberal rationalist' (Jahanbegloo 1992: 70). He subscribes to the enlightenment ideals of thinkers like Voltaire, Condorcet, Helvetius and Holbach: they are important liberators from oppression, ignorance and prejudice. However, according to Berlin, their ideas are too simplistic. Just how simplistic can be learned from their opponents, thinkers like De Maistre, Burke, Hamann, Vico and Herder who together form what Berlin calls the 'Counter-Enlightenment'.

Berlin is a typical Anglo-Saxon analytical political philosopher. He was originally educated in Hegelian thinking, but soon rebelled against this and turned to the 'Oxford realism', whose most important exponents were thinkers like Russell, Moore, Price, Ryle and Kneale. Here, clarity was of the essence: 'Above all it stressed clarity of thought and language, and that was a great relief after the metaphysical rhetoric and mists of idealism' (Jahanbegloo 1992: 153). However, as we shall see, Berlin's occasionally somewhat archaic 'Russian' use of language, has not always contributed to an easy communication of his ideas. A large part of the discussion raised by Berlin consists therefore of an accumulation of differences of opinion on the right exegesis of his position.

In what follows here, Berlin's most important propositions will first be discussed; then his concept of liberty will be specifically examined. The critique of his original standpoints, which Berlin has unfolded or incorporated, will be borne in mind as much as possible. I will finish with a summary of the central differences of opinion which have arisen on the basis of this conception and which will be comprehensively treated in the following chapters.

BERLIN'S PHILOSOPHY

Epistemology and theory of science

One of Berlin's most famous political–philosophical essays is 'Does political theory still exist?' which appeared (originally in French) in 1961. In this, he launches a frontal attack on the behaviourist idea that with the acceptance of the logical gap between facts and values within political science, there was no longer any place for normative political theory. The behaviourists, inspired by Wiener Kreis's logical positivism, considered it useless to concern themselves further with questions which cannot, in their view, be answered in a scientifically correct manner. This was particularly true of the problems with which normative political theory has always been concerned: if the logical gap is accepted, the answers developed for these questions can never have an empirical or logical foundation. In the view of the behaviourists, therefore, answers and questions could be rejected as 'unscientific' and therefore useless. Just like breeding budgies, political theory was a nice hobby for after working hours, but for the rest should be excluded from the serious practice of science. (For an account of the restructuring of the political sciences, of the critique of this by the so-called revisionist philosophy of science, and Berlin's position in this discussion, see Bernstein (1976).)

Berlin powerfully disputes this overstated and somewhat arrogant conclusion. He harps on the continual, even primary importance of normative questions, points out the determining role which metaphysical, epistemological and ethical assumptions play in the perception, description and explanation of reality, and calls the idea that it is possible to eliminate this debatable element an epistemological misunderstanding (Berlin 1962: 154–8).

In Berlin's vision, heavily influenced by Vico, human thought and action are based on the image that people have formed of themselves and others, an image which is inherent to a particular way of looking at the world. If these images, models or paradigms change, then their perception and interpretation of 'reality' and their behaviour also changes. The models constitute social and political life and if you want to understand, explain or criticize this life it will therefore be necessary to investigate these models. It is not possible, as the logical positivists claim, to make a firm distinction between empirical and normative statements, and then confine oneself to the former category. Empirical statements are also permeated by normative assumptions, and it is thus impossible to ban these from the serious practice of science. The same can be said with regard to concepts like freedom, equality and justice. These, as we have already seen in Chapter 1, are after all an element of a particular model and therefore acquire divergent meanings within different *Weltanschauungen*. In order to be able to say something about these concepts, it will therefore be necessary to further investigate the visions of the world behind them.

Whether or not a particular model is accepted is determined by the degree to which it is capable of describing and explaining in a usable or acceptable manner the reality we experience, and by the degree to which it hereby does justice to a number of essential characteristics of man and the world which he can regard as being more or less permanent and universal. Berlin, referring to Kant, labels these 'permanent features of man and the world' as 'categories'. Of necessity, people think in terms of these categories, with the consequence that they assume them to be a matter of course. Examples of this are human traits such as rationality, the ability to make choices and arrive at moral judgments, the awareness of being somehow 'different' from the non-human world around us, and 'worldly' traits like three-dimensionality, causality and the irreversibility of time. These rather stable categories, which enable communication between different cultures and periods, are not logically necessary or a priori true, they must be regarded as 'brute facts' or as 'simply given' (Berlin 1962: 164–6). Political philosophers have always had a special interest in these categories. The more adequately they can incorporate these into their theories, the greater their reality value and persuasiveness (Berlin 1962a: 169–71).

However, it should not be deduced from the emphasis which Berlin lays on the role of subjective premises in the perception and explanation of events that he is a sceptic or a relativist. We can rightly dub as subjective empirical statements which are insufficiently supported by the 'facts' regarded as reliable and verifiable within a specific group of people. Terms like 'objective' and 'true' do have a meaning. While it is true that this is not definitively defined and can shift, this will remain within limits which are reasonably stable over longer periods of time, limits which are proposed and accepted by large, relevant groups of people. Where the line between 'objective' and 'subjective' must be drawn, therefore, writes Berlin in 'Historical Inevitability', nine years before the theorist of science Thomas Kuhn became famous with comparable ideas:

> is a question for ordinary judgment, that is to say for what passes as such in our society, in our own time and place, among the people to whom we are addressing ourselves, with all the assumptions which are taken for granted, more or less, in normal communication. Because there is no hard and fast line between 'subjective' and 'objective', it does not follow that there is no line at all.
>
> (Berlin 1953: 95; see also 96–104)

In the context of his epistemology, Berlin now sees two important tasks assigned to political philosophy. In the first place, it tries to make explicit the categories, concepts and models on which people's thinking and actions are based, without them generally being aware of this. In the second place, it attempts to critically evaluate these categories, concepts and models and, if necessary, adjust or replace them with more adequate ones (Berlin 1962a: 9; 1962b: 159; 1979: 27–31).

In the light of these two tasks for philosophy, what then are Berlin's own central principles?

Pluralism

In Berlin's vision, since the Greeks, Western thinking has been under the spell of value cognitivism, monism and rationalism. Numerous leading thinkers, from Plato and Aristotle to Augustine and Thomas Aquinas, and from Montesquieu and Condillac to Hegel and Marx, have assumed that there is a knowable, rational order present in the cosmos which bestowed sense and meaning on our life, that the values defined by this cosmic order were objective, universal and absolute and fitted into one harmonious whole in a logical and hierarchical manner, and that conflicts between truly rational people were in fact not possible and would be completely banished in the realizable, perfect, ideal society. (These principles are gone into further later in the chapter). Throughout his entire oeuvre, Berlin wages an unrelenting, impassioned battle against this main current in Western thought.[2] In the last section of 'Two Concepts of Liberty', he writes candidly: 'One belief, more than any other, is responsible for the slaughter of individuals on the altars of the great historical ideals . . . This is the belief that somewhere . . . there is a final solution. This ancient faith rests on the conviction that all the positive values in which men have believed must, in the end, be compatible, and perhaps even entail one another . . . But is this true?' (Berlin 1958: 167). Berlin thinks not. He is aware that he cannot *prove* that no order reigns in the cosmos, inspired by God, nature or reason. But from his concept of science it has already emerged that, in his view, it is possible to say something about the *plausibility* of this sort of premise: it is ultimately determined by their 'empirical' support or relevance. Our daily experience, argues Berlin, is that there are many values, each in itself worthy of respect, that these values regularly come into conflict with each other, and that in such a case choices must be made. The realization of one goal is often at the expense of the other; values must be constantly weighed up against each other; too much individual freedom leads to inequality; the enforcing of equality generally leads to unfreedom; nobility is often at daggers drawn with justice, rightness and justification with efficiency, etc. The hope that there is a theory in which all these values can be realized simultaneously and harmoniously is, in Berlin's view, false. There are many worthy yet incompatible goals and there will therefore always be a chance of conflict. This fact is unavoidable for Berlin: 'The necessity of choosing between absolute claims is an inescapable characteristic of the human condition' (Berlin 1959: 169). 'That we cannot have everything is a necessary, not a contingent, truth' (ibid.: 170; see also 1969: li; 1988: 11–8).

Considering this metaphysical principle, it is not strange that Berlin ascribes great significance to freedom: people attach so much value to the freedom to choose independently precisely because, according to him, this is the characteristic fact of the human condition. If ultimate universal values *did* exist and, therefore, there were never conflicting choices, then the continual wrestling with problems of choice would disappear and with it too the primary importance of freedom of choice (Berlin 1958: 118–20, 168). This also makes understandable why Berlin attaches so much value to pluralism, tolerance, the ability to see things in their proper perspective and incrementalism, and why he is warmly disposed to thinkers like John Stuart Mill and Alexander Herzen. Berlin discusses the two with so much devotion, esteem and understanding that it is clear that he feels strongly attached to their ideas. His essays on these authors therefore also give a picture of his own thought.

In 'Herzen and Bakunin on individual liberty' (1955), for example, Berlin lashes out fiercely at Bakunin and is full of admiration and esteem for Herzen. He dubs Bakunin, among other things, a 'childish', 'a-serious' and 'slovenly' thinker, and for him his writings consist mainly of 'hollow formulas', 'radical gibberish' and 'glib Hegelian nonsense'. In his view, Bakunin was often no more than a political adventurer, who driven on by an indiscriminate hatred of the established order and of every possible limitation of individual freedom, developed the most striking and irresponsible political ideas, or rather, slogans.[3]

Herzen, on the other hand, is in his eyes 'a political and therefore also moral philosopher of great significance', a senior, erudite, nuanced thinker of lasting importance, but also equipped with great imagination and passion. Berlin first encountered his work in the 1930s when 'Herzen became my hero for the rest of my life' (Jahanbegloo 1992: 13). It was Herzen who aroused his interest in the history of social and political thought. In contrast to Bakunin, Herzen craved to examine real political problems. These problems are, according to Berlin:

> the incompatibility of unlimited personal liberty with either social equality, or the minimum of social organization and authority; the need to sail precariously between the Scylla of individualist 'atomization' and the Charybdis of collectivist oppression; the sad disparity and conflict between many, equally noble human ideals; the nonexistence of 'objective', eternal, universal moral and political standards, to justify either coercion or resistance to it; the mirage of distant ends, and the impossibility of doing wholly without them.
>
> (Berlin 1955: 105)

Something more of Berlin's vision of man and society can be learned from his essay on John Stuart Mill. In his opinion, Mill's central principles are still valid (Berlin 1959: 201). (For the relation between Berlin and Mill, see also Wollheim 1979). He supports, among other things, Mill's belief that our knowledge is always restricted and provisional, that there is no universal, knowable, ultimate truth, that people are constantly developing towards something new and unique in a spontaneous interaction with their environment, that this capacity to make independent choices and develop oneself is the essential characteristic of mankind, and for precisely this reason people need a demarcated private sphere within which they can do what they elect to do, free from the intervention of others (Berlin 1958: 188–90, 206). Furthermore, Berlin shares Mill's fear of the pressure exerted by the mass on the individual in modern society to conform to the standard of the largest common denominator. Berlin also has understanding for his fear of tyranny by an intolerant democratic majority, and his fear of an anonymous mass, which from impotence and fear of making choices itself, of having to itself create values which in earlier periods were handed down by temporal and spiritual authorities, can look for peace and order, security and organization, and which believes it can find all this in an authority which, while clear and recognizable, is also extremely dangerous, undemocratic and irrational. But just like Mill, Berlin sees no other way out of this precarious situation except to argue for more democracy, more freedom and more education. 'Reason, education, self-knowledge, responsibility', Berlin echoes the classical humanist thinkers, 'What other hope is there for man, or has there ever been?' (Berlin 1958: 199).

Berlin, to put it briefly, is on the whole in agreement with Mill's vision of humanity. For him, too, the essence of man is his capacity to make independent choices and to be master of his own life. In this continuous process of choice, man realizes himself, and Berlin therefore regards it as a denial of someone's humanity when the party involved is not given the necessary space to lend direction to his life independently. Man is an autonomous being who is capable of formulating his own goals. Because, says Berlin, confirming Immanuel Kant, he is the source and creator of all values, man is an end in himself and therefore may never be used as a means for bringing the realization of other values closer, no matter which authority has defined these values (Berlin 1955: 87, 95, 101; 1958: 127, 137, 138, 157; 1964: 190). But to explain why freedom is so valuable, says Berlin, it is actually sufficient to state empirically that people in practice have always held that the freedom to make choices oneself is an indispensable element of being human: 'it is sufficient to say that those who have ever valued liberty for its own sake believed that to be free to choose, and not to be chosen for, is an inalienable ingredient in what makes human beings human' (Berlin 1969: lx).

Value relativism?

Finally, to complete these introductory remarks on Berlin's thought, it is necessary to investigate the question of whether Berlin is a value relativist.

The British political philosopher Bhikhu Parekh and the American Robert Kocis have interpreted him as such (Parekh 1982: 34, 43, 44; Kocis 1983: 374–5, 387), and it must be admitted that Berlin perhaps gives grounds for this in a number of statements. It is not for nothing that Richard Wollheim suspects that in years to come the question will increasingly arise: 'Did Berlin believe, or did he not, in a common human nature?' (Wollheim 1991: 64).[4]

As stated, Berlin sees man as the source of all values. There is no knowable authority which is higher than the individual, and we do not possess an objective criterion against which the correctness of values chosen by different people can be measured. All values, which are not a means to realize another, higher value are therefore, writes Berlin, 'equally ultimate and sacred' (Berlin 1953: 102). In the essay 'Equality' he can therefore state that equality is an important value within liberalism which 'is neither more nor less "natural" or "rational" than any other constituent in them. Like all human ends it cannot itself be defended or justified, for it is itself that which justifies other acts – means taken towards its realization' (Berlin 1956: 102; see also p. 96).

From this, Parekh and Kocis now deduce that Berlin holds the opinion that all ends are equally valuable and are even elevated above criticism. In Berlin's view, suggests Parekh, the values cherished by Hitler and Stalin would therefore be as 'sacred' and 'natural' as the values of the average Western social democrat.[5] Parekh thus accuses Berlin of 'radical pluralism' and 'pluralistic absolutism'. Kocis also ascribes to Berlin the belief 'that there are no rational grounds for preferring one value (not even liberty) over any other' (Kocis 1983: 375). Because for Berlin, in Kocis's interpretation, all ends are equally valuable, he could not give any reason why some may not impose their preferences on others (ibid.: 374).

This is not fair on Berlin. His earlier (perhaps careless) statements quoted must be seen in the light of his aversion to value absolutism and monism. It would be in conflict with Berlin's own working method and epistemological ideas if they were intended as an argument in favour of value relativism. If Berlin was really of the opinion that it was not possible to dispute values, then he would never have made an attempt, as in 'Two concepts of liberty', to convince his reader through a fifty-page-long, reasoned argument of the value of (non-perverted forms of) negative and positive freedom. He would then have been satisfied with the simple statement that he is in favour of freedom.

Because Berlin is not a relativist or a sceptic in the field of empirical understanding, nor is he, considering his idea of science, a relativist in the field of normative judgments. Just as the insight that contestable, normative principles play a leading role in the perception and explanation of empirical phenomena does not lead to the conclusion that every statement on empiricism is equally 'true', so too the recognition of the impossibility of finding a basis for normative statements which is acceptable to everyone or verifiable, does not lead to the idea that all values are equally 'correct'. Just as with 'empirical' theories, according to Berlin, the tenability or the reality value of 'normative' theories (in which framework values are justified) are ultimately determined in their confrontation with empiricism, this reveals the extent to which they are capable of describing and explaining in an acceptable and usable manner the reality we experience (Berlin 1962: 160). (It will be abundantly clear that in Berlin's view, in this empirical verifying of normative theories, it is not the *logical*, but the *actual* or *empirical*, gap between 'facts' and values which is being bridged.)

Thus, for Berlin, it is a given that people in practice, in their daily lives, attach great value to a personal area in which they can go their own way unhindered by others. Normative political theories which do not include this *fact* of experience, this category, in their principles, pay for it by loss of reality value and therefore persuasiveness. These theories, therefore, just like all other theories which fail to do justice to a number of essential characterists of man and world, generally quickly disappear into obscurity. Empirically, it would now appear in Berlin's view that the values adhered to by people, looked at through the centuries and over different cultures, are rather stable. The communication between different eras and cultures runs far more successfully than would be possible with extreme value relativism. We are capable, in a manner advocated by Vico, to empathize, to have imaginative sympathy with other cultures. People have quite a lot in common, share numerous values, and normative statements based on these shared principles and with a reasonable range of reference are therefore very possible (Berlin 1953: 96–103; 1969: xxxi, xxxii, lii; 1988: 14–8).

In his withering reply to Kocis – he simply cannot understand how it is possible that such an 'intelligent', 'scrupulous', 'well-read' and 'basically sympathetic critic' can produce such a strange interpretation of his ideas – Berlin writes along these lines that one can always give *reasons* for one's actions:

> What rationality means here is that my choices are not arbitrary, incapable of rational defence, but can be explained in terms of my scale of values – my plan or way of life, an entire outlook which cannot but be to a high degree connected with that of others who form the society, nation, party, church, class, species to which I belong . . . Men, because they are men, have enough in common biologically, psychologically, socially, however this comes about, to make social life and social morality possible.
>
> (Berlin, 1983: 390–1)

The singularity of, and the differences between peoples and cultures which were rightly emphasized by Herder, can also be exaggerated, states Berlin in his interview with Jahanbegloo:

> There are universal values. This is an empirical fact about mankind, what Leibniz called *vérités du fait*, not *vérités de la raison*. There are values that a great many human beings in the vast majority of places and situations,

at almost all times, do in fact hold in common, whether consciously and explicitly or as expressed in their behaviour, gestures, actions.

(Jahanbegloo 1992: 37)

Relativists, Spenglerians, Positivists, deconstructivists are wrong: commu-nication is possible between individuals, groups, cultures, because the val-ues of men are not infinitely many; they belong to a common horizon – the objective, often incompatible values of mankind – between it is neces-sary, often painfully, to choose.

(ibid.: 108)[6]

In a certain sense then, Berlin too believes in universal moral values: 'I believe in moral rules which a great many people, in a great many countries, for a long time have lived by. This acceptance makes it possible to live together' (ibid.: 108). For example, he believes within all existing human cul-tures up to now it has been assumed that a minimum of 'human rights' existed: 'There may be disagreements about how far to expand this mini-mum . . . but that such rights exist and that they are an empirical pre-condition of the leading of full human lives – that has been recognized by every culture' (ibid.: 39).

But none of this means that Berlin also believes in *absolute* values: he does not know how you could establish or prove these in an unambiguous fashion. Berlin, therefore, does not understand those philosophers who see Reason for example as 'a magical eye, which sees non-empirical universal truths' (ibid.: 113). Fundamental values are not rationally justified: 'The norms don't need justification, it is they which justify the rest, because they are basic.' From the empirical observation that people want to live according to certain values and concepts, it is therefore possible to further build up a normative theory, which partly justifies these fundamental values (ibid.: 113). According to Berlin, we therefore believe in human rights because in practice our experience is that, thanks to the recognition of these rights, people live together in a 'decent' manner. 'Don't ask me what I mean by decent,' says Berlin finally to Jahanbegloo. 'By decent I mean decent – we all know what that is. But if you tell me that one day we will have a different culture, I can't prove the contrary' (1992: 114).

In his recent study *Contingency, Irony and Solidarity*, the American prag-matist Richard Rorty formulates a defence of Berlin's standpoint in a man-ner that Berlin could probably subscribe to up to a point, and which is worthwhile dealing briefly with here. Rorty looks at Michael Sandel's posi-tion (1984) that Berlin's vision has a terrible tendency towards relativism: what, wonders Sandel, is the 'privileged status' of the value 'freedom', and with it, of liberalism, when, as Berlin argues, there are many significant, often irreconcilable values which are 'only relatively valid'?

Rorty answers that this sort of question can only be asked by people who see the rationalist principles of the Enlightenment – there is a single knowable reality – as self-evident. Only then can you have a fixed point of reference, a criterion, with the help of which it is possible to define the rightness of, and hierarchy among, different values. Berlin's central a priori, and the basis of Western liberal thought, however, is that there is no fixed standard, no knowable cosmic order with a single truth. There are merely, states Rorty, various what Wittgenstein called 'language games' and Nietzsche 'mobile armies of metaphors'. He writes: 'since truth is a property of sentences, since sentences are dependent for their existence upon vocabularies, and since vocabularies are made by human beings, so are truths' (Rorty 1989: 21).

The liberal open society, therefore, has no 'philosophical basis'; there is no truth 'outside' or 'inside' us, it is made by us, by our language. As a consequence, says Rorty:

> there will be no such activity as scrutinizing competing values in order to see which are morally privileged. For there will be no way to rise above the language, culture, institutions and practices one has adopted and view all these as on a par with all the others. As Davidson puts it, 'speaking a language . . . is not a trait a man can lose while retaining the power of thought. So there is no chance that someone can take up a vantage point for comparing conceptual schemes by temporarily shedding his own.
> (Rorty 1989: 50)

However, this does not imply that no truth exists 'outside'. This, or the opposite, cannot be proved. The point is just that it is not possible to criticize those who, like Berlin, assume *no* order in the cosmos, nor to accuse them of relativism, on the basis of the paradigm, of the language game or army of metaphors, of those who do that. In short, the imputation of relativism 'should not be answered, but rather evaded' (ibid.: 1989: 50). The only justification that can be given, says Rorty, referring to Oakeshott, Dewey and Rawls, is 'a circular justification of our practices, a justification which makes one feature of our culture look good by citing still another, or comparing our culture invidiously with others by reference to our own standards' (ibid.: 57; cf. pp. 9–10). It is equally valid that moral principles (such as Kant's categorical imperative and pragmatic calculus) 'only have a point in so far as they incorporate tacit reference to a whole range of institutions, practices, and vocabularies of moral and political deliberation. They are reminders, abbreviations for, such practices, not justifications for such practices' (Rorty 1989: 59).

The question is, however, whether Berlin fully follows Rorty in his language game. He seems, in the first place, to have more faith in the possibility of verifying metaphors empirically, a verification in which communicable, universal experiences – 'categories' or 'brute facts' – form the criterion. He sees the relation between language and reality as being stronger than Rorty suggests. Likewise, Berlin presents our world of experience, of which our language is a record, as being probably considerably more stable and universal than is suggested within Rorty's language game. Finally, Berlin could hardly agree with Rorty's sombre estimation of the possibilities and tasks of philosophy and with his proposal to have this discipline absorbed into literature.

In his analysis of the concept of 'liberty' Berlin provides a demonstration of the possibilities of reasoning in the realm of political theory. This will be discussed in the following section.

POSITIVE AND NEGATIVE FREEDOM

Introduction

Why, when, and to what extent, people should obey or may coerce others are the questions which, according to Berlin, have long been central to politics. The contradictory answers which are given by the two most important systems of ideas in the twentieth century, liberalism and Marxism, also define the political conflict of our time. The conception of positive and negative liberty outlined in the following, based mainly on his famous speech 'Two concepts of liberty'[7], are in his opinion the theoretical background to this conflict.

'Coercion' means that somebody is deprived of his liberty, but when, runs the following question, can it be stated that someone is 'free'? Although the answers to this question have been very different and changeable in the course of time, nevertheless, in Berlin's view two fundamental conceptions can be distinguished. Of these two, the first, *negative* conception, concerns the answer to the question: 'What is the area within which the subject – a person or a group of persons – is or should be left to do or be what he is able to do or be, without interference by other persons?' and the second, *positive* conception, concerns the answer to the question: 'What, or who, is the source of control or interference that can determine someone to do, or be, this rather than that?' (Berlin 1958: 121–2). Although the answers can partly overlap, for reasons which will become clear later on, the questions must be kept strictly apart at all times.

Negative Liberty

Someone's freedom is defined as the area within which he can go his own way unimpeded by others. The bigger this personal domain is, the greater the individual liberty. Coercion appears when this field is consciously limited by other people: 'Coercion implies the deliberate interference of other human beings within the area in which I could otherwise act' (Berlin 1958: 122). My inability to realize a particular desire, therefore, does not mean automatically that my liberty is impaired: it would be rather odd if I were to consider the unpleasant climate in the Netherlands or my inability to jump over the Thames in London as an assault on my liberty.

A problem which is recognized by Berlin, but not elaborated upon (he gives the impression of not knowing what to do about it), arises when it must be determined in which cases there is a *conscious, human* impairment of my liberty. As long as it is a matter of innate human limitations or given natural circumstances, there are few differences of opinion. It is otherwise with the idea, also quite plausible for Berlin, that my inability to buy bread, for example, or to go on holiday – because I am too poor – and, argued further, my inability to enjoy classical music or modern painting – because, due to my social background, I am not familiar with it – is the consequence of a social order created and maintained by people and therefore can be seen as an impairment of my negative liberty. Berlin states that acceptance or non-acceptance of this reasoning is determined by the socio-economic theory adhered to:

> It is only because I believe that my inability to get a given thing is due to the fact that other human beings have made arrangements whereby I am, whereas others are not, prevented from having enough money with which to pay for it, that I think myself a victim of coercion or slavery. In other words, this use of the term depends on a particular social and economic theory about the causes of my poverty or weakness.
>
> (Berlin 1958: 123)

Berlin leaves implicit which socio-economic theory he himself adheres to. In the continuation of his argument, however, he subscribes to the definition of liberty given by classical, mainly liberal, English political philosophers like Hobbes, Locke, Bentham and J. S. Mill, which is also the most 'customary': man is free when within a particular personal domain he can go his own way without interference by others.

It is important to note in this context that in Berlin's view it is insufficient or imprecise to define liberty, as John Stuart Mill among others has done, as 'the absence of obstacles in the exercise of the will' or as 'the possession of the possibility to do what one wants'. In order to be able to speak of 'liberty', it would then be enough to distance oneself from all those desires which cannot be fulfilled.[8] Berlin is concerned with the *actual* availability of alternative choices; it is not important whether these alternatives are actually used or not. In the Introduction, written in 1969, to his collection of essays *Four Essays on Liberty*, Berlin adds the comment:

> The sense of freedom, in which I use this term, entails not simply the absence of frustration (which may be obtained by killing desires), but the absence of obstacles to *possible* choices and activities – absence of obstructions on roads along which a man *can* decide to walk. Such freedom ultimately depends not on whether I wish to walk at all, or how far, but on how many doors are open, how open they are, upon their relative importance in my life, even though it may be impossible literally to measure this in any quantitative fashion [italics HTB].
>
> (Berlin 1969: xl; see also Berlin 1964: 193)

The absence of this liberty, writes Berlin, in a following phrase which raises many problems of interpretation:

> is due to the closing of such doors *or failure to open them*, as a result, *intended or unintended*, of *alterable human practices*, of the operation of human agencies; although only if such acts are deliberately intended (or, *perhaps*, are accompanied by awareness that they may block paths) will they be liable to be called oppression [italics HTB].

(Berlin 1969: xl)

It is clear that the latter formulation leaves space for a conception of liberty in which positive, non-liberal elements play a role; the doubts mentioned earlier about the limited, negative interpretation of the concept of liberty are also to be heard here. (This will be gone into further in the section on super-human coercion later in the chapter.)

From the above it would appear that Berlin has few doubts with regard to the right answer to the question of whether freedom must be seen as, in the words of Taylor, an 'opportunity' or 'exercise' concept. For Berlin, liberty consists of the *possibility* of action, not of the activity itself. Someone who has the opportunity, therefore, of entering through all kinds of open doors, but nevertheless prefers to stay sitting quietly and vegetating, is a free man (Berlin 1969: xlii). In this, Berlin disagrees with among others Bernard Crick, Erich Fromm, Brough Macpherson, Charles Taylor, Benjamin Barber and Richard Lindley, who make the *exercise* of liberty central to their conception. Although Berlin has great sympathy for the ideals of these 'exercise' theoreticians with regard to the leading of a 'full life', he nevertheless considers it a confusion of terms when these ideals are identified with 'freedom'.

Furthermore, Berlin recognizes that someone who is too poor, too weak, or too badly educated to be able to make use of his legal liberties, or is not even aware of the roads he could take, in practice has little to gain from these kinds of liberties. But that does not negate these liberties. Berlin emphasizes that a distinction must be made between liberty as such, and the conditions under which this liberty becomes meaningful. This is to avoid freedom itself being forgotten in the struggle, also seen as just by Berlin, to fulfil the pre-conditions which make liberty effective:

> Useless freedoms should be made usable, but they are not identical with the conditions indispensable for their utility. This is not a merely pedantic distinction, for if it is ignored, the meaning and value of freedom of choice is apt to be downgraded. In their zeal to create social and economic conditions in which alone freedom is of genuine value, men tend to forget freedom itself.

(Berlin 1969: liv; cf. Berlin 1964: 192)

According to Berlin, the negative freedom of an individual is defined, as stated, by the presence or absence of impediments on the roads which he might choose to take. In an important oft-quoted footnote to 'Two concepts of liberty', Berlin makes an attempt to define more precisely what the extent of someone's individual freedom depends on. As defining variables he mentions: the number of behavioural alternatives available, the difficulty of realizing these, the opposition to be overcome from others, the importance of each in the life plan of the person involved and in the prevailing pattern of values of the society. In Berlin's words:

> The extent of my freedom seems to depend on (a) how many possibilities are open to me (although the method of counting these can never be more than impressionistic . . .); (b) how easy or difficult each of these possibilities is to actualize; (c) how important in my plan of life, given my character and circumstances, these possibilities are when compared with each other; (d) how far they are closed and opened by deliberate human acts; (e) what value not merely the agent, but the general sentiment of the society in which he lives, puts on the various possibilities. All these magnitudes must be 'integrated', and a conclusion, necessarily never precise, or indisputable, drawn from this process.
>
> (Berlin 1958: 130)

(Note that this point (d) deals once again simply with 'deliberate human acts'.)

For Berlin, once again, the negative concept of liberty is related to the question of how big the domain is within which one can make choices without, or free from, the intervention of others. Nor is there then any necessarily positive relationship between individual freedom and democracy: in a democracy the state can meddle far deeper into the personal life of its subjects than in an autocracy. John Stuart Mill, in particular, was extremely apprehensive about this possible dictatorship of the democratic majority over the individual which smothered all progress and individual development, an apprehension with which Berlin, as we have seen, can sympathize deeply. Berlin emphasizes therefore that the answer to the question, Who governs me? must logically be distinguished from the question, To what extent does the government interfere with me?[9] In his opinion, it is precisely in that distinction that the basis of the contrast between the positive and negative conceptions of freedom is to be found. The advocates of the positive conception are, in Berlin's eyes, so preoccupied with the former question that they completely overlook its logical distinction with, and the primary importance of, the latter. With all the consequences of this (Berlin 1958: 130–1).

Positive Liberty

Positive liberty is described by Berlin in the following way, as ornately as always:

> The 'positive' sense of the word 'liberty' derives from the wish on the part

of the individual to be his own master. I wish my life and decisions to depend on myself, not on external forces of whatever kind. . . . I wish to be somebody, not nobody; a doer – deciding, not being decided for, self-directed and not acted upon by external nature or by other men as if I were a thing, or an animal, or a slave incapable of playing a human role, that is, of conceiving goals and policies of my own and realizing them. . . . I wish, above all, to be conscious of myself as a thinking, willing, active being, bearing responsibility for my choices and able to explain them by references to my own ideas and purposes. I feel free to the degree that I believe this to be true, and enslaved to the degree that I am made to realize that it is not.

(Berlin 1958: 131)

Although this positive conception of liberty – the capacity to make your own choices – seems logically to be not far removed from the negative conception – the area within which one can impeded come to these choices – *historically*, the two conceptions increasingly grew apart to such an extent that they ultimately came into irreconcilable conflict.[10]

A first step along the path leading to the parting of the ways was taken, in Berlin's view, when people started to wonder whether being one's own master could be frustrated, apart from by the deliberate intervention of others, by inner, irrational drives, instincts and passions which could hardly be controlled. Only with truly free people, it was then suggested, would these drives, derived from a 'heteronome' or 'empirical' ego, be kept under control by a 'true', 'rational' or 'autonomous' ego. In this fashion, a distinction was made between a higher and a lower ego, the latter 'swept by every gust of desire and passion, needing to be rigidly disciplined if it is ever to rise to the full height of its "real" nature' (Berlin 1958: 132). In a next step, the 'higher' ego was identified with a social entity which transcends the individual (a church, race, nation, class, party, culture) or with vaguer quantities such as 'the general will', the 'enlightened forces of society' and 'history'. On the basis of this authority, wishes and aspirations considered undesirable by the rulers or ascribed to a lower nature could then be negated or oppressed in the name of freedom. In justification, an appeal was made here to the 'real' or 'rational' ego which, once released from the grip of animal passions and instincts, would retrospectively sanction the coercion which had made possible the ultimately enlightened state of liberty. Looked at properly, there had never been any question of coercion: the temporarily overruled 'rational' ego had actually wanted the imposed choice all along.[11]

Berlin takes up the cudgels against this postulation of a higher ego, which according to him is at the basis of all theories of self-realization (Berlin 1958: 133). In his opinion, it is ultimately justification for the subjugation and repression of all kinds of desires and objectives, dismissed as 'unreal' or 'false', but essentially deeply felt and authentic. If, at a particular moment, someone does not see what is best for him, coercion can sometimes be justified; in this way, the freedom of the coerced individual can even be increased eventually. But it is a 'monstrous' denial of individual dignity, of someone's capacity for self-determination, when it is postulated that as soon as something is for someone's own good there is actually no question of coercion, the party involved being deemed to actually have 'really' wanted it himself (Berlin 1958: 132–4; 1969: xliv).

Berlin accepts that in principle, even within the negative conception of liberty, a distinction can be made between a lower nature bent merely on short-term sensations and a superior ego striving for self-realization, and that here too the latter could be identified with supra-individual entities. History shows, however, that in both theory and practice, positive conceptions are much more apt to be used for this. Ultimately, this fact is decisive for Berlin (1958: 134; 1969: xliv).

Historical derailments of positive freedom

The consequences of distinguishing two souls in one breast become clearer when we look at the two forms which the desire to become master over one's own life have historically acquired.

The first form was mentioned earlier: it is possible to feel free by divesting oneself of desires or goals which cannot be realized within the existing relations. If freedom is defined as merely the possibility of doing what one wants, then in this case it is indeed freedom. The desires which one has in mind here, particularly in practice, concern matters which are relatively simple to frustrate, and mostly material, ascribed to an earthy, empirical ego. Recommended is withdrawing into a superior inner world and devoting oneself to the realization of the 'spirit'. This liberation method, propagated by stoics and Buddhists among others, is seen by Berlin as sticking one's head in the sand, and as such rejected.

The second form demands more attention: this interpretation of the concept of freedom is provided by Rationalism, against whose assumptions Berlin, as mentioned in the Introduction, has waged a real crusade in all his works. Here, freedom means that life is directed according to one's own plan and that the desires and objectives included in this are attuned as much as possible to the laws governing reality. The greater the understanding of these laws, the freer one is, the more one is freed of irrational fears, preconceptions and frustrations caused by striving after impossibilities. After all, one does not attempt to change that which one understands to be necessary. It is more rational to bring the will in line with that which inevitably must happen. According to Marxists, among others, just as it is ridiculous to resist the laws of gravity and to want to fall upwards, it is ridiculous and irrational to resist the inevitable course of history. In this view, the universal, immutable rules or laws on the basis of which we have to organize our lives, do not reduce our freedom of choice. Freedom consists of the conscious and voluntary choice of the relevant life.

According to Berlin, this belief in reason as a liberating power can still be recognized, although in a weakened form, in all kinds of schools of thought. Reason enough to investigate his principles somewhat more deeply.

Thinkers with a rationalistic background (Berlin mentions, among others, Spinoza, Montesquieu, Rousseau, Burke, Locke, Kant, Fichte, Hegel and Marx) hold, according to Berlin, the belief that only one right answer can be given to all questions, also ethical and political ones; that in principle all these truths could be superseded in a rational manner – that is, via empirical observation or logical deduction – even though some are in a better position to do this than others; that all values are compatible with each other and together form one harmonious whole; that conflicts are the consequence of not being familiar with, or not familiar enough with, this universal, harmonious pattern of values and are actually unthinkable between completely rational beings; that everyone has a single main objective in his life, that is, 'rational self-direction'; and that if the universe is guided by rational laws which are given by God, Nature, History, the Finite, there can never be coercion when people who are aware of these laws ensure that the ignorant, too, organize their lives on this basis (Berlin 1958: 145, 147, 151, 154; see also 1973: 1–3; 1974: 80–3; 1964: 173–9). After all, man is free when he lives according to reason, that is, when he follows the rational laws of the cosmos which apply to everyone. Only someone who is not right in his mind, is not master of his own life, wants to deviate from these laws and can – or should – therefore be protected from himself for his own good, for his 'higher', 'real', 'rational' ego: 'Freedom is not freedom to do what is irrational, or stupid, or wrong. To force empirical selves into the right pattern is no tyranny, but liberation' (Berlin 1958: 148).

Where people who have not yet seen the light can never understand the best intentions of their teachers, coercion is often the only solution. However, the formerly underdeveloped brought into an enlightened rational mental state thanks to enforced education will later see that coercion was inevitable and sanction this in retrospect. Berlin summarizes it as follows: 'The reason within me, if it is to triumph, must eliminate and suppress my "lower" instincts, my passions and desires, which render me a slave; similarly . . . the higher elements in society – the better educated, the more rational . . . may exercise compulsion to rationalize the irrational section of society. For . . . by obeying the rational man we obey ourselves' (Berlin 1958: 150). In this manner, Rationalism's original plea for individual responsibility and self-determination has, via an *historically* and *psychologically* understandable rationality, whose foundation is the conviction that in principle there is only one right way to live, slowly but surely changed into a justification of totalitarianism (ibid.: 152). For Berlin, there is therefore reason enough to doubt the principles of Rationalism.

He develops this scepticism in, among other places, his essays 'Historical inevitability' and 'From hope and fear set free'. The arguments developed by him in these are characteristic of his idea of science and *Weltanschauung*, commented upon in the Introduction. Berlin aims his fire mainly at the assumption that history proceeds according to particular patterns or laws laid down by a transcendental authority. The discovery and application of these laws would also imply, as we have seen, the justification of the events explained by them: something which necessarily happens beyond the will of man can after all hardly be criticized on moral grounds. However, because every ethic assumes freedom of choice, in Berlin's view belief in the order of things is also the denial of morality (Berlin 1953: 57, 58, 76–80). However, this is difficult to reconcile with our daily experiences, and in particular with our ordinary use of language as developed over the centuries.[12] Our custom of praising, judging, honouring, vilifying, rewarding, punishing people for their actions and our daily use of concepts like 'merit', 'virtue', 'responsibility', 'justice', 'guilt' and 'punishment' indicate that we presume a high degree of freedom of choice and thus, indeterminism. The real acceptance of the idea that everything is fixed would bring with it a complete metamorphosis of our use of language and our moral categories. In practice, however, even the most dogmatic adherents of determinism are not prepared for this or capable of it (Berlin 1953: 69–73: 89; 1955: 86, 92, 101; 1964: 173–89; 1969: x–xxxvii). Naturally, Berlin realizes that this does not *prove* that determinism is incorrect. He merely claims – contrary to the interpretation of, among others, E. H. Carr – that it is *implausible* (Berlin 1953: 71; 1969: x, xxvii, xxxvii).

One last argument, which is important when considered historically, and which in the view of Berlin has led to comparable non-liberal conclusions such as the Rationalistic conception of freedom, is the one in which freedom is confused with equality and brotherhood. Man, it is argued here, is a social being who is dependent to a large degree on his social surroundings, not only economically, but also for his consciousness of identity. Having a particular place in a social structure, and the recognition and appreciation of this place by others, gives the individual a sense of security and self-esteem. However, this feeling is often, in Berlin's view, confused with freedom. What, in practice, is called 'unfreedom' or struggle for freedom is then, in a large number of cases, based more on a striving towards more recognition, appreciation and sense of community, than the ambition to get more control of life within a delineated personal domain.[13] It is crucial that an increase of the feeling of self-esteem, of consciousness of identity, can also be achieved within a totalitarian regime. A dictatorship, for example, can break the humiliating influence of a liberal democratic, but foreign, power, tightly organize its citizens in people's committees which bring a sense of community and ascribe to them a unique place in world history. At the same time, however, it will not leave its citizens a moment's peace and will deny them all privacy.

In history, Berlin relates almost regretfully, people have seldom gone to the barricades for more negative freedom, for more *Lebensraum* for the individual. They have fought more often for the positive freedom to be able to participate themselves – directly or indirectly, actually or illusively – in the political decision-forming which concerns them, or for more equality, justice, status, security, welfare, brotherhood or power. And no matter how worthy these goals may be in themselves, emphasizes Berlin, they are something else than, and often irreconcilable with, the striving to allow the individual a personal domain in which to go their own way unimpeded by others.

In practice, it is irrelevant for the individual who or what restricts their freedom; whether this restriction is sanctioned by a dictator, a king, the general will or a democratically elected parliament, in all cases it remains a reduction of their freedom. However, in Berlin's view, liberals have always sought to create a society in which a border is defined around the individual, which cannot be encroached upon by anybody, or only very exceptionally. For Berlin, how this border is theoretically justified – by a reference to God, natural rights, utility, etc. – is not of primary importance. It is important that the rules which define this border are generally accepted, even to such an extent that those who break those rules without a troubled conscience are regarded as 'abnormal':

> What these rules or commandments . . . have in common is that they are accepted so widely, and are grounded so deeply in the actual nature of men as they have developed through history, as to be, by now, an essential part of what we mean by being a normal human being. When I speak of a man being normal, a part of what I mean is that he could not break those rules easily, without a qualm of revulsion.
>
> (Berlin 1958: 165–6)

The degree to which the borders around the individual are respected, ultimately defines for Berlin the extent of the (negative) individual freedom within a society. For him therefore the crucial difference between the advocates of negative and positive freedom lies in the importance ascribed to these borders. In principle, the former want to give no one or nothing the authority to cross these; for the latter, according to Berlin, the question of authority is more important:

> The former want to curb authority as such. The latter want it placed in their own hands. That is the cardinal issue. These are not two different interpretations of a single concept, but two profoundly divergent and irreconcilable attitudes to the ends of life. It is as well to recognize this, even if in practice it is often necessary to strike a compromise between them.
>
> (Berlin 1958: 166)

Necessary balancing of values

It is sometimes deduced from Berlin's argument in favour of negative free-dom, and his warning with regard to the aberrations of positive freedom, that Berlin is of the opinion that negative freedom is the only value in life, or by far the most important, or that every striving after positive freedom must be completely rejected. In a reaction to Berlin's 'Two concepts', Macpherson writes: 'It is of course Berlin's main thesis that (the whole concept of posi-tive liberty) should be abandoned.'[14] This is unfair (see Berlin 1958: 125, 169; 1969: xlv–xlvi, l–lviii; 1964: 194; 1956: 96, 102; Jahanbegloo 1992: 41). In his 'Introduction' of 1969, Berlin states: 'The issue is not one between negative freedom as an absolute value and other, inferior values. It is more complex and more painful' (Berlin 1969: lvi).

The problem is complex and painful because different, equally meaning-ful values can be in conflict with each other, and because in this conflict choices must be made whereby one value must be partially sacrificed in favour of another. The negative freedom of 'non-intervention' can come into conflict with the positive freedom 'democracy' or 'self-realization'; negative freedom can clash with equality and justice; justice with mercy; democracy with efficiency; etc. In all these cases they must be balanced against each other, a balancing whose result is ultimately determined by our image of mankind, by what in our view forms a good and significant human life (Berlin 1958: 169). Berlin's vision of man is not of such a nature that he gives priority under all circumstances to one particular value, such as negative freedom. In his 1956 essay 'Equality', for example, he states that equality can, as much as other values, be involved in a bal-ancing of the pros and cons and declares it one of the central elements in liberal thought: 'Equality is one value among many: the degree to which it is compatible with other ends depends on the concrete situation, and can-not be deduced from general laws of any kind; it is neither more nor less rational than any other ultimate principle' (Berlin 1956: 96).

Berlin also explicitly states that negative freedom can be reconciled with great social injustice – such as glaring inequality – and is also often used to justify this. In practice, freedom for the wolves all too often means death for the sheep, and Berlin is very much aware of this. The criticism of MacFarlane and Marshall Cohen, for example, that Berlin implicitly assumes that every limitation of freedom is objectionable, is therefore mis-placed (Cohen 1960: 218, 224–6; MacFarlane 1966: 79). He is certainly not making a plea for *laissez-faire*: such a socio-economic system, it is all too clear to Berlin from the nineteenth century, is not capable of creating for large sectors of the population the minimum conditions with which real use can be made of acquired negative freedoms. Berlin therefore certainly considers government interventions to guarantee these conditions as justifi-able, as we have already seen in the earlier section on negative liberty: 'Legal liberties are compatible with extremes of exploitation, brutality, and injustice. The case for intervention, by the state or other effective agencies, to secure conditions for both positive, and at least a minimum degree of negative liberty for individuals, is overwhelmingly strong' (Berlin 1969: xlvi).

Negative freedom, which people cannot make use of due to a lack of income, knowledge or health must be secured through positive intervention. But once again, the conditions for freedom may not, according to Berlin, be confused with freedom itself (see the earlier section on negative liberty). Also, it must be realized that sacrificing a part of negative freedom for the sake of other values, means, at all times, no matter how high-minded or urgent the reasons are, a *restriction* of freedom:

> To avoid glaring inequality or widespread misery I am ready to sacrifice some, or all, of my freedom: I may do so willingly and freely: but it is freedom that I am giving up for the sake of justice or equality or the love of my fellow men. . . . a sacrifice is not an increase in what is being sacrificed, namely freedom, however great the moral need or the compensation for it.
>
> (Berlin 1958: 125)

It is important to note that pleas for intervention, for planning and social legislation and even for the welfare state and socialism can, according to Berlin, be based equally on negative and positive freedom. (This idea will be raised for discussion in Chapter 4.) (Berlin 1969: xlvi). That this has not happened in practice must once again in Berlin's view be explained *historically*: formerly, the most important opponent of the advocates of negative freedom was not *laissez-faire*, but despotism. And the protagonists of positive freedom were not combating excessive state intervention, but unbridled market capitalism.

Positive freedom, being master of one's own destiny, is regarded by Berlin as a legitimate, worthy value. But just like its negative counterpart it can be perverted, in this case into a totalitarian theory. The way in which a plea for negative freedom can result in a justification of a jungle where might is right, has in Berlin's view been adequately demonstrated in the last century. However, this does not apply to the aberrations of positive freedom. The latter, even now, hidden in the sheep's clothing of a promise of more freedom, continues to be a threat to individual freedom. For Berlin this fact was ultimately the reason to aim his fire in 'Two concepts' mainly at the aberrations of the positive concept of freedom (Berlin 1969: xlvii).

SOME THEMES FOR DISCUSSION

To close this chapter, six related questions which have played a central role in the debate on the concept of freedom opened by Berlin will be formulated in this section. With each theme, Berlin's standpoint will be briefly summarized and where this contains imprecisions, or is ambiguous, it will be attempted to clarify various matters. The discourse elucidated in the following chapters will be structured partly on the basis of the subjects below.

Privacy, self-determination, self-management and self-development

If the negative concept of freedom defined by Berlin is still comparatively unambiguous, it is different with the positive concept. Here, Berlin has brought together under a single name a number of dimensions of freedom which, for a proper understanding of the concept of freedom, it would be better to distinguish. In this section therefore the various possible answers to the question of when someone is 'free' are briefly outlined once again.

Privacy

As we have seen, the first fundamental answer is formed by the negative concept of freedom. This form of freedom, which is often equated with the notion of 'privacy', consists of a private domain within which people can do as they please, free of 'public interference'. It is the centre of liberalism, which is mainly an argument about the questions of where the borders of the private domain lie and how these can be best protected (Held 1987: 41–2; Lukes 1973: 62; Williams 1981: 161–5).

How Western and modern is the notion of negative freedom?

Negative freedom is generally regarded as a rather modern and also typically Western value, which was hardly if at all subscribed to in antiquity or the Middle Ages, nor in 'primitive' societies. Berlin also writes that the notion of privacy, of a private domain with an intrinsic value, is derived from a conception of freedom which is not much older than the Renaissance or the Reformation (Berlin 1958: 129). The modernity of this notion is well expressed in an anecdote by the psychiatrist Anthony Storr. In his book *Solitude* he writes:

> Pre-industrial societies have little notion of a person as a separate entity. A Nigerian psychiatrist told me that, when a psychiatric clinic was first set up in a rural district of Nigeria to treat the mentally ill, the family invariably accompanied the sufferer and insisted upon being present at the patient's interview with the psychiatrist. The idea that the patient might exist as an individual apart from the family, or that he might have personal problems which he did not want to share with them, did not occur to Nigerians who were still living a traditional village life.
>
> (Storr 1988: 78)

A general awareness of the uniqueness of the individual first developed in self-portraits and write autobiographies. The Reformation, the rise of

Protestantism, by emphasizing the personal conscience and the personal relationship with God, gave an important stimulus to individualism. The same can be said of the growing division of labour and the growth of the cities: a growing specialization led to a greater differentiation between people, and the urbanization made social relations looser, increased anonymity and with it the consciousness of personal identity, or the lack of it. The consequence of all these influences 'is the abstraction of the individual from the complex of relationships by which he had hitherto been normally defined' (Williams 1961: 93). This development is accompanied by a comparable abstraction of 'society': this concept no longer refers to concrete, existing relations, but to the 'system' in which social life is organized. Linguistically it is striking in this context that the concept of 'individual' originally meant 'indivisible' or 'not to be separated' and could be used to indicate a married couple, for example. It is equally significant that a word like 'self' and composites like 'self-knowledge', 'self-consciousness', 'selfish', 'self-sufficient' and 'self-interest' were only incorporated into English linguistic usage in the seventeenth century.

The notion that freedom is a *modern* value is also disputed, for that matter. The American sociologist Orlando Patterson, for example, argues in his *Freedom in the Making of Western Culture* that freedom 'has been the core value of Western culture throughout its history' (Patterson 1991: xiii). His central thesis is that the notion of freedom arises from the experience of slavery or serfdom and that this experience constitutes a leitmotiv in Western civilization.

Patterson, however, does subscribe to the opinion that freedom is a typical *Western* value, which is not adhered to as a matter of course: 'For most of human history, and for nearly all of the non-Western world prior to Western contact, freedom was, and for many still remains, anything but an obvious or desirable goal. Other values and ideals were, or are, of far greater importance to them . . .' (Patterson 1991: x). According to him freedom was 'socially constructed – not discovered, for it was an invented value . . . in a specific pair of struggles generated by slavery' (Patterson 1991: 3). This happened, according to him, in Greek antiquity during the sixth and fifth centuries before our era. After the Greeks, freedom also met with a great response among the Romans, thanks to the presence of large-scale slavery. The Middle Ages then saw an expansion of both Christianity, with its emphasis on surrender to God, and serfdom. The result, according to Patterson, was that at the end of the Middle Ages:

> Europe had been not only formed as a cultural unity but, in the process of its creation, infused, body and soul, with the value of freedom. . . . The modern history of freedom . . . is merely a long series of footnotes to the great civilizational text that was already complete, and almost fully edited, by the end of the Middle Ages.
>
> (Patterson 1991: xvi)

Whatever the case, by emphasizing that freedom is a modern or in any case a Western value, it seems as if this value is being made conditional. Patterson, for example, has strong tendencies in this direction.[15] However, this is not necessarily the case. In the first place, it must be noted that the fact that a certain value is not explicitly *formulated*, is no proof that this value does not play a role in the world of experience of the parties involved. Generally, a value is first put into words when it is contested or assailed. Thus, the emphatic formulation of positive freedom took place, as Berlin had already remarked, in reaction to *laissez-faire* and the expression of negative freedom was a reaction to absolutism and despotism. Equally, it is possible to imagine that in a society which consists entirely of altruistic personalities, no concepts and profound theories with regard to the justice of sharing are developed.

Also, the conclusion cannot logically be drawn from the observation that in different cultures and periods different values are adhered to, that all these values are therefore relative, subjective and exchangeable for others. It is possible to argue in a plausible, intercultural manner that some values, cultures even, are more significant than others (cf. pp. 6–10, pp. 19–24; Taylor 1982a, 1992). After having observed that freedom is a modern, Western value, Berlin then rightly says: 'Yet its decline would mark the death of a civilization, of an entire moral outlook' (Berlin 1958: 129). There is the possibility that when people have experienced certain values, they no longer want to return to the situation in which they were still unfamiliar with the relevant values. We will come back to this in an expanded form in Chapter 5.

Self-determination and self-government

The second fundamental response to the question of what freedom means, is formed by the positive conception. This consists, as already remarked, of various dimensions. In the first place it can be stated that someone is free when his actions are based on his own decisions and choices, which are not the result of external and internal forces that are outside his will. According to Lukes, this ideal of autonomy or self-determination can be put on a par with Berlin's conception of positive freedom. Thomas Aquinas was one of the first to give it expression. After that Luther and Calvin followed, among others. In the political domain, it is a central value of the Enlightenment and of present-day liberalism. Furthermore, it is an inspiration to all those people, from Marcuse to Riesman, from Kafka to Huxley, from anarchists to neo-Marxists, who are apprehensive of the bureaucratization and uniformization of society (Lukes 1973: 52–8, 127, 128).

Self-determination can take place on a collective or political level. It is possible to take one's personal, strictly private life in one's own hands. And one can enlarge one's grip on one's own existence by attempting, together with the people with whom one forms a socio-political system, which partly determines the development of one's own life, to influence collective behaviour. An ambiguous element of Berlin's exposition of the positive conception of liberty consists of this: that he fails to distinguish sufficiently between this political and individual level. This leads him to make statements about contradictions between negative and positive freedom, which apply on the first level, but not on the second.

Berlin deals with the positive conception primarily on the individual level when, for example, he gives a first definition, quoted earlier, of positive freedom: freedom implies that man is master of his own life (Berlin 1958: 131). Nevertheless, with his (correct) statement that inner inhibitions of this freedom are linked by some theoreticians in the positive tradition, via the notion of a 'true' or 'real' ego, to entities which are often based on rationalistic assumptions such as 'national spirit', 'class' and 'enlightened powers', he leaves this level and enters the social or political field. It is important to state that it is only when this link takes place that there is a contradiction between negative and positive freedom (on an individual level): only then can the desire to be master of one's own life – a desire which could first be realized with the help of people or institutions which have seen the light and the truth – be a threat to the desire to possess a private domain within which one is left in peace by everyone.

A second, and logical, cause of a possible contradiction between the two conceptions of freedom is formed by the desire to participate in the collective decision-making.

The two questions formulated by Berlin, to be logically distinguished, to which the negative and positive conception of freedom form an answer ('What is the area within which the subject – a person or a group of persons – is or should be left to do or be what he is able to do or be, without interference by other persons?' and 'What, or who, is the source of control or interference that can determine someone to do, or be, this rather than that?'), are originally generally formulated and applicable on both an individual and social level. However, at other places in his essay they are narrowed to the political questions 'How far does government interfere with me?' and 'Who governs me?' (Berlin 1958: 130, 166). The point now is that Berlin's thesis that the deviating responses to the two questions first mentioned are at the basis of the contradiction between negative and positive freedom, answers which are even expressions of 'two profoundly divergent and irreconcilable attitudes to the ends of life' (ibid.: 166), is only valid on the political, collective level. Here, and here only, is positive freedom, seen logically, a potential threat to its negative counterpart: there is indeed no necessary, directly proportional connection between democracy and negative freedom, where in a democracy the state can intervene much more far-reachingly into the personal life of its subjects than for example in an autocracy or oligarchy.[16]

Although the idea of democracy and self-government forms a not unimportant element of positive freedom, in this book it will only be dealt with obliquely. Political participation, the taking part in democratic decision-making in the social system of which one is a part, can be an important instrument for becoming master of one's own life and for developing individual talents. These problems however can, for a large part, be analysed independently of the questions being dealt with here, and also deserve a separate study.

Self-development

A second dimension of positive freedom is the idea of self-development or self-realization. Someone is free to the extent that he succeeds in developing his own capacities, talents or capacities, or 'makes the best of himself'. This ideal of self-development, with its emphasis on uniqueness and individualism, dates from Romanticism and is most developed by early German Romantics like Schleiermacher, Schlegel and Humboldt. This ideal was also included in the liberal tradition, above all by the work of John Stuart Mill, and is also to be recognized in the ethical basis of Marxism. Marx saw man as a being gifted with many creative capacities, who is driven by a strong inner need to develop these talents. For him, too, the romantic vision of man as artist was the starting-point. In socialist society the functional capacities of the individual would no longer just be developed for the production process: the fully developed man, capable of all kinds of creative activities, would replace the specialized worker. An important difference between Marx and John Stuart Mill is, after all, that the former's conception of self-development, in contrast to that of Mill's, has a strongly communal character. According to Marx, individuals can only realize their talents in, and thanks to, a community. Mill's conception is more 'extra-social', and that of the early Romantics strongly anti-social (Lukes 1973: 67–72, 129, 130).

Self-determination and self-realization are naturally closely related: there can only be self-development if one has some control over one's own life, and it is only possible to be autonomous when one has developed to some extent. There is something to be said, therefore, for bringing these two dimensions of positive freedom under one title. However, it is different for the individual and collective components of the self-determination ideal: these must be distinguished from each other for the reasons given above.

Inner impediments and higher goals

The next subject for discussion consists of the questions of whether, apart from external there could also be inner obstacles to freedom, and whether 'higher', 'deeper' or 'second-order' goals or desires could be distinguished. Logically, the latter question precedes the former, because an internal obstacle to freedom implies the existence of an equally internal entity – the 'real', 'higher' ego – which is impeded by this. It could be deduced from Berlin's account of the perversion of the positive conception of freedom, a degeneration where the distinguishing of inner impediments formed a first step towards the realization of 'higher' goals, that under absolutely no conditions does Berlin want to recognize the existence of these sorts of impediments and goals. This is not the case. His warning formulated in 'Two concepts' about what the distinction between inner obstacles and higher goals can lead to, does indeed leave nothing open to doubt, but lacks nuance, something to which the polemical character of this essay probably contributed. In 'From hope and fear set free', which appeared six years later, Berlin is singing a different tune. There he states that impediments to the realization of our goals can come from both 'outside' and 'inside', and that it would even be absurd to deny the existence of the latter, psychic obstacles, whose great importance has only become clear in this century:

> freedom is to do with the absence of obstacles to action. These obstacles may consist of psychical power . . . or . . . they may be psychological: fears and 'complexes', ignorance, error, prejudice, illusions, fantasies, compulsions, neuroses and psychoses – irrational factors of many kinds. Moral freedom – rational self-control – knowledge of what is at stake, and what is one's motive in acting as one does; independence of the unrecognized influence of other persons or of one's own personal past or that of one's group or culture; destruction of hopes, fears, desires, loves, hatreds, ideals, which will be seen to be groundless once they are inspected and rationally examined – these indeed bring liberation from obstacles, some of the most formidable and insidious in the path of human beings. . . . It would be absurd to deny the validity of this sense of the concept of freedom.
>
> (Berlin 1964: 190–1)

However, Berlin emphasizes that these psychic impediments form only a single category of obstacles, and that the weight lent to this can never be at the expense of the other categories. In his view, however, this is done by those theoreticians who have equated freedom with 'self-determination'.

No matter what the case may be, the question remains how these inner impediments must be included in a consistent conception of freedom. Berlin, in any case, has made hardly any attempt in this direction, and as we shall see this has invited criticism from, among others, Charles Taylor, Joel Feinberg, Benjamin Barber, John Kleinig and Robert Young.

Positive freedom and rationalism

From Berlin's work, a large number of authors have understood that he believes that, on the one hand, positive freedom and, on the other hand, rationalism, value cognitivism and monism always, or even, necessarily, go together. For example, Noel Annan writes without flinching that, according to Berlin, advocates of positive freedom hold the conviction that all objectives can be united without friction in a single highest value: that is, positive freedom, and that the state can determine without any problems, in the present instance, what people *really* want in their life:

> Positive freedom is the benign name given to the theory which maintains that not merely wise philosophers but the state, indeed governments themselves, can identify what people would really want were they enlightened . . . What people say is the mere rumbling of their lower self, a pathetic underdeveloped persona insufficiently aware of all the possibilities of life, often the slave of evil passions.
>
> (Annan 1980: xvii)

Others too, including Marshall Cohen (1960: 216–7, 221–4), Robert Kocis (1983: 379), Beata Polanowska-Sygulska (1989: 123–7), Alan Ryan (1979: 5), Hillel Steiner (1983: 81–2) and Bhikhu Parekh have interpreted Berlin in this way. For Parekh, Berlin's critique of rationalism and positive freedom have even become practically interchangeable:

> According to Berlin, the concept of positive liberty rests on, and derives its plausibility from several basic assumptions. First, it rests on the theory of the two selves. Second, it assumes that reason is an objective principle rather than a human faculty. Third, it equates 'what X would choose if he were something he is not . . . with what X actually seeks and chooses'. Fourth, it assumes that the true ends of man can be determined independently of human choices. Fifth, it assumes that there is one and only one true way of living a good life. And, finally, it assumes that there are men who can claim expertise in moral and political matters.
>
> (Parekh 1982: 36–7)

Parekh then shows that positive freedom, in spite of Berlin's claim, does not necessarily have to be based on these assumptions. But, of course, it is not difficult to appear especially intelligent when one summarizes the ideas of political opponents in Parekh's manner.

Nevertheless, more conscientious authors like MacFarlane (1966), Megone (1987), MacPherson (1973) and Gray (1984) have also interpreted Berlin in this style. They have therefore gone to great lengths to disprove the alleged logically necessary relation between positive freedom and rationalism. It must be admitted that Berlin has also stimulated this interpretation through a number of careless statements.[17] Nevertheless, the chief line in his argument remains, as emphasized in various places in the foregoing, that the growing apart of negative and positive freedom must be *historically* explained and that where positive freedom and value cognitivism, monism, and ultimately despotism come together, there is a perversion of the positive conception of freedom, a degeneracy which must be understood psychologically and historically, and not logically.[18] All the same, it is still worthwhile subjecting the relevant relations to a closer study. While it is true that Berlin's warning has been too extremely interpreted by some, its power is undiminished.

Freedom as a state or as an experience

Berlin's answer to the question of whether freedom, in the words of Charles Taylor, must be regarded as an 'opportunity' or an 'exercise concept' is, as we have seen, brief and to the point: freedom consists of the *opportunity* to act, not of the activity itself. Numerous theoreticians – including MacPherson, Bernard Crick, Charles Taylor, Richard Lindley, Joel Feinberg, Benjamin Barber, Richard Norman and Frithjof Bergmann – have opposed this idea. In their view, freedom is first real when it is actually exercised. Because the latter can often only happen if one is in possession of material and non-material resources, the relevant authors generally refuse, in contrast to Berlin, to make a hard distinction between freedom and its conditions.

Superhuman coercion: social structures

The question that concerns us here is whether coercion is only exercised by other people or also by particular social structures and processes, which are the product, intentional or unintentional, of a large number of individual behaviours.

As we saw earlier in the chapter, Berlin originally took the position that there is only coercion in the case of a purposeful, human limitation of someone's freedom. However, he then adds to this that whether this is considered to be so in these cases is ultimately dependent on the socio-economic theory followed. Because the debate on the question of the extent to which the poverty or weakness of particular groups of people can be explained by the behaviour of others, or by particular social structures supported by the others, is still undecided, and will probably remain so for the time being, the question of when exactly there is coercion cannot be answered unambiguously either. (This question will be gone into further in Chapters 4 and 5.)

That the social-liberal Berlin has not completely resolved it to his own satisfaction either, could be seen from his remarks quoted earlier from his Introduction to *Four Essays on Liberty* (1969) ('alterable human practices', 'perhaps'). Does Berlin regard only the calculated and sought, freedom-limiting effects of a consciously created and changeable social structure as coercion, or here in his vision is it also a case of people being aware of these effects, but not having explicitly sought them? An example of the first case is feudalism, and of the second case, capitalism: it is known that within a capitalist system large groups of people are not in a position to open numerous doors offering access to freedom, but this was not the conscious aim. When Berlin wants to speak of coercion in the latter case too, he comes close to the ancient doctrine of socialism, and this, as we will see in Chapter 4, has far-reaching consequences for the distinction made by him between freedom and its conditions. Berlin has his doubts, and perhaps for this reason in the rest of his 1958 argument he stays on the familiar path of social liberalism.

Fewer doubts on this question are to be found in socialist circles. Socialists have always pointed to the freedom-limiting effects of certain structures, capitalist ones in particular, and have agitated against what they considered to be liberalism's too limited definitions of freedom and coercion. Present-day representatives of this tradition of thinking, who partly for this reason have also opposed Berlin's conception of freedom, include Steven Lukes, Richard Lindley, G. A. Cohen, Richard Norman and C. B. Macpherson.

Besides, not only is it a problem to determine the extent to which particular economic structures form obstacles erected by people to someone's negative freedom, a question which Berlin in any case recognizes, the pressure of public opinion, the tyranny of the majority, which struck terror in the hearts of Mill and Tocqueville in particular, also forms a problem for the negative conception. Marshall Cohen in particular refers to this (one of the few critical remarks in his discussion of Berlin which is not unwarranted). He states that Berlin's distinction between, on the one hand, conscious or deliberate, and on the other, unconscious or inadvertent, and even between the 'I' and the 'other' is not applicable and is irrelevant in this context. The power of public opinion or of habit does not show itself through "deliberate interference'. Whoever is directed or coerced does not have to be aware of this at all. Cohen writes:

> Indeed, not only does the 'other-directed' man not feel constraint, he feels liberated, and often has an ideological defence of his conformism. It would appear, then, that it will be even more difficult than it was in the case of economic oppression to decide whether the external forces which oppress the individual do so deliberately or not. More important, it will be impossible to decide whether the forces which impair his individuality are external or internal.

> (Cohen 1960: 227)

Barber, Lukes, Connolly, Benton, Smith and Lindley, among others, have pointed out the problems of this exercise of power, which Lukes has called 'three-dimensional' for the concept of freedom. This problem will be dealt with in Chapter 5.

Paternalism

Berlin makes no attempt to define what precisely he means by paternalism. It may be assumed that in broad outline he links up with the connotations which are evoked by this concept in daily practice: paternalism is a conscious limitation of someone's freedom of choice by people or institutions, which in this case claim to possess a greater capacity of judgment and who justify their intervention by an exclusive reference to the welfare, happiness or best interests of the individual concerned. (Possible definitions of this concept will be returned to extensively in Chapter 5.) The two central, related questions here are: first, whether the individual is always the best judge of his own interests or whether there are cases in which an external authority is more capable of doing so, and, second, when and how is paternalism justified.

On the basis of the foregoing, it is not difficult to predict how Berlin regards paternalism:

> Paternalism is despotic, not because it is more oppressive than naked, brutal, unenlightened tyranny, nor merely because it ignores the transcendental reason embodied in me, but because it is an insult to my conception of myself as a human being, determined to make my own life in accordance with my own (not necessarily rational or benevolent) purposes, and, above all, entitled to be recognized as such by others. For if I am not so recognized, then I may fail to recognize, I may doubt, my own claim to be a fully independent human being.

> (Berlin 1958: 157)

Naturally, Berlin states, in imitation of John Stuart Mill, it is the case that people sometimes make very stupid choices in life. But even in those cases they learn, they develop themselves and do justice to the essential characteristic of man: the capacity to make autonomous choices. If someone is treated paternalistically, this is a denial of his dignity, a treatment which could only be justified by a value higher than the individual. As the individual is the source of all values, this does not exist and paternalism is therefore never more than coercion (Berlin 1958: 137). This coercion is generally exercised at the beginning with the best intentions, but soon degenerates into pure contempt for the wishes, goals and intellectual capacities of the individual. Berlin writes:

> the central reason for pursuing liberty in the first place [is] that all paternalistic governments, however benevolent, cautious, disinterested, and rational, have tended, in the end, to treat the majority of men as minors, or as being too often incurably foolish or irresponsible; or else as maturing so slowly as not to justify their liberation at any clearly foreseeable date (which, in practice, means at no definite time at all). This is a policy which degrades men, and seems to me to rest on no rational or scientific foundation, but, on the contrary, on a profoundly mistaken view of the deepest human needs.

> (Berlin 1969: lxii)

Nevertheless, from these powerful swipes – the polemical character, not always properly appreciated, of Berlin's essays was already mentioned – it cannot be deduced that Berlin in principle rejects every limitation of freedom justified on paternalistic grounds. Children are forced to go to school, public lynching parties are forbidden by law. These restrictions on liberty are justified by values which we consider more valuable in these cases. In order to combat things like ignorance, impotence, bad upbringing or education, public expressions of sadism and hysterical bloodthirstiness, we are prepared to sacrifice a part of our freedom – or rather, the freedom of others. How we balance these sorts of values against each other is ultimately determined by what in our view forms a decent existence. Because our views on this differ from one another's, we also consider paternalism justified under different conditions. In what follows it will become evident that others go further in this than Berlin, and perhaps rightly so. Berlin's warning about what paternalism can lead to, however, remains valid.

3 Freedom of the individual

INTRODUCTION

As we have seen in his discussion of positive freedom, Berlin considered chiefly the objectionable sides of this conception. He lays particular emphasis on what, according to him, is the opportunity of justifying totalitarianism provided by this theory. It hardly needs to be said that Berlin invited much criticism here from advocates of the positive conception. Partly on the basis of this critique, in this chapter it will be attempted to further develop the positive conception of freedom which has only been scantily defined by Berlin. This will, in so far as that is possible, be done from the perspective of the individual. The question will be, therefore, which requirements must the individual meet before he can be called 'free' in the positive sense. In the next chapters, we will then examine how society must be organized in order to make this form of freedom possible. In other words: how can someone's positive freedom be inhibited or furthered by his social environment and, in the case of the latter, how realistic are the chances of degeneration into totalitarianism.

Certainly, from the viewpoint of the positive conception of freedom, where the individual in general is looked at more in terms of his relation to the community, it is theoretically disputable to deal with the positive freedom of the individual, as is being done in this chapter, free to some extent of this relation. The difference in approach between the present and the next chapter is therefore only analytical. The most important reason for this approach is that the majority of theoreticians have concentrated mainly either on the individual or on the organization of society. This comparative one-sidedness will therefore also be expressed in the next sections. Later, it will be attempted to incorporate both angles of approach into a single conception.

In this chapter, a concrete study is made of the ideas which have generally been considered important for individual autonomy in the literature. Furthermore, it is attempted to bring these together as consistently as possible within a single conception. We will be looking at the ideas of Frithjof Bergmann, Harry Frankfurt, Charles Taylor, Robert Young, Benjamin

Barber, Bruno Bettelheim, Richard Lindley, S. I. Benn, John Benson, Gerald Dworkin and Joel Feinberg, among others. The choice of these authors is based above all on the consideration that they complement each other and *together* give a rather complete picture of the positive conception. The working method in all this will be of an eclectic and, in painting terms, 'pointillist' nature. First, a number of matters will be emphasized from close by; after which, when we look at the whole from a somewhat greater distance quite a coherent image will emerge. That, at least, is the intention.

Before embarking on all this, however, a brief look is taken at the question of which demands may be made of a plausible interpretation of genuinely disputed concepts. This is done to supplement what was already stated about this subject in Chapter 1.

The interpretation of fundamentally disputed concepts

It is not only the present writer who has been driven to despair by the attempt to define freedom or autonomy. Langerak, for example, begins his essay 'Freedom: idea and ideal' with the significant remark: 'freedom seems easier to die for than to define' (Langerak 1979: 39). In his treatise 'The concept of autonomy', Gerard Dworkin comes to the same not very encouraging conclusion: 'Autonomy is a term of art introduced by a theorist in an attempt to make sense of a tangled net of intuitions, conceptual and empirical issues, and normative claims' (Dworkin 1981: 204). In order to be rid of the entire puzzle, Ronald Dworkin even came up with the suggestion of letting the concepts of freedom and autonomy 'go up in smoke'. He judged that it was more reasonable to continue to talk of intuitions only, and the normative and empirical questions to which these concepts refer. However, such a radical solution to the problem does not seem necessary and is also undesirable: to no longer use these concepts would unjustifiably evoke the suggestion that they are actually superfluous, their contents being covered completely by other concepts (Gray 1984: 334–5). Within the context of a particular philosophy, attempts can be made to develop a conception which connects our intuitions, experiences and ideas together in an acceptable manner. Our demands with regard to, among other things, the unambiguity of this conception cannot be too ambitious, however. As argued in Chapter 1, fundamentally disputable concepts like autonomy have acquired too many and often too contradictory connotations for this. However, we can lay down a number of pre-conditions for the conception to be developed (cf. pp. 9–10); Dworkin 1981: 204–7; Feinberg 1986: 44–7; Lindley 1986: 2–5).

Thus, in the first place, it can be demanded that this conception be logically consistent and therefore contains no inner contradictions. However, this does not necessarily rule out tensions between some elements of a conception. For example, it is generally expected of an autonomous individual that he hold on to his conviction or identity, even under difficult circumstances. At the same time, however, it is also expected of the relevant party that he be to a large extent open to different ideas and thoughts. The rigidity necessary for the first can now have a tense relationship with the required suppleness. To resolve this tension by excluding by definition one of the two elements seems undesirable: it only robs the conception of an essential component.

In the second place the conception must be empirically feasible, it may not require things of people which they could never accomplish. For example, it is difficult to want an autonomous person to have completely authentic values and goals. To demand that autonomous individuals develop or choose their values completely independently would be to fail to understand that man is a social being.

Nevertheless, in the third place, the conception must also be able to make clear why autonomy in general is seen as something to aspire to, as a normative ideal. The conception must in this way link up as much as possible with the way in which the concept is used in everyday linguistic usage. The basic principle here is that the contents which are ascribed to concepts like freedom and autonomy in the course of time are an indication of what can be regarded as essential for these values. Here language is seen as a report of our empirical experiences and normative ideas. It reflects what we in general consider to be important in life. In order to make statements about values plausible, we can therefore refer to the way in which we generally use certain concepts (cf. Taylor 1989: 57, 69).

Finally, for our purpose, the conception must be politically relevant. Political structures and processes must therefore either contribute to its realization or not. After all, this book is about political theory, not psychology.

With these four conditions as a starting-point, therefore, in what follows we will be studying which notions have generally been considered important in the literature for autonomy, and we will attempt to bring these together as consistently as possible under a single conception.

To bring this introduction to an end, a few words on the use in this text of the concepts of 'freedom', 'negative and positive freedom' and 'autonomy' are given. In practice, only a few authors have taken up the distinction between negative and positive freedom as defined by Berlin. This is particularly true of the theoreticians who discuss positive freedom according to Berlin's definition. The reasons for this are obvious: in the first place, Berlin has laid so strong an emphasis on the possible rationalistic principles of, and the totalitarian tendencies within, the positive conception, that for advocates of this conception it is not very attractive to characterize oneself as such. They count perhaps on gaining more sympathy by presenting themselves as defenders of, for example, 'personal liberty' (Young), 'developmental liberty' (Macpherson), 'autonomy' (Lindley), freedom as an 'exercise-concept' (Taylor), or just 'freedom' (Bergmann, Norman, Barber). Berlin's attempt to bring some order to the definitions of freedom in circulation, has been counterproductive as far as this is concerned. In the second place, the word 'freedom' has such a positive ring in everyday speech, that the authors who write on this subject like to sail under this flag of convenience. In order to avoid the terminology in the quotes misleading the reader, in what follows the concepts 'freedom', 'positive freedom' and 'autonomy' will be used to a great extent interchangeably. In so far as it is not otherwise indicated by the context, 'positive freedom' is meant in these cases. The differences between these concepts will be gone into further at the end of this chapter.

FRITHJOF BERGMANN: THE NECESSITY OF AN IDENTITY

Because Berlin's conception of freedom is also ultimately based on a particular vision of man, fundamental criticism of this conception can usually be traced back to a deviating view of the essential traits of man. An obvious way to begin a discussion of criticism of Berlin, therefore, is with a few words on the relationship between views of man and conceptions of freedom. A good starting-point for this is the 'meta-theory' on conceptions of freedom developed by the American philosopher Frithjof Bergmann in his book *On Being Free*.

Identification as a condition of freedom

Bergmann states that the concept of 'freedom' as it is used, and above all misused, in our language, now only creates confusion. Because it is associated with an increasing number of matters, its meaning has become increasingly comprehensive and therefore unusable. Thinking about freedom, in Bergmann's view, must therefore be built up once more from the bottom. To this end, he studies in the first place which notions are shared by three fundamental and partly contradictory conceptions of freedom distinguished by him (Bergmann 1977: 15–40).

The first conception is best represented by the neurotic clerk from Dostoevsky's *Notes from Underground*. For this civil servant, freedom means that one is completely independent of any imaginable power. For him an act is first free when it is not determined or explained by any influence or determinant. He also experiences his own emotions and reason as inhibiting forces which are separate and even hostile to his own 'real' self. Reason only forces him to conform to the immutable natural laws, the same for everyone, as if he were a 'will-less piano key'. According to Dostoevsky's character, freedom can only be found in a causeless, absurd and irrational expression of the will which opposes every self-interest, every value, emotion or custom.[1] In his opinion, it is also a profound human need to free oneself from all coercive forces. According to the *homme révolté*, this uncompromising drive explains the incomprehensible behaviour, opposing all best interests and not containable in a theory, which people regularly display.

The second conception has best been expressed by Plato and Kant and includes the interpretation of freedom against which Berlin agitates with his critique of the rationalistic variety of positive freedom: an action is only free when it is dictated by knowledge and reason. What is unfree is behaviour which is not explained by reason but by emotions or instincts. It is obvious that within this conception reason is not perceived as an impersonal voice which issues orders to the individual from out of nowhere, but rather as the most authentic interpreter of the true 'self'. Here, self and reason are identical, in contrast to what is the case with the first conception.

Just like Berlin, Bergmann sees this linkage of freedom and rationality, which from the very beginning guarantees that irrational or socially unacceptable behaviour is not judged to be free, as the leitmotif in the history of thought on freedom (Bergmann 1977: 26). From the naturalness with which we judge a crime inspired by passion to be less reprehensible than a crime committed with malice aforethought, can be seen how central this conception still is in our thinking about freedom. Yet why, Bergmann wonders, is a particular action more 'mine' to the extent that I have thought more deeply about it. Even when this has arisen from a surge of anger, it remains my action. My rage can even be considerably more authentic than my thinking.

Bergmann traces the third and last conception of freedom back to Aristotle. Berlin will probably feel most at home with this one, at least as far as the political implications are concerned. Here, the individual is free when his behaviour arises from powers which are released by his own body. Coercion can only be exercised by actors who are literally situated 'outside' the body. There is no appreciation of the various grounds on which behaviour can be based: whether one is driven by reason or by emotions, instincts, customs, etc., all these motives are regarded as belonging to one's own self and as being of equal value. The consequence of this way of seeing it – or rather of experiencing it – is that one must also bear full responsibility for everything one does. A *crime passionnel* will be judged as harshly as a considered crime. There is no room for the idea of 'psychological coercion'.

A comparison of these three conceptions of freedom, according to Bergmann, teaches us that they have a single fundamental characteristic in common: the border between what one can or cannot identify with, is the same as that between freedom and coercion. Actions and ideas with which one identifies, are regarded as expressions of the 'true self' and experienced as 'free'. Behaviour which is not considered an expression of one's own self, is experienced as the result of coercion. Having an identity is therefore a necessary condition for every experience of freedom. Because the neurotic clerk can identify with really nothing, he feels constantly unfree; because the Platonic observer cannot identify with his emotions, he experiences the behaviour arising from this as the product of coercion. Bergmann formulates his 'meta-theory' as follows:

> An act is free if the agent identifies with the elements from which it flows; it is coerced if the agent disassociates himself from the element which generates or prompts the action. This means that identification is logically prior to freedom. The primary condition of freedom is the pos-

session of an identity, or of a self – freedom is the acting out of that identity. Tell me a man's identity and I will tell you his freedom, tell me its limits and I will tell you when he is coerced.

(Bergmann 1977: 37)

For the same point, see also Dworkin 1970, 1976; Frankfurt 1971; Feinberg 1973; and some 2350 years ago, Aristotle, *Ethica Nicomachea*, Book III, ch. 1.

The definition of identity

What exactly is someone's identity? The 'self', states the existentially inspired Bergmann, is no immutable, a priori existing entity which can be located somewhere 'deep inside us'. The 'self' does not exist as such, it cannot be 'discovered'; it first becomes a reality through an act – an identification with particular elements from the rising stream of experiences. Bergmann writes:

It is crucial to understand that the self is literally 'constituted' through this act of identification. There is no self apart from this or prior to it. The self . . . has its being only in the fact that something is given that significance. To render this thought more concrete one could envision a flow of elements that are initially 'neutral'. Then, gradually, some of these undergo a process of 'attachment' and are invested with a special status; they receive an added significance. In a fashion analogous to this, the self is by degrees eventually constructed.

(Bergmann 1977: 82; cf. 148–52)

According to Bergmann, therefore, the self is constituted not 'from inner to outer' but precisely the other way round: an anonymous, neutral reality, in which, as with a baby, there is still no distinction between the self and the other, slowly but surely is exchanged, through a linking up of identifications, for a world in which significance is ascribed to experiences from a personal point of view. There is therefore no deeper, inner, 'real self'; there are merely identifications. Furthermore, identifying oneself, the genesis of the self, is not necessarily a conscious, reflective process of choice. In Bergmann's view, the self forms itself 'behind our backs' so to speak. Experiences are organized into new structures, meanings are ascribed and 'we' are told nothing of this activity. It happens unnoticed in the background.

We never, states Bergmann, have an exact, clear idea of what our identity is; this always remains intangible and always presents itself as changeable. It is as if we look at the 'self' as through a veil, always surmising, knowing that we can be wrong. It is often difficult enough even to define what we feel, think or want. It is even more difficult, however, to determine whether a particular feeling, idea or desire is really 'ours'. The notion may have been picked up from someone else, from a book or a film. It can also be merely a response to a stimulus or just a form of 'wishful thinking'. Do you 'really' love someone or does the feeling 'merely' arise out of sympathy, respect, guilt, habit or from the personal need for attention? Someone's identity is therefore difficult to express in the ideal types outlined earlier: in practice we rarely identify ourselves completely with our reason, with our emotions, instincts, passions, etc. We identify with all this to a constantly changing degree. Apart from this, according to Bergmann, people have the capacity to want to identify with something else and are also capable of succeeding in this.[2] Someone's identity can therefore change through an expression of the will, something which we will also see below, with Frankfurt and Taylor among others.

Freedom is the expression of those qualities and characteristics with which we identify. It is achieved when one can identify completely with the life one leads, when this life is in harmony with one's own identity. The effort, difficulty and heavy burden which is supposed to accompany freedom, the lonely heroism of the solitary autonomous person, which is usually emphasized, does therefore not tally either, according to Bergmann, with how freedom is really experienced. A free existence is in fact light and bearable and is characterized by the absence of tensions and stress: 'Freedom should connote a natural flow, neither cramped nor forced, a shift away from the need to control, to compensate and to correct, and toward the exuberance of actions and words at last taking shape quite effortlessly, as if by themselves. This is, in the end, the most authentic prototype of the experience of freedom' (Bergmann 1977: 92).

Thanks to this 'effortless' flow of acts and identifications, through this process of 'acting out', one also discovers the limits of one's identity. The experience of freedom is therefore not only a consequence or by-product of our self-expression, it forms the guide on our voyage of discovery to our identity: we see ourselves in the mirror of our freedom. The possibility of expression is therefore, according to Bergmann, a necessary condition for the discovery and the formation of personal identity (ibid.: 103). From this, it is clear that Bergmann, despite his refusal to distinguish the negative conception of freedom, cannot get around the realization that people need a form of privacy in order to be free in the sense defined by him.

Some comments

Bergmann brings a new perspective to numerous axioms in Western thinking about freedom, and adds nuances in a refreshing manner. An example would be the usual equating of freedom with the absence of coercion or inhibitions, or the presence of behavioural alternatives. However, he often goes too far in qualifying these. Bergmann's linkage of the idea of identification with the concept of freedom, is a valuable one, as shall become obvious. Yet while identification is perhaps necessary to be able to speak of freedom, it is not a sufficient condition for it: this criterion opens up the possibilities that a slave, who identifies with his chains, who drapes his handcuffs in flowers, must be classified as a free man. Because this already conflicts with our 'common sense', this criterion for freedom must be regarded as insufficient.

Also important is the nuance which Bergmann adds to an already over-rigid idea of the 'self'. As it will be argued in the following chapter, the self is not a fixed, immutable entity, but forms itself or develops in an interchange with its social environment. However, Bergmann too often suggests that there are merely identifications (constantly changing), which take place into the bargain 'behind our backs'. This is untenable. Here, Bergmann is in two minds. On the one hand, he states that freedom consists of an 'acting out of one's identity', which therefore presumes an existing personality. On the other hand, like Sartre, he states that identification appears first, and identity is therefore first formed after one has acted. On the basis of what, therefore, does one identify? After all, it is only possible to identify with something when there is a point of reference, a personality.[3] Bergmann's position also conflicts with, first, his own social view of man (see Chapter 4), second, with the empirical fact that someone's identity or personality is generally relatively stable over time, and third, with the intentional essence of man: man is to a high degree what he makes himself, he chooses his identity and is therefore also responsible for this.[4] The theories of Frankfurt, Taylor and Barber, as will become clear, possess more reality value in this area.

HARRY FRANKFURT AND THE ESSENCE OF MAN: SECOND-ORDER GOALS

Harry Frankfurt's thesis links up with the connection made by Bergmann between identification and freedom. According to him, the essential characteristic of people is that apart from the so-called first-order desires, they also have second-order desires or wishes. This distinction has been much imitated (by, among others: Dworkin 1981; Feinberg 1973; Lindley 1986; Taylor 1979; Young 1986; cf. Dworkin 1970). Its acceptance clears the way for the recognition of higher goals and, with this, of inner inhibitions.

In his essay 'Freedom of the will and the concept of a person', Frankfurt asks the question of what must be understood by the concept of 'person' or 'mankind'. The criteria for calling a particular being a 'person' are, according to him, determined by what we regard as the most 'essential', important or valuable in human existence. In theory, non-people could also meet these criteria, but because, in practice, we only regard fellow members of the *Homo sapiens* species as people, a person must possess one or more characteristics which are unique to the human species. It is not specific to people that they have desires or make choices: that is also true of other beings. What is unique, in Frankfurt's view, is only that they are capable of developing second-order desires – desires about desires:

[Men] are capable of wanting to be different, in their preferences and purposes, from what they are. Many animals appear to have the capacity for what I shall call 'first-order desires' or 'desires of the first order', which are simply desires to do or not to do one thing or another. No animal other than man, however, appears to have the capacity for reflective self-evaluation that is manifested in the formation of second-order desires.

(Frankfurt 1971: 7)

Someone has a desire of the second-order when he or she desires to possess a particular desire, or when he or she desires that a particular desire is his *will*. A desire is only someone's will when this desire is also effective; that is, when this desire also really moves – or will move or should move – the persons involved to behave in a particular way. Someone's will is therefore not the same as his intention to do something: someone can have the intention to lose weight, but in practice actually eat more. His desire for calories turns out to be stronger than his desire for a smaller clothing size. Only when the desire to eat less is a second-order desire and when he desires the desire to eat less to also be his *will*, is there a chance to really lose weight. Only in this last case does one, in Frankfurt's eyes, meet the essential characteristic of man:

Someone has a desire of the second order either when he wants simply to have a certain desire or when he wants a certain desire to be his will. In situations of the latter kind, I shall call his second-order desires 'second-order volitions' or 'volitions of the second-order'. Now it is having second-order volitions, and not having second-order desires generally, that I regard as essential to being a person.

(Frankfurt 1971: 10)

Frankfurt calls a being which has no 'second-order volitions' a *wanton*. A wanton is therefore not a person, even if he or she (or it) has first- and second-order desires. Characteristic of a wanton is that he does not care which desire becomes his will, he is not interested in the desirability of his desires. However, this does not mean that he makes no emotional evaluations of the question of how to best realize certain goals or weigh them against each other. Frankfurt reckons all animals as wantons, extremely young children, and sometimes adults.

Frankfurt illustrates the distinction between a wanton and a person on the basis of the difference between two drug addicts. The first drug addict – a person – has an aversion to his addiction and constantly struggles ineffectually against his desire for the drug. This addict has contradictory first-order desires: on the one hand, he wants to use the narcotic; on the other hand, he wants to refrain from it. As well as this, however, he has a second-order 'volition': he is not indifferent to the two first-order desires, he wants his desire not to use the drug to be effective, to become his will. The second addict – a wanton – is not concerned with the desirability of his desires, he lacks the capacity to evaluate his desires or sees absolutely no importance in this evaluation. His behaviour is merely the result of the struggle for power between his different first-order desires; he has no preference with regard to which of these desires becomes his will. He has therefore no identity either outside these first-order desires. The first, the non-docile addict, on the other hand, identifies through his second-order volition with one of the two conflicting first-order desires. He regards this desire as an expression of his true self, of his identity. He experiences the desire for the drug as a hostile power, foreign to him, which forces him to do something against his free will.

It is generally assumed that someone is free when he does what he wants. On the basis of the foregoing, Frankfurt opposes this with the notion that the *action* of the person involved in this case is perhaps free, but that this says nothing about the freedom of his *will*. The latter is only the case when he is free to have the will he wants. We can therefore first speak of free exercise of the will if there is no discrepancy between someone's will and his second-order volitions. Frankfurt writes: 'the statement that a person enjoys freedom of the will means . . . that he is free to will what he wants to will, or to have the will he wants. . . . It is in securing the conformity of his will and his second-order volitions, then, that a person exercises freedom of the will' (Frankfurt 1971: 15). A condition for the forming of second-order volitions is a certain degree of rationality: only with the help of reason is a person capable of becoming aware of his own desires and longings and critically evaluating these.

A large number of authors, with or without explicit reference to Frankfurt, have elaborated upon the idea that the essential characteristic of people is that, apart from first order, they also possess second-order desires and goals. All of them draw conclusions (sometimes far-reaching) from this with regard to the response to the question of when it can be said that an individual is free or autonomous.

CHARLES TAYLOR: QUALITATIVE EVALUATION, IDENTITY AND THE GOOD LIFE

The political philosopher Charles Taylor agrees emphatically with Frankfurt's thesis, that a being can first be called a man or person when he is capable of being objective about himself, of evaluating his own objectives and desires and forming second-order volitions (Taylor 1977: 15–6). However Taylor, in contrast to Frankfurt, makes a distinction here between 'weak' and 'strong' evaluation. As we shall see, this distinction plays a crucial role in his philosophy. It is precisely on this point that he deviates from Berlin and other liberal thinkers.

Taylor is one of the leading contemporary thinkers, but also one of the most complex. He has published in the fields of psychology, epistemology, philosophy of science, linguistic philosophy, the history of ideas and social and political theory.[5] In his work, he has been inspired by both the Anglo-American and continental philosophical traditions – a rare combination.

Taylor's ideas on freedom are, as usual, a component of a specific *Weltanschauung*. Because this deviates on a number of important points from Berlin's liberal, naturalistic vision we will take a somewhat closer look at them here. This can lead to a better understanding of Berlin too. In what follows, we will be looking at the distinction between weak and strong evaluation; the necessary connection between qualitative distinctions and our awareness of identity; our tendency to regard our lives as a narrative, and thus as a unity; the importance of the articulation of the sources of our moral convictions; Taylor's specific critique of Berlin's negative concept of freedom; and, finally, his objections to present-day interpretations of the ideal of self-realization.

Strong evaluation and identity

According to Taylor, there is weak evaluation when one balances against each other the various desires which one has at a particular moment, without the desirability of these desires itself being subject to discussion. This is the case with strong evaluation: the reflection is *qualitative*.[6] 'In this kind of case', Taylor writes, 'our desires are classified in such categories as higher and lower, virtuous and vicious, more and less fulfilling, more and less refined, profound and superficial, noble and base. They are judged as belonging to qualitatively different modes of life . . . ' (Taylor 1977: 16). The relevant distinctions are furthermore, 'not rendered valid by our own desires, inclinations, or choices, but rather stand independent of these and offer standards by which they can be judged' (Taylor 1989: 4). According to Taylor, moral intuitions are involved here whose effect is so deep, powerful and universal that there is a tendency to compare these to instincts. Everyone, for example, has the intuition that you are supposed to help someone in danger. As we saw earlier, the agnostic Berlin leaves open the question of where these intuitions come from. It is sufficient to note that they exist. Taylor, on the other hand, as a Catholic *believes* that they are dictated by a Divine authority.

The relevant intuitions are given a deviating *translation* in various cultures. This is determined by our ideas about why people earn our respect. This can be, for example, because we regard people as God's creations or as rational, autonomous beings who have the capacity for self-determination. Our moral reactions in the field of strong evaluations have therefore two facets, so to speak: on the one hand, an 'instinct' compared by Taylor, among others, to our fear of falling and, on the other, a rational articulation of this: a particular ontology, a totality of ideas on the nature and the status of man (Taylor 1989: 5). This is examined later in the chapter.

In Taylor's view, it is precisely the strong evaluations which are characteristic of man (1976: 287). We define ourselves against a background of qualitative distinctions. Taylor elaborates this thesis in particular in his *magnum opus Sources of the Self: The Making of the Modern Identity* (1989).

According to Taylor, the question 'Who am I?' is answered by what is of crucial importance for us, by where we stand in a 'moral space'. 'To know who you are is to be oriented in moral space, a space in which questions arise about what is good or bad, what is worth doing and what not, what has meaning and importance for you and what is trivial and secondary' (1989: 28). People in an identity crisis suffer from disorientation, they are unsure about the answer to the question of which possibilities of choice are meaningful or trivial in their lives. Qualitative distinctions therefore form a necessary component of the framework within which, or the background against which, our lives acquire unity, sense and meaning. 'Stepping outside these limits', writes Taylor, 'would be tantamount to stepping outside what we would recognize as integral, that is undamaged human personhood' (ibid.: 27). Possessing a moral orientation is, in short, a condition for being able to function as a person, it is not a 'metaphysical view we can put on or off' (ibid.: 99).

Life as a single narrative

According to Taylor 'to be connected to, or in contact with, what they see as good, or of crucial importance, or of fundamental value' is not only a necessity, but also one of people's most essential needs (1989: 42). We want to not only know what the correct qualitative distinctions are, but also how our life is related to the relevant moral framework. Because our life is lived in time, the question of whether we are on the right path, will thus inevitably arise. In Taylor's words: 'Since we cannot do without an orientation to the good, and since we cannot be indifferent to our place relative to this good, and since this place is something that must always change and become, the issue of the direction of our lives must arise for us' (ibid.: 47).

This makes the narrative character of human existence inescapable: we understand our lives in a narrative. In order to get an idea of who we are, we must have a notion of where we are coming from and where we are going. In the philosophical debate around the answer to the question of whether life must be understood as a unity[7], Taylor therefore distances himself from theoreticians like Parfit. They deny that someone's identity is defined in terms of his entire life: at forty, you are someone other than when you were twenty. According to Taylor, this is a misconception. Just like Locke and Hume, the parties involved see identity wrongly as an empty abstraction whose only characteristic is self-consciousness. An identity, however, cannot be regarded in neutral terms; it only exists in a context of qualitative distinctions. People define themselves by defining the direction of their whole lives with regard to what they consider valuable or the Good. People can change, naturally, but this change will then always have a place and meaning in an entire story. In Taylor's words: 'We want our lives to have meaning, or weight, or substance, or to grow towards some fullness. . . . But this means our whole lives. If necessary, we want the future to redeem the past, to make it part of a life story which has sense or purpose, to take it up in a meaningful unity' (1989: 50–1).

Articulation of the Good

The importance that Taylor attaches to qualitative distinctions implies that he emphatically wishes to concern himself with the *contents* of the Good life. According to him the debate on this within contemporary philosophy and science is completely muted. There is a strong tendency 'to focus on what it is right to do rather than on what it is good to be, on defining the content of obligation rather than the nature of the good life'[8] (1989: 3). The strong evaluations on which Taylor concentrates are given no place in this. Their relevance is even denied. There are various metaphysical, epistemological and ethical reasons for this exclusion (1989: 80ff.; 1991: 17–23).

The most important of these is the modern notion of (negative) freedom, which has developed since the seventeenth century. Central to this is the independence of the individual with regard to external authorities. Values have their origin in the will of the individual and not in a cosmic or social order outside him. The social contract theories of Locke and Grotius are an expression of this principle: a political order first becomes just when the citizens have agreed to this. Utilitarianism is another version. Within this theory, each individual is the best judge of his happiness, every form of paternalism is rejected. A contemporary interpretation is the liberal idea of 'neutrality': a liberal society should adapt a neutral standpoint with regard to the answer to the question of what forms a good or correct life. It is up to the individual citizens to formulate a response to this, and this deserves to be respected as much as other responses by an impartial state. Together, the advocates of this sort of modern theory of freedom, according to Taylor, bring the idea of qualitative distinctions into discredit. They attempt to develop a cognitive model in which these distinctions are excluded.

In this fashion, people concentrate nowadays on 'the principles, or injunctions, or standards which guide *action*, while visions of the good are altogether neglected' (Taylor 1989: 84).[9] Rationality in the field of morality, practical reason, is no longer defined substantially, but *procedurally*: one is reasoning correctly when one has followed a particular method, procedure or style, not when one has reached a conclusion which is 'good' in terms of content. If one wants to award primacy to the desires or the 'will' of the individual and at the same time maintain practical reason, then according to Taylor there is no alternative to defining this exclusively in procedural terms (1989: 86).

The consequence of opposing qualitative distinctions and of limiting practical reason to procedural rationality is, in Taylor's view, that modern moral philosophy 'has no way of capturing the background understanding surrounding any conviction that we ought to act in this or that way – the understanding of the strong good involved' (Taylor 1989: 87). The parties concerned 'leave us with nothing to say to someone who asks why he should be moral'. While their procedural theories are motivated by powerful ideals such as freedom, altruism and universalism, these themselves acquire no place in the relevant systems. John Rawls' divisive theory of justice is an example of this, according to Taylor: the two principles he deduces are ultimately considered acceptable and convincing *because* they tally with the moral intuitions we already feel. But, wonders Taylor, why is no attempt made to formulate these intuitions directly? He considers it extremely remarkable that this theory 'keeps its most basic insights inarticulate' (ibid.: 89).

Why should we articulate 'the Good'? Can we not be content – as Berlin also advocates – with our shared moral intuitions in this regard and reason further from this and enter into debate with each other (cf. Larmore 1991: 160–161)? Taylor thinks not. In the first place, a vision of the Good only really becomes first available to people when it is articulated in some way or other. Such an expression brings us closer to our moral sources and reinforces their effect (Taylor 1989: 96, 516; 1991: 22). Also, when people assume, along with humanism, that no good exists outside the individual, that a 'higher' only consists of 'facing a disenchanted universe with courage and lucidity', according to Taylor, it is still possible to speak of a moral source. 'There is a constitutive reality, namely, humans as beings capable of this courageous disengagement. And our sense of admiration and awe for these capacities is what empowers us to live up to them' (1989: 94).

Naturally, states Taylor, some articulations of our moral sources are purer, more powerful and more convincing than others. Stories, in particular, have great power, which tallies with our need to see our life in narrative terms. People therefore like to link their personal story to a larger historical pattern in which a Good is realized. Examples are the traditional *Heilgeschichte* of Christianity, Progress, the Marxist revolution and the tradition of a national cultural identity. The power of these stories arises from their capacity to lend meaning and significance to the individual existence (Taylor 1989: 97).

The articulation can take place through great epiphanic works in the field of the arts and letters, philosophy and criticism. Taylor does not want to draw any distinction between the ability of works in these different areas to cause 'something' to resonate in us. It is a matter of developing 'languages of personal resonance' and in this we cannot allow ourselves to push to one side the language of the arts and letters as too subjective: 'We either explore this area with such language or not at all' (Taylor 1989: 512).[10]

A pregnant question for Taylor in this context is whether, within a naturalistic world view, people have sufficiently powerful sources and forms of articulation to remain true to their moral imperatives. Taylor, who, as has already been noted, is himself religiously inspired (1989: 517, 521), is afraid that the answer is no. He wonders whether naturalists who attempt to expel faith from their *Weltanschauung* are not, at the same time, parasites on the religious moral sources and articulations thereof, which nourish and reinforce the shared values. No matter how great the strength of humanist or naturalistic sources may be, Taylor thinks that that of a theistic nature is incomparably greater (ibid.: 518). When, as generally happens in naturalism, the respect and the benevolence with regard to individuals are based on the admirable capacities of man, how strong, Taylor wonders, are these feelings then with regard to 'the irremediably broken, such as the mentally handicapped, those dying without dignity, fetuses with genetic defects' (ibid.: 517)?

The limitations of the negative conception of freedom

In the oft-quoted essay 'What's wrong with negative liberty' (1979), Taylor explicitly examines Berlin's ideas on freedom. He opposes the idea, linked in his mind with negative freedom, that freedom can only be inhibited by external factors, that the individual is the one best aware of his own goals, and that distinguishing 'higher' or 'deeper' desires or goals opens the way for totalitarianism.

Taylor calls positive and negative freedom an *exercise* and an *opportunity* concept respectively. The reason for this is obvious: within the positive conception one is only free when one *actively* gives direction to one's own life. One has to do something about it before one can call oneself free: 'one is free only to the extent that one has effectively determined oneself and the shape of one's life' (Taylor 1979: 177). As we saw earlier in the chapter, this activity is not sought within the negative conception of the individual: freedom is a question of what we *can* do, of which possibilities we have, it does not matter whether one actually uses these options. Freedom here, therefore, is simply the absence of inhibitions.[11]

Taylor regards this exclusive emphasis on external obstacles as a misunderstanding of the self-realization and self-determination ideal which, according to him, is also cherished within the relevant liberal tradition of thought (Taylor 1979: 177). In his reading, the ultimate justification of negative freedom is that people need a personal domain to be able to develop in their own unique manner.[12] However, as soon as freedom is related to self-realization, it must also be recognized, says Taylor, that exercise of freedom can find not only external, but also inner obstacles in its way. After all, to realize this notion of freedom a certain degree of self-awareness, self-understanding, moral discrimination and self-control is needed (ibid.: 179). One can be completely free from external obstacles, one can have countless opportunities, and still not be a master of one's life. According to Taylor in this case it is not possible to speak of freedom.

Taylor suspects that the attractiveness of the idea that freedom merely means the absence of external obstacles, lies mainly in its simplicity: freedom means that people can do what they want and the individual himself knows best what he wants. If, on the other hand, freedom is interpreted as an 'exercise concept', then answering the question of whether someone is free is less simple and uncontroversial.

In the first place, in this case, it must be recognized that an individual can also be inhibited by inner obstacles. In the second place, qualitative distinctions must be made here between motivations (Taylor 1979: 179).[13] As we have seen earlier, according to Taylor only the second-order wishes and goals are an expression of the identity, of the 'true' self of the individual. Our freedom is restricted when we are not in a position to make these wishes our will, when our wishes of the first order conquer those of the second order (ibid.: 184–5).[14] One is therefore unfree when in one's actions one is motivated by anxieties, by non-authentic, internalized conventions, by a false consciousness, by all those motivations which ultimately work against the basic goals which one strives after in life and which frustrate the realization of one's identity. They are motives which do not fit within the narrative of our life and can even threaten the continuity of this story.

What we want at a particular moment can therefore be an internal obstacle to what we really want – 'to, in Bergmann's words, 'acting out our identity'. In order to get an insight into what we really want, to be really free, however, we must have a clear view of who we are. If we want to meet these conditions, then we will first have to have developed somewhat, and have a certain amount of self-consciousness and self-knowledge. In order to be really free, in short, we must 'work' actively on our identity and our self-knowledge, and therefore freedom cannot be defined just as having opportunities (Taylor 1979: 193).

In the third place, an *exercise* conception of freedom is more problematic and controversial, because in this case the individual is not always the one who can best judge whether or not his desires are authentic. Taylor writes: 'the subject himself can't be the final authority on the question whether he is free; for he cannot be the final authority on the question whether his desires are authentic, whether they do or do not frustrate his purposes' (Taylor 1979: 180). The principle that the individual is the best judge of his own wishes would imply, according to Taylor, that these were understood as 'brute facts', as facts we could never be mistaken about (ibid.: 187–91). A large number of feelings, particularly the second-order desires, are however significantly less factual and unambiguous: feelings of shame and fear, for example, are based on a particular interpretation of our environment and these can be incorrect or distorted. However, if we recognize that this is a case of ascribing value, then, according to Taylor, we must also accept that this value can be incorrect, cannot form an accurate expression of our deeper goals, of our identity. When we ourselves have already experienced feelings or desires we would rather not have, who can say, Taylor wonders, that it is not possible that we possess more of this sort of inhibiting motivation, unrecognized by us?

Does this not pave the route, in a way warned against by Berlin, for a totalitarian society? Taylor thinks not: the identification of deeper goals and the stance that one is only free when one does what one really wants, or what tallies with these deeper goals, is not logically connected to the belief that this freedom can only be achieved in a society where the state determines how people must organize their lives. It is unreasonable to continue to use an untenable conception of freedom out of fear of the latter (Taylor 1979: 180, 193).

The inadequacy of the current culture of authenticity

In, among other places, *The Ethics of Authenticity* published in 1991, Taylor produces a cultural critique of the interpretation which, according to him, is given by many to individualism and freedom.[15] In this book, the foregoing is practically interpreted, and thus illustrated and clarified.

Taylor simultaneously links up with and opposes the ideas of cultural critics like Allan Bloom, Daniel Bell and Christopher Lasch. These condemn what they feel to be the widespread egocentrism and relativism and indifference, or even the ignorance which accompanies it, with regard to matters which transcend the individual – political, historical, religious. In his *The Closing of the American Mind*, Bloom had attacked in particular the flaccid and weak relativism of present-day American students. This implies more or less that everyone has his own values, and that it is impossible to dispute this in any meaningful way. Here, it is not merely a question of an epistemological standpoint, but also of an ethical a priori: nobody has the right to criticize how someone else leads his life. This is his or her choice and must be respected. This relativism is based on a form of individualism: everyone has a right to a personal form of self-determination and self-development, and the content of this is based on one's own autonomously determined, unique values and qualities.

Taylor can agree partially with the critique of the current practice of individualism. The critics however throw out the baby with the bath water. According to him, they do not understand that hidden behind this interpretation there is an ethical ideal which is worth defending (Taylor 1991: 15). This is the ideal of being true to oneself, an ideal that Taylor, following Lionel Trilling, calls a search for *authenticity*.

The notion of authenticity is relatively modern (Taylor 1991: 25–31; 1992: 28–32). Taylor believes that a possible beginning of this notion is in the eighteenth-century Romantic idea that people are equipped with an innate moral consciousness, an intuitive feeling for good and bad. The difference between good and evil cannot be learned, as the philosophers of the Enlightenment stated, by calculating the consequences of a particular idea or action, but by following our feelings, a voice 'deep within us'.

In the history of thought, keeping contact with the inner then acquires an autonomous value which is increasingly separate from morality. Rousseau is one of the first and most important philosophers to express this swing in our culture, in which the inner of the subject becomes central. In order to be saved in the moral sense one must restore contact with an inner, natural voice, a voice which is regularly drowned out by the passions.

A further development of the idea of authenticity appears when it is linked to the notion of *originality*. This is expressed in particular by the German philosopher Herder, who claims that every person possesses a personal, unique, original personality. Listening to this inner voice is important, because only in this way can one be true to one's identity and therefore authentic. Every individual has a unique manner of being a person, and if he wants to organize his life in a different way, imposed by others, then he is not realizing himself.

This idea of keeping contact with, doing justice to, our 'identity' or originality is, according to Taylor, the background to the present-day ideal of authenticity and of the striving after 'self-realization' or 'self-development' in which this ideal is generally embedded (Taylor 1991: 29; 1992: 31). However, he wants to demonstrate that the contemporary interpretation of individualism prevents a realization of the original ideal of authenticity. It is, then, mainly a question of egocentrism and the related relativism which also, according to Taylor, characterize contemporary individualism.[16] In this culture of authenticity no values are recognized which transcend the wishes and desires of a specific individual. In addition, our connections with others are ignored.

In his critique of egocentrism, Taylor refers to the 'dialogical' character of the human identity. We become full, self-conscious human beings through appropriating to ourselves a full range of languages of expression. Language must be here understood in the broadest sense of the word: it refers to all means of expression with which we define our identity, including the 'languages' of love, the gesture and art. These languages are a social product and are acquired through interaction with others. The acquisition of a language and the definition of identity continue throughout life and always take place in dialogue with what George Herbert Mead called *significant others*. This dialogue is therefore not confined to a phase in which people learn languages of expression, after which they go their own way. People are indeed expected to develop their ideas and opinions in solitary reflection. But, writes Taylor, 'this is not how things work with important issues such as the definition of our identity. We define this always in dialogue with, sometimes in struggle against, the identities our significant others want to recognize in us' (Taylor 1991: 33). The egocentric forms of self-realization which deny the connections with others, or interpret these in the purely instrumental fashion, therefore have difficulty in relation to the quest for authenticity.

In reaction to the relativism of the current culture of authenticity, Taylor states that if people want to define themselves in a significant manner, this must necessarily take place against a background or 'horizon' of qualitative distinctions (Taylor 1991: 37–9). We have already seen that in the section on evaluation and identity. According to Taylor this indispensable horizon is currently being neglected. All choices are judged to be of equal value, with the consequence that all options lose their significance (ibid.: 39).[17] The prevailing forms of self-realization therefore obstruct each other: they try to realize the relevant ideal in opposition to the standards which are preferred and the questions which are asked by society, tradition, nature, the community. The necessary conditions for the realization of authenticity are thus undermined. Taylor writes:

> I can define my identity only against the background of things that matter. But to bracket out history, nature, society, the demands of solidarity, everything but what I find in myself, would be to eliminate all candidates for what matters. . . . Authenticity is not the enemy of demands that emanate from beyond the self; it supposes such demands.
>
> (Taylor 1991: 40–1)

If self-realization is not to end up as emptiness then, to put it briefly, there must be a number of matters which transcend the self: 'A total and fully consistent subjectivism would tend towards emptiness: nothing would count as a fulfilment in a world in which literally nothing was important but self-fulfilment' (Taylor 1989: 507).

Some comments

It can be seen as a limitation to Taylor's ideas that, in contrast to his own scientific theoretical principles, they are chiefly philosophical with hardly any empirical support. For example, he scarcely takes the trouble to confront his vision of man with psychological and sociological insights (cf. Rosenberg 1990: 92–3). Taylor thinks that people have intuitive contact with, and strive for, the Good and he criticizes the current philosophers because they concern themselves solely with procedures and the 'right'. However, Judith Shklar states that Taylor himself does the same: when he gives examples of our intuitions – mutual respect and respect for the integrity of others' lives – these also turned out to refer to 'the right' and not 'the Good'. In addition, he incorrectly makes no effort whatsoever to empirically research whether ordinary people are indeed guided by the relevant intuitions. Precisely because shared moral intuitions play such an important role in his rejection of utilitarianism, naturalism and individualism, it is insufficient for measuring the existence of this to only refer to literary and philosophical texts. Not researching the actual thinking and action of everyday people, writes Shklar, 'leads him to impute attitudes to the obdurate which they simply do not hold or to accuse them of false consciousness' (Shklar 1991: 108). Relevant empirical questions here are, among others, whether people actually want to know how their life relates to a particular moral horizon and whether people really experience their life as a single story with a plot.

Another problem is that Taylor, although he leaves room for change, threatens with this latter assumption to force people into a straitjacket of a 'life plan'. This jacket becomes even tighter when he suggests that the moral intuitions on which our identity is based are already fixed. Taylor perhaps fails to recognize sufficiently that numerous values and goals which can be cherished and pursued in life, inevitably and irreconcilably conflict with each other, and that it is thus inherent to the human condition that many often difficult choices have to be made, and that these choices (in the course of the years) turn out to not always be equally consistent. Taylor is thinking in terms of harmony. Perhaps this exists, but the question is whether this principle also tallies with most people's experiences in the here and now. Nevertheless, it may well be that although the picture painted by him of man is not an accurate description of the average mortal, this naturally does not prove that this image is not worth aspiring to. People who are known in life as 'impossibly shallow characters' should also be branded as such. Taylor provides a justification for this here.

Another central theme of Taylor's is that relativism prevents a realization of the ideal of authenticity, because people can first fix an identity against a background of qualitative distinctions. Taylor regards full freedom, in which everything is open to discussion, as 'empty' because in that case nothing would be worth the trouble of choosing any more. Furthermore, freedom will always be 'situated': one is bonded by personal relations and thus bound to others, and one is an element of a cultural tradition which provides qualitative standards.

However, the question is how urgent or inevitable the latter takes place. Communitarian thinkers like Taylor, Walzer and MacIntyre go further into this than liberals. Liberals assume to a higher degree that people can shake off the prevailing values of their cultural community and can decide autonomously to absorb these or not. The importance of negative freedom lies partly in this. In response to Taylor's critique that liberals assume an empirically untenable 'abstract' image of man, Kymlicka, for example, suggests that they only *imagine* the individual free of a moral horizon 'in the sense that no end or goal is exempt from possible re-examinations' (Kymlicka 1989: 52). If the latter is to be possible in a meaningful sense, then it is necessary to be able to see the individual separate from his current preferences. In short, communitarian thinkers threaten to make individuals not only the product, but also the victim, of their culture.

However, none of this alters the fact that a principle must always be taken as a 'given', because otherwise one has no criterion on the basis of which the considerations necessary for choosing between values can be made. Taylor emphasizes above all this necessity of possessing a principle and does not choose a single specific cultural tradition. Moreover, he is an advocate of making the moral horizon as broad as possible, by studying other traditions (Taylor 1992: 67–73).

Finally, a big problem with the conception of freedom, as Taylor develops it in his critique of the negative conception, refers exactly to the question which, according to him, must still be answered: what is the political relevance of the fact that people often do things which they actually do not want to or which frustrate the realization of their long term goals? This question is gone into further in Chapter 5.

ROBERT YOUNG: LIFE PLAN

> Once upon a time there lived in Berlin, Germany, a man called Albinus. He was rich, respectable, happy; one day he abandoned his wife for the sake of a youthful mistress; he loved; was not loved; and his life ended in disaster. This is the whole story and we might have left it at that had there not been profit and pleasure in the telling; and although there is plenty of space on a gravestone to contain, bound in moss, the abridged version of a man's life, detail is always welcome.
>
> (Vladimir Nabokov 1961: 5)

Even more pronouncedly than Taylor, the Australian philosopher Robert Young has related autonomy to the execution of a life plan. In his view, autonomy demands not only that one can act freely in a particular situation, without the intervention of others, but also that, seen in the long term, one can lead a life which is given direction by a life plan designed by the individual himself: 'An autonomous life is one that is directed in accordance with an individual's own conception of what he wants to do in and with that life' (Young 1986: 49). The more one succeeds in directing one's life in this sense, the more autonomous one is.

Impediments to autonomy can come not only from 'outside', but also from 'inside', and paternalism can sometimes be desired to remove these obstacles. Paternalism is the restricting of someone's freedom in order to avoid him damaging himself, or to promote his welfare. The preoccupation with external restrictions on autonomy which exists in Western thought, according to Young, has given paternalism a bad image. The autonomous individual is supposed to be always able to make his own choices, no matter how stupid or bad they are, without the intervention of others. Young states that here, unjustly, no distinction is made between two dimensions of autonomy: 'Such a position is confused in so far as it fails to keep distinct the occurrent sense of autonomy, autonomy of the moment, from the more important dispositional sense of autonomy, where the focus is on the autonomous person's life as a whole' (Young 1986: 5). Because some of the individual's choices can, in the long term, endanger his autonomy, it can sometimes be necessary, in order to guarantee the realization of his life plan, to limit his ('occurrent') autonomy at a particular moment. An example would be someone who decides to use heroin, who wants to sign a contract making himself a slave, or who wants to participate in unnecessary and very risky experiments. Even though the parties involved in these cases have consciously chosen how to act, and even though they will therefore – also in retrospect – give no permission for paternalism, even then, in Young's opinion, intervention must be carried out (ibid.: 69). As far as he is concerned, people may be coerced into leading an autonomous life. (In Chapter 5, we will return extensively to this conception of autonomy and justification of paternalism.)

BENJAMIN BARBER: INTENTIONALISM

In his essay 'Forced to be free, an illiberal defense of liberty' (1971), the American political philosopher Benjamin Barber emphasizes an aspect of autonomy which already played an important background role in Young, Frankfurt and Taylor: autonomous behaviour is *intentional.*

Freedom and coercion, says Barber, are generally seen as each other's opposites: freedom is the absence of coercion. Rousseau's stance that people can be forced to be free, is thus illogical from this viewpoint. However, Barber wants to show that the relation between freedom and coercion is more complex than liberalism would have us believe. To this end, he distinguishes two models in which these concepts are given a particular definition.

Two models of freedom

The first, *abstract physical–mechanistic model* is, in Barber's eyes, ideally typical of liberalism. Theoreticians like Hobbes, Locke, Hume, Bentham, John Stuart Mill, Godwin, Dahl and Berlin make use of it. According to Barber, characteristic of this mechanistically-inspired model[18] is that freedom is seen as a movement towards a certain goal, unimpeded by external obstacles. In addition, the body is imagined as an indivisible, discrete entity with given motives which are not open to discussion (Barber 1971: 41; 1984: 26ff.; cf. Lukes 1973, ch. 11; For a defence of this model, see Day 1983). Just as no distinction is drawn within this model between the motivations which an individual can have, nor is any distinction drawn between the various sorts of coercion. Exercise of coercion ultimately boils down to the use of physical force or the threat thereof. Defined like this, it is indeed never possible to be free through coercion. However, Barber emphasizes that coercion can also consist of persuasion, socialization, manipulation, brainwashing, authority, and even of education. The mechanistic model offers no room for this notion and, says Barber, can only appear acceptable as long as:

> the objects of men's actions are viewed as non-contradictory, monolithic, and unambiguous; for at the instant we begin to speak of diversified and possibly contradictory goals held simultaneously by a single individual, that individual ceases to be a single, indivisible particle and becomes a complex entity made up of different and conflicting parts. We can no

longer speak of the entity being coerced or being free as a whole; we must specify which parts and which objects are in question.

(Barber 1971: 47–8)

The second ideal–typical paradigm, the 'concrete psychological–intentionalist model', does take into account, according to Barber, this increasingly assumed fact and shows that 'forced to be free' is not necessarily a contradiction. In this model, self-consciousness, the capacity to regard oneself 'from the outside', so to speak, is seen as the essential trait of man. Through this consciousness, man is permanently split into two parts. This split does set in motion feelings of alienation, but also makes it possible to reflect on one's own existence and, in this way, to be an intentional being. In this light, according to Barber, a distinction can be made between conscious, intentional and free acts, and unfree behaviour, which is merely an impulsive or conditioned response to an external stimulus: 'When we merely "do", we react as animals; only when we are conscious of what we do and thus take an attitude toward it . . . do we act intentionally, as men' (Barber 1971: 52). Therefore, it is only the man who acts intentionally who acts freely: 'A man is unfree in behaving impulsively not because he would necessarily have chosen to act otherwise, but because he did not choose to act at all, his behaviour was really not his action at all, whatever the motives, causes or origins of the behaviour' (ibid.: 57).[19]

Not only is the individual split into two parts – usually alienated from each other – through his capacity for self-reflection, he is also as a rule tossed back and forth between deviating and often conflicting goals, feelings and considerations. It is generally extremely difficult, even for the party involved, to define what he or she really wants. For Barber, and equally for Bergmann, the answer to the question of whether the action which ultimately results can be called 'free', is not determined by whether one has been able to do what one wants without impediment, it is more important whether one can identify with this action, or regard it as one's own action. Before one can identify with one's own behaviour, one must first be aware of the motivations behind it. The difference with someone who acts unfreely, is therefore not only that one identifies with one's actions, but also, and here Barber deviates from Bergmann, that one is aware of and identifies with the motives for it: one does not act impulsively, but intentionally (Barber 1971: 58).

Three forms of coercion

As stated, in this psychological–intentionalist model, coercion appears in more forms than in its abstract, physical–mechanistic opposite. Barber distinguishes three types: coercion which is explicitly aimed at the body of the subject is the first, most obvious form. This was taken as the starting-point in the first model. Someone who is tied to his chair or is threatened with this, is naturally not free.

Coercion which is aimed at the conscious self, the ego, is the second type. Positive and negative sanctions, which are imposed by others to direct the behaviour of the subject in a direction pleasing to them are, in Barber's view, an attempt to undermine the conscious, intentional self and can therefore limit the freedom of the subject. The father of children threatened with starvation will possibly allow himself to be bribed to do something which he himself does not approve of. The relevant act, however, will never be *his*, will not be free. He is merely a coerced instrument of another – another who uses him as a means to realize his goals.

The third type of coercion, the most serious in Barber's view, is aimed at the non-conscious 'reactive' self or selves. (Compare the 'radical' conception of power of Lukes and Connolly, dealt with in Chapter 5.) It attempts to influence this in such a way that its behaviour tallies with the wishes or goals of the manipulator. The decision to concentrate on 'the reactive self' can be due to the fact that this is simpler to condition and easier to impose habits on, than the conscious self: the latter acts each time once again open-mindedly – without preconceptions and is therefore the enemy of habit. What is bad about this type of coercion – socialization, advertising, propaganda, and also education – is that, in contrast to the other types, it can permanently change individuals: all their future behaviour can be influenced by it.

Freedom due to suppression of non-intentional behaviour

Nevertheless, according to Barber, it cannot be said that all forms of socialization, education and persuasion are meant to be an attempt to undermine the self-consciousness of the self. In fact, the same means can be used to try to enlarge this consciousness:

It is no longer impossible to think that if coercive influence can be applied to the reactive self to inhibit consciousness, it can also be applied to the active self to generate and nourish consciousness, and if this is possible, then – at least from the perspective of intentionalism – we may be able to say with conviction that men can be forced to be free.

(Barber 1971: 72)

Education must aim to replace the impulsive reaction to external stimuli by the unconscious, with chosen, free action by the self-conscious self. In Barber's view, coercion, the suppression by others of these impulses, can be necessary for this:

In liberating consciousness, impulses must be repressed; such repression aims not at the creative inputs into the process of consciously forming and implementing intentions, but at the irresistible springs to reactive behaviour which, by-passing self-awareness altogether, remove from the subject his capacity to make his own future.

(Barber 1971: 73)

'Non-perverted' education or therapies can realize this liberation.

According to Barber, empirical research must be able to show which education this applies to. Criteria here include: the effect of a particular form of training on the experience of freedom of the individual concerned; the degree to which he can indicate reasons for his behaviour (impulsive reactions can at best be clarified, but never rationalized or justified); the degree to which the individual can process stimuli from his surroundings or, in any case, can postpone the reaction to them; and the degree to which he lives according to ossified habits or is constantly creating new opportunities.

It is therefore a question of teaching people to act *consciously*, and not *'correctly'*. All the same, according to Barber, this does not necessarily imply that their behaviour will ultimately be different from the behaviour which would have arisen from urges, instincts, habits, etc., or that free people are less easily manipulated or persuaded. Research actually points to the opposite (see the section on Bettelheim later in this chapter).

Freedom as struggle and regret

We may well wonder why the act of 'choosing', why conscious, intentional acting, is so important for freedom. Bergmann, for example, states that one is also free if one 'lets everything wash over one' or 'lets oneself be swept along by events'. The only condition is that one can identify with the latter. He points out that in some cultures and religions it is actually this surrender and acceptance which opens the way to wisdom. In the West, in his opinion, people are too concerned with whether one chooses personally, or is forced (Bergmann 1977: 55–61).

The fact that one, possibly after lengthy weighing up of the pros and cons, has chosen something, is according to Bergmann no guarantee of freedom, for yet another reason. What we think, the ideas we have of our choices, is actually influenced and limited in countless ways. In addition, we certainly do not always have our thoughts under control. Why is it suddenly freedom, Bergmann wonders, when 'the decisive event happens to be a thought occurring in my consciousness?' (Bergmann 1977: 16–5).

While Bergmann thus associates freedom mainly with an effortless and anxiety-free 'stream of identifications', in Barber's view, freedom is actually always accompanied by the (laborious) creation of and choosing between new possibilities and with the overcoming of tensions (Barber 1971: 58–63, 75–9).

In imitation of Sartre, he states that with intentional action there is a double negation, causing tensions. In the first place, through choosing something new, one denies what one was and is. In this, the future does not consist, as in the deterministic, mechanistic model of freedom assailed by Barber, of a fixed number of options from which a choice must be made: the future is actually being created. By acting consciously and intentionally, therefore, one is not making a selection from among existing alternatives, one *creates* them.

In the second place, through the choice ultimately made one negates all the other possibilities formed by consciousness. A large number of imaginable 'projects' are therefore unused, do not become reality. Thus, freedom brings with it dilemmas, inner conflicts and tensions. One must choose from among the self-invented alternatives, and the awareness that so many options are being neglected causes a sensation of constant regret and inadequacy. Unconscious behaviour, impulsive reaction, on the other hand, is completely linked to the here and now, considers no possibilities and never has such feelings. It is therefore, in Barber's view, completely unfree. In this, he distinguishes himself from Bergmann. Freedom, the creation of and choosing from among projects, is not characterized by passivity, but by activity, or at least that is what we can deduce from the above. In Barber's view, too, it is therefore not an *opportunity*, but an *exercise* concept.

Freedom therefore requires one to overcome one's own past and the dilemmas and regret which accompany the creation of the future. It does not consist, as Christian Bay and Bergmann suppose, of the absence of inner inhibitions or the harmony between 'basic motives and overt behaviour'. According to Barber, freedom actually means 'permanent and necessary tension, ineluctable conflict. It requires not the absence but the presence of obstacles; for without them there can be no tension, no overcoming, and consequently, no freedom' (Barber 1971: 60). Barber approvingly quotes Sartre, who in his *La Republique de Silence* stated that he was never so free as during the German occupation:[20] the greater the reluctance which must be overcome, the greater the experience of freedom; the stronger we are shackled to the present by all kinds of conditions, the more intense is our sensation of freedom when we overcome this.

To recapitulate, if, for Barber, the conscious creation of and choosing between alternatives is central, an activity which is always accompanied by tensions, conflict and regret, Bergmann is – to some extent – at the other extreme: making choices is not what is most important, it is also possible to allow oneself to be carried along by the flow of events and a choice is often no more than the product of socialization, ignorance and chance. Both viewpoints have a certain plausibility.

PROVISIONAL CONCLUSIONS

Where have the insights of a number of representative advocates of the positive conception of freedom brought us up to now? In the first place, we have seen that only actions with which one can identify, actions which one regards as an expression of the 'true' self, are perceived to be 'free'. Having an identity is therefore a necessary condition for every experience of freedom: freedom is the expression of this identity. We then concerned ourselves with what is held by a number of authors to be essential to our identity or our humanity. In general, all subscribed to the belief that someone who, throughout his entire life, is at every moment only propelled by the first desire or impulse can hardly be a master of his own life. Autonomy requires one to be objective about one's own desires and wishes, to be capable of making a qualitative evaluation of which of these wishes and desires in his life or life plan is essential or valuable, or not, and can therefore be considered an expression of his identity; that on the basis of this one forms wishes about desires – wishes that certain desires become one's will and others not – and that, finally, one is also really capable of making these second-order desires one's will. Autonomous action is therefore conscious, intentional action; one is aware of one's motives, evaluates these on the basis of their 'deeper', more central values and only then takes well-considered action. Free action is therefore not impulsive, is not based exclusively on acquired codes, habits, instincts, etc. Furthermore, the more one checks one's wishes against one's central values, the more depth or personality one has and the more autonomous one is. Qualitative evaluation therefore presupposes self-consciousness or self-knowledge: one must be aware of one's motives and one must know which values occupy a central position in one's own life, what one's identity is. That, in all this self-reflection, the autonomous person must also possess a certain degree of rationality, is obvious. Finally, we have seen that positive freedom, in contrast to negative freedom is not an opportunity, but an exercise concept: it is necessary *to do* something in order to become master of one's own life.

It seems important in all this to beware of freedom or autonomy becoming a constrained, over-conscious wrestling of a tormented self with its desires and wishes. Freedom, Bergmann rightly emphasizes, is in practice actually experienced as light, bearable and harmonious. In addition, freedom is certainly connected with the autonomous creation of, and the choice between, new possibilities: our experience of freedom is often greatest when the trails we follow have not yet been blazed for us. The existentialist idea that we are constantly creating new options and can decide every moment to be someone else, however, is too extreme: this would become a rather tiring activity, and conflicts in reality with all our sociological and socio-psychological findings. The formation of an identity is a 'dialogical' process and takes place necessarily against a horizon of qualitative distinctions. The individual does not ordain these latter standards autonomously, they are also proffered by society and its cultural tradition. Freedom requires that this be partly assumed and, at the same time, can be always open to discussion. In reaction to existentialism, the 'self', finally, must also not be regarded as an all too rigidly delineated entity which hardly, if ever, changes, with a clear conception of what it wants from its life. People are more flexible, are less the prisoner of their own personality, wrestle more with opposing desires and conflicting values, than Young's 'life plan' conception and, to a lesser extent, that of Taylor, tend to allow (cf. Chapters 4 and 5).

Finally, it has become clear that the different definitions of freedom given in the course of time deviate from each other, in the first place, in the identification of the 'self', and that the fixing of what counts as an inhibition of freedom is determined by where one draws the boundaries of the self. The distinction generally made between inner and outer inhibitions of freedom, where the human body is regarded as the boundary, is lent nuance by this: properly regarded, there are only external inhibitions, obstacles which can also be thrown up in one's own body and mind. However, because the danger of distortion – as Berlin has demonstrated – becomes greater as soon as a theory of political freedom permits personal desires to be characterized as 'unauthentic', 'false' and not originating from the 'true' self, it is useful to continue making a distinction between inner and outer inhibitions. In this way the defensive ring around the individual remains as strong as possible.

A number of important elements of autonomy have not yet been dealt with. These are independence of mind, steadfastness and integrity, being open to new experiences and ideas, and originality. In the following section, more attention will also be devoted to the question of whether all these requirements for autonomy can still be met by ordinary mortals.

BRUNO BETTELHEIM: INTEGRITY AND WILLPOWER

I know with scientific certainty that everyone carries it in him, the plague, because no one, absolutely no one, is not susceptible to it. And that one must be always on one's guard to avoid being driven in a moment of distraction to breathe in another's face and infect him. The microbe really exists. All the rest, health, invulnerability, uprightness, even hygiene, is the result of willpower and of a willpower which can never falter. The decent person, the one who infects almost no one, is the one who allows himself to be the least distracted. But what a willpower and power of concentration is necessary to never be distracted!

Albert Camus (1942: 183)

Autonomy can also be explicitly understood as, in the words of Robert Young, a 'character ideal' (1986: ch. 2) – in this case, as the possession of the willpower to hold on to one's own integrity, one's own inner convictions, under difficult circumstances. In a certain sense, this is a strengthened version of the ideal of authenticity which was described by Taylor: genuineness or being faithful to one's own identity. This idea is perhaps best represented by Bruno Bettelheim. This Jewish psychiatrist was born in Vienna in 1903. During the years 1938 and 1939 he was a prisoner in the German concentration camps of Dachau and Buchenwald. Just before the start of the Second World War he was able to get to the United States of America. He became mainly known for his treatment of autistic children, and his studies of camp experiences, education and 'the truth' of fairy tales. He committed suicide in 1990.

In his book *The Informed Heart* (1960), Bettelheim gives an impressive report of his experiences in the concentration camp. By trying to continue to exercise his profession, he attempted to ignore the daily reality in the camp and in this way resisted the attempts to break his identity and willpower. To this end, Bettelheim made a psychoanalytical study of the deviant behaviour of a number of groups of prisoners.

Of these groups, including 'gentile political prisoners, Jewish "political" or "workshy" prisoners, Jehovah's Witnesses, non-political middle-class prisoners', the latter were the ones least fitted to keep their bearings in the degrading situation they found themselves in. They lacked the inner strength or conviction needed for this. Bettelheim wrote of these German apolitical bourgeois:

> No consistent philosophy, either moral, political, or social, protected their integrity or gave them strength for an inner stand against Nazism. They had little or no resources to fall back on when subject to the shock of imprisonment. Their self esteem had rested on a status and respect that came with their positions, depended on their jobs, on being head of a family, or similar external factors.
>
> (Bettelheim 1960: 120–1)

From the moment that these people lost their social status, they usually lost all self-respect and their personality completely disintegrated. They became rudderless, tried to imitate other prisoners, or attempted through exaggerated submissiveness to get on good terms with the SS, which only increased the contempt of the latter. Many of these prisoners became depressive and the number of suicides in this group was the highest.

The political prisoners, generally social democrats and communists from the 'lower' socio-economic classes, turned out to be better able to withstand the Nazi terror. They were psychologically prepared for imprisonment, could explain the situation in which they found themselves in terms of their *Weltanschauung* and saw no reason at all in imprisonment to lose their self-respect.

However, the least disturbed group was the Jehovah's Witnesses, people who are seldom seen as a model of autonomy. They retained their integrity thanks to their profound, but extremely rigid, religious conviction. Members of this group, wrote Bettelheim, 'were generally narrow in outlook and experience, wanting to make converts, but on the other hand exemplary comrades, helpful, correct, dependable . . . they were the only group of prisoners who never abused or mistreated other prisoners' (Bettelheim 1960: 123). These Jehovah's Witnesses never exploited their key positions within the camp, given to them by the SS because of their correct and diligent work habits, to acquire privileges or harm the interests of other prisoners. Because, in the eyes of the SS, their only crime was to refuse military service, they were regularly offered their freedom, with as the only requirement that they change their views about this service.

Despite the atrocious conditions which they too had to endure in the camp, they consistently refused this.

Partly on the basis of these personal experiences in a concentration camp, in his description of autonomy Bettelheim laid great emphasis on values like integrity, steadfastness and personality. Autonomy, he wrote:

> has to do with man's inner ability to govern himself, and with a conscientious search for meaning despite the realization that, as far as we know, there is no purpose to one's life. It is a concept that does not imply a revolt against authority *qua* authority, but rather a quiet acting out of inner conviction, not out of convenience or resentment, or because of external persuasion or controls.
>
> (Bettelheim 1960: 72)

For Bettelheim, a precondition and characteristic of individual autonomy is a balanced integrated personality with a strongly developed sense of identity, based on the conviction of being a unique respected being with a number of profound significant relations with others.

S. I. BENN: AUTARCHY OR BROADMINDEDNESS

The idea that the Jehovah's Witnesses, generally regarded as rather narrow-minded, must also be regarded as autonomous personalities – in fact, precisely for this reason – has bothered a number of authors. They made tough demands on the autonomous individual, demands which some of them simultaneously soften.

For example, Benn explicitly refuses to characterize dogmatic Marxists and Jehovah's Witnesses as autonomous: the qualification 'autarch' seems more suitable to him. In his view autonomy is confined to critically-minded, all-round developed and broadly informed representatives of the Western, pluralistic tradition of thought. He finds it difficult to include the above groups in this. Benn says: 'autonomy is an ideal available only to a plural tradition. However massive the personality integration and principled coherence of tribesmen and some religious sectarians, they cannot qualify as autonomous if they cannot claim to have actively made the nomos their own' (Benn 1975: 128).

All the same, it seems useful here to make a distinction between the *cognitive* and *conative* qualities of individuals. The capacity to form second-order 'volitions' and maintain integrity under difficult circumstances, is a conative quality which is partially separate from the cognitive capacities which Benn wants from an autonomous personality. Intellectual narrow-mindedness can therefore go very well together with moral steadfastness.

RICHARD LINDLEY: ACTIVE THEORETICAL RATIONALITY

The English political philosopher Richard Lindley considers both aspects important for autonomy. Strongly inspired by John Stuart Mill, he states that someone is cognitively heteronomous with regard to a particular conviction when he holds this on the basis of a lack of 'passive or active theoretical rationality', or when this is untrue (Lindley 1986: 45–52, 70; cf. Mill 1859: ch. 2). The latter speaks for itself: someone whose action and thinking is based on mistaken information can hardly be master of his own life. The former requires some more explanation.

Passive theoretical rationality is the tendency, on the basis of the available information and generally accepted principle of reasoning, to make the correct deductions. This form of rationality is a necessary condition of autonomy, but is not in itself enough. After all, the citizens of Aldous Huxley's *Brave New World* have this rationality. Few, however, would call them autonomous personalities. For this, they lack the will or drive necessary for autonomy, to search for the truth or other truths, to check whether what has been assumed up to now is true or correct. Lindley calls the latter inclination 'active theoretical rationality'.

It is naturally not necessary to take this form of rationality to the extreme: it is not possible to doubt everything. Although it is thus perhaps irrational to be exaggeratedly self-assured about the trueness or correctness of certain ideas, it is not necessarily unreasonable to be content with convictions for which one has no hard proof of oneself. This is particularly true in the field of our theoretical scientific beliefs: it is senseless to desire of someone that he produce proofs for all this sort of knowledge. It is not always irrational to accept the authority of others in this. However, it is different in the field of our religious, moral and political convictions, called 'opinions' by Lindley, after Mill. The importance of these opinions in our attempts to lend direction to our life is much greater and, therefore, also the necessity to evaluate these independently. This is certainly the case if we consider the enormous pressure exerted upon the individual to fit in with the opinions of the public at large or the rulers. This creates a real danger of people, not so much giving their life the direction which is best for them, but one which is the product of social pressure to conform. This can best be prevented by constantly looking for alternatives and raising one's own opinions for discussion. According to Lindley, active theoretical rationality also requires 'that one not only have good reasons for one's own opinion, but also give proper consideration to rival opinions. In matters of opinion, an autonomous person should be in a position to refute opposing views' (Lindley 1986: 50).

An important reason for this active form of rationality is also to be found in the knowledge that our fundamental moral intuitions are mainly formed during our childhood years, a time in which our critical, rational capacities have hardly been developed. Precisely because our opinions are, to a large degree, the product of our upbringing and therefore originate from others, a critical evaluation of them is extremely desirable. Only then can we rightly say that the fundamental values we uphold are 'ours', that we (as far as this is concerned) are autonomous.

JOHN BENSON: THE COURAGE TO BE FREE AND TO TRUST IN OTHERS

Autonomy demands, in short, active rational capacities. However, and this brings us back to Bettelheim, once again one needs self-confidence and personality to dare use these: to think independently, to choose and to act and, if necessary, to deviate from what is generally regarded as 'normal' or 'desirable', courage is indispensable. Someone's cognitive and conative qualities can therefore not be completely separated from each other. John Benson's answer to the question formulated in the title of his essay 'Who is the autonomous man?' is:

> To be autonomous is to trust one's own powers and to have a disposition to use them, to be able to resist the fear of failure, ridicule or disapproval that threatens to drive one into reliance on the guidance of others. . . . autonomy is closely allied to courage. Intellectual skills cannot exist without qualities of character. . . . If autonomy calls for a supple mind it also calls for a stiff neck.
>
> (Benson 1983: 9, 15, 16)

Nevertheless, Benson, too, opposes the demands which Benn and many others make on the autonomous individual. They associate too strongly autonomy with an over-conscious, extremely critical stance with regard to their own convictions and principles. Only a few will be capable of this profound and ongoing self-examination (Benson 1983: 5). Benson is also extremely doubtful whether it would be such a pleasant experience to meet such a person, constantly concerned to question the (few) certainties we cherish in life. Socrates, too, was ultimately condemned to the poisoned goblet, we might add.

It is a practical impossibility, writes Benson, to collect independently all the proofs of our knowledge. Nor is this necessary. When the state says that smoking is bad for our health, then we generally regard it as such a dependable source that it is unnecessary to personally check the proof of this statement. Autonomy can therefore be reconciled with authority, with the trusting acceptance of the knowledge of others. The criterion for autonomy is then shifted to the question of the extent to which one is capable of justifying this faith. Blindly following the word of just anybody is not exactly an expression of autonomy. It is necessary to have good reasons for ascribing authority to someone and remaining always prepared to investigate oneself in the event of doubt. This is particularly true in the case of ethical questions (Benson 1983: 13). In this field, too, one can naturally turn for advice to more experienced, wise men and women. And, if one accepts their conclusions, one perhaps possesses praiseworthy opinions. However, a morality first comes to life when one has also 'followed through' its justification:

> What is at stake . . . is not only the truth of the opinion but the character of the assent . . . one should not just take over the conclusions of the practically wise man but try to follow through the process of deliberation that he has followed, so that by appreciating the force and relevance of his reasons one makes the conclusion one's own.
>
> (Benson 1983: 14)

GERARD DWORKIN: QUALIFYING MORAL ORIGINALITY

A qualification of the authenticity which is considered by many to be necessary for moral autonomy, in particular, is to be found, among others, in Gerard Dworkin. If Taylor, as we have seen, gives a transcendent basis to morality in the final analysis, Dworkin has strong tendencies towards a sociological justification. The latter makes a qualification possible.

In general, strongly divergent philosophers such as Kant, Kierkegaard, Nietzsche, Hare, Popper, Sartre and Wolff regard someone as morally autonomous 'if and only if his moral principles are his own' (Dworkin 1978: 157). More specifically, writes Dworkin, this can then mean, among other things, that an autonomous individual is the source, the creator of his moral principles; that he has chosen these principles autonomously; that his will is the ultimate source or authority with regard to his principles; that he alone decides which principles are binding for him; that he bears full responsibility for his conviction; and that he never adopts a moral judgment from someone else without having first thought it over autonomously and therefore never accepts others as moral authorities. Dworkin considers that all these formulations of autonomy are too strong.

The idea, for example, that moral autonomy requires people to create or invent their principles themselves, or that one is influenced by nobody in choosing principles is, in his view, untenable on both empirical and conceptual grounds:

> On empirical grounds this view denies our history. We are born in a given environment with a given set of biological endowments. We mature more slowly than other animals and are deeply influenced by parents, siblings, peers, culture, class, climate, schools, accident, genes, and the accumulated history of the species. It makes no more sense to suppose we invent the moral law for ourselves than to suppose that we invent the language we speak for ourselves.
>
> (Dworkin 1978: 158; see also: Dworkin 1981: 208–9)

In addition, according to Dworkin, it is a logical or conceptual problem that a fundamental feature of moral principles is that they refer to the relations between people. Principles, which are created free of all the above-mentioned influences, can therefore hardly be social or moral in nature. In his opinion, they are more a personal ritual.

It is therefore unrealistic of people to desire to create their values completely autonomously, influenced by nobody. However, people can always decide for themselves whether to accept or reject existing values. Although the choice of alternatives can, to a large extent, be given, each person can, or must, ultimately always make the choice himself (cf. Young 1986: 35–42). The problem now is to give the latter an interpretation which is neither trivial (who else could make my decisions?) nor unrealistic (choices can never be seen separately from authority, tradition and community) (Dworkin 1978: 160–70). The fact that someone is also influenced by others in his choices between existing values is therefore no proof, for example, of a lack of autonomy: this applies to almost all our convictions and decisions.

In the article 'The concept of autonomy', Dworkin tries to solve this problem by making a distinction, just like Bergmann, between goals, desires and values with which one can identify or not. Only when one is propelled in one's life by the former motivations, is there autonomy. However, even someone's identifications can be the product of such influencing that we no longer regard these as 'his'. That is why Dworkin adds an extra, procedural requirement:

> The full formula for autonomy, then, is authenticity plus procedural independence. A person is autonomous if he identifies with his desires, goals and values, and such identification is not itself influenced in ways which make the process of identification in some way alien to the individual. Spelling out the conditions of procedural independence involves distinguishing those ways of influencing people's reflective and critical faculties which subvert them from those which promote and improve them.
> (Dworkin 1981: 212; cf. Dworkin 1970; Benn and Weinstein 1971: 210)

This last point brings us back to the ideas of Barber: influence or education must aim to replace unfree, reactive behaviour with conscious, intentional action.

JOEL FEINBERG: THE NEED FOR A STARTING-POINT AND THE RIGHT CENTRE

A final warning against requirements for autonomy which are set too high comes from the American legal philosopher Joel Feinberg. In his book *Harm to Self* he formulates twelve related virtues which are generally associated in our culture with autonomy (Feinberg 1986: 32–44). Each of these can be traced back to a greater or lesser extent to a conception of self-determination.

The great majority of these virtues formulated by Feinberg have already been discussed here, even if under other names. For example, among others, he mentions 'distinct self-identity', which means that an autonomous person possesses his own individuality and that he is not completely defined by his relations with others. 'Authenticity', which means that he can independently justify his opinions and preferences and therefore not allow them to be determined by the pressure to conform. 'Moral independence', he is an 'uncommitted person' who makes judgements independent of the questions or claims of others. 'Integrity', he sticks to his own principles. 'Self-control', he has himself under control, by which it is usually understood that reason is master of the passions. 'Self-legislation', he makes, in Kantian or anarchistic manner, the law for himself. 'Self-reliance', he is capable of surviving without the help of others. 'Initiative', the way he lives his life is not completely based on reaction to the actions of others, he develops his own plans and projects. 'Responsibility for self', not only does he take responsibility for his actions, he is also reliable, incorruptible and steadfast.

All these virtues associated with autonomy are qualified by Feinberg. He does this in the first place by pointing out that none deserve to be pursued unconditionally. For example, 'self-reliance' is certainly a virtue but, if interpreted too extremely or dogmatically, can end up in an anti-social or non-social attitude which makes participation in groups impossible. The same can be said of 'self-control': this can result in the suppression of valuable elements of identity, as when 'reason' is always given primacy above 'the passions'. 'Integrity' can equally become moral fanaticism and 'moral independence' can become the tendency to avoid deep relationships with others and the accompanying commitments. In all these cases, writes Feinberg, 'They are virtues only when their elements exist in just the right degree, neither too little nor too much' (Feinberg 1986: 46). It is also worth emphasizing that autonomy is not the only value in life and that an autonomous person is not by definition a 'good' or morally upright person: he can be simultaneously egoistical, heartless, cruel and ungenerous (ibid.: 45).

What Feinberg qualifies, in particular, is the expectation that autonomous personalities have 'formed' themselves through rational reflection, that they are self-made. He emphasizes that every person must first possess an identity, no matter how rudimentary, before he eventually can choose or develop a new one (Feinberg 1986: 34). Certain principles, also the tendency to rational (self) reflection must be taught to children if they want to play a role in their own self-development. Rational reflection, in addition, boils down to the application, according to certain rules of reasoning, of already accepted principles: these are used to test other as yet unaccepted principles, to make certain judgements or take decisions. This reflection therefore presupposes having a point of departure which is not debatable. If one did not have this then there could be no rational reflection feasible. In Feinberg's words: 'Rational reflection presupposes some relatively settled convictions to reason from and with. If we take autonomy to require that all principles are to be examined afresh in the light of reason on each occasion for decision, then nothing resembling rational reflection can ever get started' (Feinberg 1973: 26; 1986: 33). Equally, someone can only evaluate his values and goals, his identity, against the background of a number of certainties, a number of principles which are not in doubt. The idea that autonomy requires all values and convictions to be thrown open to discussion every time, as if earlier discussions had no significance at all, leads in Feinberg's view only to anomie: 'The "cognitively anomic" man has no firm direction in his reasonings, nothing unquestioned with which to compare and test the questionable. . . . If that is what autonomy is, then it is neither an ideal state nor a virtue appropriate to free status' (ibid.: 26).

Feinberg also stands emphatically behind Dworkin's objection to the requirement that autonomous people must be completely morally authentic. He subscribes to Dworkin's thesis that a morality is a social entity and that it is therefore unthinkable that the individual discovers his own alternative rules for playing the public game. The autonomous person is severely limited in his choice of moral principles. With regard to general values which are borne by a culture, it can even be said, according to Feinberg, that 'he has scarcely any choice at all. Choosing and deciding come in at lower levels of generality when principles conflict. But we hardly ever select among rival moral principles at a general level' (Feinberg 1986: 38). This last fact could also show, Taylor would probably remark, that morality is less determined by social factors than Feinberg and Dworkin are apparently inclined to assume.

In general Feinberg emphasizes – and this brings us to the angle of approach of the following chapter – that it is unrealistic and dangerous to discuss in an abstract manner people's ideal qualities. This threatens with oblivion the sociological truth that people are social beings. Individuals are components of an already existing cultural community characterized by mutual moral dependencies and duties, shared traditions and institutions. This fact imposes limits on what we can define as the characteristics of personal autonomy (Feinberg 1986: 47).

FINAL CONCLUSIONS

As we saw earlier, a number of provisional conclusions have already been made with regard to the answer to the question of what can be considered characteristic of autonomy. Here we will elaborate further on those conclusions.

In the provisional conclusions, we saw, among other things, that only actions which are regarded as an expression of individual identity are experienced as 'free' and that having one's own identity is therefore a necessary condition for autonomy. In the following section, this was further elaborated: autonomy demands a balanced, integrated personality and implies, in the words of Bettelheim, 'a quiet acting out of inner conviction'. Willpower, an element of someone's 'conative autonomy', is closely related to this: it requires willpower to hold on to one's integrity even under difficult circumstances. An ethics only acquires practical significance when one has the inner strength to make sacrifices, which are the inevitable accompaniment of putting morality into practice.

Autonomy also requires some qualities in the cognitive field, especially, in Lindley's terminology, 'active theoretical rationality'. By autonomously looking for the truth, or alternative truths, one reduces the chances of giving a direction to one's life less suited to one's talents or identity and which one would not choose if one was aware of the alternatives. This is all the more desirable because the pressure to conform to the values of the masses is very great and because fundamental moral intuitions are to a large extent formed during childhood – a time in which the critical faculties have hardly developed. That our conative and cognitive qualities are not completely separated from each other is obvious: it requires self-confidence and steadfastness to dare to doubt, to raise the existing and learnt conventions for discussion and to withstand the pressure not to do this from one's social surroundings – to leave the familiar behind and go in search of the unknown.

The requirements with regard to someone's active theoretical rationality however, must not be raised too high: autonomy cannot demand that absolutely *everything* is open to discussion, as there must always be something which remains as starting-point, which can serve as a basis for this discussion. Possessing an 'open mind' is therefore praiseworthy, but this must not be so open that in fact every thought blows out of it again as quickly as it blew in.

Also, the independence of mind or *originality* required from autonomous personalities must not be exaggerated. Certainly, in the field of empirical knowledge autonomy can be reconciled with authority, with the acceptance in good faith of the knowledge of respectable others. In the field of ethics the requirement of full authenticity, however, is equally misplaced. It would mean denial of both the social being of man and of morality. The disavowal of a first principle presented by the culture in which one lives, can ultimately only lead to emptiness and anomie, as Taylor pointed out. It is possible, however, to require of autonomy that someone ultimately decides independently whether he wishes to accept or not the values proffered by his environment. It is also possible to wish that the contemplation preceding this decision takes place as independently as possible. In this, the relevant values are checked against the moral intuitions we use, no matter how these have arisen. The last requirement is particularly important because a morality only really acquires significance when one has not only accepted its conclusions, but has also followed through its justification.

With regard to wellnigh all virtues which one can associate with autonomy, it can be said that possessing to an increasing degree a particular virtue is not in itself a cause for celebration. Beyond a certain level the relevant quality gets in the way of itself or other qualities associated with autonomy. In addition, an autonomous person is not necessarily a 'good' person.

There are other significant values in life against which autonomy must be weighed.

Finally, in general it is worth remembering that people are social beings who develop their identity in the context of a cultural tradition borne by a particular community. This fact imposes limits on what we can and may expect from autonomous people.

Once again: negative and positive freedom

As announced in the introduction to this chapter, we will end here by once more examining the differences between negative and positive freedom. There is as yet no reason to review the distinction between the two concepts made by Berlin. However, in Chapter 2 we saw that within the positive conception he did mistakenly bring together under a single term the notions of, on the one hand, political self-government and on the other, individual self-determination and self-realization. Furthermore, in the next chapter it will emerge that Berlin has not consistently developed and applied the present distinction, especially as far as the difference between freedom and its conditions is concerned. Together with the reasons already advanced in the introduction, this perhaps explains why his conceptions have gained so little following.

To supplement Berlin's definitions, we can say the following about the two conceptions of freedom. Negative freedom, the area in which the subject can go his own way unimpeded by others, is a purely *interpersonal* or social concept which refers to the relations between people at a particular, limited moment. Positive freedom, or autonomy, the capacity to independently lend direction to one's own life, is a much broader concept, which negative freedom partly includes. It is broader, in the first place, because it is not only an interpersonal, but also an *intrapersonal*, concept: someone's attempts to be master of his own life can be frustrated by inner inhibitions as well as external ones. In the second place, it is broader because the question of the degree to which someone is autonomous, in contrast to the question of the extent to which someone is free, cannot be answered at *one* particular moment, but only across a certain time span. Autonomy partly includes freedom because someone who is not free can hardly be master of his own life. It is possible, however, and this is a possibility which will be discussed in Chapter 5, that someone's personal domain can be limited by others in order to protect his long-term autonomy. If this happens with his permission, then it will probably be a case of desires he cannot identify with and which he therefore wants to suppress with the help of others. It is not then possible to speak of limitation of freedom. This is the case, however, when he or she had given no permission and limitation is imposed on the instigation of others, others who are of the opinion that the relevant desires are against the deeper goals of the individual now being coerced and must therefore be suppressed. If this suspicion is valid then the freedom of the relevant individual is limited at that moment, but his autonomy is guaranteed. Because some-thing cannot be simultaneously limited and remain the same size, freedom is not entirely included by autonomy.

Finally, an important difference between negative freedom and autonomy is that the former is an *opportunity* and the second an *exercise* concept: someone who elects to leave unutilized all the opportunities which life offers him, and is also not inhibited by anyone in this inactivity, must be called 'free'. However, he cannot be easily described as an autonomous person-ality: as we have seen in this chapter, people must do quite a lot before they can with justice claim they are masters of their own lives. Thus, one must search diligently for alternatives, for other ideas, values, styles, tastes; one must evaluate the position one's wishes and desires to occupy, or should occupy in one's life; and one must suppress desires which are in conflict with one's deeper life goals or which undermine one's integrity.

4   Freedom and society

INTRODUCTION

In the previous chapter it was attempted to flesh out further the positive conception of freedom which Berlin mainly discussed in a perverted form. It appeared that differences of opinion on the definition of this concept were not insurmountable. This was despite the different, but not necessarily contradictory, emphases laid. Within Western culture there exists a reasonable consensus on the characteristics of an autonomous personality and, the impression is, on the desirability of individual autonomy also. It is a different situation in responding to the question of how society should be organized to enable realization of this value. This is the problem we concentrate on in this chapter. If the individual above all was central in the foregoing, here attention is focused on his relations with others.

Before the role of politics arises, however, we first go deeper into the question of *when* it can be stated that someone's freedom increases or decreases. In general the answer emphasizes either inhibitions of freedom or the available choice alternatives. The discussion can therefore perhaps best be begun with a discussion of the crux of whether or not freedom can be characterized as a 'triadic relation', consisting of an actor, a possible inhibition, and a goal or alternative choice, and whether the positive and negative conception can be traced back to this relation. This is done in the next section.

In the following sections a number of representative positive conceptions of freedom will be dealt with in which the 'real' availability of alternative choices is central and where in the latter an important, stimulating role is ascribed to the community. In succession, the ideas of the following are discussed: Crawford Brough MacPherson, Steven Lukes, Charles Taylor, Frithjof Bergmann and Richard Norman. Each of these authors emphasizes, within the positive concept of freedom, a particular aspect of the relationship between individual and society, and together they produce an image of this which is rounded to some extent. It will be attempted to sketch this in the last section.

In discussing the theoreticians mentioned, and inspired by their thinking, a large number of subjects and questions will arise. We will just mention the following: Does someone's freedom increase directly and proportionally with the number of possibilities of choice available to him? Are there any costs involved with the growth of the number of options? Does freedom increase proportionally with the reduction of the number of constraints? Can an individual become autonomous alone or must this occur in an ensemble of social relations? What is the importance of the capacity and the possibility of isolation for individual autonomy? To what extent is self-development of individuals bound to fixed patterns? Is an alternative choice relevant if one is not aware of its existence? To what extent are the possible choices given, or can one create these oneself without limits? How value-free is a definition of a constraint or a worthwhile goal? Can social structures exercise coercion? In which way do notions of 'rationality' and 'common sense' play a role in answering the question of whether someone is free? To what extent is Berlin's distinction between freedom and its conditions tenable? Are equality and freedom conflicting or complementary values? Does society have a moral duty to help individuals to develop their autonomy and do citizens therefore have a right to the conditions for freedom? How is a right given a basis? Do citizens also have duties to society? To what extent are conflicts between values and interests determined by society and therefore solvable? Does a pluralism of values lead naturally to a liberal idea of politics or is there also room for a communal conception?

From this summary, it will appear that in this chapter the definition of the contents of, and the difference between, the two conceptions of freedom will continue.

ABSENCE OF CONSTRAINTS AND/OR PRESENCE OF OPPORTUNITIES

Different parties can be distinguished in the debate – unfortunately rather abstract – on the question of whether freedom can be characterized as a 'triadic relation' or not. *First*, a party which assumes that freedom is always a triadic relation and that in principle there is no difference between the positive and negative conceptions. In addition the *raison d'être* of the distinction between, on the one hand, absence of constraints and, on the other, availability of alternative choices, is denied. It is generally stipulated, however, that within the negative conception the constraints are emphasized and within the positive conception the absence of real possibilities. *Second*, there is a party which says that there are conceptions of freedom, such as the positive one, that cannot be defined by the triadic relation.

In this section, some representatives of the first party will first be dealt with. After that, it will be the turn of those who see the difference between positive and negative freedom mainly in the number and nature of the obstacles which are distinguished. We then look at the theoretical fixedness of the definition of constraints and real possibilities. Finally, we deal with the criticism of the idea of a triadic relation and it will be attempted to draw some conclusions.

Freedom as a triadic relation

In an influential essay dating from 1967 the American political philosopher Gerald MacCallum rejects the distinction, made by Berlin among others, between positive and negative freedom. He calls this distinction a misunderstanding which only diverts attention from the real differences of opinion on political freedom. In his opinion, freedom must be regarded as a 'triadic relation':

> freedom is always *of* something (an agent or agents), *from* something, *to* do, not do, become, or not become something; it is a triadic relation. Taking the format 'X is (is not) free from Y to do (not do, become, not become), Z', X ranges over agents, Y ranges over such 'preventing conditions' as constraints, restrictions, interferences, and barriers, and Z ranges over actions or conditions of character or circumstance.
>
> (MacCallum 1967: 314)

If, according to MacCallum, no actor X, restriction Y, or a behavioural alternative Z is mentioned, it can always be deduced from the context of the relevant discussion how X, Y or Z must be fleshed out. The expression 'freedom of opinion', for example, leaves open in principle who or what could restrict this freedom. However, as it is generally used in a political context, it can be assumed that here it is a question of restrictions which can be imposed by the state. Even with the expression 'freedom from hunger', according to MacCallum, it is not difficult to fill in the unmentioned objective on your own. It is therefore reasonable to assume that an empty stomach is an obstacle for someone who wants to work hard or concentrate well.

The real differences of opinion in the freedom debate have their origins, according to MacCallum, not in the existence of different forms or concepts of freedom, but in deviating ideas about what can be regarded as actors, goals and above all restrictions. In order to be able to debate meaningfully on 'freedom' these must be made explicit (MacCallum 1967: 320).

Steven Lukes, without mentioning MacCallum, incidentally, has also spoken to this effect. He subscribes to the definition by John Rawls of the difference between a concept and a conception. In his *A Theory of Justice*, Rawls states that a concept of justice expresses what the different conceptions have in common. A concept is the generally accepted notion that like should be treated as like and non-like in a non-like manner. The different conceptions use divergent criteria to determine when this is the case and to consider the importance of the possible unlikenesses. In this spirit, Rawls also argues in his book that only one concept of freedom exists, that is: MacCallum's triadic relation. He claims here also to base himself on Berlin, but that is difficult to defend (Rawls 1971: 5–6, 201–5).

Likewise, Lukes claims that there is only one concept of freedom: freedom consists of the degree to which *an actor* can realize his *objectives* unimpeded by any *constraints*. The different conceptions give a deviating interpretation of the three elements from which the concept is constructed (Lukes 1985: 71–2). The difference between, for example, Marx, Spinoza, Rousseau, Kant and Hegel, on the one hand, and, on the other, the majority of liberals (John Stuart Mill and Humboldt are exceptions, among others) is, according to Lukes, that the conception of freedom of the former group is wider, more complex or richer than that of the latter. This is because, in the first place, constraints here can also be inner or impersonal in nature and can also consist of the absence of something (money, knowledge, etc.); second, because a qualitative discrimination is made between different objectives or preferences; and, third, because the individual, in the words of Barber, is not regarded 'abstract-mechanically', but as a self-defining being who realizes himself in interaction with others (Lukes 1985: 72–80).

Positive freedom: distinguishing a larger number of constraints

MacCallum's thesis that only one concept of freedom exists and that this is triadic in character, has found much support and application (Benn and Weinstein 1971; Barber 1971; Rawls 1971; Feinberg 1973a; Crocker 1980; Young 1986; Goodin 1988). Lawrence Crocker states that the difference between positive and negative freedom lies chiefly in the fact that advocates of the first conception argue 'for a longer list of preventing conditions as constituting limitations on liberty. For example, poverty typically will not be included among liberty's preventing conditions on the negative account, while it will on the positive' (Crocker 1980: 5). And Robert Young writes that advocates of the negative notion 'take a less generous view of what constitutes an interference with a person's options, for according to them only the part played by other human beings in bringing into existence arrangements which interfere with those options is to be seen as restrictive of liberty' (Young 1986: 4).

In a book in which he analyses, among other things, the relation between the welfare state and individual freedom, Goodin comes to comparable conclusions in a largely intuitive manner. In imitation of MacCallum, he says that positive and negative freedom are not fundamentally opposed 'conceptions' (he means 'concepts'), but merely differ in emphasis. He tends to think that advocates of the positive conception, in contrast to their opponents, also take notice of whether someone can really make use of available options: 'Whereas their opponents focus narrowly on freedom as "opportunities", advocates of the positive conception also take notice of people's capacity to exercise those options. . . . negative liberty refers to the set of opportunities available to a person, whereas positive liberty refers to his capacity to make use of them. Positive liberty determines . . . the "worth" of negative liberty' (Goodin 1988: 307–8; cf. Held 1987: 71). In Goodin's view, freedom – the possibility of choosing from different alternatives – only really acquires meaning when the options are realistic and do not exist only on paper. Negative freedoms as such 'opportunities without the means of making use of them' are worthless.

A second important difference related to this between the two conceptions of freedom is, Goodin feels, that advocates of positive freedom, again in contrast to their opponents, take into account that anonymous social structures can also restrict individual freedom: 'negative freedom emphasizes the coerciveness of human agents exclusively, whereas positive freedom also takes note of the coerciveness of social structures and other impersonal forces' (Goodin 1988: 307).[1] In terms of MacCallum's X (actors)–Y (restrictions)–Z (alternative actions) scheme Goodin concludes that within the negative conception the relation between X and Y is emphasized, and within the positive conception the relation between X and Z.

The theory-laden definition of obstacles and possibilities

We see in the position of Joel Feinberg that within MacCallum's scheme there is no logical difference between the absence of a particular obstacle and the availability of an alternative choice. According to him, having an alternative indicates the lack of any obstacles. Equally, an imposed obstacle implies not having available a particular alternative:

> A constraint is something – anything – that prevents one from doing something. Therefore, if nothing prevents me from doing X, I am free to do X; and conversely, if I am free to do X, then nothing prevents me from doing X. 'Freedom to' and 'freedom from' are in this way logically linked. Thus, there can be no special 'positive' freedom to which there is not also a freedom from.
>
> (Feinberg 1973: 6–7)

Feinberg does draw a distinction between positive and negative, and between inner and outer constraints. Naturally, where the border is drawn between inner and outer obstacles is determined by the way in which the 'self' is demarcated from its surroundings (see Chapter 3). However, according to Feinberg, within a political context it is simplest to regard all constraints which come from literally outside the body (including 'the mind'), as external, and all obstacles 'inside' the body as inner.

Negative constraints consist of the absence of something – money, power, skill, knowledge, talent; positive constraints from the presence of something – obsessions, headache, closed doors, chains welded fast, pistols to the breast.[2] Freedom from a negative constraint means the absence of a lack, and thus the presence of, a condition which makes it possible to do something. Feinberg calls the presence of such a condition 'outside' the body an *opportunity* and 'inside' the body an *ability*. Not every absent condition is a negative constraint. Feinberg writes: 'Only those whose absence constitutes a striking deviation from a norm of expectancy or propriety, or whose absence is in some way an especially important consideration for some practical interest either of the subject or of some later commentator can qualify as constraints' (Feinberg 1973: 6). Properly regarded, this states that the socio-political ideology adhered to determines what is regarded as a constraint. After all, this theory is at the base of which state one perceives as 'normal' or as a 'deviation'.

Comparable notions are developed by Weinstein and Benn. Not everything, they write, can be regarded as a worthwhile goal and can be said to be an intervention in someone's freedom. Every conception of freedom is, as far as this is concerned, bound up with what, at a particular moment, one generally experiences as reasonable and plausible. Not every constraint on the number of choice alternatives can then be called 'coercion': it must be possible to make plausible that this restriction is the consequence of the conscious choice of another. Real constraints on freedom, state Benn and Weinstein, 'are not natural, unalterable, given, but rather . . . some rational being (or beings) can be held responsible for them, for bringing them about, or for allowing them to continue' (Benn and Weinstein 1971: 199).

We could also say that as politics has to do with the relations between people, a constraint on someone's freedom is then first politically relevant if others can be held responsible for this. Those restraints which are considered to have been created by others, and are thus removable, can in any case change in the course of time. Benn and Weinstein illustrate this on the basis of the altered ideas on unemployment: while in the nineteenth century this phenomenon was generally regarded as a natural fact which could not be influenced, nowadays it is to a high degree regarded as a manipulable variable. (Benn and Weinstein wrote their article during the heyday of Keynesian economics.)

An (unintentional) illustration of the cultural definition of the distinguishing of constraints is provided by William Parent's critique of MacCallum. He writes: 'The most serious difficulty with MacCallum's analysis is that there are meaningful statements of the form "X is (is not) free from Y to do Z" which do not imply any assertions about the social freedom (unfreedom) of agents. MacCallum's thesis that if a statement can be translated into this triadic schema it can be understood to be about human freedom is false' (Parent 1974: 154; cf. Gray 1984: 327–8). As examples, Parent gives among others the statements: 'X is free of prejudice to judge the case', 'X is free from poverty to take a world cruise', and 'X is free from time-consuming duties to take a vacation'. According to Parent, an *American*, none of these statements concerns *social* or *political* freedom. He believes that in general none of the relevant constraints is regarded as a threat to individual freedom. Nevertheless, he thinks that MacCallum's essay has some value, 'because it does emphasize a much overlooked truth: translatability into the XYZ schema is a necessary condition of the intelligibility of any claim about social freedom. Whenever we use 'freedom' in the social sense we ought to specify or at least be able to specify who is free from what conditions to perform what activity' (Parent 1974: 154).

How difficult and subjective it is to distinguish between the personal and political sphere and, with it, between 'individual' and 'political' freedom, can also be seen from Parent's examples: after all, looking for the cause of someone's prejudices or poverty in social structures created or maintained by others can easily be defended. As Berlin, too, argues (see Chapter 2), ultimately the socio-political theory adhered to determines the answer to the question of to what extent others can be held responsible for one's poverty or ignorance, for example, and in which case it is therefore possible to speak of an intervention into the personal sphere (see also Chapter 5 and Gray 1984: 339–41; Norman 1987: 45–7). What is understood by political, or the political sphere, is thus equally defined by this ideology. The naturalness with which Parent considers his examples to be exclusively applicable to individual freedom, and makes a distinction between 'political' and 'personal' freedom, and thus considers his own normative principles to be generally valid, is therefore remarkable.

Balance

Parent's objections against MacCallum's (and Lukes') thesis seem thus to be refutable. More problematic is the logical criticism which can be applied to it. For example, in a reaction to MacCallum, Berlin says that wanting to remove a constraint is not necessarily directly linked to aiming at a particular goal: one can fight against one's chains, without knowing what one is going to do with any freedom achieved. Berlin writes: 'A man need not know how he will use his freedom: he just wants to remove the yoke. So do classes and nations' (Berlin 1969: xliii). In this case, there is an actor (X) and an impediment (Y) but no goal (Z), and there is therefore a two-sided relation.

Related to this critique, it must be said that a theory of freedom in which freedom is defined as a triadic relationship has the shortcoming that obstacles are only noticed or recognized if one pursues the goal or alternative belonging to the relevant obstacle. If a prisoner does not wish to escape, then the prison wall is no constraint and he is therefore free. The less you want, the freer you are.[3] MacCallum's conception of freedom therefore offers the possibility of a 'retreat to the inner citadel'.

The logical problem which precedes this is remarkably enough not mentioned by Berlin himself. This problem is that the two questions which, according to him, are at the basis of positive and negative freedom, differ fundamentally from each other and can therefore only be joined with great difficulty in a single concept under a single name. The negative notion referred to the question of how big the private realm is in which one can do, without interventions by others, that which one wants or which one is capable of. The positive notion referred to the question of who or what 'is pulling the strings' and can therefore determine what someone does or is (see

Chapter 2). That these are clearly two different questions, is expressed by among other things the fact that within the negative concept of freedom, in contrast to its positive counterpart, one does not have to do anything to be free: negative freedom is an 'opportunity' and positive freedom an 'exercise' concept. The thesis that there is only one concept – in Lukes' words: 'the non-constraining of the realization of agents' purposes' contradicts this fact. What this concept omits is that within the negative conception one does not have to aim at any (frustratable) goals in order to be free. After all what is at issue here is that one is left alone by others, not whether one is also going to do something with this. There are therefore, in the terminology of Rawls and Lukes, two concepts of freedom, each of which has different conceptions in mind. The rationalistic version of positive freedom, for example, is a conception of the positive concept of freedom.[4] These two concepts are, as Berlin stated rightly, 'clearly different', even though the answers to the questions posed by these concepts overlap to a large extent (Berlin 1958: 121–2, 131–2).

In short, the XYZ system only recognizes obstacles when the individual actually wants something, and the removal of obstacles first acquires meaning when the individual knows what he wants to do with his freedom. The solitary person – and this is the biggest objection to this scheme – is the starting-point from which everything begins. One can also regard the individual in his relation to his social environment: one could imagine seeing this environment less as an inexhaustible source of possible constraints and more as a condition for acquiring and exercising autonomy. The community does not have to be, under all circumstances, a barrier which must be overcome by the individual for the sake of his freedom. As we will see in the coming sections, it can also be the source of material and non-material conditions of freedom which are considered indispensable. From this viewpoint, having an alternative does not always mean the same as the absence of an obstacle. One can often only acquire an alternative choice thanks to the active involvement of these others and *not* by removing an obstacle, formed by these others. As the more logical critique of MacCallum's thesis shows, his scheme primarily assumes possible restrictions, not stimuli. He takes the individual as starting-point far too much and with this atomistic principle it fits better into the negative than into the positive tradition of thinking about freedom.

In this context Feinberg can only maintain that an available alternative is the same as an absent obstacle[5] by distinguishing – somewhat forcedly – a category of *negative constraints*: not possessing certain capacities could be seen as the result of a lack of training. If one sees the receipt of training more or less as a right or a matter of course (as MacPherson, Taylor, Lukes and Norman do, among others) then you could interpret the non-receipt of this as a constraint imposed by others and thus politically relevant. The available alternative 'capacity' is then the same as the missing obstacles 'lack of education'.

The extent to which one regards education as a right or matter of course and in which cases one thinks that a constraint is caused by others and is thus politically relevant, is again determined by the socio-political theory followed. Parent's (misplacedly natural) examples already illustrated this. Under the condition that, just like Feinberg, we distinguish a category of negative constraints, Parent however is (unwittingly) right when he says, that a statement on freedom is only politically relevant when it is translatable into MacCallum's XYZ scheme. Because politics concerns the relations between people, a constraint of someone's freedom is first political, as we have seen in Berlin, Feinberg and Benn, and Weinstein, when others can be held responsible for this. In short, what MacCallum's scheme makes clear once more, is the decisive importance of images of man and society in determining what can be called a constraint of autonomy or freedom. Berlin, too, emphasizes in this context that the two questions on which the concepts of freedom distinguished by him are ultimately based, are perhaps not far apart logically speaking, but have fundamentally grown apart historically, under the influence of opposed *Weltanschauungen* (cf. Chapter 2).

The relevant principles differ mainly with regard to the role which society plays or must play in acquiring individual autonomy. Within the negative conception, which was developed in a period in which the citizen needed urgent protection against a powerful state not committed to civil rights, people have faith, more than within its positive counterpart, in the ability of the individual to develop under his own steam, that is: to independently possess the alternative choices necessary for autonomy. One has therefore the tendency to emphasize the possible interventions in the private sphere of the individual and to see freedom mainly as the absence of (positive, external) constraints.

Within the positive conception of freedom, which was mainly worked out in an era of unbridled market capitalism, in an age thus with formal freedom of choice but with little to choose from for many, there is more interest in the availability of alternative choices. The community can play not only an inhibiting, but also a stimulating, role in this. MacCallum's scheme only offers space for this approach when the negative constraints distinguished by Feinberg are also included in it. If this is done, then Crocker's stance is correct that an important (but by no means the most important) difference between the positive and negative conceptions of freedom lies in this, that within the first conception one distinguishes a longer list of possible constraints.

If within the positive conception one regards the individual as a social being, distinguishes negative constraints and thus ascribes a certain stimulating role to society in the acquisition of individual autonomy, then Goodin's suspicion is correct, that within this conception one has more interest for the means which someone needs to really be able to use his 'opportunities', and that within this conception it is above all the relation between actor (X) and alternative (Y) which is central. Another question to be answered has then become to what extent the distinction made by Berlin between, on the one hand, freedom, and on the other hand, its conditions, is still tenable.

In the following sections we will look at a number of conceptions of freedom, in which the relation between individual and community in the acquisition and exercise of autonomy is made central.

CRAWFORD BROUGH MACPHERSON: THE RIGHT TO (CONDITIONS OF) FREEDOM

The Canadian political philosopher MacPherson has developed a conception in which no distinction is made between freedom and its conditions. Not possessing the latter is therefore seen as a constraint on freedom. His ideas are interesting because he provides a Marxist-inspired critique of thinking about freedom and democracy within the liberal tradition, without moving too far beyond the framework of the latter school. He attempts to breathe new life into the lost humanist inspiration of liberalism and to show that the ideals of this political tendency cannot be realized in the current state. MacPherson feels therefore linked with 'those who accept and would promote the normative values that were read into the liberal-democratic society and state by J. S. Mill and the nineteenth and twentieth century idealist theorists, but who reject the present liberal-democratic society and state as having failed to live up to those values, or as being incapable of realizing them' (MacPherson 1977: 224, 227).

Self-realization, democracy and scarcity

According to MacPherson, every normative political theory has as its basic principle that man possesses a number of unique qualities with which he distinguishes himself from other beings. This principle is empirically testable and, thanks to its entanglement in our language and our thought in general, forms a justified basis for normative claims.[6]

MacPherson's starting-point is comparable to that of, among others, Barber and Taylor: in principle man is an actor, a creator, an enjoyer of his abilities. Different qualities can be characterized in this as essential: the ability to think rationally, to make moral judgements and act morally, to aesthetic creation and contemplation, to friendship and love or to the undergoing of religious experiences. However, whatever capacities one regards as essential, according to MacPherson all that is important is the perception that man is more than the passive 'consumer of utilities' which the prevailing utilitarian liberalism[7] takes him to be: 'Whatever the uniquely human attributes are taken to be, in this view of man their exertion and development are seen as ends in themselves, a satisfaction in themselves, not simply a means to consumer satisfactions. It is better to travel than to arrive. Man is not a bundle of appetites seeking satisfaction but a bundle of conscious energies seeking to be exerted' (MacPherson 1967a: 4–5).

The quantity of physical, mental and psychic talents or qualities which someone possesses is not necessarily the same as his capacity to use these talents. The latter is determined by the current external constraints, the former by innate gifts and earlier external barriers. The degree to which someone is capable of using and developing his presumed talents and has access to the means needed for this, are defined by MacPherson as his *developmental power*. The ability to use the capacities of others for your own ends, to take advantage of others, he calls *extractive power* (MacPherson 1973a: 40, 42, 52).

A democracy is seen primarily by MacPherson as a way of living together, and only in the second place as a procedure for choosing and legitimizing governments. The egalitarian principle inherent in democracy requires according to him not only a decision-making procedure which is based on the principle of 'one man, one vote', but also the implementation of the right enjoyed by all to develop their talents. In a real democracy therefore all citizens possess an equal amount of 'developmental power', and the more a society maximalizes the development of its members, the more democratic it is (MacPherson 1973a: 51).

Furthermore, within a democratic society only those talents of the individual are developed which do not obstruct the development of the talents of others. According to MacPherson, only these gifts are 'essential' or 'human'. That this harmony can be achieved, and the obstacle formed to this by presumed scarcity can be overcome, is a fundamental principle of a democratic theory for MacPherson. If the maximum development of everyone's capacities only led to even more conflict and destruction, then there would no longer be any sense in pursuing a society in which this development is made possible (MacPherson 1973a: 54, 55, 73; 1973b: 111, 112).

It follows from the foregoing, that within the context of a democratic theory someone's capacity to use and develop his talents must be measured in terms of the absence of external constraints. If there is no external obstacle then, in MacPherson's view, he will develop fully:

A man's power . . . is to be measured in terms of the *absence of impediments* to his using his human capacities. For we have seen that a democratic theory rests on the assumption that everyone is at least potentially a doer, an actor, a user and developer of his capacities. His ability so to act, which is what democracy claims to maximize, is at its maximum when there are no external impediments to such action.

(MacPherson 1973a: 58)

For MacPherson, too, therefore the individual is the starting-point who can only encounter impediments on his route to self-realization. Someone's 'developmental power' must then, in his opinion, be calculated *from* the maximum. Which possible constraints can be identified here? MacPherson emphasizes that within a political theory only socially created, and therefore politically influenceable, obstacles are relevant. He distinguished three categories in this: 'lack of adequate means of life', 'lack of access to the means of labour', and 'lack of protection against invasion by others' (MacPherson 1973a: 59–70). Berlin, writes MacPherson, is wrong to recognize only the latter category.

Because development of talent is always accompanied by the application of material and non-material 'energy', a lack of prosperity and culture is an impediment to this development. The same is true of the insufficient access to the resources which one needs to be able to use one's talents: to be able to do justice to one's creative being one cannot do without tools and materials which can be worked upon. In theory, MacPherson understands work in the broadest possible sense. He is therefore not only concerned with the paid production of commodities. (In practice he turns out to actually have paid work mainly in mind.) That one, finally, can only use and develop one's talents when one is not impeded in this by others, is obvious. The last possible obstacle can be removed relatively easily, by civil rights guaranteed by the state. This has, MacPherson recognizes, also happened in the existing liberal democracies. The case is more complicated with the other categories of impediments.

It can be asked whether the available resources and work opportunities are sufficient to provide everyone with his basic needs. Is there not always a scarcity? MacPherson does not seem to be too pessimistic about this. Permanent scarcity of material and non-material means only exists when one assumes that needs increase as quickly as their satisfaction. This scarcity is merely postulated by the prevailing utilitarian liberalism to justify market capitalism and to keep it going (MacPherson 1967a: 16–9; 1967b: 25–31). However, this principle only applies in a society in which the people are conditioned to think that they are insatiable consumers. Nevertheless, within a real democratic society the needs, according to MacPherson, will be identical to the means needed to enable everyone to use and develop his capacities. The quantity needed for this is not unlimited. Within a democracy a scarcity of necessities is thus not a natural given.

Shortages of land, materials and tools which may arise are also in MacPherson's view ultimately a human, or more precisely, capitalistic, construction. How the ownership and thus access to the 'means of labour', is divided is determined by the way in which a specific group of people have organized society. Within the Western world, there is in principle no lack of capital and land. As a consequence of private ownership of the means of production, access to this is divided extremely unfairly. Most people are forced to obtain these by selling a part of the 'developmental power' to the relevant owners.

According to MacPherson this transaction reduces the possibilities of using and developing one's own talents in three ways. In the first place, during working time one loses control of the use of one's own capacities. Others determine what one must do. Because the capacity and the will to self-determination is an essential characteristic of man, this also damages his dignity. In the second place, the employee loses the profit which the employer makes on the hiring of his capacities. This amounts to the difference between the wages received and the market price of his product. And in the third place, this transaction reduces the will and the enthusiasm of the employee to develop his talents outside working hours. Because during working hours one cannot and may not use one's capacity for self-determination, for 'creativity' and choice, – the work is generally monotonous and routine – in the free time one also becomes a passive and soulless consumer.[8]

The connection between freedom and its conditions

In an essay which is analytically one of the most thorough reactions to Berlin's 'Two concepts', MacPherson relates the above notions to the concept of freedom. Individual freedom, as we have already seen, in his view means the absence of impediments created by others to the use and development of capacities considered essential for man. Here impediments are formed not only by deliberate, direct interventions by others, but also by the absence of 'means of life and labour'. According to MacPherson, Berlin denies the importance of these last obstacles (MacPherson 1973a: 96). The latter is, as we have seen, the question. Berlin states explicitly that ultimately the socio-political theory adhered to determines what one sees as a constraint on one's freedom, and that it is therefore possible to argue for social facilities and market intervention with an appeal to negative freedom. The social liberal Berlin would also certainly support these pleas. The problem with his stance, however, is that he does not want to base these pleas on freedom, but on the conditions of freedom: Berlin continues to draw a hard distinction between freedom and its conditions. Is this consistent? MacPherson thinks not.

He wonders whether there are any theories of any standing which regard the poverty of particular groups of people *not* as the consequence of social structures created by others and therefore as a constriction of their freedom (MacPherson 1973b: 100). The unequal division of the access to the means of life and labour which is inherent in capitalism is, in his view, a constraint on the negative freedom of those with little access. As we have seen earlier, these people are coerced to sell an important part of their 'developmental power' on the labour market. The area 'in which they cannot be pushed around' is considerably reduced by this relation of dependence to the possessors of capital (MacPherson 1973b: 101).

The insight that social structures supported by others can also limit the freedom of the individual is, according to MacPherson, inconsistent with the distinction made by Berlin between freedom and its conditions. Despite the implicit acceptance that a lack of access to the means of life and labour limits someone's negative freedom, Berlin's conception of negative freedom does not include access to these means. Or rather, in Berlin's terminology, he recognizes that the poverty or illness of some – a lack of means, conditions

not being fulfilled – can be explained within a particular socio-political theory by the actions of others and can therefore be seen as a limiting of the
negative freedom of the former but, at the same time, he continues to
emphasize that freedom is something completely different than the means
which are needed to be able to make use of it. Unless Berlin were to declare
the relevant socio-political theories to be lacking in all plausibility – and he
does not – this would be inconsistent.[9] According to MacPherson, a plea for
the welfare state or socialism based on negative freedom is then only possible when Berlin drops his distinction between freedom and its conditions.

That Berlin himself also has difficulty with his conception of negative
freedom – in MacPherson's view far too restricted and strictly mechanistic –
can be seen, among others, from the footnote already quoted (see p. 27) in
which he contemplates how the size of someone's negative freedom can be
estimated. On the basis of this, MacPherson rightly claims:

> When he comes to consider how the amount of negative liberty can be
> estimated, he lists five factors on which its extent depends, including '(a)
> how many possibilities are open to me', and '(b) how easy or difficult
> each of these possibilities is to actualize'. The (b) seems to admit by the
> back door those factors which he had pushed out as mere 'conditions' of
> liberty.

> (MacPherson 1973b: 104)

Contradictions between, and perversions of, freedoms

Earlier, in Chapter 2, we have already looked at some analytical problems
with Berlin's positive conception of freedom. There we saw that, properly
regarded, Berlin has brought a number of different notions together in this
conception under a single name. MacPherson, too, refers to this. He distinguishes three notions: Positive Liberty 1 (PL1), the capacity to be master of
one's own life, a capacity that MacPherson equates with someone's 'developmental power'; Positive Liberty 2 (PL2), the rationalistic variation of PL1 so
disputed by Berlin; and Positive Liberty 3 (PL3), the right to participate in
and exercise influence on the political decision-making.

MacPherson has no difficulty in recognizing that a distinction must be
made between negative freedom (NL) and PL3; there is a logical difference
between the question of who or what rules me and the question of to what
degree the relevant government is intervening in my personal realm.
However, he disputes emphatically that NL and PL1 are conflicting or even
differ clearly from each other: 'there is no . . . clear distinction between negative liberty and the apparently basic sense of (Berlin's) positive liberty (conscious self-direction)' (MacPherson 1973b: 96, cf. 110, 118). This difference
exists when positive freedom (PL1) degenerates into its rationalistic variation (PL2). MacPherson does not see the necessity of this: 'It is *not* necessary for an advocate of positive liberty to assert or assume that there is a

single universal harmonious pattern in which the ends of all rational beings must fit' (MacPherson 1973b: 111). There is, states MacPherson, a big difference between the conviction that there is something like a knowable cosmic order, which must be enforced upon others, and the conviction that the many divergent lifestyles which would be seen in a truly democratic society, are not necessarily conflicting. He does consider the latter, however, as an essential starting-point for positive freedom. Why, wonders MacPherson, would we otherwise aim at a society in which everyone possesses a maximal 'developmental power'? Conflicts, including those between values, only exist in a society characterized by scarcity and class struggle. However, according to MacPherson, these phenomena are not necessary.

In MacPherson's view, positive freedom is only perverted in PL2 when, in the first place, conservative liberals (MacPherson here mentions Hegel and T. H. Green) refuse to accept that a condition for a maximalization of positive freedom (PL1) or 'developmental power' is that one has access to the means of life and labour and that this can only be realized for everyone by abolishing capitalism. As within the existing relations of ownership, PLI is never realized; while one nevertheless believed that this was possible, it was necessary to believe that it could and should be enforced by an authoritarian elite.

In the second place, according to MacPherson the positive conception degenerates where radicals (like Stalin and to a lesser degree Lenin) saw no route but the authoritarian to convince their opponents of the importance or the justice of access to the available means. In both cases, the cause of the perversion of PL1 and PL2 is therefore not in the positive conception of freedom (MacPherson 1973b: 116).

Nor has MacPherson much good to say about Berlin's interpretation of positive freedom: he considers this conception, because here, too, Berlin does not recognize the importance of access to the means of life to be even more devoid of content than its negative counterpart:

> positive liberty, in its basic sense of ability to form and follow one's own conscious purposes, requires even more clearly than negative liberty that there be no indirect domination by withholding the means of life and labour. Berlin's formulation of positive liberty neglects this, so his positive liberty has nowhere to go except into the clouds. It becomes an abstraction, emptied of any content: it has not even the narrow but concrete content which his negative liberty has – 'no chains'.
>
> (MacPherson 1973b: 117)

MacPherson proposes a different definition of positive and negative freedom, which, in his opinion, has a greater reality value. The first concept (PL1) – the degree to which someone has access to the means which are needed to use and develop his presumed capacities, he renames *developmental liberty*. The latter concept – the absence of the need, or the coercion, to make available his 'developmental power' to others – he renames 'immunity from the extractive power of others' or, in short, *counter-extractive liberty*.

To the others, he also emphatically reckons the state, because this is often nothing more than an instrument of the owning class.[10] It forms an instrument to continue the relations of ownership and the widespread belief in an unquenchable longing of man for more. The possible constraints of the two freedoms 'turn out to be much the same'. There is then hardly any distinction between the two concepts, it is merely a matter of differences in emphasis. This modest difference also makes it clear that possessing 'counter-extractive liberty' is a primary requirement for 'developmental liberty' (MacPherson 1973b: 118–9).

Discussion

On the basis of MacPherson's ideas, a number of subjects important for freedom can be raised. At the beginning of this section, it was noted that MacPherson provides a Marxist-inspired critique of liberalism while not moving too far beyond the ideological framework of the latter tendency in doing so. This is both his strength and his weakness. For example, in contrast to numerous liberals he has devoted attention to the great importance of economic structures and processes for individual freedom, but he is so preoccupied by this that he neglects the significance of social and political relations outside the economic sphere. In practice, his *Weltanschauung* turns out not to deviate much from the 'abstract' vision of man held by liberalism, so disputed by Marx. Just like Marx, he underrates the contradictions which can always arise, even in a socialist society, between individuals among themselves, between individual and community, and between the different values which can be held simultaneously by the same person. We will deal with these three matters in reverse order.

The inevitability of conflicts and politics

MacPherson damages the plausibility of his theory by introducing, actually completely superfluously, a number of rather forced (Marxist) assumptions with regard to the character of a truly democratic society. For example, he postulates that only the faculties which do not obstruct the development of talents by others, are essential for man or are 'human' and that therefore only these will be developed in a democracy. However, there is sufficient 'empirical' support as desired by MacPherson for an alternative list with 'essential' human qualities. Steven Lukes mentions in this context the capacity for competition, malice, greed, contempt, lust for power, jealousy, destruction and all possible forms of cruelty. These talents too have been reflected in 'the very structure of our thought and language' and numerous authors have therefore made them the basic principles of their political theory. MacPherson makes it easy for himself by excluding, by definition, all these qualities which normally demand some regulation, by appealing to a moral theory which is not made explicit (Lukes 1979: 147–8).

He expects, furthermore, that the many deviating lifestyles and value patterns which will be displayed by a democratic society (or classless society) do not necessarily conflict with each other. In a society where scarcity has been abolished, the different values are in harmony with each other, no value has to be sacrificed for another or balanced against another. Looked at in this way, it becomes understandable why negative freedom in its original meaning – a private space within which one must be left alone – disappears when MacPherson formalizes his own definitions of freedom: in a society without value conflicts it is not necessary to protect people from others or from other values.

However, this seems to be an over-optimistic interpretation of the nature and the reason of the relevant conflicts. The contradictions of interests (between capital and labour) could decrease perhaps in a 'truly democratic society'. However, it remains unclear how MacPherson thinks he can solve value conflicts if they occur between equality and negative freedom; security and freedom; efficiency and equality or justice; nobility and justice; democracy and negative freedom; happiness or innocence and knowledge or truth, etc. (Berlin 1969: xix, l; cf. Chapter 2). MacPherson shows himself to be a typical Marxist by exhibiting little interest in ethical questions. Just like Marx, he seems to think that egotism and conflicts of interest between individuals and between state, society and citizen are only characteristic of capitalism. This is a misunderstanding. Lukes writes about Marx's indifference to morality:

> Not only are scarcity, conflicting moralities and limits upon knowledge and understanding here to stay; minorities will always need protection from the most democratic procedures, interpretations of shared goals will always differ, and there will always be a need to secure public goods and provide for future generations in a way that will not be immediately apparent and compelling to all individuals.[11]

(Lukes 1985: 94)

In this context, it can be mentioned that MacPherson's standpoint is inconsistent with his earlier acceptance of the contradiction between negative freedom and PL3 or self-government. For the latter form of positive freedom, which MacPherson distinguished so sharply in his critique of Berlin, his new definitions offer no room either, however. Perhaps he is here assuming implicitly that the state in a classless society 'withers away' and that therefore, in a real democracy, there will be no politics and therefore no PL3. This would be in accordance with the denial of the right of politics to exist which is normal within traditional Marxism. Because all power and all contradictions are traced back to class and property relations, in a socialist society there is no further need of an organized decision-making process on the correct definition of the general interest. However, David Held remarks on this: 'if not all differences of interest can be reduced to class, and if differences of opinion about the allocation of resources are for all practical purposes inevitable, it is essential to create the institutional space for the generation of, and debate about, alternative political strategies and programmes' (Held 1987: 135). When differences of opinion are not accepted as 'real', and politics is thus robbed of its legitimacy, one is preparing the way for political oppression.

Freedom in an 'ensemble' of social relations

Another criticism of MacPherson's ideas concerns his portrayal of man. Here, MacPherson shows himself to be a 'real' liberal. He, too, takes the solitary individual as his starting-point: man is a 'bundle of conscious energies seeking to be exerted' which, on their way to self-realization, can only encounter obstacles. Because MacPherson regards possessing the necessary means for self-development as a right, he sees their absence as an impingement on someone's freedom. This is the relation he makes between individual and community. To the question of *how* the development of someone's capacities must take shape in practice, he devotes no attention.

Just like the liberalism he so disputes (of which he considers Berlin a typical exponent), MacPherson assumes that the individual realizes himself as long as he has the access to means of life and labour. However, a large number of capacities, the ones defined by him as essential, only develop to a high degree outside the economic relations which MacPherson concentrates on. An example of this is the capacity for rational thought and the making of moral judgements, friendship and love, and the experience of religious or aesthetic experiences. It is unclear how the development of these capacities is related to the possession, or not, of material means and access to the means of production. Bhikhu Parekh and Steven Lukes in particular have pointed out this one-sidedness of MacPherson's thought. In reaction to MacPherson, Parekh emphasizes, for example, 'Human capacities cannot be developed and exercised by an individual in isolation. They are located within, and sustained by, the framework of social relations and are developed when the latter make them both possible and necessary' (Parekh 1982: 71).

Lukes expresses himself in similar terms. According to him, MacPherson uses an abstract, atomistic *Weltanschauung* which offers no space to the question of which forms of social, cultural and institutional activities and relations enable man to develop his capacities. With these specifications lacking, all that remains of MacPherson's theory of democracy is only a promise of an 'abstract, anti-utilitarian, individualistic moral perfectionism' (Lukes 1979: 149). This theory, says Lukes, 'bears the stamp of the liberal individualism it so acutely criticizes. Individuals and their powers and capacities are conceived in abstraction from the social relations and forms of community which, on the one hand, impede and, on the other, facilitate and constitute their further development.' And he adds: 'Social relations structure human activities and potentialities, which cannot be conceived independently of them' (Lukes 1979: 151–2). By basing himself entirely on the individual, according to Lukes, MacPherson remains trapped in the abstract humanism of which Marx had already accused Feuerbach. In his 'Thesen über Feuerbach', he had written: 'the human essence is no abstraction inherent in each single individual. In its reality it is the ensemble of the social relations'.

In the following sections, we will concentrate on this 'ensemble' of social relations, necessary for the development of individual autonomy.

STEVEN LUKES: THE SOCIAL CONDITIONS OF INDIVIDUALISM

> A conservative is a fellow that if he sees someone drowning, will throw him a rope that is too short and tell him that it will be good for his character to swim for it. A liberal will throw him a rope that's long enough, but when the drowning man gets hold of it he'll drop his end and go away to look for someone else to help.
>
> (Lukes and Galnoor 1985: 97)

Lukes belongs in the positive tradition of thinking about freedom. Constraints on freedom are, in his view, not merely the result of direct interventions by other people, but also of social structures created or maintained by others. In addition, real respect for human dignity is first shown when one supports others in obtaining the realistic alternative choices indispensable for freedom. Lukes therefore also identifies what Feinberg calls external negative constraints.

In his view, four conceptually and logically closely linked values form the basis of the ideal of equality and freedom. The idea of human dignity is the first value. It is the centre of the value 'equality'. According to Lukes, people are worthy of our respect because every individual possesses the capacity for freedom. Freedom consists of three components: autonomy, privacy and self-development. Together with the idea of human dignity these form the fundamental values of individualism. Respect for the human capacity for freedom consists of awarding equal (effective) rights to autonomy, privacy and self-realization (Lukes 1973: 125; see also Lukes 1974a: 75ff.).

In what follows, we will first look at Lukes' analysis of the concept of freedom and equality. After that come his ideas about a true respect for human dignity. His rejection of the abstract *Weltanschauung*, which according to him is at the basis of traditional individualism, is a part of this. This view will be dealt with in the final section.

Three elements of freedom

In the first place, according to Lukes one can state that someone is free if his acts are based on his own decisions and choices that are not the result of external and internal powers separate from his will (Lukes 1973: 52–8, 127, 128). This ideal of autonomy is associated by Lukes with Berlin's positive conception of freedom. Crucial for autonomy is that one is to a certain extent capable of (critical) self-consciousness and that one possesses alternatives from which choices can be made.

A second answer to the question of what freedom means is formed by the negative conception of freedom, called 'privacy' by Lukes (Lukes 1973: 59–66, 128, 129). This aspect of freedom consists of a personal realm in which one can do what one chooses, or not, free of 'public interference'.

A third component of freedom is, in Lukes view, the idea of self-development (Lukes 1973: 67–72, 129, 130). This idea has two constituent parts: in the first, someone is free to the extent that he autonomously determines and controls his life, and, in the second, to the extent that he also succeeds in realizing his own capacities – 'that is, to make out of himself the best of what he has it in him to be'. Naturally, much discussion is possible with regard to the question of what these qualities are precisely. Still, Lukes emphasizes that everyone has one or more talents which are worthy of being developed and admired.

These three components of freedom are closely connected to each other. The exercise of autonomy and the development of individual talents requires a minimal negative freedom. Talking about negative freedom presumes autonomy: the inhibition of actions which do not arise out of personal choice is, according to Lukes, not a restriction of someone's freedom in the strict sense of the word (Lukes 1973: 136). Finally, self-development presumes a certain degree of autonomy, as it cannot otherwise be *self*-realization.

The last connection made by Lukes, however, can also go in another direction: one can only be autonomous when one has developed one's capacities somewhat. Autonomy and self-development therefore are related to such an extent that there is much to say in favour of bringing them together, as Berlin did, under a single term. The acquisition of autonomy can perhaps best be regarded as a self-reinforcing, cumulative process: the more one develops, the greater the chance of individual autonomy (which again promotes the capacity for self-development) and the bigger will be the need for negative freedom. Again, more privacy can (under certain social limiting conditions, which Lukes also refers to) promote individual autonomy and self-realization. And so on.

True respect for the individual

As stated, according to Lukes, the idea of human dignity is the centre of the ideal of equality. This idea is based on the conviction that *everyone* must be respected as a valuable being, as an end in itself. People deserve this respect because they possess one of a number of admirable essential traits. These are, in the first place, the capacity of human beings 'to act autonomously, to become (relatively) self-determining, to become conscious of the forces determining or affecting them, and either to submit to them, recognizing their necessity, or to become independent of them' (Lukes 1973: 131; 1974a:

77). This capacity is naturally not equally strongly developed in all. However, every person potentially possesses it. In the second place, people have the capacity 'to think thoughts, to perform actions, to develop involvements and to engage in relationships. . . . Intellectual activities, artistic creation, love, friendship are examples: all these may be said to require a private space free of public interference or surveillance in order to flourish' (Lukes 1974a: 78; 1973: 132).[12] In the third place, every individual is, in principle, in a position to develop one or more unique human talents which are worthy of admiration and respect.

Respect for the individual implies, according to Lukes, that everything possible must be done to promote these three capacities. In practice, this means that people are treated as potentially autonomous beings who have the capacity to realize themselves, and who are permitted a private space within which they can develop undisturbed activities and relations valued by them. One can be deficient in this in various ways.

First, people's dignity is not only assailed when their capacity to choose, and with it, self-determination, is denied. This also occurs when the number of alternatives from which they can choose are unreasonably restricted. This restriction can take place on the social, political or economic level (Lukes 1974a: 78–9). Here Lukes quotes Tawney in agreement. He saw the ultimate goal of the quest for equality as the increase of 'the range of alternatives open to ordinary men, and the capacity of the latter to follow their own preferences in choosing between them' (Tawney 1931: 260, quoted by Lukes 1974a: 79). Obstructing people from getting a proper understanding of their own situation is, according to Lukes, the most important and damaging denial of their autonomy. This happens by the continuation of the social structures and processes which reduce consciousness to the *status quo* (Lukes 1974a: 80; cf. MacFarlane 1966: 78; Chapter 5). He refers to the widespread belief in the inevitability and naturalness of a social hierarchy. This belief is definitely in the way of the establishment of a 'single status society' which in his view is necessary for a serious respect for autonomy.

Second, someone is not, or is insufficiently, respected as a person if others, without good reason, intervene in activities and relations he/she experiences as meaningful. Lukes emphasizes that meddling in someone's activities and relations also take place in ways of which liberals are generally less aware. He is thinking here of 'class discrimination, remediable economic deprivation and insecurity, and what Hayek has called "the hard discipline of the market", where nominally equal economic and social rights are unequally operative because of unequal but equalizable conditions and opportunities' (Lukes 1974a: 80).

Finally, according to Lukes, people's dignity is assailed when they are impeded in the development of their capacities. This can take place in various ways and in diverse fields. In a stratified society, however, the weakest experience a systematic and cumulative restriction of their possibilities.

Structural inequalities must therefore be combated. A layered system of education which sanctions existing social inequalities is an example of this. A denial of human dignity also takes place in a political system which offers its citizens no, or insufficient, opportunities to participate in the political decision-making process and, in doing so, to develop their capacity for self-government. Another example is a system of production which condemns people to monotonous, one-sided and slavish work in which they are given hardly any, if any, opportunity to develop their own professional skill or feeling of responsibility (Lukes 1973: 134–5; 1974: 80–2).

Abstract conception of the individual

If one wants to take individual freedom seriously then, according to Lukes, another core idea of individualism must be rejected: this concerns the 'abstract conception' of the individual, and is at the basis of a number of other central ideas of individualism – the economic, political, epistemological and methodological individualism. Within this conception the individual is seen 'abstractly': as a being with *given* immutable needs, interests, goals, rights, desires, talents, etc., all of which are seen completely separately from every social context. The individual is only the bearer of these traits which determine his/her behaviour, and society is merely a constructed instrument to realize certain individual goals (Lukes 1973: 73–9).

The abstract idea of man plays an important role in the thinking of the theoreticians of 'natural rights' and 'social contract', of the early utilitarians and the classical economists, and had its heyday between the middle of the seventeenth century and the beginning of the nineteenth century. It was disputed by many nineteenth-century thinkers, including anti-revolutionary and Romantic conservatives, Hegel, Marx, Saint-Simon, Comte, and their followers, German historians, English idealists, sociologists and social psychologists.[13]

This abstract view of man must be rejected, according to Lukes, as we have already seen from his critique of MacPherson. The abstract view of man is at loggerheads with all the lessons which the human and social sciences have taught us. People must be regarded as the source of intentions and goals, decisions and choices still to be discovered, as 'people' who have the capacity (still to be fulfilled) of entering into valuable relationships and developing activities, and who are capable of all kinds of forms (still to be discovered) of self-development. Furthermore, real respect for the individual requires that both the strictly individual and the social aspects of human personality be taken into account. True esteem can be seen, thus, from the recognition that individuals are dependent for their development on both the stimuli of or socialization through their social environment, and on the space which the community allows at a particular moment to use their acquired freedom and, if necessary, to deviate from the norm. Lukes formulates the emancipation dilemma as follows:

on the one hand, such respect requires us to take account of them as social selves – moulded and constituted by their societies – whose achievement of, and potential for, autonomy, whose valued activities and involvements and whose potentialities are, in large part, socially determined and specific to their particular social contexts. On the other hand, it requires us to see each of them as an actually or potentially autonomous centre of choice . . . able to choose between, and on occasion to transcend, socially-given activities and involvements, and to develop his or her respective potentialities in the available forms sanctioned by the culture – which is both a structural constraint and a determinant of individuality.

(Lukes 1973: 149)

CHARLES TAYLOR: CRITIQUE OF ATOMISM

Charles Taylor's criticism of 'atomism' links up closely with Lukes' objections to the abstract view of man, an image which is at the basis of the 'market' tendency within liberalism. The beginnings of this tendency can be ascribed to thinkers like Smith, Locke and Bentham, and its end can be located in Hayek, Friedman and Nozick. Taylor's most important objective is to demonstrate that it is inconsistent, on the one hand, to award people rights (of freedom) and, on the other hand, to be indifferent to the question of whether these rights are of any use to them. In relation to this, he wants to show that people have not only rights with regard to society and their fellow citizens, but also duties. He gives therefore an argument for the stance that not possessing the conditions or means needed for positive freedom is also a politically relevant (negative, external) constraint on freedom. Where Lukes defensively and still carefully formalizes the implications of a real respect for human dignity (people are constrained when they have no opportunity of coming in contact with alternatives), Taylor goes further: people have a *right* to the help of others in the development of their capacity for freedom.

The impossible self-sufficiency of the individual

According to Taylor, the term 'atomism' refers to, among others, the theories of the social contract which were developed in the seventeenth century and the doctrines which implicitly or explicitly further this. This includes some forms of utilitarianism and all those contemporary theories which, in one way or another, try to defend the precedence of the rights of the individual over the rights of society, or who ascribe a purely instrumental value to society (Taylor 1979: 39). As ideal and typical representatives of this atomic mode of thought, Taylor mentions Hobbes, Locke and Nozick. According to him, these thinkers assume the primacy of the rights of the individual and consider society only valuable because it enables man to realize private goals. Beyond the duties which the individual has agreed to (contractually), he has no duties with regard to society. Thus, every 'principle, of belonging or obligation, i.e. a principle which states our obligation as men to belong to or sustain society' is denied (ibid.: 40).

According to Taylor, this doctrine is founded on the conviction that the individual is 'self-sufficient', that he does not need society in order to reach full growth as a' person and to be able to function. Because the image of man subscribed to, ultimately determines which rights one ascribes to the individual, and images of man can be criticized on empirical grounds, one can challenge the 'primacy-of-rights' doctrines by demonstrating the limited reality value of the atomistic view of man (cf. Chapter 1). If one sees images of man and the rights based on this as irrefutable a prioris, or if one denies every connection between images of man and rights, then further discussion is naturally useless. However, Taylor does not assume this.

To his mind, people are ascribed rights because they possess capacities appreciated and respected by us, capacities which we consider essential for human life and which therefore have a special moral status for us. Our image of man, our idea of what is essential for man,[14] therefore defines the rights we ascribe to people. Because, for example, we regard the capacity to make moral judgements and for religious contemplation to be essential for human existence, as these capacities have a special significance for us, require our respect, we have the 'intuition' that people have the right, or should have, to freedom of opinion and religion.

The normative consequences of this reasoning, however, go further than the postulation of the 'primacy-of-rights' theoreticians that people have certain rights which cannot be infringed. Taylor states:

> To say that certain capacities command respect or have worth in our eyes is to say that we acknowledge a commitment to further and foster them. We do not just acknowledge people's right to them, and hence the negative conjunction that we ought not to invade or impair the exercise of these capacities in others. We also affirm that it is good that such capacities be developed, that under certain circumstances we ought to help and foster their development, and that we ought to realize them in ourselves.
>
> (Taylor 1979: 46)

The belief that the human capacity to make moral judgements is worthy of our respect therefore implies more than the recognition of everyone's right to his own opinion. It also means that one must try to become someone who is able to form an opinion independently and remain true to his conviction, despite the costs which this can imply. After all, true respect for the capacity for moral judging cannot be combined with a casual and superficial opportunism. It implies, furthermore, that one tries to help others to develop this potential. According to Taylor, it would be inconsistent and without credibility, on the one hand, to ascribe rights to people on the basis of a number of unique respectable potentials, and, on the other hand, to be indifferent as to whether these are developed or not.

'Ultra-liberals' are opposed to the linkage of rights and the possession of certain capacities. According to Taylor, they are afraid that recognition of duties (to develop one's own talents and also help others to do so) opens the way to the limitation of freedom. They make the notion of choice central to their concept of freedom and refuse to discriminate between right and wrong choices, at least, not on the basis of the concept of freedom. We have already seen in Chapter 3 that this position is untenable in Taylor's view. Not all choices are realistic or meaningful. Also, the freedom to choose is only valuable if we have achieved a level of self-consciousness and autonomy in which we really, consciously, choose and are not directed by fear, greed, ignorance or superstition.

This level of self-consciousness, however, cannot be achieved alone: unlike what the atomistic psychology of ultra-liberalism would have us believe, the capacity to choose is not innate, but a potential which must be developed. When the awarding of rights is based on the recognition of the worth of particular human qualities, and if that implies that we must develop these capacities in ourselves and others, then every proof that these qualities can only develop in a community or in a particular form of society is, in Taylor's view, also a proof that we must support the relevant society. If the social view of man is correct, it can no longer be maintained that people have merely rights, and no duties with regard to society: awarding rights implies that one also takes on duties.

Duties to society

What does this mean for the concept of freedom? The theoreticians who make individual rights central are mainly in pursuit of the right to freedom, by which they mean, according to Taylor, 'freedom to choose life plans, to dispose of possessions, to form one's own convictions and within reason act on them, and so on'. And: 'freedom by which men are capable of conceiving alternatives and arriving at a definition of what they really want, as well as discerning what commands their adherence or their allegiance' (Taylor 1979: 53, 55).[15] In Taylor's opinion, this freedom is unachievable for someone whose horizon is so limited that he can only imagine one way of life. It is equally unfeasible for someone with such a fear of, or aversion to, the unknown – a fear and aversion which is stimulated or not by the other members of his, by definition, limited group – that he will never get acquainted with alternative views. Freedom is, according to Taylor, the capacity to give, independently, direction to one's life on the basis of well-founded choices. The capacity to choose and the self-awareness needed for this can only be developed within an entirety of social relations:

self-understanding is not something we can sustain on our own . . . our identity is always partly defined in conversations with others or through the common understanding which underlies the practices of our society. The thesis is that the identity of the autonomous, self-determining individual requires a social matrix.

(Taylor 1979: 60; cf. Chapters 3 and 5)

This matrix is formed by an entire civilization which consists of a complex pluriform whole of groups, movements, tendencies, of public and academic debate, of a great number of institutions – museums, universities, libraries, orchestras, newspaper and weeklies, broadcasters, representative bodies, political parties, church organizations, associations, schools, courts, publishers, etc. In order to make freedom valuable, in order to make it possible, it is necessary to maintain this totality.

If we now have the duty to respect individual freedom, then we have, says Taylor, also a moral duty to the group, the bearer of the necessary condition of freedom – the culture. This does not tally, however, with the atomistic principle that society has a purely instrumental value for the individual and that people are not impeded by any 'obligation to belong to or to sustain society'. Atomism ignores the social character of man and his freedom, denies that the individual has duties to society as well as rights, and properly regarded, therefore, forms a threat to the freedom of the individual. Taylor recapitulates:

> The crucial point here is this: since the free individual can only maintain his identity within a society/culture of a certain kind, he has to be concerned about the shape of this society/culture as a whole. He cannot . . . be concerned purely with his individual choices and the associations formed from such choices to the neglect of the matrix in which such choices can be open or closed, rich or meagre. It is important to him that certain activities and institutions flourish in society. It is even important to him what the moral tone of the whole society is . . . because freedom and individual diversity can only flourish in a society where there is a general recognition of their worth.
>
> (Taylor 1979: 58)

FRITHJOF BERGMANN: IDENTIFICATION WITHIN THE COMMUNITY

Frithjof Bergmann also criticizes the abstract or atomistic view of man. As we have seen he connects the notions of identification and identity to the concept of freedom: an act is free if the actor experiences it as an expression or objectification of his identity and one can therefore first feel free when one has an identify. The formation of identification is therefore a condition for the ability to experience freedom. The essence of freedom consists of the desire of the ego to objectify itself ('to act itself out in the world') and of its identification with the creations of this activity.

The consequence of this conception, according to Bergmann, is that freedom, in contrast to what many liberals think, requires no absolute independence or complete absence of 'obstacles'. This applies only for those who, like the neurotic clerk from Dostoevsky's *Notes from Underground*, lack all identity: they must indeed 'throw off' everything, even their own reason and feelings, in order to feel free. However, in Bergmann's opinion, as long as one can identify with that on which one is 'dependent', there is no constraint on freedom:

> 'dependency' on something does not in any way diminish one's degree of freedom as long as one truly identifies with the thing on which one is 'dependent'. If I am in harmony with something – if in fact it is me . . . then I need not be isolated from it, and need not be protected from it, to be 'free'. The demand for freedom takes the form of an insistence on total independence only for those who lack identity. For all others the claim is not compelled to this extreme – and yet, in terms of freedom, they have not compromised and do not receive less.
>
> (Bergmann 1977: 48)

According to Bergmann, one can only acquire an identity by absorbing, to some extent, the culture in which one lives. Freedom can thus not be acquired by shutting oneself off from one's social environment. 'We do not see man as solitary, autonomous, or independent', writes Bergmann, 'he is for us inseparable from his culture' (Bergmann 1977: 102). Many people who cherish the ideal of total freedom envisage an open limitless space where everything is allowed and is possible. The only thing he will find in this vacuum, warns Bergmann, is a 'desert of self-disassociation'. In his opinion, which relates to Taylor's objections against the present-day culture of authenticity (see Chapter 3), the individual in the (former) 'free West' is now roaming in this desert.

> It is true that in the pursuit of freedom one has destroyed ever more obstacles – social, ethical and religious frameworks – but the emptiness thus formed makes it even more difficult to identify with anything and in doing so feel 'free'.[16]
>
> (Bergmann 1977: 161–3)

Bergmann illustrates these notions with a critique of the thought of Herbert Marcuse. As we know, in his *One Dimensional Man* (Marcuse 1964), he claims that our modern civilization exercises a more deceptive form of repression, mainly due to its use of the mass media, than earlier, bloody tyrants. While the latter systems of coercion first came into action after the desires and goals had been formed, the modern systems can manipulate people in such a way that every open and violent suppression has become superfluous: the cherishing of desires which cannot be fulfilled is simply avoided. If repression used to be aimed at outward behaviour, nowadays, according to Marcuse, even the inner is no longer safe: man is formed in such a way from his earliest youth that open repression can be avoided, properly regarded an extremely inefficient means of enforcing conformism.[17]

Bergmann recognizes that the instruments of influence have become more numerous and effective, but the difference with former times is, in his opinion, less than Marcuse would have us believe. A culture has never confined its interference with the individual to his outer behaviour. All civilizations begin, and this is both inevitable and desirable, to form the inner man, his needs and desires, from the moment that he is born (Bergmann 1977: 51). With his suggestion that it was once different, according to Bergmann, Marcuse seems to be implicitly basing himself on the psychology of the 'underground man'. His ideal image of autonomy and independence is an illusion. Not so much because Marcuse asks more from people than they can produce, but because he seems to have a totally mistaken conception of what 'freedom' means. Freedom, once again, is not the absence of every influence: in practice, making oneself independent of all influences means that one must, like an onion, peel away so many skins from one's ego – layers which are socially influenced and which therefore can no longer be regarded as authentic – until nothing more of the 'ego' remains. Freedom in this sense requires thus the total self-destruction of the ego. However, the peeling of onions and egos only leads to tears (cf. Taylor, Dworkin and Feinberg in Chapter 3).

DISCUSSION

Enculturation

> We are born weak, we need strength; we are born totally unprovided, we need aid; we are born stupid, we need judgment. Everything we do not have at our birth and which we need when we are grown is given us by education.
>
> (Jean-Jacques Rousseau 1762: 38)

The relation between individual and group, as we have repeatedly seen in the foregoing, is characterized by tensions: on the one hand the former can always be threatened in his negative freedom by the latter; on the other hand, the individual can only become autonomous thanks to, and within, the community. Society is the source of material and cultural conditions indispensable for positive freedom. This is not merely a question of the actual presence of all those institutions from which a culture is constructed (newspapers, libraries, political parties, universities, museums, theatres, action and pressure groups, and church communities, etc.). Also important is something that is especially emphasized by Lukes and Norman (see Chapter 4), which is that the formal and informal education which people receive is such that they can really make use of these institutions.

Furthermore, the formation of a personality, of an identity, as argued by Taylor, Feinberg, Bettelheim and Bergmann, among others, precedes autonomy. Getting to know, absorbing the existing culture is a requirement for this. It is therefore not a question of uncritical adoption of old ideas, of a one-sided choice between conformism and non-conformism, but of an inter-active, dialectic process, propelled forward by the knowledge that one's own perspective becomes bigger and broader when one stands on the shoulders of others. This process could be designated by the word *enculturation*. Enculturation encloses *socialization*. We speak of the latter when there is an educating party present who 'incorporates' the individual into a particular culture.

This has all been splendidly expressed by the English cultural philosopher and sociologist of culture, Raymond Williams. We have become accustomed, he writes in *The Long Revolution*, to draw a sharp distinction between indi-vidual and society, between 'man' and 'world'. The product of this, the abstract conception of the individual, has indeed had a liberating effect for man, but the limitations of this viewpoint have become increasingly great. Through its preoccupation with the naked individual it forms a denial of the mutual dependence of individual and community and with it an obstruction to the development, the individuation, of man. According to Williams, indi-vidualism has become 'selfishness and indifference by the facts of its own incompleteness'. Our fellow man has become part of the 'masses' for us, and at the same time we have condemned ourselves to a similar anonymity and emptiness (Williams 1961: 89–119).

Human identity, says Williams, is essentially a 'social structure' which develops in a constant interaction between innate qualities and social envi-ronment. These are the basic individualizing factors, but again, writes Williams, as both interact:

> the very fact of the growth of self-consciousness produces a distinct orga-nization, capable both of self-scrutiny and self-direction. This 'autonomous' self grows within a social process which radically influ-ences it, but the degree of gained autonomy makes possible the . . . next stage, in which the individual can help to change or modify the social process that has influenced and is influencing him.
>
> (Williams 1961: 100–1)

Open-ended self-development

> Human nature is not a machine to be built after a model, and set to do exactly the work prescribed for it, but a tree, which requires to grow and develop itself on all sides, according to the tendency of the inward forces which make it a liv-ing thing.
>
> (John Stuart Mill 1859: 188)

The idea of 'self-development' or 'self-realization' should not be understood strictly teleologically: the end result is uncertain. However, sometimes it is presupposed that the theoreticians who emphasize the self-realization of the individual assume that the final goal is fixed, just as with a seed which becomes a tree. Considering the necessity of following one particular path through life, the behavioural alternatives would be extremely limited and the individuals would therefore not be very flexible either.

Such an interpretation of the self-development ideal of the positive tradition of thinking about freedom applies very much to the rationalistic variant of this ideal. In this, in the words of Isaiah Berlin, freedom is seen as 'the unimpeded fulfilment of my true nature'. The link between self-development and rationalism, however, is not at all logical. It is unnecessary to suppose a mysterious, invariable 'self' which directs our life with or without our knowledge in a particular fixed direction and which we must discover. Our actions, our identity, are to an important extent the product of our choices and we can and may not avoid the responsibility for this (cf. Berlin 1964: 176).

Furthermore, as Williams stated, since each individual possesses a number of unique innate qualities and has a unique personal history, his self-development, no matter how much this is socially dependent and influenced, is an open-ended process and with unlimited possibilities. The individuality develops in an interaction between innate qualities and the 'ensemble' of social relations. Which talents develop or not is very much dependent on the random and deliberate stimuli which one receives from one's environment. Someone who is not challenged or stimulated to acquire particular capacities, will never develop them either. The more people have developed, the greater the mark can be that they themselves set upon their life and identity (cf. Kleinig 1983: 67; Bay 1958).

The value of isolation

Finally, attention must be focused on the importance for individual development of the capacity for, and the possibility of, isolation or being alone. We repeatedly refer here, and will continue to do so, to the necessity of people 'absorbing' the culture in which they live. This is because culture, knowledge of alternative ideas, tastes, values, is a condition of autonomy. Formal and informal education are indispensable in this. However, this does not argue that people should be constantly surrounded bodily by others, that people are uninterruptedly taught, told by others what is worth knowing about. Enculturation, acquisition of knowledge and those activities which are also characteristic of autonomy – the development of talents, the creation of new possibilities, keeping contact with identity – are, to an important extent, efforts which take place in isolation.

In this context, in his book *Solitude*, the English psychiatrist Anthony Storr defends the value of being alone. In the first place, he points out the important role which social relations play in the development of one's own identity. 'Personality' is a relative concept: one can first become aware of one's identity when one can reflect upon it, can contrast it with that of others. Storr writes: 'One cannot even begin to be conscious of oneself as a separate individual without another person with whom to compare oneself. A man in isolation is a collective man, a man without individuality' (Storr 1988: 147). This applies to both children and adults. Extremely introverted, creative people – some artists, philosophers, composers – can perhaps define themselves and develop by using their own past, the earlier developed identity or works produced, as a frame of reference. However, it is true for these people, too, that they must have a starting-point for their personal voyage of discovery, a starting-point formed by their earlier, socially and culturally defined identity (Storr 1988: 147–154).

It is not strange therefore that modern Western psychologists generally attach much value to social relations. For example, in general, one regards the capacity to enter into meaningful relations with others on the basis of equality as the most important criterion for mental maturity, as a condition for the development of the individuality, and as a condition of general mental health or contentment. People who isolate themselves or who go through life solitary are, in general, certainly in the Freudian tradition of thinking, suspect.

Storr wants to refine this idea. He does not detract from man's social essence, but points out the importance that work carried out in solitude can have for individual development and for making life meaningful. He emphasizes the value of solitude, of being able to withdraw, for self-reflection, for staying in contact with one's own identity, for rediscovering a new balance after changes in life (after the loss of loved ones, for example), for contemplation, learning and creativity. The capacity to be alone, something which is developed by few, and to go beyond Storr, the possibility of being able to make use of this, are therefore conditions for individual autonomy (Storr 1988: 28).

In this context, one can wonder whether education is organized in our Western culture in a pedagogically correct manner. Within this education, students generally are given little opportunity to pursue knowledge and the borders of their possibilities at their own tempo, in solitude and independently. Usually, they are told what, when and how (and rarely why) they must learn, and an extensive system of incentives and punishment is used to enforce this learning process. Ultimately, this means that the acquisition of knowledge is threatened with becoming associated with sanctions. The satisfaction which knowledge and self-realization can provide, and the naturalness of development, can be undermined from an early age in this way with a consequence that sanctions are needed literally to keep the children in the lesson – the vicious circle is closed – and the acquisition of culture after the end of the schooldays and the removal of the coercion is often abruptly brought to an end. The compulsion imposed on pupils to attend school thirty to thirty-five hours a week, in a busy class full of distraction, is an illustration of this. This commandment is at loggerheads with the fact that the acquisition of knowledge and personality development take place, to an important extent, in solitude. It seems not impossible that students could attain greater learning achievements if the number of compulsory learning hours was sharply reduced.

RICHARD NORMAN: FREEDOM AND EQUALITY

The idea that freedom of choice first acquires meaning when one really has something to choose and that the community has a stimulating role to fulfil in the latter, is particularly emphasized in the positive tradition of thinking about freedom. We have already discussed this earlier in this chapter. The standpoints of Lukes and Taylor illustrated this. Another example of this conviction are the ideas of the English political philosopher Richard Norman. He developed these mainly in his *Free and Equal, a Philosophical Examination of Political Values*, which appeared in 1987.

Norman offers a further broadening of the image already sketched of the positive conception of freedom because he explicitly examines the relation between freedom and equality. The concept of 'equality' is naturally worthy of separate study; it is after all as essentially disputed as 'freedom'. However, by briefly looking at this value, we can also learn something more about freedom: both conceptions are, within the positive conception of freedom, closely connected and the justifications of both are organically related, certainly for Norman.

An important principle of Norman's is that he refuses to see politics as a matter of course as the continuation of social conflicts by peaceful means, or as a form of defence of interests in which acquisition of power and exercise of it is central. In the first place, he associates politics with a communal attempt to make the best of ourselves. He thus refers regularly to the idea of 'community', a value which, for a long time, was regarded in political thinking as an artefact, but which in recent years has received new life. It could be said that this community division of politics and society is characteristic of the positive tradition of thinking about freedom.

Negative and positive conditions of freedom

According to Norman, it is the notion of 'choosing' which forms the centre of the concept of freedom. Other aspects of freedom are, in his view, only derived from this one (cf. Benn and Weinstein 1971: 209). This applies, for example, to the wish to own a private space in which we can go our own way unimpeded by others. Normally speaking, this desire is not based on the wish to be abandoned by everyone, but on the conviction that the principle of non-interference offers us the possibility to make autonomous choices. The absence of constraints or force is thus not of central importance in the concept of freedom. According to Norman, it only forms a 'negative' condition for freedom:

we wish not to be interfered with by others precisely because, and only because, that will enable us to make our own choices for ourselves . . . the central element in the concept of freedom is the positive one of being able to make choices . . . the negative fact of non-interference is related to it as one of the conditions for our being able to make choices.

(Norman 1987: 37)

For Norman, this choosing only becomes significant when one has different, relevant possibilities of choice. The more this is the case, the freer one is. In an article he writes: 'freedom I take to be the availability of, and capacity to exercise, meaningful and effective choice' (Norman 1982: 90). Enjoying alternative choices, therefore, is seen by Norman as a 'positive' condition of freedom. Within this he again distinguishes three categories: political, material and cultural.

When people can exercise more influence on the *political* decision-making of the community in which they live, they will also have more control of their own lives and they therefore enjoy a greater freedom (Norman 1987: 41–3).

The second category is *material* in nature. More money means more behavioural alternatives and therefore greater freedom. With a higher income more luxury goods are available, one can travel more often and further, one can afford to take more leave, etc. Certainly, when one lives below the poverty line, a rise in material welfare is important. The less one has to fight for a bare existence, the more time and energy is released which can be devoted to other, cultural matters.

Technological progress too, says Norman, brings with it an increase in freedom. Not merely through the rise in prosperity, but also through the opening up of all kinds of new possibilities. Thanks to modern means of transport and communication, for example, numerous goods and cultural expression are accessible (in principle) to far more people. Norman also emphasizes that freedom and material prosperity are not identical. A dictatorship with a high standard of living remains a dictatorship. However, he does oppose Berlin, who in his view suggests too much that freedom and prosperity have absolutely nothing to do with each other.

The last category identified by Norman concerns cultural conditions. The possibility of making choices is not only determined by the actual options present, it also depends on the degree to which one is able to discern, articulate and assess these. The extent to which this capacity is developed in the individual is strongly dependent on the quantity and quality of the formal and informal education he receives. Education of a poor quality is characterized in Norman's view by resulting in an unconscious, uncritical acceptance of the prejudices and thought patterns of one's own society. In order to allow people to really choose they must be taught to question these dominant, obvious values and ideas.

Norman emphasizes that freedom is a relative concept – one is never

completely free or unfree. Its extent depends on the degree to which the positive and negative conditions mentioned are fulfilled. None of these conditions is a sufficient condition in itself. All that is really necessary, argues
Norman, is the negative condition 'non-intervention': extremely large coercion makes someone completely unfree, even if the positive conditions are
fulfilled. The relation between freedom and its conditions is thus, in
Norman's view, of a causal nature: the conditions are not part of the definition of freedom, but are closely related to it (Norman 1987: 50).

Because the material and cultural (and, by definition, political) conditions can exclusively be met by living together with others, according to
Norman, one can only be free within the community. He therefore criticizes
the contradiction between individual and society supposed by John Stuart
Mill, for example.

In *On Liberty* Mill defines freedom, according to Norman, in the first
place as self-determination and self-development. However, when he goes
into the question of how society must be organized to enable the realization
of these values, he turns out, in Norman's reading, to see the community
merely as a source of constraints. This is expressed in Mill's famous 'harm
principle': the individual should be left alone by society as long as he does
no harm to others (Mill is discussed in Chapter 5). However, in Norman's
view it is inconsistent first to define freedom as a positive concept, but then
to deny the individual the political, material and cultural conditions necessary for this. This occurs by exclusively emphasizing the non-interference
principle when the relation between society and individual is raised for discussion (Norman 1987: 11–7, 54–5; cf. Taylor pp. 107–10).

Equality as a natural value within a cooperative

Where people together create the positive conditions for freedom, a division
problem arises: it may be decided how the communally produced goods and
services must be distributed among the participants in the society. Norman
considers the principle of equality to be the most justified here: 'everyone
should have as much freedom as is compatible with the same degree of freedom for everyone else' (Norman 1987: 55).

Norman wants to justify this value by showing that just like freedom it is
emotionally rooted in our world of experience. He therefore rejects the formal and utilitarian arguments which are generally produced in favour of
equality. For example, utilitarianism is insufficient because it looks merely at
the *consequences* of equality and inequality: if it emerges empirically that
equality leads to greater happiness for a greater number of people then this
principle is justified, from this viewpoint. But equality, says Norman, is not
important because of its consequences, but for what it is: it refers to the way
in which people should be treated, in our view, a treatment which they have
a right to because it is just (Norman 1987: 66).

In this context, he examines extensively John Rawls' theory of justice, a theory that according to him is in broad outline egalitarian in character. Norman argues that Rawls uses two contradictory arguments in his book. In the first argumentation, which he rejects, contract thinking is central: principles of justice are here chosen by rational, egoistic individuals who do not know which position they will later occupy in society. The idea of cooperation is central to the second argument. The idea here is that everyone's welfare is dependent on the cooperation with others and that, therefore, the division of the benefits must be such that all are prepared, even the least endowed, to cooperate with the relevant cooperation. The latter train of thought is certainly present in Rawls' theory, but in Norman's view is undermined by Rawls as he connects it with the notion of a hypothetical contract. Norman wants to take the idea from this context and tries to develop it further.

If people bind themselves to a form of cooperation this has, according to Norman, two implications. In the first place, this commitment has consequences for the way in which decisions are made: it will be attempted to come to a decision communally, a decision which all can support and in which everyone's interests and ideas are respected as much as possible. Interests can conflict, and difficult decisions will have to be taken, but these will work out in such a way that the commitment of the individual to the group is strengthened and is not exploited.

In the second place, there are consequences for the content of the decision: on the whole, everyone must benefit equally from the cooperation. Equality is thus the leading principle of justice in a cooperation, which is expressed in the division of power, and of the burdens and benefits of the cooperation. The members of a cooperative framework could naturally decide for an unequal division, but Norman thinks that in practice an 'a priori equality' applies: as long as there are no weighty reasons not to do this, in principle, people must be treated equally. An unequal division would be irrational; it is precisely the equal division of the burdens and benefits which makes a cooperative of a particular institution (Norman 1987: 73).

Equality as the promotion of egalitarian social conditions

In practice, equality does not mean, emphasizes Norman, that everyone has the same functions and receives the same rewards. It is a matter of creating the *social conditions* which enable every person to lead an equally valuable and gratifying life. Naturally, there is no guarantee that this can be realized. For this, people differ too much in innate qualities and the course of their lives is too characterized by randomness. However, according to Norman, it is possible to aim at having the social conditions at least as equal for all as is possible:

> though we cannot guarantee to everyone an equally good life, we can
> organize our social arrangements so that they do not give anyone less

chance of a good life than anyone else, and the differences in the quality of people's lives are simply the outcome of their particular choices and temperaments.

(Norman 1987: 103)

In order to promote equal chances for a satisfactory life, special burdens or heavy or unpleasant work may be compensated for by higher rewards. This idea of compensation is after all egalitarian in character: extra burdens are repaid by extra benefits. However, people do not need additional (material) rewards when they have done something 'good': the appreciation and admiration which they will receive from others for this, is considered sufficient by Norman. The use and development of their capacities gives people generally so much satisfaction that even without an extra financial reward they would be prepared to carry out the relevant work.

Furthermore, egalitarians do not aim to have everyone become equally mediocre, to create a grey grim mass. The diverse development of talents is actually promoted and acclaimed. However, they refuse to translate the appreciation of this into structural differences in power or incomes, all the more so as these undermine the chance of development of many. Finally, the pursuit is not focused on an 'equality of opportunity' either. This view, says Norman, echoing Tawny, has little to do with egalitarianism, as the ideas of a hierarchical society remain intact. People only get equal chances to compete for a limited number of prizes, an equal chance to be unequal. This inequality obstructs a real respect for the individual, expressing itself in the creation of equal chances for a dignified life (Norman 1987: 101–4, 120–4; cf. Lukes 1974a).

Conditions of equality

In short, Norman is concerned with an equality of opportunities to enjoy a satisfactory life, in so far as this can be promoted by an equality in socially determined conditions. Here, he makes a distinction in conditions that runs parallel to the distinction in positive conditions of freedom made earlier.

First, political power must be divided equally, which does not rule out responsibilities being delegated to chosen representatives. Norman considers the division of power to be of primary importance because this is at the basis of the other relationships within a society.

Second, every individual must profit equally in material terms from his participation in a cooperative community. Special needs or particular burdens may thus be compensated for by extra profit: the goal is that everyone's profit is equal on the whole.

Third, in education everyone must be given equal opportunities to develop his talents. Once again the aim here is not that everyone gets an equal chance to become unequal, via a system of education which reproduces inequalities. Norman completely rejects the idea of a 'social ladder'.

While it is true that people are unequally talented, each individual has an equal need to develop his talents. In order to disseminate the chance of a decent life, everyone must also get the opportunity for this.

For that matter Norman considers the existence of equal chances to participate in the culture to be closely related to educational equality. This is necessary, says Norman, as does Raymond Williams, if every citizen is to participate socially and politically in the society to which he belongs. People who cannot participate in the culture, which is formed by the quality newspapers, journals and TV stations, the literature, the art, etc., cannot participate either in the 'democratic' decision-making, because the debate which accompanies this is always carried on in terms of the 'elite culture'.

Freedom and equality as harmonious values

Socialists are often accused of being a threat to individual freedom in their pursuit of equality. People differ so much in their talents and capacities that, if left undisturbed by others, they will inevitably become unequal. Equality can therefore only be realized by limiting the freedom of the individual to employ his talents according to how he sees fit. Norman opposes this reasoning by thinkers like Hayek, Friedman and Nozick. Freedom and equality are, in his view, not irreconcilable or conflicting, but *complementary*.

Norman emphasizes that egalitarians have never sought to make everyone equal on all levels – a quest which indeed could only be realized with force. The goal has always been to create the social conditions which would enable everyone to lead an equally valuable and satisfactory life. These conditions are, in practice, the same as those for freedom: an equality in power, income and education as the goal. By working for equality, therefore, in the view of Norman, one also promotes freedom: 'Egalitarians have in practice aimed at equality of social power, equality of wealth and equality in education – and . . . I can then claim that, in these various ways, what egalitarians are aiming at is equality of liberty' (Norman 1982: 97; cf. 1987: 134).

Finally, does the realization of equality not form an assault on our fundamental rights to freedom? Robert Nozick suggested that imposing taxes to redistribute incomes can be equated with forced labour. Norman considers the idea of inviolable basic rights to be problematic. According to him, the notion of a 'right' has no meaning as long as it is no privilege or claim which is guaranteed in some way or other by an institution or convention. The idea of a 'natural right' is therefore a contradiction (Norman 1987: 139ff.). The term 'rights' can, at most, indicate certain fundamental human needs or traits, which we consider so important that we think they should be respected in all societies. In general, this concept lends special status to rights of negative liberty in particular, and that is why Nozick suggests that equality-promoting taxation is an assault on fundamental rights. The ethical basis of the rights of negative freedom is no different or stronger than those of positive rights and, according to Norman, there is therefore no reason to reserve the qualification 'rights' exclusively for these negative appeals. Conflicting freedoms will inevitably have to be balanced against each other and this balancing cannot be avoided by declaring a random number of freedoms to be inviolable rights.

BALANCE

The democratic community versus liberal politics

Norman can be criticized because he is in danger of losing sight of the negative condition of freedom. This arises from his thesis that the notion of 'choice' is the core of the concept of freedom. 'Choice', however, implies an activity and this, as we have seen, is only a characteristic of positive freedom. Negative freedom, on the other hand, is based precisely on that which Norman considers so improbable: the desire to own a private space where one is simply left alone by everyone. This can be combined with complete apathy: one does not have to do anything to enjoy this form of freedom. Positive freedom, self-realization and determination, is a more comprehensive and fundamental value in human life than 'privacy', but this does not make the latter value unimportant. Through his emphasis on the activity of 'choice' Norman runs the danger of neglecting this.

This is expressed in his treatment of the contradiction between freedom and equality. Norman makes it plausible that the positive conditions of freedom are the same as the conditions for equality and that socialists in their pursuit of social equality are thus working simultaneously for individual freedom – however, for *positive* freedom and not for freedom in general. Norman has not demonstrated that there is no contradiction between, on the one hand, negative freedom and, on the other, positive freedom and equality. He is hardly concerned with the question of how negative freedom for the wolves can lead to an unequal division of incomes, power and knowledge, in which way this inequality can reduce the positive freedom of the sheep, and how in order to avoid this the negative freedom of the wolves must be restricted. Just like Tawney and Lukes, in the first place, he makes an ethically and communitarian inspired plea to realize those social conditions which offer everyone an equal opportunity to realize his capacity for autonomy. The degree to which people get the opportunity for this, determines the ethical level of a society. The plausibility of his argument, notwithstanding, Norman cannot get around the fact that negative and positive freedom must always be balanced against each other, even in a cooperative community. He recognizes this implicitly with his critique of the natural right argument of Nozick.

Furthermore, in a somewhat broader context, we can ask ourselves whether there is a tension between the individualistic and community motifs in the thinking of socialistic theoreticians like Norman and MacPherson. Marx, too, assumed that people could only develop into unique individuals

in community with others, and that everyone's individuality is defined to
such a degree by his relations with others, that all personal tendencies, goals
and projects will, as a matter of course, establish the community relations.
However, what will the relations be in a 'true' community? Are the contradictions not already contained in the concept of 'community'? After all,
people always belong to different communities at the same time (family,
extended family, circle of friends, work, home, motherland, people, culture,
class, religion, race, etc.). These communities bring with them deviating loy-
alties which can conflict with each other. How, and on the basis of which
normative considerations, must these conflicts be settled (see Lukes 1985:
98)? Norman does not solve these problems, which concern the conditions
of freedom, by simply appealing to the idea of community.

In short, Norman (and before him MacPherson) devotes too little attention to the contradictions which can always arise between individuals,
between individual and community and even between different identifications of the same person. These contradictions are the ultimate consequence
of the incompatibility of numerous significant values. Ethical pluralism is
therefore closely connected with negative freedom: the knowledge that in life
there are diverse conflicting values which must inevitably be weighed up
against each other, and the conviction that, as a consequence of the logical
gap between facts and values, it is not possible to demonstrate in a formal or
empirical manner the right or wrong of the supremacy of a particular value,
stimulates the desire for the individual to be allowed a private space in which
he can profess his own truth, undisturbed and unpunished.

Value-non-cognitivism and pluralism, however, do not have to be a reason to declare the values of the individual sacred and to assume in advance
an insurmountable contradiction between the values of the individual and
the society and to avoid every debate about values, every attempt to reach a
consensus. Pluralism is something different to atomism and nihilism, and
democracy – political participation – does not have to decay as a matter of
course into the exercise of power. As emphasized by Berlin, people, certainly
within a bordered culture, have sufficient in common not to make a discussion about values useless by definition. On the basis of a number of shared
principles or intuitions there are always good demonstrable *reasons* why a
particular value must be given priority above another at a particular
moment.

Norman's importance therefore lies in his refusal to postulate in advance
an insoluble conflict between the values of individual and community, and
in his attempt to base a political theory on the idea of cooperation and not
necessarily on conflict and power. The development of everyone's capacity
for autonomy, or in another field, a collective good – like a clean environment – will be considerably easier to realize within a conception of politics
such as that of Norman's, than within a liberal *Weltanschauung* in which private interests, conflicts and power call the tune.

To recapitulate, the individual and the group have a relationship full of tensions: on the one hand, the individual can always be threatened in his negative freedom by the group; on the other hand, the individual can only become autonomous in, and thanks to, the community. Where theoreticians like Norman and MacPherson are too light in their treatment of the former, numerous politicologists, liberals and contemporary social democrats preoccupied by power can be accused of having too little interest in the latter.[18] For that matter, in recent years there has been a remarkable revival of more community-based conceptions of politics. This is taking place mainly in the context of the debate about the future of the welfare state. It is the belief of many that this is threatened with defeat from atomism, anomie and social disintegration and it is therefore due for revision. In the relevant debate, the idea of 'citizenship' plays an important role.

Freedom and the number of options: a proportional relation?

As has been expounded in Chapter 3, the idea that one must search for, or possess, alternative choices is an important element of the positive conception of freedom. Autonomy requires, in the words of Lindley, 'active theoretical rationality': by getting to know other ideas, lifestyles, values and tastes one reduces the chances of giving one's life a direction which fits less well with one's talents or identity and which one would not choose if one was more aware of the alternatives. One really only chooses – one is first really in control of one's own life – when one is in a position, through education and socialization, to see one's own horizons in the proper perspective and to expand them.

The idea that freedom of choice first gains significance when one also really has something to choose and that the community has a constructive role to play in this is, as stated earlier, mainly emphasized in the positive tradition of thinking about freedom. The standpoints of Lukes, Taylor and Norman were an illustration of this. Lukes stated among other things that it is an expression of a lack of respect for the individual if the number of alternatives from which to choose is unreasonably limited. Taylor argued that only within the context of a culture can one have the opportunities of choice which are indispensable for freedom, and that everyone who wishes to respect the individual capacity for freedom therefore also has a moral duty with regard to the community, the bearer of the culture. Norman, finally, saw the notion of 'choice' as the centre of the concept of freedom. According to him, individual freedom increases in proportion to the number of alternative choices. On the basis of these connections generally made between freedom, choice and the possession of possibilities of choice, it is interesting to look at these relations again.

A first question we can ask concerns the status of (the number of available) alternative choices. Bergmann argues that the presence of alternatives is no guarantee of freedom, that it says nothing about the *context* in which the choice must be made. When one can only choose from two extremely unattractive possibilities – working in the mines or starving – then it is rather misleading to speak of 'freedom' (Bergmann 1977: 55–9).

From this we can conclude that 'choice' first acquires real significance when one has various *relevant* options. It is not just a question, says Norman, of the quantity but also of the quality of the choices. However, when are there 'meaningful alternative choices'? What is a relevant alternative for one (white or red wine), can seem mere superfluous luxury to another (the beer drinker). Norman recognizes this problem, but emphasizes that people, certainly within a limited historic period, have enough in common to be able to reach a certain consensus on the answer to the question concerned. For example, nowadays we generally agree that thirty instead of three different television stations enlarge our freedom less than the possibility of choosing from more political parties or religious tendencies (cf. Benn and Weinstein 1971).

Does freedom, as suggested by Norman and Berlin (1958: 130, see Chapter 2), grow in proportion to the number of relevant options? Barber admits that freedom assumes familiarity with alternatives and that the increase of the number of possibilities stimulates consciousness, but, like Bergmann, he adds a number of caveats to this relationship (Barber 1975: 75–9). In the very first place, Barber asks how long one can continue with the augmentation of the number of alternative choices before it becomes counter-productive. People's privilege in a free market economy to choose from sixty different makes of cars can have the effect that they can no longer imagine how one can live without a car.

In addition, there are also psychic limits to the number of alternatives which a person can bear without becoming completely disoriented. In practice then, people seem to be very attached to a minimal certainty in order to be able to constantly pursue new opportunities.

In this context, Bettelheim emphasizes that having increasing numbers of options does not necessarily cause the experience of freedom to grow. On the psychological level, processing this demands an increasingly integrated personality. In order to solve his dilemmas of choice the individual can look for external authorities through which his autonomy can ultimately be drastically undermined (Bettelheim 1960: 78). In this manner, one could explain the rise of fascism in the beginning of this century: the disappearance of traditional contexts like church, village and family, the transition from a *Gemeinschaft* to a *Gesellschaft* caused an ethical vacuum which many could only fill by surrendering themselves to a Führer (cf. De Kadt 1939; Fromm 1941).

With regard to the psychic limits which are imposed on the number of options, another case is the consequences of the bombardment of information to which the present-day Western citizen is constantly exposed. The consequence of this flood of snippets of information about events from all over the world can be that people can no longer distinguish the really important matters. The image of the world that people have can therefore become, through a surplus of information, increasingly incoherent and superficial, which does not further the possibility of giving rational direction to one's own life. The American media scientist Neil Postman claims, in this context, that the Western media no longer provide us with information, but with *disinformation* (see Chapter 7).

Barber also wonders whether the constant presentation of new options does not undermine the creativity needed for individual freedom. In this way a speaker or writer who only shows one side of the story, is often considerably more interesting and stimulating than the one who exhaustively presents all the nuances possible. In Barber's view, this is explained by the fact that freedom means not choosing between, but the creation of alternatives.

Berlin, too, in his essay 'From hope and fear set free' asks whether knowledge can always be reconciled with freedom. Does an increase in knowledge always lead to more open doors, or does it also close doors (1964: 194–8)? A poet can be dependent for his inspiration on particular illusions and myths. If these are disproved then he is liberated from superstition and ignorance, from irrational forces which exercise power over him. Through this, his autonomy grows; he can now give a more rational justification of his convictions and have a greater insight into the motivations behind his behaviour. On the other hand, however, his freedom to write poetry, to create, is reduced. His increased knowledge has become an obstacle (Berlin 1964: 195). On the one hand, people who drink from the fountain of knowledge are thus liberated from false hope and fear; from superstition, from ignorance, from dark forces which exercise an influence over them without them being aware of it. They thus become more autonomous. But, on the other hand, in this way they could face life less unconstrainedly, they might express themselves less spontaneously and authentically and, as Bergmann imagines, allow themselves to be carried along by events. Their freedom or capacity to carry out creative work is thus reduced. This alternative has always been able to rely upon great sympathy in our civilization: romantics like Rousseau, Tolstoy and Gauguin are interpreters of this.

In his essay 'Is more choice better than less?', Gerald Dworkin states nevertheless that in economic theory and in political philosophy it is generally assumed without question that having more options must be seen as positive. He, too, points to the costs which this sometimes implies, however, costs which can exceed the gains (Dworkin 1982: 47–57).

The more opportunities, the more time and energy is demanded, in the first place, to make a choice and the more one is psychically burdened by this. The doubt about whether one has chosen 'correctly' becomes constantly greater. In the second place, more options cause the responsibility for the ultimate choice to increase (George Bernard Shaw wrote: 'Liberty means responsibility, that is why most people dread it.'). Third, the social pressure to conform can become stronger through new alternatives. When, for example, the technical possibility arises of determining before the birth whether a child is mongoloid or not, society can put pressure on the mother concerned to have an abortion due to the economic costs which mongols bring with them. New possibilities can, in the fourth place, cause the value of the old ones to decrease. Titmuss points out that the freedom to give blood to other people disappears when there is also the possibility of selling blood. The freedom to give something which is not regarded as merchandise is destroyed in this case.

Although the costs mentioned by Dworkin do not always mean a decrease in someone's freedom, possessing more options is not always to be desired. Nevertheless, Dworkin does not want to belittle the importance of being able to choose (Dworkin 1982: 58–60). First of all, possessing more possibilities enlarges the chance that people can realize their own desires. In addition, being able to choose can give an intrinsic satisfaction. Furthermore, making choices can have an instrumental value for developing particular potentials or character traits. In this way, the capacity for judgement only develops through having often to choose. Finally, choosing has an intrinsic value where it is an expression of the essential characteristic of man: the capacity to self-determination. Restriction of someone's possibilities of choice is thus an infringement on his human dignity (cf. Megone 1987: 616).

The distinction between freedom and its conditions

Earlier in the chapter, we saw, on the basis of MacCallum's thesis, that every meaningful statement on social freedom is triadic in character, that the positive and negative conceptions of freedom differ chiefly in their emphasis. The former conception emphasizes the availability of real alternative choices and the latter the absence of impediments. Because, in the positive conception, one does not take the solitary individual as the starting-point, but rather looks at man in relation to his environment, here one is more interested in whether someone can really also use his 'opportunities'. As Norman and Taylor argued, one can only have the material and cultural conditions desirable for autonomy within and thanks to the community.

Because one generally regards the meeting of these conditions within the positive conception to a greater or lesser degree as a matter of course, or even a right, here one furthermore distinguishes a longer list with possible obstacles than within the negative conception. This was also stated by Crocker, though not in the context of these considerations. One therefore recognizes also what Feinberg calls 'negative, external impediments'. In practice, it would appear, this boils down to the fact that within the positive conception, unlike the negative, one recognizes that social structures maintained by others can also limit the autonomy of the individual. Goodin, among others, has made statements to this effect. In Norman's terminology, these structures are always the cause of the absence of particular 'positive conditions of freedom'.

We saw earlier that Berlin did actually recognize that the poverty or weakness of certain people can be explained with the help of social structures created or maintained by others. This statement must then be formulated within the framework of specific socio-political theory which he does not qualify in advance as unacceptable. It is therefore possible to regard poverty as a limitation of the *negative* freedom of the parties involved.[19] Berlin then also emphasizes that intervention in the market, social facilities and even socialism can be justified by appealing to negative freedom. John Gray considers precisely this aspect of Berlin's theory to be of vital importance. He writes: 'the important point about Berlin's account is that it allows that even "impersonal social forces" may be restrictive of (negative) freedom, always providing they are demonstrably avoidable and remediable' (Gray 1984: 341).

The problem with this position of Berlin's, however, is that it undermines the distinction he makes between freedom and its conditions: one cannot posit simultaneously that poverty is a constraint on someone's negative freedom and that freedom and material prosperity must be seen as separate from each other. This was amply demonstrated by MacPherson, as we saw earlier.

The most important reason for Berlin to make this distinction was his fear that people in their striving to meet the conditions for freedom would forget the freedom itself, that a dictatorship with a high level of prosperity would declare its citizens 'free'. The question is whether he is comparing the right matters here: a prosperous dictatorship must not be implicitly compared to a poor democracy, but to a poor dictatorship. The negative freedom which people enjoy in a prosperous totalitarian state is as big as that in a poor totalitarian state. However, it is smaller than in a poor or rich liberal democracy. Their positive freedom, on the other hand, is greater in a prosperous than in a poor dictatorship and greater in a prosperous than in a poor democracy. Whether someone's autonomy is greater in a prosperous dictatorship than in a poor democracy depends on how one weighs up the lack of negative freedom, and with it autonomy (negative freedom is, as appeared in Chapter 3, partially an element of positive freedom) under the relevant totalitarian regime against the autonomy which is greater due to the higher standard of living.

One could therefore make a distinction between freedom and its conditions only in the negative and not in the positive conception of freedom, were it not for the fact that no conditions are needed for negative freedom. Material prosperity increases the opportunity to give life direction autonomously, but has little to do with the degree to which one is left alone by the state and by others. It is not an obvious move therefore to base pleas for market intervention, social facilities or socialism on negative freedom. Equally, it can be concluded that within the positive conception, thanks to its social view of man and holistic view of society, there is more room for the perception that social structures too can limit individual freedom.

Properly regarded, the ideas of Norman illustrate the above. If 'privacy' forms a negative, and material facilities a positive condition for freedom, then the conclusion follows that material prosperity is separate from, is not a condition of, negative freedom. For MacPherson, too, negative freedom is a part or a condition of positive freedom. When he discusses how the size of someone's 'developmental liberty' or autonomy must be measured, he turns out to regard 'lack of protection against invasion by others' as one of the three factors to be discounted. Equally, MacPherson sees the absence of a lack of means of life and of access to the means of production as important components of someone's autonomy: in order to be able to use and develop his capacities, the material and non-material basic needs must be met and one must have tools and materials available to one.

In short, negative freedom simply means that one is in possession of a private space in which one can go one's own way undisturbed by others. While, for autonomy one needs the community, for negative freedom one needs nobody. Free in this sense, one is preferably on an uninhabited island. Negative freedom or 'privacy' is thus exactly what Norman considers so improbable – the possibility of being left alone by everyone or withdrawing at all times to a private space where one can deviate from the norm unpunished.

The desire to possess a private space, however, does not need to exclude the awareness that for the material and cultural conditions of autonomy one is mostly dependent on 'the others'. This is probably based on the insight that enculturation, and the activities which are also characteristic of autonomy, are, to an important extent, solitary efforts. Examples here are self-reflection, keeping in touch with one's identity and the creation of new possibilities. In addition, this desire is based on the knowledge that a contradiction can always arise between the individual and the society. MacPherson, Bergmann and Norman are wrong to pass so lightly over this.

Norman makes plausible that the positive conditions of freedom are the same as the conditions for equality and that socialists, in their pursuit of social equality, simultaneously agitate for individual freedom. In the course of his argument, however, he increasingly loses sight of the negative condition of 'privacy'. For example, he does not go into the question of how the positive freedom of the sheep is related to the negative freedom of the wolves. In addition, he fails to see adequately a conflict between 'privacy' and the positive freedom to influence political decision-making or, in MacPherson's terminology, between NL and PL3.

MacPherson appeared originally to have no difficulty in recognizing that the question of who or what rules over me can and must be distinguished from the question of to what degree the relevant government intervenes in my private space. However, when he later converts NL into 'counter-extractive liberty' this important component of freedom – NL as a defensive wall against the state and society – disappears utterly.

Right to the conditions of freedom?

The question arises of whether people can also lay claim to *rights*, to the material and non-material conditions needed for self-determination and self-realization. We have already seen earlier that within the positive conception of freedom a longer list with possible constraints is generally identified because here there is more of a tendency to regard the presence of certain conditions of freedom as a right or natural.[20] The theories of MacPherson, Lukes, Taylor and Norman did indeed turn out to have this characteristic. The justification which Taylor gives for his stance that individuals should be helped by others in acquiring autonomy, here resembles closely that of MacPherson and Lukes. Unlike what he would have us believe, this does not conflict with that of Norman.

Taylor claims that individuals are granted rights because they possess a number of capacities which we consider fundamental for human life and which therefore have for us a special moral status. Taylor does not see why these rights should be exclusively of a negative nature and therefore concern merely the principle of non-intervention. Usually, people can only really use and develop their qualities with the help of others. If our respect is thus really earnest, we also have a moral duty to give this help to people and therefore give people rights of positive freedom. It is, in short, inconsistent and lacking in credibility (this was also Norman's critique of John Stuart Mill and Nozick), on the one hand, to ascribe rights to people on the basis of a number of qualities worthy of respect and, on the other hand, to be indifferent as to whether they can also really develop these qualities.

Lukes' argument is closely related to this. In his view, too, each individual has the right to our respect on the basis of a number of unique essential capacities which all people share. For Lukes, these qualities are the capacity for self-determination and self-development. A lack of respect is expressed not only through unjust intervention in someone's personal life, but also through a denial of his potential for autonomy and self-realization.

Norman's justification of equality and with it, indirectly, of freedom, does not conflict with that of MacPherson, Taylor and Lukes. This is despite his rejection of (formal) arguments based on references to the notion of universality and to unique, human capacities (Norman 1987: 60–1). He labels the idea of an inviolable natural right as a contradiction, because rights first acquire meaning when they are guaranteed in one way or another by a convention or institution. A right is, for him, nothing more than an empirical generalization of what people generally consider important in life. The epistemological status of negative and positive rights of freedom is, as far as this is concerned, identical and there is therefore no reason to ascribe to people merely the former rights.

The point now is that Norman, by placing freedom and equality in a concrete social context, and by appealing to those experiences and feelings which make those values meaningful for us, ultimately offers no other justification or basis for these values, and the rights based on them, than Taylor,[21] MacPherson and Lukes. Respect for the individual and for his qualities, to which the last two authors appeal, is equally an empirical, socially determined and bounded fact. That applies also to the normative charge of our use of language, to which MacPherson refers to justify his principles: a language can be interpreted as the reflection of the 'experiences and feelings' which make certain values meaningful within a language community. Berlin, too, as we have seen, uses this fact. At most, the difference is that Norman gives the impression of having smaller communities in mind. He therefore expects perhaps more variety in moral intuitions and, as a consequence, in allotted rights and duties.

In this context, Alan Carling makes the predictable criticism of Norman that by basing his justification of values on existing sentiments in a concrete limited community, he makes solidarity difficult with 'unknowns' outside the relevant cooperation (the Third World, for example) (Carling 1988: 91–2). The existing lack of solidarity between the rich and poor communities, however, could be seen as a proof of Norman's stance, that rights first get practical meaning within an actual context of society. As long as the feeling of being a member of a 'world community' is only experienced by few, the idea of 'human rights' for the inhabitants of the Third World will remain rather meaningless. In practice, they will benefit more, Norman would reply, in the development of a global feeling of community here, than in once again proclaiming a formal 'declaration of the rights of man'. It can be argued against this that the practical significance of rights is not fully dependent on an actual guarantee. Their value can lie in the fact that they function as a rudder for our daily efforts and as a criterion for measuring existing societies. Finally, one can only speak of a violation of human rights in the Third World if one has first awarded rights to the people involved.

Whatever the case may be, an important perception is that none of the authors dealt with appeals to the rationalistic principles which Berlin so opposes, for his justification of positive rights of freedom.

The inevitability of notions of common sense

For these writers, 'rationality' turns out to have no other meaning than the one Berlin ascribes to it: rationality means that one can explain and defend in a rational manner one's choices by referring to one's own values or goals. He assumes that these are shared to a high degree, and thus considered plausible, by the people with whom one shares a society, civilization or even species. Of course, writes Berlin:

> some values are higher than others, so that a 'lower' value will be set aside in favour of a 'higher' one; and in some cases of serious conflict 'trade-offs' or compromises can constitute rational solutions. But this does not

entail the belief that there can be no rational choice of ends save within a
single scheme of life valid for all men.

(Berlin 1983: 391; cf. Chapter 2)

Although some explicitly reject cultural relativism (Taylor 1982, 1992: 67ff.;
Lukes 1982), none of the discussed advocates of the positive conception of
freedom defend such a universal 'single scheme of life'. They all, more or
less, define values in a social or cultural context.

This brings us to the last subject of this balance sheet: the indispens-
ability of notions of 'common sense' or rationality for answering the question of when someone can be characterized as 'free' or 'autonomous'. We
saw in the second chapter that Berlin is extremely afraid of a linkage
between freedom and rationality, certainly where the latter concept boils
down to value cognitivism and monism. The reasons for this were evident:
references to notions of rationality have always made it possible for those in
power to negate or suppress the often deeply-felt and genuine desires and
goals of their subjects, which happen to be displeasing to them, under the
cloak of freedom, education and emancipation. An important value of negative freedom is this, that one can do what one wants or not, unimpeded and
unpunished by the authorities and 'the others' who together determine what
can be said to be 'rational'. John Stuart Mill in particular emphasized this
value. Within one's own private space one must have the possibility of deciding oneself what is rational and irrational. This is better for the individual
concerned and presumably better, in the long term, for the community.
Social progress and dynamics are promoted by this.

However, the problem is that in his definition of freedom, Berlin cannot
do without a notion of rationality either, a notion as this is defined within a
particular cultural community. For example, we saw that he refused to
regard as 'free' a slave who adjusts his wishes and goals to his situation, or
someone who frees himself from earthly, relatively easily-frustratable desires
and withdraws imperturbably into an inner world he considers superior.
Bergmann and Cooper, on the other hand, argued in favour of the latter and
associated what Berlin called 'ostrich' politics with wisdom, or, one could
say, with 'eastern rationality'. In his critique of contented slaves, stoics and
Buddhists, Berlin appealed therefore to that which we, in the Western world,
would generally regard as normal or rational to pursue in life. As has been
said earlier, we expect a slave with any intelligence to try and free himself of
his chains, and we find Buddhists generally to be somewhat odd.

We see a similar appeal again when Berlin deals with what the size of
someone's negative freedom depends on. In his already mentioned footnote,
where, as it shall have become clear by now, he gives not a definition of negative, but of positive freedom,[22] he defines not only the available number of
behavioural alternatives as determining variables, but also: 'what value not
merely the agent, but the general sentiment of the society in which he lives
puts on the various possibilities' (Berlin 1958: 130; see p. 27). Just like

Norman therefore he sees individual freedom rising with the number of 'meaningful' possibilities of choice and what must be understood by this is partly determined by 'the general sentiment' in the society where he lives. One needs a criterion, says Taylor (see Chapter 3), in order to be able to determine whether the absence of freedom of religion in Albania was a greater or lesser assault on individual freedom than the duty current in England to drive on the left-hand side of the road. This criterion is provided by 'common sense' notions.

Finally, we find a reference to that which one generally regards as 'normal' or 'rational' within a particular society as a plausible definition and explanation of the reality experienced, in Berlin's treatment of 'coercion'. In Chapter 2, we have seen that originally Berlin took the position that this only occurs in the case of a deliberate, direct limitation of someone's freedom by other people. However, he later adds to this that ultimately the socio-economic theory adhered to determines when one declares this to be the case. It is possible to render plausible that certain social structures which are created or maintained by others are the cause of my poverty or weakness, and that others therefore in this case are coercing me in an anonymous fashion. What one sees as coercion therefore depends on what one regards as plausible within a certain community, and this can change in time. An example of this is how people have regarded unemployment over the years: if one considered the economic situation to be the result of human choices then the unemployed was the victim who had the right to support; if one regarded the market as being balanced in principle by an 'invisible hand', then he was an idler.

In short, it constantly seems that notions of 'rationality' are indispensable in order to contain the range of the various definitions of freedom. If this does not happen, then these lose all plausibility in their one-sidedness. Earlier, in Chapter 3, we have seen this already with regard to the virtues which are generally expected of an autonomous personality: these must be weighed up against each other and against other values. An unlimited increase in a particular virtue leads to a situation where it eventually gets in its own way after a certain level. This must also be the criticism of all those authors who thought they could contain the essence of freedom in a single attractive slogan. The feverish search for a single correct meaning of 'freedom' which characterizes some, seems to be an expression of the implicit ontological principle that there is a knowable, logical order in the cosmos in which all concepts have a precisely defined place (cf. Chapter 1).

Therefore, in spite of Bergmann, 'identification' is not an adequate condition for freedom, as this criterion implies that the slave who decks his chains in flowers does not need to be freed. Equally, Norman, Lukes, Berlin and Lindley do correctly state that having more alternative choices enlarges individual autonomy, but this only applies up to a certain point. One should not exaggerate, as argued earlier. 'Freedom', writes Bergmann correctly, 'is not absolute independence, it is not the having of a choice, and it is not the absence of constraints' (1977: 78). The last nuance is valuable in so far as it contains a critique of atomism. Individual autonomy does not increase proportionately to the removal of external obstacles. At a given moment, there remains only a social vacuum where no single being can be happy: Kaspar Hauser is not an ideal image for human development. It may well be that freedom, as Barber imagines it, is always accompanied by the overcoming of inner constraints, that our experience of freedom is greater the higher the impediments, but it cannot, and should not, be deduced from all this that if we want to promote the autonomy of the individual, we should raise the number of obstacles without limit. Freedom is more than the absence of constraints or the presence of alternative choices, but that does not make these unimportant.

Finally, freedom does not consist merely of *choosing* between options, but also of *creating* them. However, the latter should not be understood too literally. Bergmann and, to a lesser degree, Barber thus exaggerate somewhat with their postulation that we are incessantly creating for ourselves the possible choices and can decide any moment to be someone else. This could become a rather tiring business and conflicts in actuality with all we have learned from sociology and social psychology. In practice, the human personality turns out to be fairly stable during its life. This picture of the matter is also inconsistent with Bergmann's (and also Barber's) own thesis that the 'self' is, to a high degree, determined socially and that only the identity-less resistance fighter pursues full authenticity and this total independence. However, it is a good point on a more subtle level: our experience of freedom is greatest when the trails we follow have not yet been blazed by others. Furthermore, we regard someone whose behaviour is completely predictable not as a model of human freedom, but rather as a prisoner of his own personality.

Also important is that this idea, normatively seen, places the responsibility for our actions where it belongs – with the individual. By rejecting every form of determinism and emphasizing that ultimately it is the person himself who chooses his values, apologies such as *Befehl ist Befehl*, and *Doch die Verhältnisse, sie sind nicht so*! (Bertolt Brecht in *Die Driegroschenoper*) will be radically destroyed. Ethically speaking it is not unreasonable to proceed in principle from Sartre's thesis 'that man is condemned to be free. Condemned because he did not create himself, yet, in other respects free; because, once thrown into the world, he is responsible for everything he does' (Sartre 1946: 23). A coward is thus 'responsible for his cowardice. He's not like that because he has a cowardly heart or lung or brain; he's not like that on account of his psychological make-up; but he's like that because he has made himself a coward by his acts' (ibid.: 34). In brief, if the situation of man is 'defined as a free choice, with no excuses and no recourse, every man who takes refuge behind the excuse of his passions, every man who sets up a determinism, is a dishonest man'. And in this vale of tears 'honesty' is the only 'strictly coherent attitude' (ibid.: 44–5). Thus, coercion – a threat – does not make someone unfree either: it 'merely' means that the costs of particular alternatives are raised. To what extent this existentialist principle must be implemented in practice, is again a question of weighing up the pros and cons, or rationality. There are always 'mitigating circumstances' to be found. However, it can do no harm as a principle, it prevents some opportunism and hypocrisy – and perhaps even a few concentration camps.

5 Emancipation and paternalism

INTRODUCTION

In the foregoing it was suggested that man can only develop his own individuality if he first incorporates the culture around him. This acculturization takes place both intentionally and unintentionally, both specifically and randomly, both from his own free will and more or less under coercion. Certainly, in the first years of life it is a passive, unconscious and also often compulsory *learning* process, rather than an intentional, deliberate *self*-realization. This is not directly regrettable or objectionable: without education and socialization, after all, there is no culture, and without culture, no autonomy.

The socialization which is necessary to become free in the positive sense, however, raises a problem, which can be identified as *the first dimension of the dilemma of emancipation*: to what extent can this be continued without the negative freedom of the individual being unacceptably impaired? It can be said, it is true, that to a high degree one only develops thanks to the education or the stimuli which one receives from one's environment, but this development first becomes valuable when one is then allowed the freedom to also do something with it. This is a problem (particularly with regard to the immature) for which every serious socio-political theory must find a practical solution.

Theoreticians who want to introduce change into the coexisting culture or preferential structure, characterized as objectionable or not optimal, then run up against an additional question, which can be identified as the *second dimension of the dilemma of emancipation*. The relevant social critics, who in the Anglo-American literature are often branded as 'radicals', believe that the values, goals, desires and preferences of the individual are, to a high degree, the product of the social interactions with his environment. The authenticity, and with it the political status, of the individual preferences can therefore be qualified to some extent. The radicals can claim that the individual has developed preferences which, while he himself experiences them as valuable and original, are in fact a random product, whether objectionable or not, of the existing social structures, and which are not optimal:

there are wishes and accompanying gratifications which the individual would prefer above his present preferences, if he were familiar with these alternatives. As these authors generally have democratic and egalitarian inspiration with regard to the regretted preferences, however, they are wrestling with a dilemma. This consists of the following: on the one hand (because of their professed democratic principles), they must respect the existing preferences of the individual, but, on the other hand (if they want to do justice to the developmental ideal they cherish), they must break up the existing structure of references and socialization. The question is once again to what extent the latter can happen without restricting – unacceptably – the negative freedom of the individual. This question will be central to this chapter.

Taylor and Barber, as we saw in the third chapter, claim that the individual is not always necessarily the best judge of his own interests. In the following, we shall see this translated by Steven Lukes and William Connolly among others, into a 'radical' conception of power and interests. Both of them claim that the preferences of the individual do not always run parallel to his 'real' interests, but can only be the 'undesirable' product of social structures and processes which he cannot grasp. There is therefore also a relationship between the radical conception and the Marxist idea of alienation. As was demonstrated at great length by Berlin, this idea is open to heavy criticism. In the first part of this chapter, the relevant debate will be further explored. This will be done once again on the basis of a number of representative standpoints which together give a picture of the various questions and answers which form the core of the discourse.

In the second part, we will investigate the problem of paternalism, on the basis of the ideas of John Stuart Mill. Within Anglo-American philosophy there has been an extensive debate on this over recent decades. However, just as we will find with regard to the discussions on the concepts of 'power' and 'freedom', this debate is hardly, if at all, linked to that on freedom. All the more reason to look at this somewhat more extensively. A finding important for our aim will be that here, too, 'rationality' (that is, that which ordinary people of sound judgement will generally consider worth emulating or reasonable) ultimately forms the criterion against which the plausibility of the various conceptions of paternalism are measured.

ON POWER AND 'REAL INTERESTS'

'Power' is one of the central concepts of contemporary Anglo-American political science. Where power is exercised, someone's freedom is limited, and the two concepts are thus closely related. It is striking therefore that in Anglo-American political science they are generally studied independently of each other. People are either concerned with power (the behaviouristic-oriented political scientist) or with freedom (the social or political philosopher) and seldom with both at the same time. This is probably explained by a misunderstanding prevalent among both behaviourists and a number of political philosophers, that the question of when one can speak of 'freedom' is of a normative, prescriptive and thus non-scientific nature, and the question of when there is 'power' is of an empirical, descriptive and thus non-philosophical nature.

Whatever the case may be, it is meaningful for two reasons here to go briefly into the discussion carried on within political science on the concept of power. In the first place, because it gives a deepening of the question postulated earlier in Chapter 4 of which way individual freedom can be restricted. In the second place, because it forms a suitable introduction to a number of increasingly urgent questions on the emancipation dilemma, that is, on the status of the individual's preferences, on 'real interests' and on paternalism.

Dahl, Lukes, and Bachrach and Baratz on conceptions of power

A good starting-point is a discussion on power and restrictions of freedom in which Lukes participated with his *Power, a Radical View*. In this Lukes distinguishes three different conceptions of power which, according to him, are based on a single concept. (Here, Lukes takes up the distinction made by Rawls between a concept and a conception: see Chapter 4.) According to him this concept can be formulated as: 'A exercises power over B when A affects B in a manner contrary to B's interests' (Lukes 1974b: 27).[1] Because people always influence each other, however, a criterion is needed to determine when this is significant enough to be called 'power'. It must therefore be determined what someone's interest is and when this is infringed. Lukes states that three divergent answers can be given to this question, answers which each form an 'essentially contested' conception of power and interests.

Within the first *one-dimensional conception*, the interests of the individual are equated with the preferences indicated by him during a political decision-making process. One exercises power when one can push through one's preferences against the wishes of others. In the research (on a behaviouristic basis) into division of power in a particular society one concentrates therefore on the *behaviour* of individuals or groups during the decision-making with regard to issues over which a *perceptible* conflict has arisen, a conflict that is presumed to expose the different policy preferences. Typical representatives of this approach are the American political scientist Robert Dahl and his students Nelson Polsby and Raymond Wolfinger. The three of them attempt to justify Dahl's polyarchy conception of the Western political system by carrying out empirical research into political decision-making in the town of New Haven, Connecticut.[2]

The research by Dahl and his associates forms a contribution to a debate on the division of power in American society, which has been going on within sociology and political science since the end of the 1940s. This debate between *elitists* and *pluralists* has even, to an important extent, defined for decades the image of the practice of political science. It was in the 1980s that interest in this subject faded into the background, without incidentally, any shared standpoint being reached. The elitists, who were mainly to be found among the sociologists, were of the opinion that a single socio-economic elite controlled society on all important levels. The pluralists, on the other hand, claimed that there are a number of elites opposing and competing with each other. Both camps collected, on an extensive scale, empirical research material to support their own standpoints and to undermine that of their opponents. This took place mainly in local communities. The contradictory research results made the discussion increasingly methodological in character.

A weakness of many of the first researches was, among other things, that these were based only on the so-called 'reputation method'. In this, various people were asked who they regarded as influential in certain fields within the community. The more someone is mentioned, the more powerful he is presumed to be. The sociologist Floyd Hunter, among others, who carried out one of the first studies into the power structure in a local municipality, reached an elitistic conclusion with the help of this method (Hunter 1953). Dahl rejects this methodology and therefore the conclusion too (or, to put it perhaps more realistically: he rejects the conclusions and therefore also the methodology). In an article from 1958 he says that too many people want to believe too much that 'they run things' (Dahl 1958: 463). According to him, frustrated idealism often finds an easy outlet in a cynicism suggesting worldly wisdom, in which the insight is central that a shadowy group is pulling the strings and obstructing the good intentions of the parties involved.

Dahl's most important objection to the elite theory is that this can always be formulated (and reformulated) in such a way that it is impossible to refute it: behind every group which, thanks to further research, turns out not to be the elite, a new 'real' ruling class can be assumed. It must be possible, however, to translate a scientific elite theory into unambiguous concepts and testable hypotheses. In order to show what such a theory should look like, Dahl himself formulates what is, according to him, a usable definition of a ruling elite and some hypotheses with which the existence of such a group could be made plausible.

A ruling elite is, according to him, 'a minority of individuals whose preferences regularly prevail in cases of differences in preferences on key political issues' (Dahl 1958: 464). It must be possible to specify to a greater extent the composition of this group, in order to avoid an endless regression of explanations. An unusable test confuses a ruling elite with a group which possesses a high *potential* power. After all, the political effectiveness of a group is crucial and this is not determined only by its potential power, but also by its unity. Also unusable are the tests where the influence on a particular field is generalized: 'Any investigation that does not take into account the possibility that different elite groups have different scopes is suspect' (ibid.: 465). A group with much influence in one field is often hardly, if at all, active in other fields, or is too divided internally to be politically effective. Furthermore, a scientific insight into the real power position of a group can first be obtained through a 'careful examination of a series of concrete decisions' (ibid.: 466). Hunter, and also C. Wright Mills in his *The Power Elite* (1956), have neglected this. For Dahl, it is a matter of course that in these decisions on 'key political issues' there must be a difference of opinion or conflict between a minority getting what it wants and a majority. If there is no conflict, but great consensus, then no fundamental political subjects, and also no elites, can be identified.

It is naturally possible, recognizes Dahl, that the ruling elite exercises so much influence on the ideas, attitudes and opinions in a society that there is a sort of false consciousness among the citizens, a 'manipulated and superficially self-imposed adherence to the norms and goals of the elite by broad sections of a community' (Dahl 1958: 468). He suspects that C. Wright Mills postulates something similar. But this hypothesis too can only, according to Dahl, be really tested in the way he proposes:

> For once again either the consensus is perpetual and unbreakable, in which case there is no conceivable way of determining who is ruler and who is ruled. Or it is not. But if it is not, then there is some point in the process of forming opinions at which the one group will be seen to initiate and veto, while the rest merely respond. And we can only discover these points *by an examination of a series of concrete cases where key decisions are made.*
>
> (Dahl 1958: 169)

The research by Dahl and his associates has been sharply criticized by, among others, Peter Bachrach and Morton Baratz (1962, 1963; see also Crenson 1971). They do subscribe to a large extent to the critique of the elitists by the pluralists, but at the same time state that the pluralists also use principles and research methods which lead naturally to the conclusions which they wanted. In particular, they point out that power is not just exercised directly and openly in the case of a concrete conflict, but also when an individual or group succeeds in keeping a particular subject, threatening to him or her, from the political agenda: 'power is also exercised when A devotes his energies to creating or reinforcing social and political values and institutional practices that limit the scope of the political process to public consideration of only those issues which are comparatively innocuous to A' (Bachrach and Baratz 1962: 948). Thanks to this 'non-decision-making' – it is decided by the rulers that no decision-making will take place about a particular problem – there is no perceptible confrontation. Researchers working in a one-dimensional tradition would conclude, incorrectly, on the basis of this that there are no differences of opinion on the relevant subject. Within what Lukes calls the two-dimensional approach, on the other hand, one does bear in mind potential conflicts, questions which are consciously kept outside the political system.'

A second critique of Bachrach and Baratz, related to this, is that Dahl and other pluralists do not indicate what must be understood by 'key decisions'. Dahl studies *existing* conflicts but has absolutely no assurance that these are about real matters. In order to obtain this certainty, he will first have to make an analysis of the 'mobilization of bias in the community; of the dominant values and the political myths, rituals, and institutions which tend to favour the vested interests of one or more groups, relative to others' (Bachrach and Baratz 1962: 950). Only then can he judge whether a particular issue is merely a routine matter within the existing order or raises this order for discussion. The critics recognize that normative principles play a role in such a judgement. However, this can only be avoided by unjustifiably ignoring important sociological and politicological insights on power.

Although Lukes considers the approach of Bachrach and Baratz a progression with regard to that of Dahl, nevertheless, he has a number of closely related objections (cf. Connolly 1972 and Benton 1982). With this critique is defined the *three-dimensional conception* of power which he advocates.

In the first place, he considers the two-dimensional conception to be still too behaviourist. According to him, there is a one-sided focus on existing behaviour, on concrete decisions and perceptible conflicts. Decisions, says Lukes, are not always taken by individuals who consciously make a choice from various alternatives. They can also be the products (unwanted or unexpected) of anonymous social structures and processes (Lukes 1974b: 22).[3]

In the second place, power is expressed not only during a concrete, perceptible conflict. It can also be exercised without any confrontation, when A can influence, form or determine what B wants. Lukes wonders whether controlling the thought and desires of others is not actually the most important form of power. Power, as Aldous Huxley's *Brave New World* tells us, is always at its most effective when one is able to avoid conflicts:

> is it not the supreme and most insidious exercise of power to prevent people, to whatever degree, from having grievances by shaping their perceptions, cognitions and preferences in such a way that they accept their role in the existing order of things, either because they can see or imagine no alternative to it, or because they see it as natural and unchangeable, or because they value it as divinely ordained and beneficial?[4]
>
> (Lukes 1974b: 24)

The power of 'non-decision-making' therefore includes not only being able to bring about that some existing desires or grievances are kept outside the formal political system. In Lukes' view, Bachrach and Baratz assume too much that dissatisfaction or disgruntlement must be *articulated*. If this has not happened, they must then also conclude, that there are no grievances and, as a consequence, no conflicts or exercise of power. Lukes regards this as highly unsatisfactory: 'What one may have here is a *latent conflict*, which consists in a contradiction between the interests of those exercising power and the *real interests* of those they exclude. These latter may not express or even be conscious of their interests' (Lukes 1974b: 22). As soon as those over whom power is exercised become aware of their real interests, the latent conflict become a reality.

Lukes and Connolly on 'real' interests

The question now arises of what someone's 'real' interests are. The definition of interests also takes place within the context of a particular normative political theory. According to Lukes, one can roughly say that the *liberal*, on the basis of the one-dimensional conception of power, equates the individual interests with what people actually want, which boils down to what they indicate as their policy preferences through political participation. In political terms, this is considered most reasonable as it offers the least room for rationalizations in which people, under the pretext of 'false consciousness', have all kinds of desires ascribed to them which in fact they do not hold at all. With this standpoint, we recognize the vision of Isaiah Berlin. The *reformist*, who can be placed in the two-dimensional conception, demands attention for the fact that wishes or interests can reveal themselves in a more indirect, concealed, 'sub-political' manner too. The *radical*, finally, who bases himself on the three-dimensional concept, links the interest of the individual to that which *he would want* if he found himself in the situation where he could make a *real* choice: 'The radical maintains that men's wants may themselves be a product of a system which works against their interests, and, in such cases, relates the latter to what they would want and prefer, were they able to make the choice' (Lukes 1974: 34). This choice must then be made 'under conditions of relative autonomy', a state in which the individual involved is free from the power of others.[5]

William Connolly's approach to the concept of 'interest' shows strong similarities to those of Lukes, who also refers approvingly to Connolly. He, too, considers it unsatisfactory to base oneself merely on actually articulated preferences or needs, whether experienced or not. The last angle of approach, which is not discussed by Lukes, is represented by, among others, Amitai Etzioni, Christian Bay and James Davies. The principle here is that people possess a number of universal needs which must be satisfied, because otherwise their functioning and development is inhibited. Bay (1958), for example, says that neuroses, psychoses, addiction to drugs and alcohol, criminality, suicide, etc., can be symptoms of a long-term frustration of higher order needs such as self-development, love and self-determination. In this context, Wright Mills (1959: 11) speaks of 'troubles' which are not (yet) translated into concrete wishes, never mind into political demands: 'Instead of troubles defined in terms of values and threats – there is often the misery of vague uneasiness, instead of explicit issues there is often merely the beat feeling that all is somehow not right.' Even when people do not recognize certain needs themselves, it can be in their interests for these to be satisfied anyway. An unwanted policy is therefore in their interests when it enlarges the chance of this.

As stated, Connolly regards this approach also as too limited. He points to the possibility that people can have all their needs satisfied, not be troubled by neuroses, psychoses or floating feelings of dissatisfaction, but, at the same time, lack every capacity for critical thought, self-determination, love and empathy. Although these people can experience absolutely no drive to develop this capacity, nevertheless, it is possible that they would prefer the state in which they would have done so. Connolly writes:

> human beings might, in some settings, lack inclinations or urgings of any sort to achieve states they would prize for themselves once attained; they might possess strong dispositions to resist the attainment of those very modes of life; they would find them most gratifying once having experienced them; and they might even find that certain arrangements prized for themselves necessarily include tensions and anxieties as part of the prized condition.
>
> (Connolly 1972: 470)

When the effort is aimed at the discovery/rediscovery of more gratifying lifestyles, a conception of interests, which is based exclusively on existing wishes and (conscious or not) needs, is in Connolly's view insufficient:

> Any view which anchors interests exclusively in felt behavioural tendencies runs the risk of celebrating uncritically those inclinations cultivated by dominant socialization processes while deflecting conceptual attention from possible gratifying modes of existence bypassed by those same processes. If the intellectual enterprise aims to recover worthy aspirations that have been lost, to render intelligible modes of life that are now only dimly glimpsed, then a definition of interest *restricted* to felt behavioral tendencies can hardly suffice.
>
> (Connolly 1972: 471)

He proposes therefore a definition (often quoted in the literature), which in his view comes closer to meeting these requirements: 'Policy X is more in A's interest than policy Y if A, were he to experience the *results* of both X and Y, would *choose* X as the result he would rather have for himself' (Connolly 1972: 472).[6] An important feature of this definition is, in short, that it is a question of appreciation *in retrospect* and not *in advance* of a particular policy. It therefore allows the postulation that a policy is in someone's interest, even if the party involved does not desire it at that moment or is even strongly opposed to it.

Problems of the radical conception

The adherent to the radical conception of power and interests finds himself faced with a number of problems. First, his expectation that people would want something else if they had the choice must be justified. Second, it must be made comprehensible how they are kept from this choice by others. Third, if criticism of this exercise of power wants to be politically relevant, it must be indicated why the alternative wishes and desires are to be preferred above the existing ones (Lukes 1974b: 42; Benton 1982: 11).

To begin with, how can one justify the position that in reality people want something else than what they say? If people do not rise up in a political system which from the outside one regards as unjust, can this not be an expression of a consensus on deviating values? In speaking about 'real interests' is there not a threat that one becomes guilty of ethnocentrism or value cognitivism?

Lukes thinks that this does not have to be the case. There is sometimes empirical support for the view that the contentment and consensus displayed is not authentic, but imposed. For example, in what Antonio Gramsci called 'abnormal times' (periods in which the old system of power is dysfunctioning briefly and the social and political control is somewhat lightened) people sometimes 'suddenly' turn out to hold values and objectives which are completely different to what their former passivity led one to believe. Here (in 1974b), Lukes was thinking of, among other things, the 'Prague Spring' of 1968. Another indication of dissatisfaction is, according to Lukes, people's attempts to work themselves up within an existing, rigid and apparently generally accepted, social hierarchy such as the caste system in India. People who really subscribe to an order will never try to improve their position. The degree to which social mobility is aspired to can therefore give an impression of the real wishes and interests of those at the bottom of the ladder (Lukes 1974b: 46–50).

A second problem which has to be solved within the radical conception was that one had to make plausible that the behaviour or thinking of B was the result of A exercising power. Lukes mentions three characteristics of the three-dimensional model, which make the empirical perception of the latter difficult.

First, to exercise power it is not always necessary for one to *actively* involve oneself with something. Research by Crenson (1971) provides an illustration of this: the failure of the question of air pollution to reach the agenda was often not the *consequence* of the (perceptible) action of a company, but simply of its presence, its reputation of power.

Second, the exercise of power does not need to be conscious or intentional. The real, deeper motive for his actions can after all also remain unconscious for the actor involved (in the Freudian sense). In addition, one cannot be aware how others interpret one's behaviour, nor can one be aware of the consequences of one's action. Only, however, where this ignorance is the result of a 'remediable failure to find out' (Lukes 1974b: 51) can one reasonably say that power is being exercised. There is therefore no question of this if knowledge of the consequences is just not available.

Finally, there is the problem of the radical conception offering space to the insight that social structures and processes too – that is, collectivities (groups, classes, institutes) – can exercise power. A question here is naturally how the line must be drawn between, on the one hand, the structural determination always present and, on the other, exercise of power. Simply because people are social beings, they are always influenced by others. One therefore makes the term 'power' completely meaningless if it could accommodate all forms of influence, socialization and education.

Structural determination or exercise of power

Lukes deals with this last problem by going extensively into the debate, famous in the Marxist literature, between the determinist Nicos Poulantzas and the more voluntaristically inclined Ralph Miliband. Lukes' standpoint is that the freedom of action of individuals within a collectivity is indeed structurally tied to limits, but that a certain autonomy always remains to act differently. The future is not completely open, nor is it completely fixed. If the latter were the case then there could never be any question of 'power': exercising influence on events which are completely determined, is a contradiction. Lukes therefore states: 'that to identify a given process as an 'exercise of power', rather than as a case of structural determination, is to assume that it is *in the exerciser's or exercisers' power* to act differently. In the case of a collective exercise of power, on the part of a group, or institution, etc., this is to imply that the members of the group or institution could have combined or organized to act differently' (Lukes 1974b: 55).

Responsibility, power and, to supplement Lukes, freedom, therefore go hand in hand. The purpose of localizing power then is that one also fixes responsibilities. In a later work, Lukes quotes approvingly C. Wright Mills in this context, who was of the opinion that power too had to be ascribed to people in strategic positions, who are capable of initiating changes which are in the interests of large groups in society, but who nevertheless fail to do so. Mills (1959: 100) postulated that 'it is now sociologically realistic, morally fair and politically imperative to make demands upon men of power and to hold them responsible for specific courses of events'.

In a reaction to this standpoint of Lukes, Bradshaw states that there is a contradiction between, on the one hand, Lukes' methodological critique of Dahl (by merely looking at the behaviour of individuals he overlooks power exercised by structures) and, on the other hand, his refutal of the structuralism of Poulantzas because, in his opinion, there is only an exercise of power when the relevant person could have acted differently. Thus, writes Bradshaw, 'in the last resort, it seems that all observations must be observations on individuals, not groups' (1976: 126). In his reply, Lukes repeats that statements on power do not necessarily have to be traceable back to the behaviour of individuals and that groups therefore can also exercise power. However, the point is that the members of the group, in that case, could have decided *together* as a *group* to act differently. Social structures therefore only exercise power if people could have decided individually or collectively to change these structures. (The readiness of the individual to change collective behaviour together with others, is therefore properly regarded determining the degree to which it bears responsibility for the power of the group.) Lukes admits that the circumstances under which this possibility exists are subject to discussion. However, he rejects Poulantzas's structuralism because of Poulantzas's inability to make a connection between individual actions and social processes and, in doing so, to give meaning to individual responsibility on the collective level.[7]

SMITH: THE INCONTESTABILITY OF 'REAL' INTERESTS

Lukes and Connolly emphasize again and again that each of the three conceptions of power, and the related conceptions of interests which have been distinguished, is equally 'ineradicably valuative' and 'essentially contested' in character: from the entire spectrum of existing and potential wishes or desires a certain selection is made within each conception, to which a special moral status is given and this choice is always contestable (Lukes 1967: 146–8; 1974b: 23, 26, 34; 1986: 4–5; Connolly 1972: 459–60). The British political scientist G. W. Smith (1981: 406) disputes this: in principle 'an empirical decision procedure on the basis of which the radical conception is superior to its rivals' exists. In his opinion, the disputable character of the three conceptions of power is not caused by the random ascription of interests, which are completely separate from the actual wants cherished by people. After all 'in each of the three conceptions of power, interests are defined in terms of the agent's expressed or expressible wants – in the case of the liberal, actual manifest wants; in the case of the reformist, actual manifest and hidden wants; and in the case of the radical, hypothetical but in principle realizable wants, that is, wants he would elect for if he were given the chance' (Smith 1981: 407).

In order to determine the plausibility of the various concepts, Smith confronts these with the case of the happy or contented slave, a touchstone much used for conceptions of autonomy and paternalism (see, among others, Bergmann 1977: 7–10; Berlin 1958: 139–41; Connolly 1972; Dworkin 1971, 1983; Feinberg 1971: 121–8; Kleinig 1983: 157–65; Mill 1859: 236–7; Young 1986: 72–4; and, in a more general sense, Elster 1982). Only a conception within which a contented slave remains a slave, is plausible in his view. The liberal and reformist conception does not stand up to this test. As their advocates assume existing (hidden, if necessary) wants, they are forced to qualify a slave, who always sees his desires met because he never desires anything which is beyond his possibilities, as a free man over whom no power is exercised. The supporters of the radical conception, on the other hand, who also define the interests of a slave in terms of his hypothetical desires, cannot go along with this. A slave is in the power of his master, no matter how contented he is, because 'he is prevented from doing or being many things he would want to do or be if he were made aware of what he is missing' (Smith 1981: 408).

After all, says Smith, it is completely legitimate, and also precisely the reason behind the three-dimensional conception of power, to look at the *conditions* under which someone's desires are developed or not (Smith 1981: 411). The absent desires of a contented slave cannot serve as guidelines as these have not come into being free of unacceptable psychic and social influences, influences which impede a correct understanding of the real possibilities.

Properly regarded, within the radical conception there is an expectation of the desires and wishes which a slave would have if he were freed. This prediction, which is based on the behaviour generally shown by liberated slaves, can be refuted: a freed slave can choose to become a slave again. Is he then no longer a slave? And if people say that this choice was not made 'freely', is one then not basing oneself (implicitly), as Lukes also predicted, on a contestable ideal of autonomy?[8]

This would certainly happen, says Smith, with 'strong radicalism': on the basis of a particular ideal of human development, the relevant choice is rejected as being *by definition* irrational and heteronomous. However, Smith chooses 'weak radicalism': it is stated that a real choice must be made free of influence, and one expects that no one would choose under these circumstances an existence as a slave. If this happens all the same, then the circumstances will be studied: was there indoctrination, brainwashing, manipulation, etc.? In contrast to its strong counterpart 'weak radicalism' is therefore no definition, but a *theory*[9] – a theory which can be refuted. If it turns out that there was no unacceptable influence, it must be concluded that the choice has been made in freedom. Smith writes:

> we might have views about what men capable of autonomous choice should choose . . . and we might properly initiate investigations into their backgrounds when they act contrary to our convictions, but what we must not do is to go on to insist (in the absence of independent evidence of indoctrination or brainwashing) that they cannot be choosing rationally because they are not choosing as we think a rational person should.
>
> (Smith 1981: 413)

In Smith's view, the case of the slave therefore provides at the least an indication of the untenability of Lukes' proposition that all conceptions of power are equally fundamentally disputable. It appears, in the first place, that even the methodologically most problematic radical conception can be given an interpretation which is empirically testable, and, second, that this conception is also theoretically more plausible than the other, as it continues to call a contented slave a slave.

The most important reasons which Lukes has for his 'contestability the-sis', can be found, according to Smith, in an earlier essay by him, entitled 'Alienation and anomie' (1967). In this, Lukes looks at the Marxist view of alienation. It is obvious that this shows a close relationship with the radical conception of power: the happy proletarian is the victim of the power of a capitalistic system which alienates him from his real interests. The desires and accompanying gratifications of the people in a communist society will, according to Marx, be then qualitatively superior to those in capitalism. However, Lukes says that this conviction only acquires meaning if it can be empirically tested. To do this, it is necessary to get to know inside out both a communist and a capitalist society: only then could one objectively define which experiences are superior. According to Lukes, this test is not possible. The most important reason he gives for this is that no one can ever occupy a position from which he can compare objectively, unconditioned, different cultures or societies with each other. Everyone's viewpoint is, after all, a sub-jective social product. Lukes writes: 'If one believes, as Marx and Durkheim did, that man is largely conditioned by social circumstances, that new needs are generated by the historical process, that his very picture of himself and others is a function of his situation, then . . . no one is in a position gen-uinely to compare and evaluate alternatives' (1967: 147).

However, even if this were then the case for Smith, it still does not under-mine the weak radical standpoint: 'It would be relevant only if we had to find some individual, or group of individuals, capable of authoritatively deciding human needs and interests for humanity at large . . . This, however cannot be the point of the exercise . . . the aim is basically a matter of showing how it is possible for an individual or group of individuals to recog-nize their own interests for themselves, rather than to legislate interests for others' (Smith 1981: 420). To this, he adds that the result of such a study would naturally give an indication of the real needs and interests of others. Nevertheless, 'its prime function is not and cannot be that'.

This standpoint of Smith's is not without problems. In the first place, he has insufficiently understood the range of Lukes' remarks on Marx and Durkheim: not only is an individual incapable of making the relevant deci-sions for *others*, properly understood, he cannot do this for himself either. The individual who has to compare the two systems of desires and gratifica-tions is not a fixed point of reference. There is a large chance that he is socialized in each system to such an extent that he will always choose that system in which he finds himself at the moment of choice. Connolly had already pointed out that people *change* by participating in different cultures. As a consequence of this, the alternatives are assessed from the perspective of the last culture experienced, while it is precisely this which must be raised for discussion:

a different person is making the choice and that affects its status as evi-dence. For [the] recent experience is mediated through new orientations, expectations, and investments which themselves are supposed to be part of the conditions to be appraised. Even under ideal conditions of choice, then, elements of conjecture and speculation will enter into our assessment of the extent to which alternative modes of social life are more or less in our interests.

(Connolly 1972: 477)

Certainly when it is a case of appreciating various forms of society, of complete 'lifestyles' – Connolly is thinking of, among other things, participation research in a kibbutz, and in various forms of pre-, post- and industrial societies – it is necessary to take into account the paradox that 'the very process of preparing oneself to make the most reflective choice about one's interests affects the evidential status of the choice one makes' (Connolly 1972: 476; cf. Lindley 1986: 176; Young 1986: 37–42).

In short, Smith's objection that individuals must decide the alternatives they prefer for themselves only and not for others, is doubtful where the individual who ultimately makes the choice is different than the one who has not yet been in contact with the alternatives. If this problem was set absolutely, however, one would fall back into an extreme ethical relativism[10], a relativism which Lukes and Connolly certainly do not adhere to. Smith fails to recognize sufficiently that Lukes' remarks were formulated in a critique of Marx. In his historical materialism or sociological determinism, the latter is not consistent because he only considers it applicable to the ideas, norms and values of his opponents. A consistent application would lead, furthermore, to a moral nihilism of which Lukes has declared himself to be a pronounced opponent (see in particular Lukes 1985 and Popper 1945).

The second difficulty, from Smith's viewpoint, is that unlike how he wants to appear, it is very much about the preferences or the consciousness of *others*: a justification must be found for the suspicion that this is false or non-optimal, and the desire to change this. Smith, too, after all, will have to come up with an argument for why he wants to study the genesis of the preferences of the one, but not of the other. He needs a criterion for this. The same is true of Connolly and Lukes: they, too, have to justify why they want others to first experience an alternative culture before they can accept their preferences as authentic. The necessary criterion is inevitably normative in character and consists of what people fit to judge generally consider to be a worthy aspiration.

TED BENTON'S EMANCIPATION PARADOX

On the basis of such considerations as those of Lukes and Connolly, the English sociologist Ted Benton, already quoted in the introduction to this book, formulated his 'paradox of emancipation'. Benton, too, points out that the 'radical' critic must justify why he wants to study desires which are not at all present at the relevant moment. This critic usually does this with the standpoint that the existing structures and processes frustrate the development of particular, significant desires. 'Significant in what way?', is then the question, 'If the answer is just that *different* states and activities would have resulted, then the critique loses its political sting' (Benton 1982: 13). The radical therefore, according to Benton, will assume that the potential desires are to be preferred in one way or another to the existing ones. He can say that the alternative desires are more valuable either in terms of content or 'procedure', the latter because they are the *consciously chosen* preferences, which have come into being independent of power structures, of autonomous individuals. These justifications therefore are based, says Benton, on a particular ethical or political conviction. Autonomy is also a normative ideal after all.

In this context, it turns out that Lukes and Connolly try to avoid the notion of 'real' interests acquiring a totalitarian application by demanding that the subject ultimately defines his interests himself. Benton, however, points out that he is, by definition, not capable of this; as a consequence of the challenged exercise of power or social processes, he has never been in contact, or will be, with the alternatives. The choice must therefore be made *for* the subject (Benton 1982: 25).

It can be argued against this that Lukes and Connolly are not concerned with a contents-oriented choice of particular alternatives, but with the creation of conditions under which one can make real choices 'relatively autonomously'. Even apart from the question of how it must be determined in practice when there is 'relative autonomy', Benton considers it equally a problem that the conditions demanded by the radicals are based on a normative ideal image of individual autonomy.

For example, according to him, Connolly is implicitly assuming that there is a positive connection between, on the one hand, experience or knowledge and, on the other, the capacity to judge one's interests. However, according to Benton, one can equally argue that more experience and knowledge 'may dull the sensibilities and lead to a loss of judgement' (Benton 1982: 27). Equally, Benton claims, Lukes uses the disputable principle that making free choices is an essential characteristic of the ability of man, and that promoting this is therefore always in his interest.

In short, the problem with the radical conception, according to Benton, is that not only must it be decided on behalf of another to come in contact with alternatives, from which he himself may then make a choice, it must also be decided for him that being able to choose from alternatives is desirable. This decision is inevitably based on a normative idea of man. Benton concludes therefore that the definitions which Connolly and Lukes give of 'interest' have a normative charge. (Incidentally, both would agree with this conclusion.)

The radicals' unwillingness to regard the existing desires and wishes as given, is not without political dangers. Berlin has gone extensively into these. The radicals discussed here, who are, on the whole, democratic, egalitarian and libertarian in their inspiration, are also aware of this. Nevertheless, it is not possible for them to completely ward off these dangers. After all, they can hardly drop the sociologically and social-psychologically-based perspective and critique of the existing preferences without ceasing to be a radical. These radicals are therefore, in the words of Benton, prisoners in a paradox:

> if they are to remain true to their political values they may implement no changes without the consent of those who are affected by them, and if they seek to implement no such changes, then they acquiesce in the persistence of a political system radically at odds with their political values. This paradox I shall call the paradox of emancipation.
>
> (Benton 1982: 15; cf. Benton 1981: 162)

Because this contradiction between the principles adhered to is *real* and not apparent, it is for the rest more correct, as has already been said in Chapter 1, to call it a *dilemma* of emancipation.

The paradox of emancipation can, according to Benton, only be solved in a gratifying manner when the radicals try to link up with the 'counter-preferences', which are developed into a particular structure of preferences during every socialization. Thanks to these alternative identifications, the latent consciousness can be present in someone, that his interests are more or less in conflict with the preferences imposed on him. If they are absent, then there is no basis on which others can be convinced of their (presumed) interests. The *democratic ideological struggle* favoured by Benton thus also consists of the attempt to stimulate, with the help of political parties, social movements and other forms of social relations, the counter-preferences. In this way, it can be attempted to *convince* others of their interests. He concludes:

> To deny, or to overlook, the counter-tendencies to the social production of consensual wants and identifications is to deny the possibility of ideological and political struggle which is simultaneously democratic and genuinely radical and emancipatory. It is to remain locked within a strategic perspective which offers only imposition of 'solutions' on an unwilling population, or feeble acquiescence in the *status quo*.
>
> (Benton 1982: 33)

RICHARD LINDLEY ON DILEMMAS

For the most part, Lindley accepts Benton's critique of the conceptions of interests of Lukes and Connolly. However, he, too, does not want to lapse into a feeble acquiescence in the existing, in his opinion, non-optimal wants and desires of the majority of the citizens in Western democracies. The key to a way out of the dilemma of emancipation is to be found, according to him, in the respect which liberals have for individual autonomy. On the basis of this, far-reaching social changes can be justified, even though there is a widespread acquiescence in the *status quo*. He concentrates mainly on those liberals, who while they accept the idea that autonomy is a central value in human life, in his view, do not draw the full consequences from this (Lindley 1986: 169, 177).

Just like MacPherson, Lindley thinks that the most important justification of the liberal political systems is in the claim that everyone has an equal right to autonomy. This is based on the idea that every individual is worthy of our respect. Autonomy, the underlying notion of which is 'self-determination', has two dimensions, according to Lindley. In the first place, someone is autonomous when he has developed his own identity on the basis of which his behaviour can be explained and justified. In the second place, autonomy requires that one is free of extreme inhibitions or coercion. The latter form of freedom is important, but the 'main rationale for favouring a large sphere of negative liberty is that it may be essential for the promotion of autonomy, which is a more fundamental value' (Lindley 1986: 8). Lindley considers negative freedoms like freedom of expression of opinion, of assembly and association, to be 'very important, [but] they are not intrinsic values. Their main worth consists in being necessary conditions for the development, maintenance and exercise of autonomy' (Lindley 1986: 186; cf. Norman in Chapter 3). Unlike the assumption of the utilitarians, autonomy is not an instrumental, furthermore, but an intrinsic value. This can be seen from the fact, according to Lindley, that no one regards living in Huxley's *Brave New World* as an aspiration (ibid.: 74).

The question now is how respect for the individual autonomy, which, according to Lindley, is axiomatic in liberal democracy, is to take shape in reality. Here Lindley occupies a 'neutralistic' standpoint: 'moral judgements should be made from a standpoint of strict impartiality – both in regard to times and to people' (Lindley 1986: 84).[11] This implies that one must promote one's own or another's autonomy over the *entire* life. In this context, Lindley rejects Kant's categorical imperative – one should at all times regard the other as an end and not a means. That provides no space for the temporal dimension. In order to respect someone's autonomy in the long term, it can sometimes, emphasizes Lindley again and again, be desirable to restrict it in the short term (ibid.: 76, 82, 88, 92, 102, 112, 184). The exercising of autonomy in the present, can after all seriously restrict the possibility of this in the future:

> there may be an intertemporal clash of autonomy interests within a person . . . if I give full reign to my current autonomy . . . this could restrict my future autonomy, either by bringing it about that my autonomy capacity is diminished, or that opportunities for its exercise are foreclosed by present conduct.
>
> (Lindley 1986: 88)[12]

Respect for individual autonomy also means, according to Lindley, that one promotes not only the exercise of this capacity, but also its development.

(He produces no arguments for the latter point, but they could resemble those of Charles Taylor in Chapter 4.)

By way of illustration, Lindley narrates the life of a worker, an existence which in its hopeless misery seems to be something from a song by Bruce Springsteen: 'John' grows up in a village where nearly all the adults have a job with the nearby car factory. As is right and fitting, he leaves school at sixteen to go to work for the 'Johnstown Company'. His prospects are to spend the rest of his life doing unskilled work on the production line. He marries the girl next door ('She sits on the porch of her daddy's house with the eyes of one who hates for just being born' (Springsteen 1978)). They have children immediately. Within five years he has got used to having his own television, video, stereo and car. In the meantime, however, he finds the work becoming increasingly monotonous and stultifying. In order to be able to continue paying for the consumer goods he has learnt to appreciate, however, he has to keep going. He had imagined before that it would all turn out differently.

Given his wants pattern and the available alternatives, it is probably in John's interests to keep his job and continue to live in the old way. On the other hand, however, in Lindley's view, there is much to be said for raising for discussion the process of socialization and the socio-economic system which laid out the main course of his life for him. On turning twenty-one, he is already so tied down to an existence which does not satisfy him by all kinds of expectations, dependencies and conventions, that it is difficult to speak of autonomy. Perhaps, says Lindley, his capacity for critical thought, to open up conventions for discussion, the courage for non-conformism, has been insufficiently stimulated. Perhaps, also, this has been exploited by commerce by the creation of an image of normality and the accompanying desires and gratifications which people do not dare to deviate from.

Lindley makes a comparison with the attitude of liberals with regard to heroin dealers: because they take the existing desires as the starting-point, they generally do not want to have the heroin addicts compulsorily detoxicated. On the other hand, a liberal does want to prosecute the dealers as he considers the way in which the relevant wants have been created to be objectionable and to be combated. In the same way, one can now state that, according to Lindley, these processes and structures, which create wants and needs in a society and frustrate the development of individual autonomy, must be rejected. The most important failure of the contemporary liberal democratic societies, in this context, is not that the *exercise* of autonomy is inhibited – the lack of any appreciable obstacles in this field in fact forms the most important justification of these systems. Their most important failure is then that the *development* and maintenance of the capacity for autonomy of the majority of the population is frustrated (Lindley 1986: 181–2).

INTERMEDIARY CONCLUSIONS

Someone's interests can be defined in various ways. One can, as is usual within liberalism, equate personal interests with what the individual indicates to be his preferences and wants (through political participation). An important advantage of this approach is that no room is offered for rationalizations in which, under the guise of 'false consciousness', desires are ascribed to people which, in reality, they do not at all cherish. A disadvantage is that one is uncritical with regard to the way in which the relevant preferences come into being. One may wonder whether these have been consciously chosen on the basis of a reasonable knowledge of the alternatives, or whether they are the product, either arbitrary or desired by another, of certain social structures and processes. A second important disadvantage is that by taking the current wishes exclusively as the starting-point, one can never create a situation which, if the parties involved were familiar with it, they would choose in preference to the existing one. It is therefore better to have a definition in which someone's interests are equated with what he would want if he himself had experienced the possible alternatives and therefore could make a real choice.

However, this definition, too, is not without its problems. The most important problem is that the specific group of people which the radicals are most concerned with have, by the nature of things, no knowledge of the possible preferable alternative choices. This can, in the first place, be the consequence of the exercise of power. In this case, it must be made comprehensible how they are kept from this knowledge by others. It can also be the consequence of the circumstance that the parties involved have not been looking for alternatives of their own free will, that they display a lack of 'active theoretical rationality' (which can also be a consequence of exercise of power). The problem in both cases is that the decision to come into contact with alternatives – alternatives which at that moment they possibly do not at all appreciate – must be made for, and not by, these people. This can be justified in terms of content or form; one can say that the alternatives *as such* are more valuable than the possibilities the people involved are familiar with, or one can say that a choice is first significant if one is sufficiently familiar with the relevant options.

It will be clear that this last formal or procedural justification is not value-free. It is based on the ideal of positive freedom. The formal argument is also limited in content. It is after all difficult to keep presenting people with new alternatives. We already referred in Chapter 3 to the problems related to this, such as the human need for security and continuity. In order to be able to make a choice between alternatives which are worth considering or not, one must therefore have a normative criterion.

Both this criterion and the formal justification can be partly empirically based. One bases oneself then, as Smith also remarked, on the experiences of others. It is to be expected here that those who one wants to examine the alternatives, or to whom one generally wants to offer the opportunity to choose, will share those experiences. Ultimately, thus, the reference is to what is generally held to be rational and valuable in life by those within a particular society who are aware of the alternatives and capable of judgement.

Both justifications are thus, in short, normative in character and in both cases therefore it can be said that someone is attempting to pass on his norms and values to another. However, this does not immediately have to be an insurmountable objection. Making normative choices, choosing for oneself and for others, does not necessarily result in an authoritarian or totalitarian system. In addition, in Taylor's terminology, having a 'horizon of qualitative distinctions' is a condition for possessing an identity and holding a standpoint. For this reason, the attempts by the various authors to avoid the necessity of choosing between, or rather, for values,[13] make a somewhat forced impression. Ultimately, they cannot get around this either.

Although Lukes himself emphasizes that all conceptions of power and interests are 'essentially contested', looked at properly the avoidance of normative choices began already with him. He demands that 'real interests' be empirically identifiable and that the parties involved do this themselves under 'relatively autonomous' circumstances. The possible indications which he then gives that people actually want something different from their acquiescent support of the *status quo*, would lead us to expect (sudden popular uprisings; the pursuit of vertical mobility within a caste system) are rather limited in their extremity. They offer no solution to the forms of three-dimensional exercise of power, generally inspiring little excitement, with which we are confronted in Western democracies. With Lindley, one can here think of the social structures and processes which are the cause of many seldom coming in contact with lifestyles and ways of thinking which are strange to their milieu of origin and the education, rearing and career associated with this. Furthermore, Lukes himself notes, socialization structures can be so successful that there is no development of what Benton calls 'counter-preferences'. Finally, the indications named by Lukes offer no solace for the problems emphasized by Connolly, in particular, that people sometimes perceive absolutely no need to come in contact with alternative ideas, tastes and styles, a contact which in retrospect, they would probably appreciate highly, once it had actually taken place.

If Lukes and Connolly still want to intervene in these cases, if they first want to make others aware of an alternative culture before they are prepared to accept their preferences as authentic, then they will have to make normative choices. They will have to assume that there are particular preferences and accompanying gratifications with which the parties involved are not familiar at this moment in time, but which they would also prefer to their current ones. Or they must assume that the parties involved can first make a real choice when they are familiar with additional options, worthwhile in the views of Lukes and Connolly.

Smith, likewise, tries to get around the normative problems surrounding the emancipation dilemma. He postulates that with the radical conception of interest too, it is a matter of empirically observable desires. His proposal boils down to studying people with a 'deviant' pattern of wants to see if their desires have arisen under 'normal social and psychic' conditions. If there is nothing to be found here (Smith assumes that agreement can be reached on this subject), then one will have to accept the relevant desires. It is therefore, according to Smith, not at all the case that people have values imposed on them, within his conception.

Naturally, what is crucial here is the answer to the question of what forms a 'normal' pattern of wants, and, arising from this, under which social and psychic circumstances this can be developed. If one were to define normality empirically, that is, statistically, this would lead to a noticeable homogenization and uniformization of our culture. For example, the few people who nowadays participate regularly in cultural activities, would in this case have to be urgently subjected to a social and psychic examination. This is probably not what Smith intended. As a criterion to define what normal wants and desires are, he probably cherishes a normative ideal of what people should pursue in life.

Radicals like Connolly and Lukes desire, in short, on the one hand, that people define their own interests themselves, and, on the other hand, perceive that they are often not in a state to do this as a consequence of the existing socialization structures. On the basis of this contradiction, Benton formulates his 'emancipation paradox'. When solving this dilemma, he too tries to avoid deciding on behalf of the people involved which goals are worth pursuing in life, and thus he too tries to get around normative choices. For example, we saw he regarded it as an objection that the conceptions of power and interests of Lukes and Connolly are based on an ideal image of human development, something he himself tries to avoid. Benton does not succeed in this. His plea for the development through 'democratic ideological struggle', of counter-preferences, should of course be the most important instrument for social change in every democracy. However, this too is based on a normative image of man which one is attempting to impose on others.

If Benton wants to convert people to other wants and goals, than he must assume after all that these are more valuable for one reason or another than the existing ones. Furthermore, when does this 'persuasion' turn into 'talking round', 'exerting pressure', 'manipulation', 'coercion' and 'brainwashing'? When does acculturation turn into socialization, paternalism, propaganda or manipulation? At which moment does one here no longer take the existing preferences as the starting-point? The instruments for changing preferences form a sliding scale between suggestion and manipulation, a scale on which Benton is somewhat closer to the pole first mentioned than Connolly and Lukes. However, there is absolutely no rift in principle. The difference in position is probably explained by the fact that the last mentioned ascribe greater influence to the existing structures of socialization, or are more pessimistic with regard to the inertia into which many are supposed to have fallen. They have therefore less faith in the counter-preferences on which Benton has pinned his hopes. To what extent these latter preferences are present is a question which can be partially answered empirically. Partly, because ultimately it is again normatively determined which counter-preferences one hopes to find.

Lindley too, finally, wrestles with the fact that some within the radical conception are, by definition, not able to decide to become familiar with alternatives, and he too tries to remove as much as possible the impression that this normative choice must therefore be made on behalf of those people. It turned out that he wants to change the structures which ensure that people develop insufficiently their capacity for autonomy. Here he makes an appeal, over the heads of a part of the population assumed to be heteronomous, to those liberals who realize that negative freedom is not sufficient to become free in the positive sense. However, the question remains of what must happen with the people who are already socialized in the relevant culture. What if they fail to approve of the changes in the structure of which their preferences are after all a product?

A distinction must be made here perhaps between paternalism and socialization. With paternalism *already existing* situations are countered, as we shall see in the following sections. This is not the case with socialization as the preferences must still be formed to a large extent. With regard to new generations, one can say that it must not so much be justified that people become socialized, but how this happens. This question therefore concerns the first dimension of the emancipation dilemma.

It is different with people who have already, under the influence of the existing structures of socialization, developed their own preferences. Changing their preferences requires people to break through the vicious circle of the existing cultural reproduction process. It is inevitable here that one makes normative choices for others. Unlike Lindley's suggestion, this is no 'solution' to the emancipation dilemma, therefore, but the ascription of a heavier status to positive freedom than to its negative counterpart. This is very defensible, but one must continue to call paternalism paternalism, even if it takes place in an indirect manner, via the changing of structures of socialization.

In short, ultimately, none of the radical authors offer a completely satisfactory solution to the problem that people, as a consequence of existing structures of socialization or a lack of 'active theoretical rationality', cannot be independently capable of making the decision to become familiar with other – possibly highly appreciated in retrospect – ideas, tastes and styles. This decision will, in this case, have to be taken by others on their behalf. Paternalism seems sometimes inevitable, therefore, in order to break up existing structures of socialization or a prevailing inertia. This concept will be analysed further in the next section.

It will emerge that the debate waged in recent years within Anglo-American political and social philosophy on paternalism, shows great affinities with the discussion of conceptions of interests, discussions which, in a remarkable manner, have taken place completely separately from each other. Also, in answering the question of when a paternalistic intervention is desirable or permissible, it will ultimately be necessary to refer to what is generally held to be rational and valuable in life within a particular society. For many theoreticians, apparently, this is, as it will turn out, an unacceptable fact. They want to take exclusively the rationality of the individual as the starting-point; only he or she is called to choose values. In its extremity, this leads to a dubious value relativism.

The rest of this chapter will begin with a short explication of what can be understood by paternalism. As the standpoint of John Stuart Mill forms the point of departure for many authors, including Isaiah Berlin, we will then be looking at his wellnigh absolute objections to paternalistic interventions. These objections can be seen equally as arguments for negative freedom. The theoreticians who are then dealt with (Feinberg, Dworkin, Carter, VanDeVeer, and Kleinig and Young) either attempt to create more space for paternalism than Mill's 'liberty principle' allows, or to confirm this principle.

PATERNALISM: SOME DEFINITIONS AND DISTINCTIONS

Before going into a number of possible justifications of paternalism, it is desirable to first demarcate this concept somewhat and make some distinctions. In a 1971 article, Gerald Dworkin defines paternalism as the use of coercion, to promote something whose value is not or insufficiently recognized by the parties involved. He says it can be regarded as an 'interference with a person's liberty of action justified by reasons referring exclusively to the welfare, good, happiness, needs, interests, or values of the person being coerced' (Dworkin 1971: 20).

It can also be that the subject does recognize the value of something, but not the means to promote it. Health and the wearing of a crash helmet and car seat belts are examples of this. In a definition which is otherwise comparable, Feinberg makes a more explicit distinction between what could be called 'negative' and 'positive' paternalism. The former is present when individuals are protected from themselves by force, the second when they are guided by force towards their happiness or welfare, whether they appreciate this or not (Feinberg 1971: 110; see also Feinberg 1986).

After this was pointed out by critics, in a later article Dworkin recognizes that paternalism is not always accompanied by coercion. Thus, the testator who lays down in his will that his children only gain possession of the inheritance when they have passed thirty, is limiting no one's freedom (Dworkin 1983: 105). In this context, John Kleinig mentions the example of a social service which gives its clients help in kind (food, clothes, housing) instead of in money. In his opinion, there is no coercion here (accompanied by possible sanctions) even if the freedom of the people involved to spend the money received as they want is limited (Kleinig 1983: 5).[14]

According to Kleinig, furthermore, there is no necessary connection between paternalism and intervening in someone's freedom of action. A dying elderly woman, who, on asking, hears from the treating doctor that her supposedly lost son is doing very well – while he knows that he has just been arrested for multiple rape and murder – is not impeded in her freedom of action. However, Kleinig recognizes that she is restricted in her freedom to 'know'. The relevant doctor, no matter how good his intentions, controls her thinking. Therefore, Kleinig supposes:

> that it is best to see in acts of paternalism a constraint on freedom, albeit not necessarily a coercive one or even an interference with liberty of action. We can speak of there being an *imposition*, for . . . one party imposes upon another. The paternalist exercises some measure of control over some aspect of the life of another – be it a thwarting of the other's desires, a manipulation of the other's beliefs, or a channelling of the other's behaviour.
>
> (Kleinig 1983: 7)

The word *manipulation*, however, is out of place in this definition. Unlike in paternalism, the individual who is being manipulated is by definition not aware of this, which explains the association with 'betrayal'. Manipulation is also aimed at the interests of the manipulator, while in paternalism what matters are the interests of the object. Furthermore, it must be emphasized that the paternalist is trying to render himself superfluous: the freedom of the object is restricted *temporarily* in order to allow it to be so large at a later date that his benevolent interference is no longer needed. With regard to the mentally-handicapped, it is therefore better to speak of *tutoring* than of paternalism. We can roughly conclude, therefore, there is paternalism when A exercises a control limited in time over one or more aspects of the life of B, an action which he justifies by referring to the needs, interests, values, welfare or happiness of B.

Furthermore, a distinction can be drawn between, on the one hand, 'pure' or 'direct' and, on the other, 'impure' forms of paternalism (Dworkin 1971: 22; Kleinig 1983: 14). In the first case, the group of people whose freedom is being constrained is identical to the group of people whose welfare is being promoted with the help of this constraint on freedom. There is impure paternalism when the two groups do not coincide: the freedom of one group is constrained to stimulate the welfare of the other. An example of this would be the constraints generally imposed on cigarette producers by the government. In this case, the damage could also be avoided by the target group itself (by not smoking). However, as the state does not trust the people involved to make this choice, a different group, the producers, are impeded from freely selling their wares.

Feinberg makes a further distinction between 'strong' and 'weak' versions

of paternalism. It is a question of the first case, when an individual is protected against his own wishes from the damaging consequences of completely voluntary choices and actions. It is an example of the second case,
when the government protects someone from himself, on the assumption
that the action which causes the damage is involuntary (Feinberg 1971: 129;
cf. 1986: 12–6). An action is regarded as voluntary by Feinberg if it is a consciously chosen expression of one's own identity.

Finally, paternalism has to be distinguished from *moralism*. Important
differences are, first, that the reason for paternalism is in the interests of the
object, while in moralism it is rather a question of supra-individual values,
for example, those of the relevant community; second, that paternalism is
aimed at actions with which an object (temporarily) incapable of judgement
inflicts damage on itself, while moralism is not subject to these restrictions;
and third, that paternalistic interventions, unlike moralistic ones, are never
intended as sanctions for morally reprehensible behaviour (Ten 1971:
63–65).

JOHN STUART MILL'S LIBERTY PRINCIPLE

In his famous essay 'On Liberty', John Stuart Mill tries to establish a principle that decrees 'without exception' in which cases society may intervene in
the personal sphere. His 'Liberty Principle' is the starting-point for numerous authors who have written about paternalism. It embraces,

> that the sole end for which mankind are warranted, individually or collec-
> tively, in interfering with the liberty of action of any of their number, is
> self-protection. That the only purpose for which power can be rightfully
> exercised over any member of a civilized community, against his will, is to
> prevent harm to others. His own good, either physical or moral, is not a
> sufficient warrant. He cannot rightfully be compelled to do or forbear
> because it will be better for him to do so, because it will make him happi-
> er, because, in the opinions of others, to do so would be wise, or even
> right. These are good reasons for remonstrating with him, or reasoning
> with him, or persuading him, or entreating him, but not for compelling
> him, or visiting him with any evil in case he do otherwise. . . . The only
> part of the conduct of any one, for which he is amenable to society, is
> that which concerns others. In the part which merely concerns himself, his
> independence is, of right, absolute. Over himself, over his own body and
> mind, the individual is sovereign.

(Mill 1859: 135)[15]

Mill immediately adds to this that this principle naturally only applies to
people who are in a position to improve their own lot by exchanging ideas
with others. He does not so classify children, people who have not yet
attained the maturity of their mental capacities, and 'inarticulate' people
from 'backward forms of society'. Although the principle of liberty is fur-

thermore formulated in general terms and therefore is also valid on an individual level, Mill is primarily concerned with the relationship between, on the one hand, individual citizens, and, on the other, society and government. The subject of his essay is 'Civil, or Social Liberty: the nature and limits of the power which can be legitimately exercised by society over the individual' (Mill 1859: 126). Paternalism of parents with regard to their children, or of friends among each other, is therefore different to paternalism of the state.

Looked at properly, Mill gives three reasons for his almost absolute ban on paternalism. The first and, according to him, the only reason (Mill 1859: 136) is utilitarian in character: it does not contribute to the greatest happiness for the greatest number as, on the whole, the individual can judge his interests better than any paternalist. After all, no one is as well aware of his feelings and circumstances and no one has as much interest in promoting his welfare. The intervention by society must, on the other hand, be based on general considerations, which can be incorrect or not applicable to the relevant case (ibid.: 206–7, 214). The benefits of intervention at the right moment cannot be offset, therefore, against the costs of the inevitably far more numerous incorrect moments: 'All errors which the individual is likely to commit against advice and warning are far outweighed by the evil of allowing others to constrain him to what they deem his good' (ibid.: 207).

Sabine (1973), Feinberg (1971: 112–4) and Dworkin (1971: 23–8), among others, have pointed out that this utilitarian argument, which was already sharply criticized in his own century, was not sufficient for Mill either.[16] The central thesis, in particular, that the individual knows best what is good for him, caused him some doubts. In a different context, a discussion of government interference in general, Mill deals with some exceptions to this position. Just like Connolly and Lukes, he notes that there are valuable matters whose use is not always clear to the parties involved. These are matters:

> of which the utility does not consist in ministering to inclinations, nor in serving the daily uses of life, and the want of which is least felt where the need is greatest. This is peculiarly true of those things which are chiefly useful as tending to raise the character of human beings. The uncultivated cannot be competent judges of cultivation. Those who most need to be made wiser and better, usually desire it least, and, if they desire it, would be incapable of finding the way to it by their own lights.
> (Mill 1848: quoted in Dworkin 1971: 25: 459)

In addition, according to Mill, individuals, through lack of knowledge and experience, cannot always calculate well what must be done in the present to assure future interests.

One can wonder why Mill does not want to make any comparable exceptions when he discusses the question of paternalism in 'On Liberty'. Utilitarianism generally leads to more pragmatic recommendations than the (originally) absolute imperative formulated in this essay.[17] Sabine and Dworkin presume that there is an explanation in Mill's moral conviction that all forms of coercion are a denial of human dignity.[18] This conviction is the second reason for his rejection of paternalism. (The first was that individuals taken on the whole know better than others what is in their interests.) The freedom to choose is therefore, irrespective of the essence of man, an essential trait which defines his dignity (Sabine 1973: 641; Dworkin 1971: 72). Mill therefore considers it justifiable to intervene when someone chooses to sell himself as a slave: one cannot permit someone to misuse his freedom to become unfree (Mill 1859: 235–6). Seen from a purely utilitarian point of view, however, this could be a justifiable choice. (For a justification of this kind, see Feinberg (1971: 123–25).)

The third and last reason which Mill gives for rejecting paternalism is that making choices oneself, correct and incorrect, is a precondition for the development of individuality. Paternalism deprives people of this learning and development process. Mill writes among other things:

> The human faculties of perception, judgement, discriminative feeling, mental activity, and even moral preference, are exercised only in making a choice . . . The mental and moral, like the muscular powers, are improved only by being used . . . He who lets the world, or its own portion of it, choose his plan of life for him, has no need of any other faculty than the ape-like one of imitation. He who chooses his plan for himself, employs all his faculties.
>
> (Mill 1859: 187)

Despite all these objections to paternalism Mill would have no difficulty with what Feinberg calls 'weak paternalism'. His principle of liberty means that people can be rightly protected from the choices of others and therefore it also applies to involuntary actions. These are, after all, not a chosen expression of one's own identify and are therefore just as alien to the individual as someone else's choices. Often quoted is Mill's example about someone who wants to cross a rickety bridge:

> If either a public officer or any one else saw a person attempting to cross a bridge which had been ascertained to be unsafe, and there were no time to warn him of this danger, they might seize him and turn him back, without any real infringement of his liberty; for liberty consists in doing what one desires, and he does not desire to fall into the river.
>
> (Mill 1859: 229)

Nevertheless, Mill adds, when one has informed the person of the dangers, it is then up to him alone – 'unless he is a child, or delirious, or in some state of excitement or absorption incompatible with the full use of the reflecting faculty' (Mill 1859: 229) – to determine whether the risks are acceptable in relation to the goal to be achieved.

JOEL FEINBERG: PATERNALISM AND VOLUNTARINESS

Feinberg's standpoint comes close to that of Mill's: only weak paternalism is acceptable. Thus, only in the case of real involuntary behaviour, or if temporary intervention is necessary to be able to observe this, can paternalistic interventions be justified (Feinberg 1980: x, xi; 1971: 119; 1986: chs. 17, 20). A question now is when is it a case of involuntary actions. Feinberg goes deeper into this than Mill. He writes: 'To whatever extent there is compulsion, misinformation, excitement or impetuousness, clouded judgement (as e.g. from alcohol), or immature or defective faculties of reasoning, to that extent the choice falls short of perfect voluntariness. Voluntariness then is a matter of degree' (Feinberg 1971: 115; cf. 1986: ch. 20).

Feinberg explicitly distances himself from Aristotle who also characterized impulsive and emotional action and reactions as voluntary (see Chapter 3). For Feinberg, voluntariness is first present when the action is a well-considered choice, which can be seen as an expression of the identity of the actor:

> Chosen acts are those that are decided upon by *deliberation*, and that is a process that requires time, information, a clear head, and highly developed rational faculties. . . . Such acts not only have their origin 'in the agent', they also represent him faithfully in some important way: they express his settled values and preferences. In the fullest sense, therefore, they are actions for which he can bear responsibility.
>
> (Feinberg 1971: 116)

The values or the identity of the subject are therefore the basic principle in Feinberg's weak paternalism. Only if the suspicion exists that someone is not completely rational according to his *own criteria* and therefore is not acting completely voluntarily, is it justified to restrain the individual involved from this action until the opposite has been proved. The difference with Mill is that Feinberg sets higher requirements for the voluntariness of an action: for him the rationality of a choice is to the fore, while Mill wants to also leave space for 'desires and impulses'.[19]

GERALD DWORKIN: PATERNALISM AND RATIONALITY

Dworkin, too, has taken Mill's standpoint as the point of departure for his own considerations. According to him, this standpoint does leave some space for paternalistic interventions. He points out first of all that with regard to children paternalism is generally considered not only acceptable, but also desirable. One presumes that to a greater or lesser extent they are lacking in the necessary emotional and cognitive capacities to be able to rationally ascertain their interests. Therefore, it is the moral duty of the parents to protect the children's long-term interests by sometimes restricting their freedom. What is characteristic of this paternalism is that a *future* consent as such is anticipated: it is 'gambled' that the children involved will later, when they are mature, recognize that their parents were right at the time. Dworkin writes: 'Parental paternalism may be thought of as a wager by the parent on the child's subsequent recognition of the wisdom of the restrictions. There is an emphasis on what could be called future-oriented consent – on what the child will become to welcome, rather than on what he does become' (Dworkin 1971: 28).

The essence of this idea is often used for 'real-will' theories with regard to adults. They, too, at a particular moment, could lack the capacity to judge their own interests objectively, but in retrospect would agree without any doubts to the earlier curtailment of their freedom. As we have seen, what this can lead to is extensively discussed by Berlin. Nevertheless, says Dworkin, 'the basic notion of consent is important and seems to me the only acceptable way of trying to delimit an area of justified paternalism' (Dworkin 1971: 29).

Dworkin then looks for the conditions under which it may be presumed that rational people would consent (in retrospect) to paternalism. A core element of his argument is that there are 'goods' (such as health and knowledge) which everyone in principle wants because they are a precondition for the fulfilling of personal objectives in life.[20] Guaranteeing these goods, therefore, will generally be consented to retrospectively. In general, one can now, in Dworkin's view, say that paternalism will be considered most acceptable when it is not so much aimed at increasing someone's happiness or welfare, but at promoting his ability to make independent choices in his life, of his capacity to rational self-determination (Dworkin 1971: 33).

It is important then to reach agreement on which 'goods' the possession of should be promoted, even if the value of this is not seen by the parties involved at a particular moment. A problem here naturally is that values can clash. Someone can find a particular value more important than his health or even his life. For example, some religious sects are opposed to blood transfusions or inoculation. When can it be said that this is not a rational choice?

Dworkin attempts to answer this question by examining the behaviour of someone who, while he is aware of the statistical chance of sustaining injury as a consequence of not wearing seat belts, considers the inconvenience of wearing seat belts as a more weighty consideration than the risks run. Dworkin tends to regard this as an irrational consideration:

> Given his life plans, *which we are assuming are those of the average person*, his interests and commitments already undertaken, I think it is safe to predict that we can find inconsistencies in his calculation at some point . . . I am assuming that *he is just like us in all relevant aspects* but just puts an enormously high negative value on inconvenience – one which does not seem comprehensible or reasonable [emphasis added by HTB].
>
> (Dworkin 1971: 30)

In addition, it is possible that the individual involved simply fails to use his seat belts through sloppiness or absent-mindedness as a consequence of the cognitive, but not emotional, processing of the risks.

Thus, says Dworkin, one can say in two ways that someone's choice is irrational: 'In one case he attaches incorrect weights to some of his values; in the other he neglects to act in accordance with his actual preferences and desires' (Dworkin 1971: 30). Naturally, paternalism is the simplest to justify in the last case: there is here, by definition, no question of someone having alien values imposed upon him. Nevertheless, Dworkin does not want to exclude in advance normative choices of paternalistic interventions. The driver who sustains injuries because he values too highly the convenience of not wearing seat belts finally, in retrospect, calls into question the value of 'convenience'. By making the wearing of seat belts compulsory, a prediction is therefore made about the result of a future evaluation of values.

Finally, Dworkin names some conditions which also determine the answer to the question of in which cases one will consent to paternalism. First, a role is played by whether it is possible to repeal the choice which is objected to. The more difficult this is (think of the decision to use drugs), the sooner a paternalistic intervention will be considered acceptable. Second, the social and psychological circumstances under which the decisions have been taken, are important. Forced postponement of a choice which one wants to a make in a state of excitement or weakness, such as suicide, is therefore easier to justify. Third, a role is played by the degree to which the dangers accompanying the relevant behaviour are recognized by the parties involved. A consideration here is which role this behaviour plays in the life plan or the identity of the person in question. Banning alpinism or parachute jumping can sometimes mean a greater assault on someone's identity than the compulsion to wear seat belts generally does (cf. Feinberg 1971: 114–16).

ROSEMARY CARTER: PATERNALISM AND CONSENT

Carter provides a justification of paternalism which links up with that of Dworkin, and earlier, Lukes and Connolly. She postulates that people have a right to non-intervention and that this right first fails to apply when it is explicitly given up. Consent before or after, or a tendency towards this (if the subject were asked for his assessment and acquired relevant information), is therefore, according to her, a necessary condition for justifying a paternalistic intervention (Carter 1977: 134–6).

In order that the consent also be a sufficient condition, however, three conditions must be met: it may not, as in brainwashing, be the logical consequence of intervention; it may not be obtained by withholding relevant information; and it may not be given due to 'a distortion in the subject's values, beliefs and desires'. In the latter case, it is mainly a question of paternalism of parents with regard to their children. The extent to which a child will later consent to this, writes Carter:

> will depend in part on what beliefs and attitudes his parents attempted to instil, and on how successful they were in doing so. If they have been very successful he might not dissent from certain kinds of treatment which have impaired his ability to lead a full and happy life or which were undesirable for other reasons.

(Carter 1977: 137)

As an example, Carter mentions a child who has grown up within a narrow-minded religious sect, which forbids the development of certain artistic and intellectual capacities, a child, which, once it becomes mature, consents to this prohibition because it knows no better. As its ideas, desires and preferences have been distorted or deformed by his raising this consent, writes Carter, is naturally no justification of the relevant paternalism.

John Kleinig and, above all, Donald VanDeVeer, have exhaustively criticized Carter's ideas. On the basis of the example mentioned above, Kleinig wonders whether one cannot equally say that someone who is raised by 'dedicated empiricists' and, in consequence, has learned to consent to his lack of religious feelings, is a victim of a 'distortion in values, beliefs and desires'. And the same question can be asked with regard to the businessman who is raised with the idea that there is a future for him in commerce, and who also appreciates the life which he has arranged on the basis of this future perspective. Kleinig finds it objectionable that for solving this sort of problem Carter only refers to our 'intuitions': 'Talk of consent resulting from distortion presumes that an acceptable account of distortion can be or is provided. But that is not so. There is only an appeal to our intuitions' (Kleinig 1983: 62).

In this context, Robert Young (1986) says that one will probably speak of manipulation at the moment when one does not agree with the values communicated: 'Whether we acknowledge distortion or not tends to turn on what we *value*. This may circularly lead us to apply our conception of the good for a person as a criterion for the proper objects of rational and informed consent.' When precisely there is manipulation or 'distortion' cannot, according to Young, be scientifically established at this moment, but he expresses the hope and expectation that in the future a suitable psychological theory will be developed, which can bring a definite answer (Young 1986: 67).

DONALD VANDEVEER: AGAINST RATIONALITY AND VOLUNTARINESS

When Carter assumes, says VanDeVeer (1979: 637–9), that people have a *right* to negative freedom or non-intervention, then that must necessarily be valid until the moment that they explicitly renounce it. However, that is not at all the case at the moment of a paternalistic intervention. Unlike Carter's proposals, this can therefore never be rightful. Retrospective consent can be an expression of forgiveness, even of gratitude, but is no justification.

VanDeVeer, who rivals Mill in his aversion to paternalism, has most difficulty with the future-oriented character of Carter's conception of paternalism: it is predicted that consent will follow, and this prediction does not always have to come true. Carter does propose a number of guidelines for the most careful possible consideration of the chance of the latter. According to her, whether the consequences are irreversible must be involved in the consideration, as well as how the costs are related to benefits, and whether the paternalistic intervention is in accordance with the long-term goals of the party involved (Carter 1977: 141). Nevertheless, VanDeVeer is of the opinion that Carter continues to 'bet' too much on consent, and for him this forms a too shaky basis for deciding in favour of paternalism (VanDeVeer 1979: 640).

In a later article, VanDeVeer (1980: 29) also goes extensively into the views of Dworkin and Feinberg. He tries to develop a principle that curbs paternalism more than the conceptions of these authors do. In his view, they make excessive demands on the rationality or voluntariness of the choices made by the subject.

For example, it appeared that Dworkin justified making the wearing of seat belts compulsory (also for people who experience this as impractical and inconvenient) by referring to what rational people in general hold to be a worthy goal. It is reasonable to presume that people esteem health higher than a petty inconvenience such as wearing seat belts, and that therefore, normally speaking, they will consent to the paternalistic compulsion of the latter. And they will certainly do this if they were to personally experience the dangers of not wearing them. This appeal to what normal individuals hold to be normal is unacceptable for VanDeVeer as it justifies paternalism in too many cases. Nor does it do justice to the fact that choosing oneself, even if this does not happen completely rationally, has an important intrinsic value:

> The prerogative to choose for oneself, if not of unlimited value, is a distinct value to be weighed against, for example, the desirability of imposing restraints acceptable to a fully rational individual . . . My point is that the criterion of 'those restrictions which would be permissible to fully rational individuals' fails to give due weight to that good.
>
> (VanDeVeer 1980: 196; see also 1980: 200–1, 203–4)

Furthermore, Dworkin argues that in general paternalistic interventions are considered justifiable when these enlarge or guarantee someone's capacity for rational self-determination. However, for VanDeVeer this principle also lays too much emphasis on rationality. The capacity for this is merely one form of freedom and is not so important that it simply justifies intervention in freedom in general. Suicide, for example, ends someone's rationality, but can sometimes – as in the case of useless, unbearable suffering – be highly reasonable. VanDeVeer, therefore, does not agree with Mill that freedom can never mean that people are free to be unfree (such as voluntary slaves). If people choose this, that choice must be respected (VanDeVeer 1980: 197–9; 1979: 641).

Weak paternalism, such as that defended by Feinberg, can count on more consent from VanDeVeer. This principle only justifies intervention when someone acts not completely rationally – or better, not optimally – *according to his own criteria.* By postponing the action under coercion, it is checked whether this is completely voluntary or not. The requirements of freedom which Feinberg sets are considered far too heavy by VanDeVeer, however. He doubts whether he himself has ever made a decision which met all these conditions (absence of all coercion, of misunderstandings, or confusing emotions, etc.). He proposes an alternative principle, therefore, which can be seen as a mitigated version of Feinberg's 'weak paternalism':

> The principle I am defending is that paternalistic interference with generally competent adults is permissible if, and only if, it respects the *substantially voluntary acts and choices* of such persons (where it is presupposed that such an act or choice may or may not be one chosen by a fully rational person).

> (VanDeVeer 1980: 202)

Being able to choose *oneself*, is therefore so important for VanDeVeer, that, in short, he wants to make as low as possible the requirements, with regard to the voluntariness or rationality, interpreted as what people in general hold to be rational or normal. Referring to the (Kantian) method of justification which John Rawls uses in his *A Theory of Justice*, he also expresses the expectation that people who find themselves in an 'original position' (a situation in which they have to determine a principle of paternalism while they do not know if this will also apply to them themselves in the society to be formed), will be most enthusiastic about his principle (VanDeVeer 1980: 204).

JOHN KLEINIG: PATERNALISM GUARANTEE OF AUTONOMY

As we have seen, John Stuart Mill mentioned three arguments against paternalism: individuals on the whole know better than others what is in their interests; making choices oneself is a condition for the development of individuality; and restricting someone's freedom of choice is an infringement of his human dignity. Kleinig considers only the last one, to be properly regarded, tenable. That people know best what is good for them, is at best true in a very general sense. According to him, no one need be surprised any more at 'the carelessness, thoughtlessness, and stupidity of people with respect to the unelevating character or self-destructive potential of their self-regarding behaviour. For rational beings, we do some pretty irrational things' (Kleinig 1983: 29). And that is not only true of isolated individuals, but also of people in general, particularly when the consequences of their behaviour are somewhat further off in the future. While the importance of autonomous choice for the development of individuality is furthermore evident in the abstract, it does not have to be present in the concrete cases which one is speaking of in the context of paternalism. Muscles must be trained, endorses Kleinig, but overtraining can lead to permanent injury. Equally, people can sometimes make decisions which definitely undermine their capacity for autonomy (Kleinig 1983: 31).

The Kantian reasoning that the capacity for choice, for self-reflection and self-determination is unique to man, and this makes it an end in itself and an object of respect, and that paternalism is at loggerheads with this respect, is seen as convincing by Kleinig. Nevertheless, he thinks that this reasoning leaves space for paternalism – even more so, that interventions are sometimes necessary if human dignity is to be taken seriously.

In order to develop his own conception, in his book Kleinig exhaustively evaluates a large number of justifications of paternalism, most of which have already been discussed here. Wellnigh all these justifications are to a greater or lesser degree rejected by him. He does this mostly on the basis of the consideration that they show insufficient respect for man's essential qualities of self-reflection and self-determination. Kleinig calls what is ultimately left as, according to him, the strongest argument for paternalism, 'The Argument from Personal Integrity'. The relevant reasoning is, to a large extent, similar to that of Robert Young (1986: 63–79; see Chapter 3), includes elements from that of Dworkin, and links up with the ideas, incidentally not mentioned by Kleinig, of Frankfurt, Taylor and Barber.

A characteristic of this justification is that a more differentiated and less abstract conception of the ego is assumed than is, according to Kleinig, usual within liberalism. People have not only diverse, partly contradictory goals, preferences and desires, but these in their turn have a divergent status within the more central life plan of the relevant individual. Some values, goals and desires are more important and play a more continuous and central role in someone's life than others. Our concrete choices and actions, however, do not always need to do justice to our hierarchy of values. Kleinig now suggests that weak and strong paternalism are permissible if a particular action, born from a passing desire of a lower order, threatens to form a disproportionate burden for the more permanent, long-term goals which the relevant individual has set himself in life. In this case 'benevolent interference will constitute no violation of integrity. Indeed, if anything, it helps to preserve it' (Kleinig 1983: 68; cf. Young 1986: 76). Thus, within this conception, paternalism is motivated by the values and goals of the subject involved and not by what others consider desirable in life. His capacity for self-determination is, says Kleinig, fully respected here: there is no moralism or imposition of values.

Critics of paternalism, in other words, should not show respect in the first place for every random choice of the individual, but for his 'integrity'. According to Kleinig, this is 'closely related to wholeness – that complex of beliefs, dispositions, attitudes, goals, relations, and life plans that together constitute someone as the particular person he or she is' (Kleinig 1983: 60). The critics lay too much emphasis on immediate desires and choices and too little on the individual identity of which these desires and choices are an expression. This identity does not reveal itself merely in the current moment, but has to be seen as a continuity with a past, a present and a future, a future which must sometimes be secured in the present by a paternalistic intervention:

> Recognition of the individuality of others is not some respect for bare voluntary choices of rational choosers in an abstract sense, but for continuants whose capacities have found concrete expression in ongoing projects, life plans, etc. and who in day-to-day decision-making can be expected to work within the framework they provide. But as we know . . . we are often disposed to act in ways that are perilous to the projects and plans that are partially constitutive to our identity. Where this is so, paternalism may not be violative of integrity.
>
> (Kleinig 1983: 73)

Naturally, Kleinig declares himself to be no pronounced advocate of paternalism. It is no substitute for persuasion or education and only intended as a last resort. In order to limit its use as much as possible, he then proposes, just like Dworkin, Feinberg and Carter, a number of limiting guidelines. For example, there must be a maximal linkage with the values and goals of the subject. In addition, where it is not yet clear what these are, negative and weak paternalism are to be preferred above the positive and strong varieties. And finally, the degree to which the behaviour forms a threat to the general well-being of the individual, the size of the risk in relation to the importance of the action, and the possibility of later settling any damaging consequences, must be borne in mind (Kleinig 1983: 74–7; cf. Young 1986: 78).

CONCLUSIONS

> This monstrous impersonation, which consists in equating what X would choose if he were something he is not, or at least not yet, with what X actually seeks and chooses, is at the heart of all political theories of self-realization. It is one thing to say that I may be coerced for my own good which I am blind to see: this may, on occasion, be for my benefit; indeed it may enlarge the scope of my liberty. It is another to say that if it is my good, then I am not being coerced, for I have willed it, whether I know this or not, and am free (or 'truly' free) even while my poor earthly body and foolish mind bitterly reject it, and struggle against those who seek however benevolently to impose it, with the greatest desperation.
>
> Isaiah Berlin (1958: 133–4)

In this chapter, we have seen that people have non-optimal preferences when there are desires and accompanying gratifications which they would prefer to their current preferences, if they were familiar with these alternatives. That the latter is not the case, can have two origins. First, the parties involved can show, in Lindley's words, a lack of 'active theoretical rationality'. And second, and this perhaps helps to explain this phenomenon, the existing social structures and processes can make it impossible to a greater or lesser extent for the parties involved to come in contact with alternatives, or to be able to socialize them in the conviction that their current preferences are the only ones imaginable. The dilemma central to this chapter consists of the fact that radicals like Lukes, Connolly, Smith, Lindley and Benton, on the one hand, on the basis of the democratic and egalitarian principles they profess, want to respect the existing preference of the individual, while, on the other hand, on the basis of the contents or the way in which they came into being, consider these objectionable and want to change them. The desire to confront the existing preferences of people with alternatives in order in this way to promote their positive freedom, must therefore be weighed up against their negative freedom.

In the first sections we looked at a number of 'radical' approaches to this dilemma. However, again and again the difficulty appeared to be that (a specific group) of people within the radical conception, as a consequence of the challenged exercise of power by others or of their own inertia or lethargy, have no knowledge of the alternative ideas, styles, tastes, etc., and will also not choose to come in contact with these. The choice must therefore be made by others, on their behalf.

This choice is inevitably normative in character. After all, there are no objective criteria available for choosing. Even if one could avoid making choices charged with values and related to the content, one will have to draw a line on psychological and economic grounds between alternatives which are worth becoming familiar with, or not. It is hardly possible, like the autodidact in Sartre's *La Nausée*, to get to know civilization by beginning in the library at A. In addition, the procedural justification that people have to be aware of alternatives, because a choice is first significant when the subject really has something to choose, is based on a normative ideal image of individual autonomy.

We then saw how different authors attempted to avoid or mitigate the normative choice mentioned, where someone tries to pass his values on to another. None of the authors offered therefore a firm basis for breaking up the exercise of power (three-dimensional) described by Lukes and the inertia or lethargy emphasized by Connolly in which people can find themselves. People tried as much as possible to avoid having to make real choices about the Good Life. Out of fear of being branded a paternalist, the existing or latent preferences were taken as the starting-point. It was therefore obvious to subject the concept of paternalism to further study. This took place in the second part of the chapter.

There is paternalism, it emerged, when A exercises a control limited in time over one or more aspects of the life of B, an action which he or she justifies by referring to the needs, interests, values, the welfare or happiness of B. Paternalism is not necessarily accompanied by coercion or the restriction of negative freedom and is something different than manipulation and moralism. After this first conceptual definition, a number of representative conceptions of freedom are investigated with John Stuart Mill's objections to paternalistic interventions as the starting-point.

The rationality, or what Taylor calls the 'qualitative distinctions' of the *individual*, and not those of society, are wellnigh the absolute principle for Mill in his treatment of liberty. He is very concerned about the pressure which every society exercises on its citizens to conform to its customs, expectations, norms and values, to what it generally regards as rational. He therefore wants to protect the individual as much as possible from society. Mill has three objections against paternalism. First, on the whole individuals know better than others what is in their interest, and paternalism therefore does not contribute to the greatest good for the greatest number. Second, restricting someone's freedom of choice is a denial of his human dignity. And, third, paternalism deprives people of the possibility of developing their individuality through making choices, right or wrong. Nevertheless, Mill considers weak paternalism acceptable: someone who wants to cross a bridge which is about to collapse, may be restrained by bystanders to check that he is aware of the danger.

Feinberg's and VanDeVeer's justifications of paternalism are related to this. However, Feinberg, very much against the wishes of VanDeVeer, makes very high demands on what must be understood as voluntariness. For him, an action is first voluntary when it is a consciously chosen, non-impulsive expression of the identity of the actor. Where doubts exist as to whether this is the case, it is permissible to intervene. It will be clear that these requirements are implicitly based on an ideal of autonomy – an ideal that has been argued here is highly characteristic of Western culture. Feinberg's justification of paternalistic intervention is therefore based on what is generally held within our culture to be a worthy goal or rational. In his conception therefore the rationality of the individual is no longer central, but also that of society.

We found an explicit appeal to the latter rationality in Gerard Dworkin. He states that anticipating retrospective consent, as parents do with regard to their children, is an essential element of every justification of paternalism. He suspects that paternalism will generally be consented to (retrospectively) when, thanks to the intervention, certain of what Feinberg calls 'welfare goods' are secured. Everyone needs 'goods' like health and elementary education in order to realize his more personal life objectives, and guaranteeing these therefore shows respect for these goals and the person's capacity for self-determination.

There is a question, however, of which goods must be secured. To answer this, Dworkin appears to appeal to what ordinary people in general aim for in life – 'Given his life plans, which we are assuming are those of the average person . . . he is just like us in all relevant aspects'. What is generally regarded as rational within a particular society therefore ultimately determines when and how paternalism is turned to.

Dworkin's notion of retrospective consent, a notion which mainly evoked disbelief in VanDeVeer, was further developed by Rosemary Carter. She laid down a number of requirements for this consent: the approval may not be obtained by withholding relevant information, may not be the logical consequence of the intervention, and may not be given through a 'distortion in the subject's values, beliefs and desires'. In answering the question of under which circumstances the last two conditions are met[21], Carter too can do 'no different' than refer to rationality, the 'common sense' within a society.

This is to the dissatisfaction of VanDeVeer, Kleinig and Young. As Carter cannot indicate exactly when there is 'distortion' and only appeals to what Kleinig disapprovingly brands as 'intuitions', they reject her entire conception. In reaction to her illustration of children who grow up in dogmatic religious sects, Kleinig, for example, suggests that one could just as well claim that the world view of people who are raised by empiricist or business people is 'distorted'.

This relativism, which has already been noted in the intermediary balance, is misplaced, however. It does not necessarily have to be deduced from the fact that it is not possible to give an unshakable basis to particular values or lifestyles with the help of 'the scientific method', that it is not possible to argue rationally about normative questions (cf. Chapters 1 and 2). The plausibility of a normative theory in which the relevant values are justified will be determined by its empirical support, internal consistency and coherence with moral intuitions already available. In this context, we always speak of *plausibility* or *acceptability*, and not about truth. With their disdainful rejection of every appeal to common sense, plausibility or rationality, Kleinig, VanDeVeer and Young give the impression that they presume a theory should be based on more. However, this is a rather naïve concept of what we know, or can know.

The authors mentioned try (in vain) to avoid the situation in which they have to justify what a particular manner of life is preferable to another and may therefore be imposed or secured by paternalistic interventions. The fear of making normative judgements and sometimes to decide for others what is right or wrong, the fear therefore of running the danger of being called totalitarian, is apparently so deeply ingrained in them that they are trying to develop a purely procedural theory and are trying to take the values of the individual completely as a starting-point. Through the latter, they are degenerating, in theory, into a form of value relativism, which is untenable in its extremity. They recognize insufficiently the importance of what Taylor called (see Chapter 3) qualitative distinctions of the definition of the individual identity and they take too little into account the social character of the relevant 'horizons of significance'. If all choices in life, Taylor rightly notes, are seen as having equal value, all options lose their significance.

However, in practice their relativism is more flexible. For example, Kleinig's position is less neutral and procedural than he would have us believe. As we have seen, he suggests that people possess diverse, partly contradictory desires, which have a deviating status within someone's central life plan, and that weak and strong paternalism are permissible when transitory, lower-order desires threaten this life plan. Paternalism, postulates Kleinig, is motivated within this conception by the values and goals *of* the relevant subject and not by what others hold to be worth aspiring to in life. His capacity to self-determination is here therefore, in Kleinig's view, fully respected, there is no question of imposing values or moralism.

Richard Arneson has rightly called this claim 'false or misleading'. In his review of Kleinig's *Paternalism*, he writes, among other things:

> in some cases the liberal ideal is itself an alien value. If we impose paternalistically on people in order to weld the past, present, and future of each person into some semblance of unified, integrated aims, we will be imposing on some persons an ideal of cohesion they themselves do not share.
>
> (Arneson 1985: 957; cf. Blokland 1988)

Young, too, properly regarded, imposes an ideal of autonomy on people, an ideal of which continuity and coherence are important elements. This is very defensible, but it must be realized that this defence, as Lukes and Connolly note, is in the nature of things 'essentially contestable' in character.

A difficulty of another order with the justifications of paternalism which were developed by Kleinig, Young and, previously, Taylor, is that they draw an insufficient distinction between the political and the individual level. Mill, Feinberg, VanDeVeer and Dworkin, as we have seen, speak primarily of the paternalism of the state with regard to its citizens. That is also the reason for Mill's warning that interventions of society are necessarily based on general considerations, which are incorrect or, in precisely this case, are not applicable. That explains his stance that it is therefore better, taken on the whole and looked at utilitarianly, to assume that the individual knows best what is good for him. Kleinig, Young and Taylor rightly state that people sometimes bring their higher-order goals in danger by surrendering 'unwillingly' to desires of a lower order, and that paternalism in these cases can also be considered acceptable by the parties involved. However, the question is whether there is a task for the state here too. Someone who is tormented by 'weakness of will', neuroses, psychoses, etc., has to go to a psychiatrist, *not* to a political scientist, and certainly not to a politician.

To recapitulate. The second dimension of the emancipation dilemma can be interrupted if others make the choice *for* the subject to come in contact with alternative ideas, tastes, styles. This choice is made within the context of a particular *Weltanschauung* and is inevitably of a normative character. The acceptability of the relevant *Weltanschauung* is determined by its internal consistency, coherence with already living intuitions, and empirical support. It is ultimately a question of plausibility, not of truth. The instruments for breaking through the dilemma vary from the 'democratic ideological struggle' to which Benton refers, to the change in the social structures advocated by Lindley. Changing the socialization structures for people who do not yet have any preferences, is not a paternalistic intervention, but the implementation of a different form of social schooling and education. Where this change takes place against people's wishes, who are also formed by it, there is indirect, strong paternalism. Paternalism is a 'bet' on consent in the future. A bet or expectation which is justified by referring to the findings of people who are familiar with the state to be preferred, according to the paternalist, and who have not been exposed to what are, according to general criteria, unacceptable forms of influence, such as manipulation and brainwashing.

6   Final balance and synthesis
Freedom and cultural politics

INTRODUCTION

In the general introduction we set ourselves two main objectives for this study. The first broad intention was to make explicit and evaluate a number of important assumptions of contemporary Western thought about freedom. On the basis of this, it would also be attempted to formulate a somewhat consistent and coherent conception of freedom. The second, more specific, goal was to contribute to the analysis of the so-called emancipation dilemma. The question here was mainly how governments and other institutions can promote the development of individual autonomy, without the negative freedom of the citizen being unacceptably impaired. In this chapter, it will be attempted to arrive at a synthesis of the insights collected for these goals. It will also be attempted, in general theoretical terms, to instigate a relationship between the conception of freedom developed here and the subject of cultural politics. In the final chapter, cultural policy will be examined more concretely.

POSITIVE AND NEGATIVE FREEDOM

As starting-point for the discussion in this book, the two conceptions of freedom formulated by Isaiah Berlin were examined in Chapter 2. He defines negative freedom as the realm in which someone, unimpeded by the deliberate interventions of others, can do or be that which lies within his capacity. The greater this private realm, the bigger his negative freedom.

The negative conception of freedom forms the centre of Western liberal ideas. Liberalism is mainly an argument about where the borders of the private realm are to be found, and how these can best be protected. For Berlin, the justification of these conceptions of freedom lay mainly in the value of pluralism, a product of the process of rationalization which can be seen in Western civilization since classical times and Christianity. This pluralism boils down to the recognition of the impossibility of finding a defence convincing for everybody of objective, universal and eternal values, and to the insight that there are many significant, but also conflicting, ideals which must inevitably be balanced up against each other. Together, these principles stimulate and justify the desire that people be left a private realm in which they can profess their own truth.

The positive conception of freedom refers to the answer to the question of who or what can determine what someone does, or is. Positive freedom is the capacity to direct independently, be in control of, one's own life. According to Berlin, this conception arises from the desire to be able to choose for oneself, and to be able to justify the choices made, by referring to one's own identity and objectives. Positive freedom is therefore based on the desire to be someone and not just an arbitrary part of the mass, someone who is responsible for his or her deeds, and not a plaything of external forces and powers.

In Chapter 2, it was pointed out that, within his positive conception, Berlin brought a number of aspects of freedom under one heading, which it would have been better to distinguish. In the first place, a distinction could be made between *self-determination* and *self-realization*. The first occurs when someone's actions are based on his own choices, which are an expression of his identity. Self-realization occurs when someone develops his capacities, talents or skills and, in doing so, is 'making the best of himself'. However, both dimensions are strongly related. It is first possible to speak of self-realization when one has taken control of one's life to some extent, and the latter is only possible when one has developed somewhat. There is something to be said, therefore, as Berlin has done, for bringing these two aspects of positive freedom into a single conception.

However, it is different with the individual and collective dimension of the self-determination ideal. One can attempt to gain control of one's own strictly private life (in so far as this can be demarcated), and one can attempt to increase the grip on one's own life, by defining the collective action together with others.

Berlin has not always distinguished these two levels or dimensions clearly from each other. There is naturally a contradiction between negative and positive freedom if the latter value is taken to mean 'political democracy' or 'self-determination'. The questions 'Who or what governs me?' and 'To what extent does the state intervene in my private realm?' are indeed, as Berlin argues, logically different. Positive freedom on a collective level can therefore mean a very limited negative freedom on an individual level: in a democracy, the government can interfere far more profoundly in the private life of its citizens than in an autocracy. Equally, there is a contradiction between the two conceptions of freedom when possible inner constraints on someone's positive freedom are linked to social and metaphysical entities like 'class', 'people' and 'general will'. On a purely individual level, however, the desire to possess a private realm in which one can go one's own way undisturbed by others, and the desire to autonomously direct one's own life, are in line.

On the basis of the ideas of Harry Frankfurt, Charles Taylor, Benjamin

Barber, Robert Young, Bruno Bettelheim, Richard Lindley, John Benson, Gerald Dworkin and Joel Feinberg, the positive conception of freedom was further elaborated in Chapter 3. This happened on an individual level. We saw that the various definitions of autonomy, unlike what the authors concerned often wanted us to believe, did not conflict insurmountably with each other. It was mainly a question of placing different emphases. Tensions can exist between these various points of emphasis (see the Introduction to Chapter 3). However, the attempt to abolish these, by emphasizing only one facet of freedom, was rejected. This would mean an unnecessary and undesirable impoverishment of the concept of freedom. In addition, it would be an expression of the ontological principle, not held here, that every concept has a single correct unambiguous meaning, which can be sharply demarcated from other concepts.

Taken on the whole, the authors mentioned turned out to draw first a connection between autonomy and *identification*: only actions with which one can identify are perceived as 'free' and every experience of freedom therefore presupposes having an identity. Positive freedom demands, furthermore, that the party concerned can postpone or renounce the gratification of his immediate desires. In this way, he has the opportunity to evaluate which of these desires and longings are essential or not in his life and can therefore be regarded as an expression of his identity. Autonomous action is therefore *intentional* in character: one is aware of one's motives (self-knowledge or *self-consciousness* is thus required), evaluates these against the background of one's 'deeper' or central values (for which a certain degree of *rationality* is needed), and only then embarks upon well-considered action. Autonomous behaviour is therefore not impulsive, is not based completely on learned habits and conventions, or on instincts and drives.

Despite the desired self-reflection, however, Bergmann rightly emphasizes, it cannot be the intention that an autonomous personality is distinguished by a permanent, cramped, over-conscious and neurotic wrestling with constantly upsurging, spontaneous feelings and emotions. Freedom is also experienced – or perhaps especially – as light, effortless and harmonious. A more or less developed *life plan* is important, but life should therefore not degenerate into, as John Lennon once put it, 'what happens to you while you're busy making other plans' ('Beautiful Boy' 1979). This experience of freedom, 'a quiet acting out of inner convictions', is, says Bettelheim, characteristic of a balanced, integrated personality. Will-power, an element of what Lindley called *conative autonomy*, is closely related to this. After all, it demands perseverance to be able to preserve one's own integrity under difficult circumstances. Willpower is also needed to be able to meet another requirement of autonomy: *active theoretical rationality*. The independent search for alternative values, ideas and knowledge requires one to dare to question the existing and learned conventions and to be able to withstand the pressure from one's surroundings not to do this. This quest for alternatives is desirable, as in this way the chance of one giving a direction to one's life which does not do justice to one's identity or talents, and which one would not choose if one had been aware of the other possibilities, is reduced.

The insight that the ability to doubt, to ask oneself questions, is a condition for positive freedom, however, must remain attached to the awareness that not *everything* can be discussed. There should always be something left which can serve as a starting-point for an evaluation or debate. In this context, Feinberg points out that 'critical thinking' also boils down to the *application* of already accepted principles: principles not (yet) accepted are checked against this and on the basis of this decisions are taken and judgements made. Rational reflection therefore requires that one has a frame of reference. This is usually formed by the existing civilization. If one does not master these to some extent, then a process of thinking or choice can never get under way. In a comparable manner, Taylor pointed out that the development of an identity forms a *dialogical* process and inevitably takes place against a *horizon of qualitative distinctions*. These latter standards are not completely decreed by the individual himself, but are also provided by the society and the cultural tradition it forms.

In short, the independence of spirit required of autonomous personalities should therefore not be exaggerated – neither in the field of empirical knowledge, nor in the field of ethics. Dworkin and Benson also point out that this would mean a denial of both the social essence of man and that of ethics. It is possible to demand that someone decides as independently as possible whether he wants to accept the existing values and conventions: all the more so, as ethics first really acquires significance when one has not just assumed the conclusions, but has also lived through its justification.

On the basis of the above definitions, it was stated at the end of the third chapter that positive freedom is a broader concept than its negative counterpart, and partly contains this conception. The latter, because someone who has not a personal realm within which he can do or be that, undisturbed by others, which lies within his capacity, can hardly be master of his own life. There are three reasons why the positive conception is broader.

First, because it also includes a notion of 'self-realization'. People must first have developed their talents and capacities somewhat, if they want to take their life in their own hands, independent of others. Second, because it is not only an 'inter', but also an 'intra' human concept. Ultimately, attempts to be in control of one's own life can be frustrated not only by external, but also by inner, inhibitions. And third, because the question of to what extent someone is autonomous, cannot be answered at a single moment, but only over a certain duration of time. In a single glance it is possible to see whether someone has been shackled, which is impossible for the questions of whether he is master of his own life and whether this existence is an expression of his identity.

A basic difference which lies at the root of these three reasons is that negative freedom, in Taylor's terminology, forms an *opportunity*, and positive freedom, an *exercise concept*. Someone who chooses to leave unexploited all the opportunities offered him by life and is disturbed by no one in this passivity, must (in the negative sense) be qualified as a free person. With negative freedom, it is only a matter of the presence of doors which could possibly be opened; it is not important whether one is aware of the existence of these, or really opens them.

As we have seen, more is required for autonomy: one may actively guide one's life: in the first place, by looking independently for alternative ideas, values, tastes, styles, etc. Autonomy has a difficult relation to the thoughtless following of paths paved by others. In addition, it is necessary to constantly evaluate which position one's immediate wishes occupy in one's life. And finally, it is necessary to suppress feelings which are in conflict with central values and goals in life and which therefore undermine one's identity. Someone who in the course of their life is only moved forward at any moment by any random drive or urge, can therefore not be called an autonomous being.

If man is thus characterized as a 'doer', as a being that is looking for the borders of his possibilities, then it is obvious that one will distinguish more obstacles than within a conception, where an individual who has fallen completely into lethargy is also characterized as a free person. Properly regarded, after all, within the last mentioned negative conception, one can only be confronted by external obstacles. With regard to the development of talents, to the formation and implementation of a life plan, it is a different case. Here, one can also be impeded by inner, psychic obstacles such as neuroses and psychoses, and by the lack of material and non-material aids. For example, being raised in an environment poor in culture means a lack of the non-material conditions indispensable for positive freedom. One can, to a greater or lesser extent, hold others responsible for this lack or this obstacle to freedom. This depends on the implicitly or explicitly held vision of man and society. The more one regards people as the product of social structures and processes, and the more one considers these as capable of being made or influenced, the sooner one will see those lacking in material and non-material aids, with limited freedom, as the victim of coercion.

In the *fourth chapter*, the distinction between the two conceptions was further developed. This was done by examining a number of ideal–typical responses for the positive conception, to the question of how society must be organized to make the realization of both ideals of freedom possible. If therefore the individual was formerly central, here attention was shifted to his relations to others.

It was begun with MacCallum's thesis that every meaningful statement on political freedom was triadic in nature. According to him, it must always be possible to distinguish an actor, a goal or possibility of choices, and an eventual impediment. On the basis of this, we saw that positive and negative freedom differ mainly in the emphasis which they lay within the relevant triad. Advocates of the positive conception emphasize the availability of real possibilities of choice, defenders of the negative the absence of (external) impediments.

A deviating view of man and society is at the basis of this difference. Within the negative conception, there is generally more faith in the capacity of the individual to develop under his own power and to have available the alternative choices necessary for autonomy. The social environment is seen as a potential impediment rather than as a stimulus for this development. This concept of freedom is therefore ultimately intended as a defensive wall against other people, against a society and the state, and is therefore anti-social in character.

Within the positive conception, man is seen much more as a social being, who can first develop his individuality in interaction with his environment. Instead of mechanistic or atomistic, as in the negative conception, here the image of society is organismic or holistic (on the understanding that the conviction that society is more than the sum of its parts does not necessarily have to be accompanied by the expectation that this is of a metaphysical nature). Because one regards the individual more in his relation to society, understands him to be more a part of an 'ensemble' of social relations, those obstacles to individual development which can be thrown up by social structures and processes, obstacles which to a greater or lesser extent are created or maintained by others, are borne more in mind. All the more so as advocates of the positive conception of freedom generally regard the meeting of the material and cultural conditions required for autonomy as more or less a matter of course or even as a right, they distinguish a longer list with possible impediments of individual freedom than the defenders of the negative conception.

In the terms of Feinberg, these 'negative, external impediments' are also counted among these possible obstacles. Lukes, MacPherson, Norman and Taylor mention here, among other things: a lack of material means of existence; absence of means of work, of tools to employ and develop one's capacities; ignorance with regard to relevant options, or an unreasonable limitation of someone's opportunities of choice; and a lack of formal and informal education through which people are taught to distinguish alternatives, to articulate and evaluate. In Chapter 5, the idea that social structures and processes can also exercise pressure and be responsible for these external inhibitions on the basis of the thought of Lukes, Connolly, Benton, Smith and Lindley was further developed.

In Chapter 2, we saw that Berlin also recognized that the poverty or weakness of certain people could plausibly be explained by existing social structures which are created or maintained by others. He therefore considered it plausible to regard this poverty as a limitation of the *negative* freedom of the parties concerned. Berlin's thesis that it is possible to justify social facilities, interventions in the market, and also socialism, with an appeal to negative freedom, is logically tenable, if he drops the distinction between freedom and its conditions. However, he repeatedly rejects this. This justification, considering the image of man and society is generally linked to the negative conception, is also implausible in practice.

That the distinction between freedom and its conditions within the positive conception is difficult to make, can be seen, for example, from the theories of MacPherson and Norman. More material welfare and a better education here enlarge the possibilities of being master of one's own life. However, this is not to say that people in a prosperous dictatorship are free. Properly regarded, the distinction only has any plausibility within the negative conception. After all, material welfare does not immediately have anything to do with the degree to which people are left alone by others. Berlin's remark that the negative conception is the most fundamental form of freedom can also be understood in this light: 'The fundamental sense of freedom is freedom from chains, from imprisonment, from enslavement by others. The rest is extension of this sense, or else metaphor' (Berlin 1969: lvi). Classical liberal civil rights such as freedom of opinion, assembly and association are a concrete version of this. These are aspects of freedom which, with some goodwill, can be seen separately from the question of whether one has also developed an opinion to express, which is worthwhile meeting about with others.

THE EMANCIPATION DILEMMA

If the two conceptions of freedom are now brought together on an individual and social level, then the contours of the emancipation dilemma become visible. It appeared, on the one hand, that people had to search autonomously for alternatives in order to be able, in this fashion, to get a perspective on the culture, values, conventions and knowledge in which they grew, and to transcend them. On the other hand, it became clear that this personal quest can first succeed when one has a point of departure, frame of reference, or 'horizon of qualitative distinctions'. Self-determination and self-realization therefore demand that individuals first absorb a culture. The latter often happens playfully, unconsciously and from free will, but is also accompanied by education and socialization, by learning and hard work.

In brief, on the one hand, people are always the product or even the victim of their culture, of the community bound in time and place in which they live, and it demands an active theoretical rationality to overcome the limitations of their cultural background. On the other hand, however, the same culture is the indispensable source of the necessary non-material and material conditions of individual autonomy. This ever-present tension between negative and positive freedom (and the conditions for it), between individual and society, was characterized as the first dimension of the emancipation dilemma. This dilemma cannot be solved. One can only attempt to find a balance between its two elements, equally valuable or plausible.

If one wants to bring about change in existing preferences, not regarded as optimal or unacceptable, one runs up against an additional question, that was characterized as the second dimension of the emancipation dilemma. If the first dimension therefore refers to an individuality still to be developed with personal preferences, in the second dimension, naturally only analytically to be distinguished from the first, it is a question of already formed preferences. 'Radicals' like Connolly, Lukes, Benton, Smith and Lindley subscribe to the idea that the values, goals, desires and preferences of the individual are, to an important extent, the product of the social interactions with one's environment. The authenticity, and thus the status of individual preferences, can therefore be put somewhat into perspective. They can state that the individual has developed preferences, which he himself experiences as valuable and original, but which are in fact the arbitrary, if not unacceptable product of the existing social structures and processes. These preferences cannot be optimal here: there are wishes and accompanying gratifications which the individual would prefer to his current preferences, if he was familiar with these alternatives.

That the latter is not the case can have two causes. First, the parties concerned can lack the readiness required for autonomy to go in search of alternative values, to study whether that which has been accepted up to now, is really, true, good or beautiful. Second, and perhaps partly explanatory of this deficiency, the existing social structures and processes play a role. These make it more or less impossible for the parties involved to come in contact with alternatives or can cause the conviction to grow that their present preferences are the only ones possible.

As radicals are generally democratic and egalitarian in their inspiration, they wrestle with a dilemma with regard to the regretted preferences. This consists of the following: on the one hand, on the basis of the democratic principles subscribed to they want to respect the existing individual preferences, while, on the other hand, on the basis of the content or the manner in which they have come into being, they consider these objectionable and want to change them. On the one hand, therefore, they assume on the basis of the negative conception, that people should be treated as responsible beings, as mature citizens who are capable of choosing autonomously or developing preferences and should not be patronized by others. However, on the other hand, they refuse to assume entirely existing preferences. This has two disadvantages. In the first place, one is so uncritical with regard to the way these preferences have come into being and, in the second place, in this case one can never create the situation with which, if the people concerned were familiar, they would choose rather than the existing one. The question is once again how this preferable situation can be created, without the negative freedom of the individual being unacceptably limited.

The greatest difficulty for the radicals is that the people whose preferences are regretted, have, by definition, no knowledge of the alternative ideas, values, tastes, etc. The decision to actually have contact with them, must therefore of necessity be taken by others. This will be based on a normative ideal. The conviction that a choice, consciously taken on the basis of a reasonable knowledge of the alternatives, is more valuable than one which forms the non-arbitrary product of the existing social constellation is, after all, also based on an ideal image of individual autonomy.

Diverse methods for creating the preferable situation mentioned are imaginable. In the first place, as Lindley, among others, proposes, the social structures can be changed. There is also enough basis for this. For far too many people in our Western liberal democracies, the course of life is fixed as a consequence of the simple fact that they come from the lower social strata, for example: they probably have a shorter and inferior education than others, they will carry out less rewarding and less interesting work, hardly participate if at all in cultural activities, not participate in democratic decision-making, and so on. Too many people are still the victims of a socio-economic structure, which either condemns them to too much of, what Gorz calls heteronomous work, or socially marginalizes them in a workless or 'unsuitable for work' existence. Too many people are inhibited in their development by an educational system which reproduces the existing cultural and economic inequalities and which, to a high degree, only develops those limited talents which can be cashed in on the labour market. The capacity for critical thought, for questioning conventions and habits, is stimulated in too few people. The courage to not conform, to deviate from the image of a normal, happy life shaped by commerce and the mass media is encouraged in too few people. Too many people have too few possibilities to participate in the political decision-making process, to develop their capacity for self-management and exercise influence on the development of the society of which they are a part.

Thanks to conclusive socio-scientific research this effect of the existing social structures is now considered familiar. The people in strategic positions who are more or less able, alone or together with others, to initiate change in this arrangement, but nevertheless fail to do so, can therefore be considered partly responsible for the existing social inequality in the chance to develop one's talents (cf. Lukes' considerations on the basis of the debate between Poulantzas and Miliband on determinism and voluntarism in Chapter 5).

Changing social structures is a form of paternalism when this emphatically goes against the preferences of the citizens partly generated by these structures. The fewer already formed preferences there are, the more people will have to speak of an adaptation of socialization structures. The latter case thus refers to the first dimension of the emancipation dilemma, the former (changing structures against the will of the citizens) to the second dimension.

It could now be argued that people are, to an important extent, always the product of their social environment, and that it is therefore more a question of how they should be socialized than of how this can be justified. There is a threat of totalitarianism when politicians see in this reasoning a free hand to involve themselves without bounds in the formation and communication of values. Nevertheless, one should take into account the socio-logical fact that people are social beings. It is undesirable that people, out of fear of the accusation of totalitarian thinking, leave cultural formation as a matter of course completely to 'the free play of social, in this case economic, forces', and not to democratically accountable institutions such as govern-ment, parliament, political parties, educational institutions and the press.

Another method for bringing people into contact with the unknown alternatives, alternatives which they will after this not want to do without, is formed by what Benton entitled the 'democratic ideological struggle'. The attempt to convince others of the value of alternative ideas, approaches and goals, the development of counter-preferences, is, in a democracy, naturally the most important, most desirable manner, of solving the emancipation dilemma. Representative bodies, political parties, action and pressure groups, churches, trade unions, and all other possible forms of social rela-tions and societies, the media, education, science, literature and the arts, form the podia on which this 'struggle' is waged. This is done with hard and soft means. For example, publishing a book, which people can decide for themselves whether they want to buy and also read, is a less hard method of conviction than the duty generally imposed on Western public broadcasters to devote a certain part of their broadcasting time to 'culture and informa-tion'. The latter instrument is again less far-reaching than determining which knowledge, ideas and views children are confronted with during their school time. Are they to be prepared for the labour market, or also for life?

Changing the social structures and the waging of a democratic political 'struggle' merge where it emerges that a real presentation and confrontation of deviating ideas can only be guaranteed or created by changing the struc-tures. It is evident that certain institutions and bodies give more space to this than others. For example, commercial broadcasters, by definition, for mar-ket reasons, appeal to the lowest common denominator, to that with which the viewer and listener is already familiar. They are consequently less puri-form than public broadcasters like the BBC and therefore provide less opportunity for developing individual autonomy.

The harder the means, the stronger one will oppose the existing prefer-ences and the more there will be paternalism. The other way round, the less already-fixed preferences there are, the sooner it will be necessary to speak of socialization. Socialization and paternalism, and the first and second dimension of the emancipation dilemma, are therefore, in short, on a single sliding scale.

PATERNALISM AND RATIONALISM

In Chapter 5, paternalism was defined as control, limited in time, of one or more aspects of someone's life, which is justified by referring to his welfare, happiness, needs, interests or values. Paternalism thus plays, to a greater or lesser extent, a role in solving the second dimension of the emancipation dilemma. This is also to the displeasure of the radicals. Although they generally add some qualifications, they subscribe to the main outlines of the three objections to paternalistic interventions formulated by John Stuart Mill.

First, in general, individuals know better than others what is in their interest. All the more since interventions must necessarily be based on generalized considerations, paternalism therefore seldom contributes to general welfare. Second, the restriction of someone's freedom of choice is an impingement on his human dignity. In this sense, Berlin writes: 'paternalism is despotic . . . because it is an insult to my conception of myself as a human being, determined to make my own life in accordance with my own . . . purposes' (Berlin 1958: 157; see Chapter 2). And third, paternalism deprives people of the possibility of developing their individuality through making correct and incorrect choices. An absolute ban on paternalism, however, was undesirable where, in that case, it was necessary to accept completely the existing preferences, not considered optimal.

The essence of paternalism, suggested Dworkin and Carter, among others, is that retrospective agreement is anticipated. It is assumed that the parties involved do not have the necessary cognitive and evaluative skills to take a correct decision for their welfare. But it is also expected that when these capacities are available at a later date, he or she will still agree with the intervention. If one leaves out the cases where, for instance, someone harms himself in a manner emphasized by Young and Kleinig, one thus confines oneself to paternalism as a means of solving the emancipation dilemma, then it could be stated that the parties involved are impeded by the inner obstacle, 'ignorance'. It is assumed, therefore, along with Connolly, Lukes and J. S. Mill, that someone can first judge his own interests when he has experienced the relevant options. In the second chapter, however, we have seen to what the identification of this sort of impediment can lead.

We saw here, on the basis of Berlin's 'Two concepts', that in a number of cases a first step en route to totalitarianism has been taken when a division has been made between, on the one hand, a 'lower', 'heteronomous' or 'empirical' self and, on the other hand, a 'higher', really free, 'rational' or 'autonomous' self. In the next step, this 'real' self is identified with a social or semi-metaphysical entity which transcends the individual. Examples would be a church, race, nation, class, party, culture, or vaguer quantities such as 'the general will', the 'enlightened forces in society' and 'history'. On the basis of this authority, it was then possible to deny or suppress, in the name of freedom, desires and goals unacceptable to the rulers and ascribed to a lower nature. This was justified by appealing to the 'real' or 'rational' self which, once freed from the grip of irrational passions and instincts, and rescued from former ignorance, would sanction the coercion in retrospect that had made the ultimate enlightened state of freedom possible. 'This monstrous impersonation', Berlin then states, 'which consists in equating what X would choose if he were something he is not, or at least not yet, with what X actually seeks and chooses, is at the heart of all political theories of self-realization' (Berlin 1958: 133). He warned against a rationalistic perversion of the positive conception of freedom, against the historical and psychological, but not logically explicable linkage of freedom with value cognitivism and monism.

Despite numerous interpretations, Berlin did not deny that people could be impeded by inner inhibitions (see Chapter 2). Incorrectly, all the same, he did not want to conclude from this that the identifying of this sort of obstacle implies that 'deeper' or 'second-order' objectives of a 'higher' self exist, whose realization is frustrated by the relevant impediments. The threat of despotism first arises when these 'more essential' objectives are linked to a social or metaphysical authority assumed to be knowable, an authority which is credited with a monopoly of knowledge in the field of the true, the beautiful and the good. The appeal to rationality, which is made by the advocates dealt with here, of the positive conception of freedom, turned out to be of a completely different order, however. They are concerned with what could be called 'normality' or 'argued common sense'. They appeal to that which is experienced by people who can judge, as generally valuable or as an adequate, usable description of reality. In this, they do not deviate from Berlin: he, too, makes extensive use of this.

In this way, we saw (cf. Chapter 4) that Berlin refuses to qualify as 'free' people who adjust to too great an extent their wishes and objectives to the possibilities offered by their situation, or who can free themselves from earthy, relatively simple, frustratable desires and withdraw into an 'inner citadel' considered superior. He inevitably appeals here to that which is generally regarded in our Western cultures as normal, rational or reasonable to pursue in life. Berlin makes a similar appeal when he tries to determine what the scale of someone's freedom depends on. Just like Taylor, Feinberg, Norman, and Benn and Weinstein, he sees this growing with the number of 'meaningful' choice possibilities. What must be understood by this, he allows partly to be determined by 'the general sentiment' in the relevant society. We find a reference to this, finally, in Berlin's conception of 'coercion'. Berlin originally takes the stance that here there is exclusively a resolute, direct limitation of someone's freedom by *other people*. However, he later adds to this that ultimately the socio-economic theory determines whether this is considered the case. It is possible to make plausible, however, that certain social structures created or maintained by others are the cause of poverty or weakness, and that others therefore exercise coercion on one in an indirect, anonymous manner. The cases in which there is coercion thus depend on what is regarded as plausible, and as rational, within a specific community.

It would constantly appear that notions of 'rationality' are indispensable to keep the range of the various definitions of freedom under control. If this does not happen then, in their one-sidedness, these often lose all plausibility. This must therefore also be the critique of all those authors who think that they have grasped the essence of freedom with a single catchy formula. The

feverish search for a single correct meaning of 'freedom', which characterizes many theoreticians, seems an expression of the implicit ontological principle that there is a knowable, rational order in the cosmos in which all
concepts have an exactly defined place (cf. Chapter 1).

Being able to *identify* with one's acts or position is therefore not a sufficient condition of freedom, as this criterion means that the slave who covers
his chains with flowers can qualify himself as a free man. Equally, *multiple
choice alternatives* as such do not simply cause individual autonomy to rise.
It was argued in Chapter 4, that they can destroy or reduce the value of the
old ones, and lead to disorientation and an undermining of the creativity
closely related to freedom. And individual autonomy does not rise equally
with the *removal of external obstacles*. At a particular moment there is only
an atomistic social vacuum in which no single being can reach maturity.

Nor does freedom mean the complete *absence of inner impediments*. It
can be stated that freedom is actually accompanied by the conquest of this,
and that our experience of freedom is greater the higher the impediments
become. Inner impediments are also necessary to be able to come up with
the tranquillity and distance for weighing up one's own immediate desires
and wishes against one's mainly long-term projects. However, it should not
be deduced from this that if we want to promote the freedom of the individual it would be a good idea to enlarge without limit the number of obstacles.
Freedom is more than the absence of impediments or the presence of choice
alternatives, but this does not mean that these have become unimportant.

Finally, freedom does not consist just of *choosing between options*, but
also of the *creation* of them. But the latter should not be taken too literally
either. The constantly having to create and choose between new possibilities,
linked to the existentialist idea that at every moment we can decide to be
someone else (see Chapter 3), would become a rather tiring business, and
actually conflicts with the social view of man constructed by current human
sciences. However, to add nuances, it is apt: our experience of freedom is
greatest when the paths we take have not yet been blazed by others, and we
do not regard someone whose behaviour is completely predictable as a
model of human freedom, but rather as a prisoner of his own personality.

The rejection of every form of determinism, and the emphasizing of the
idea that people ultimately choose their values themselves, is also ethically
and politically important because it places responsibility for our action
where it belongs: with the individual. Coercion too, the threat of sanctions,
does not therefore make someone unfree either. It merely means that the
costs of certain alternatives are raised. To what extent this existentialist principle must be implemented in practice, is once again a question of balancing,
of rationality. The question is, then, to what extent someone is capable of
exercising influence, whether together with others or not, on the course of
events (cf. Chapter 5). However, it does no harm as a principle; it prevents
people avoiding their own responsibilities too easily.

In justifying paternalism, too, it was argued in Chapter 5, one inevitably refers to that which people within a particular culture generally consider worthy, reasonable or normal. It is not the rationality or the 'qualitative distinctions' of the parties involved which are always to the fore, as the majority of the authors discussed here desired, but those of the relevant civilization or society. If someone shows behaviour which deviates from what general criteria consider rational, therefore, then intervention is considered justifiable. This is the case when people endanger their long-term goals, their life plan by surrendering 'unwillingly' to passing wishes and desires of a lower order. Intervention is also considered permissible when individuals do not act completely 'willingly' – thus, when their behaviour is not a consciously chosen, well-considered, non-impulsive expression of individual identity – and, finally, when people have insufficient attention for the importance of their 'welfare goods': that is, goods such as health and basic education which everyone needs to realize personal life goals. All these (related) cases refer to the Western ideal of autonomy which, in general, is considered worth pursuing as a matter of course. As we have seen, continuity, balance, self-development, independence, rationality and intentionality are important elements of this ideal.

CULTURE AND AUTONOMY

> Why do we not just leave those people be who find happiness and pleasure in chicken-breeding or racing pigeons, in bicycle racing and football competitions, in tending the garden or fishing? Why, if it makes them feel good? Why should we violently and expensively try, with great difficulty, to give them something they have no use for and which they do not miss. What are we actually doing?[1]

The interpretation given in this book to the concept of autonomy is related to the *Bildung* conception of 'culture'.[2] In this conception, culture is not a purely descriptive, sociological or anthropological term, but also an evaluative one. Raymond Williams claims that this refers to an intellectual, spiritual and aesthetic developmental process to an undetermined ideal (Williams 1961: 57ff.; 1976: 87ff.).

This view of culture can be traced back to the classical Greek ideal of education (*paideia*), an ideal which since then has been a constant element of Western civilization, although it has met with a better reception in some eras than others (cf. Lemaire 1976; Bird 1976). During the Renaissance, in particular, it had much support, which was expressed in the introduction of the concepts of 'civilization' and 'culture'. The nineteenth-century bourgeoisie also cherished this ideal of personality formation, they even used it to legitimize its social position. Within socialism, it was propagated by a number of tendencies which emphasized the cultural emancipation of the working class, even if one tried, usually without much success, to give it a 'socialistic' interpretation. In the current era, its influence seems to be waning. It is quickly associated with 'bourgeois'. However, although the relevant ideal may have functioned for a while as a legitimization of the bourgeoisie, it also forms, writes the philosopher Mooij, 'the continuation of old humanistic ideals, and is as such intimately connected with the history of our civilization in the general sense' (Mooij 1987: 104).

Nevertheless, it is obvious that the content of the *Bildung*, or civilization ideal, has changed in the course of time. For example, nowadays there is a less one-sided connection made, as in the eighteenth and nineteenth century, between knowledge of the classics and personal development. Other sources and forms of knowledge are considered an expression of, and a means to, the latter. Nor is it expected, as a matter of course, that people with a bigger cultural baggage will also be morally superior. In this context, George Steiner has often pointed out that numerous camp executioners in Nazi Germany were in cultural terms extremely *gebildet* (Steiner 1967).[3] Finally, the current ideal of civilization will be more open than in former times. In this context, the historian Kossmann states:

> It is obvious that an ideal of civilization in the current situation cannot be a homogeneous, coercive and prescribed pattern of ethical and aesthetic norms and of fixed erudition. It will sooner take on the form of an inventory of possible ethical and aesthetic norms, of possible cultural goals, once realized in the history of humanity. The present ideal of civilization is not prescriptive but descriptive, it is not closed, but open.
>
> (Kossmann 1985: 23)

As stated, the ideals of autonomy and *Bildung* have many points of contact. This is already clear from the foregoing. Individuals who possess more 'culture' or 'civilization' – that is, people who are familiar with more ways in which one can regard life – have generally also a greater chance of an autonomous existence. Because they are familiar with alternative ideas, values, attitudes, tastes, styles and so on, they are, after all, in a better position to make real choices in life, choices which are therefore not determined by ignorance, prejudice or habit. In addition, we have seen that people must develop their faculties to some extent if they are really going to take control of their own lives. Participation in cultural activities can play a major role in this. In short, culture forms an extremely important condition of positive freedom. However, it is not a sufficient condition. This book has shown that positive freedom also requires, among other things, a certain degree of negative freedom, rationality, self-control, self-knowledge and willpower. Nevertheless, by disseminating culture one also increases the possibility of individual autonomy.

A 'cultural dissemination policy' is generally understood to be the attempt by governments and other institutions to have more people participate in activities in the field of arts and letters. The positive freedom of the individual, however, is dependent on his knowledge of culture in general. Science and philosophy, for example, form equally important sources and expressions of individual autonomy. Nevertheless, art and literature especially can have an emancipatory effect. Both are an 'intensified' reflection and image of human existence. Or, it can also be stated, both chiefly form (alongside science and philosophy) the material reflection of the *Bildung* conception of culture. Actual participation in cultural activities can therefore help people to realize their talents and, in particular, artwork can provide alternative insights into life, which increase the chance of positive freedom.

With regard to literature especially, it can be stated, writes Mooij, that in certain cases it 'broadens, liberates, wrings free, opposes rigidity; that it utters "redemptive words"' (Mooij 1987: 184). This is because, in the first place, literary works are a stimulus to the imagination. They offer people the possibility of freeing themselves from their generally constrained circumstances and placing themselves in strange situations and attitudes to life. (Mooij, incidentally, in contrast to Steiner, does not consider it impossible that more understanding and sympathy for others are the result of this.) In addition, literature can show people the familiar in a new way. Together, these two possible effects can create the critical function of literature: 'More understanding for the unknown and a surprising view of the familiar can lead to less "understanding" of the familiar. The obvious acceptance of what is familiar to us, can disappear. A form of critique of the world or of society has therefore been created' (Mooij 1987: 181). Literature can therefore help people to free themselves, to liberate themselves from old forms and ideas.

The philosopher Doorman expects very much, perhaps too much, from participation in activities in the field of the arts. He suspects that people develop in this way a 'cultural erudition', which consists of, among other things, the capacity of empathy, imagination, imaginative sympathy for cultural developments, and the capacity to argue. According to Doorman, this erudition is necessary to solve a number of major social problems with which we will be confronted in the near future. Among these problems he includes, among others, 'moral problems through advancing technical developments' and a 'sharpening of the world contradictions between rich and poor' (Doorman 1990). A motive for specifically disseminating knowledge of arts and letters is, for him, the conviction '"that a lively contact with the various arts" could bring about that citizens have an extensive "library" of metaphors for thinking about human realities'. According to Doorman, it is desirable to have these, as only in this way is it possible to do justice to the great diversity of practical contexts in which we are involved throughout our lives. Some flexibility of spirit and some imagination is therefore required to be able to solve problems in the field of both technology and the moral, politically and social life, etc. In a society which is increasingly dominated by the 'computer metaphor' of the natural sciences and technology, the importance of this only increases. Doorman writes: 'a culturally scanty, strongly scientific intellectual training can easily lead to a fatal atrophy of our imagination' and the conclusion is therefore obvious, that 'cultural dissemination is needed to inhibit this cultural atrophy as much as possible' (Doorman 1988: 43).

However, it would seem reasonable in all this not to lose sight of the fact that a number of important artistic expressions have an overwhelmingly *aesthetic* value. These artworks do not have primarily a vision of life or reality as message. Chiefly, they attempt to make life more pleasant. The dissemination of knowledge of this art increases individual autonomy mainly in the sense that one can really only choose to enjoy this, or not, once one is aware of its existence. The importance of this freedom cannot be overrated; it already forms sufficient reason to promote cultural dissemination.

In their attempt to make citizens familiar with cultural expressions, the cultural disseminators involved, nowadays and in the past, have, to a greater or lesser degree, taken a paternalistic stance. (Another possibility, rising or falling inversely proportionately in importance, is that to this end they tried to change the social structures.) They do not want to accept the fact that people can often work up more enthusiasm for 'chicken-breeding or pigeon-racing' than for world literature, and try to actively influence the cultural preferences of the parties involved. A number of questions arise here.

With a paternalistic intervention, it is stated here, agreement in the future is anticipated. To what extent there is a 'bet' depends on the degree in which people can base themselves on the findings of people who are familiar with the situation, which is preferable according to the paternalism. In this, they may not have been exposed to what are, according to general criteria, unacceptable agreement-guaranteeing forms of influence such as manipulation and brainwashing. The question is now whether the people who are already familiar with the cultural products from which others are excluded, as a consequence of the existing social structures and processes or from their own inertia, would like to return to the situation in which this was not yet the case. Can one simply expect that someone who is stimulated to develop his capacity for autonomy, will later be grateful for this? Can it reasonably be assumed that the people who, thanks to a cultural dissemination policy, would come in contact with alternative values, ideas, thoughts, lifestyles, tastes, and with science, art and literature, will appreciate all this in retrospect?

A romantically or anarchistically inspired desire for a natural man, who probably never existed yet has been lost, and who is as yet unspoiled by a growing doubt and insecurity with drinking from the cup of knowledge, has always been present in Western civilization. The biblical story of the lost paradise is probably still the best-known expression of this desire. But we also recognize it in diverse philosophers, writers and artists such as Rousseau, Marx, Nietzsche, Lévi-Strauss, Heidegger, Gauguin, Tolstoy, Thomas Bernhard, Salinger, Mahler, Bruckner and Johnny Rotten. Culture, knowledge of alternative ways of looking at life, is often experienced more as a burden, as an unbearable lightness, than as a liberating enrichment of life. Do people, in short, actually want to be free? Simultaneously with culture, does one not also disseminate unnecessary difficulties, useless self-laceration, uncertainty and doubt, unavoidable unhappiness? And how could this be justified? These questions have already been gone into exhaustively in this book, although usually implicitly. After all, all authors who defend a particular definition of freedom, also give a number of reasons why the aspects of the values emphasized by them are important in, or essential for, human life. Nevertheless, by way of closing off the theory, and as an introduction to the practice, it is interesting to go into these questions once again, but this time more explicitly.

THE BURDENS AND BENEFITS OF FREEDOM: AUTONOMY OR HAPPINESS?

In Dostoevsky's *The Brothers Karamazov*, Ivan tells his brother Alosha a parable in which the problem of freedom is central. The story takes place in Spain during the heyday of the Inquisition. Fifteen centuries after his promise to return, Jesus wants to spend some time among his people, who are weighed down by sin. He descends to Seville, a day after the 'Great Inquisitor', in the presence of a big, enthusiastic crowd, has brought hundreds of unbelievers to the stake. The people and the Inquisitor recognize Him immediately, but nevertheless the Inquisitor has Jesus arrested. At night, he visits the prisoner in jail where, in a long monologue, he tries to justify himself.

The core of the Inquisitor's argument boils down to this: he accuses Christ of having saddled the people with an unbearable burden – freedom. They are expected to believe willingly – not due to the promise of daily bread, not through instilled fear, not due to miracles carried out. The people must themselves choose their values, determine themselves what is good and evil, and in this can only depend on their own conscience, without outside help. 'Instead of confiscating human freedom', the Inquisitor expounds to his prisoner, 'you have enlarged that freedom and burdened the domain of the human soul for all time with the agonies inherent to freedom' (Dostoevsky 1880: 257). Precisely because man 'with such a terrible burden as free choice' is abandoned to himself, he will turn against Christ's truth, 'because it is impossible to leave him behind in greater confusion and agony than you did'. His haughty rejection of 'the only powers on earth which are capable of defeating, to their joy, the conscience of the weak rebels' – that is: 'the miracle, the mystery and the authority' shows, according to the scourge of heretics, that Jesus overrates the powers of man and actually does not love him:

> I swear to you that man is weaker and more inferior than you think. Can he achieve the same as you, can he? By raising him so high you have stopped suffering with him so to speak . . . and that is while you loved that man more than yourself!

(Dostoevsky 1880: 259)

By 'teaching people that the free decision of their heart and their love plays no role, but that it is a question of a mystery to which they must blindly surrender' the Roman Church relieved them of the unbearable freedom and therefore showed more compassion than the Saviour ever did. 'We have altered your heroic deed and based it on *miracle, mystery* and *authority*', explains the Inquisitor:

> and people were glad because they were again led like a herd and finally the terrible gift which caused them so much suffering was removed from their heart. Were we not right to teach and to act like this? Have we not loved mankind, we who were so humbly aware of our impotence, full of love lightened their load and even permitted sin to their weak nature, as long as it was within the limits laid down by us? Why have you got in our way?
>
> (ibid.: 260)

In short, the Roman church has accepted what Jesus refused: the emperor's sword, and we, says the Inquisitor, conquer an empire in which 'all are happy and have ceased to rebel and exterminate each other as was everywhere the case in your regime of freedom' (ibid.: 261). And the people will be grateful, that they can subject themselves for once and for all:

> The secrets of their conscience which torment them the most, they will present to us and we will take all decisions and they will accept our decision with joy, because in this way they will be freed from the great care and the terrible agonies of the personal and free decision as this is still demanded now.
>
> (ibid.: 262)

Only the keepers of the mystery, 'the sufferers who will take on themselves that accursed knowledge of good and evil' will be unhappy. For the happiness of millions of weaker souls they will burden themselves with their sins, and in their time they 'will stand before you and say: "Condemn us if you can or dare"'. It would have been easy, the Papal inquisitor ends his apologia, to join God's elect with the strong and the powerful, 'But I reasoned and did not want to lend my services to foolishness. I turned on my axis and joined the few who have improved on your work. I left the proud and returned to the humble to work for their happiness' (ibid.: 263).

This parable is probably not an accurate description of the reason behind, or the genesis of, the Church of Rome. However, it is valuable all the same because it exposes the spiritual costs of freedom to make one's own choices, or rather, of having to make them, of autonomy, pluralism, of what Lukacs called the 'transcendental homelessness of humanity'.

On a lower, more down-to-earth level, but with a comparable effect is the critique by the leading Dutch writer Gerrit Komrij of the people who want to bring the lower socio-economic strata in contact with art and culture. A few years ago, he stated sarcastically that it 'is ridiculous to want to disseminate culture . . . Cultural policy must actually be aimed at keeping large groups away from culture, or to just share it out very sparingly. Culture does not make you happy' (Komrij et al. 1986).

According to Komrij, art and culture, contrary to general belief, are not at all 'healthy and tasteful' because all those deviating ideas, styles, tastes, manners, in which one can look at the world only bring people doubt, uncertainty, and with it, profound unhappiness.

> Culture does not mean just wonder, apathic enjoyment, relaxation and fun, but also self-criticism, active resistance, fighting and hurt . . . Culture is . . . being able to house contradictions alongside each other in peace in your heart. And certainties in unhappiness . . . Culture means that in our inner self we fight one part with another . . . We have to kick culture away from us. Much of it has already been force-fed us and it is not apt to place it on the plate of small eaters as something healthy and tasty, with a suitable order to consume it. Very few people can digest culture. That is not something to lament, it is a statement.
>
> (Komrij et al. 1986)

The 'Grand Inquisitor' from the Netherlands then wonders whether the disseminators of culture are not motivated in the first place by feelings of envy with regard to people who are 'happy in their ignorance and unletteredness', a blessed unspoiled state which the cultural commissars themselves have lost. Is it not the case that they therefore 'not on the basis of pedagogic awareness, love of humanity or feeling of responsibility, but from hate, pure hatred, want to destroy their unspoiled world?' (ibid.: 32).

In short, it has regularly emerged in Western civilization that knowledge of, and with it the necessity of choice between alternative ways of looking at the world, that is, positive freedom, makes people unhappy and one must therefore not try to bring people in contact with culture. Komrij, and before him, the Spanish Grand Inquisitor, are exponents of this. However, they probably equate two values, autonomy and happiness, which can better be distinguished from each other.[4] One can be happy without being autonomous, and autonomy can be combined with profound unhappiness. In addition, positive freedom is a greater, a more important, value than happiness. And the stance that one can become unhappy from this sort of freedom is not necessarily a reason to stop the promotion of one's development.

What does Komrij understand by 'happiness' for example? Considering his rejection of culture, it must be a life which, in the words of Mario Vargas Llosa, 'without doubts and uncertainty, without the duty to constantly have to study reality and to have to choose between different viewpoints'. Happiness can perhaps be defined in this sense, writes Vargas Llosa, as 'a situation of harmony between people's feeling and the reality in which they live' (Llosa 1985: 26). In the same spirit, happiness can perhaps be usefully defined as 'the enjoyment of pleasant experiences'. The question now is whether people want to be happy in this sense. We will try to find an answer by way of a detour.

In the context of a critique of utilitarian justifications of a morality, the American philosopher Robert Nozick has tried to demonstrate that a philosophy based on a calculation of pleasant and unpleasant experiences cannot make it clear why we reject life in a so-called 'experience machine'. This refers to an apparatus with the capacity of allowing everyone enclosed in it to undergo every experience he desires. 'Superduper neuropsychologists', writes Nozick, 'could stimulate your brain so that you would think and feel you were writing a great novel, or making a friend, or reading an interesting book. All the time you would be floating in a tank with electrodes attached to your brain.' In order to avoid having people miss certain experiences, it could be presumed that careful research has been carried out (by private enterprise, adds Nozick subtly) to determine what are generally known as pleasurable. Every two years, one could leave the pool for a while in order to determine one's programme for the coming time, partly on the basis of these researches. If one is in the machine, then one will naturally not be aware of this. One will think it is all really happening.

The question now is why one should reject such a life. What is it, that there is more in life than the enjoyment of pleasant experiences, which causes us to decide if necessary to become unhappy?

We can ask ourselves the same question with another, more familiar metaphor. In Aldous Huxley's *Brave New World* – a world in which we already find ourselves, according to the American communication expert Neil Postman – everyone is completely happy. This is because, thanks to a far-reaching conditioning, they never have desires or goals which cannot be realized. All desires, mainly oriented to sensual pleasure, are thus fulfilled, so that the stability of the system (peace and order is the ultimate goal) is assured. If any doubt or unhappiness arises in the people, then there is always a soft drug to suppress that. They call this 'Soma', a sort of hashish, but without unpleasant side-effects.

Why, once again, does *Brave New World*, despite the complete happiness of almost all its inhabitants, symbolize for very few a society in which they would really like to live?

This is probably explained by the fact that no one is autonomous here, that no one functions as a person, none are in control of their own lives, of their thinking and desires. No single idea, no single desire or goal is, after all, authentic – the product of a personal, independent thinking or wishing. Everything is the product of a conditioning, which has already begun long before birth – in so far as you can say this, since in this 'new world' everyone comes from the test tube. What is essential to man is not his capacity for happiness, but for autonomy. Essential is his potential to distance himself from his immediate desires – and therefore not react without will to every stimulus with a Pavlov reaction. Essential is his capacity to make real choices, to develop authentic ideas and goals. In *Brave New World*, all ideas have already been thought for him and all choices and goals are already fixed.

All the same, we do not want to be linked up to an 'experience machine', because, says Nozick, we do not want to just experience things, we want *to do* them. Second, because we want *to be* in a particular manner. Someone who sails around in a barrel, does not really exist: there is no reply to the question of what kind of personality he is, whether he is clever, intelligent, funny or sympathetic. And, third, because we are embarrassed by a reality which, like the world of those linked up to the machine, is completely constructed and limited by people. Many desire to keep contact with a deeper, poetic or transcendental reality.[5] People want, in short, to live their own lives in the midst of reality. This cannot be done for them, by machines or ideal societies.

As stated, a distinction was drawn, only for the sake of the argument, between happiness and autonomy. In practice, a notion of autonomy will be missing from no single plausible definition of 'happiness'. People are not pigs, emphasizes the social democrat John Stuart Mill. They possess more elevated or noble faculties and, once they have been made aware of this, will never experience a situation as happiness in which justice is not done to these qualities. Mill writes:

> It is an unquestionable fact that those who are equally acquainted with, and equally capable of appreciating and enjoying, both, do give a most marked preference to the manner of existence which employs their higher faculties. Few human creatures would consent to be changed into any of the lower animals for a promise of the fullest allowance of a beast's pleasures.
>
> (Mill 1861: 280)

This can be explained by pride, by his penchant for or love of freedom and independence, by his pursuit of power or, most plausible, according to Mill, by his feeling of self-respect. The latter is so essential for personal happiness that nothing which conflicts with this can be a worthy aspiration for the parties involved over a longer period of time.

That people, nevertheless, can in practice often confine themselves to lower pleasures, is considered by Mill to be the consequence of a socio-economic system which frustrates the development of the more noble or higher gifts. The capacity to enter into meaningful relationships with others, to exert oneself for others and the public good, and to develop oneself spiritually; the gift to be continually surprised by, and be interested in, nature, the arts, sciences, poetry, history, and the future of man, is, according to Mill, a sensitive plant, which is often trampled before it reaches maturity (Mill 1861: 284–60).

People who assume that self-respect, the acquisition of the higher skills, is at the expense of happiness, are confusing the latter value with *content*. A being with higher, more developed capacities, Mill also admits, is possibly more susceptible to feelings of unease than a being with a small repertoire of needs. But, he continues:

> It is better to be a human being dissatisfied than a pig satisfied; better to be Socrates dissatisfied than a fool satisfied. And if the fool, or the pig, is of a different opinion, it is because they only know their own side of the question. The other party to the comparison knows both sides.
>
> (Mill 1861: 281).

Only the people who have experienced the alternatives themselves, are therefore, according to Mill – and in this he does not deviate from radicals like Connolly and Lukes – in a position to judge, and that explains his position, already quoted in Chapter 5, that 'the uncultivated cannot be competent judges of cultivation. Those who most need to be made wiser and better usually desire it least, and, if they desire it, would be incapable of finding the way to it by their own lights' (Mill 1848: 459).

To resume: we do not want to live in a Brave New World, in an experience machine or in the Spain of the Grand Inquisitor, because there our capacity for autonomy is denied, and because the realization of this potential is a necessary condition of a reassuring or happy human existence. While freedom is accompanied by costs[6], this does not weigh against the benefits. The advancement of cultural participation is not primarily about broadening pleasant experiences, but about promoting individual autonomy.[7] Dissemination of culture, of the capacity to make real choices from real alternatives, is therefore no expression of contempt or hate, but of taking people seriously. It is a proof that one ascribes to all, and not just to a handful of privileged people, the potential to be autonomous, and that one does not want to condemn anybody to a nihilistic hedonism unworthy of man.

MORE REASONS TO PROMOTE THE DISSEMINATION OF CULTURE AND AUTONOMY

> Oh, if only they could enjoy that pure, clear literature, those clear springs of fresh wisdom and lust for life, of those crystalline ideas, arising from the very human courage and the pure, far-seeing understanding of their great spirits. Oh, how many would have a new world unveiled to them – how they would see things they never saw before and which were yet always close to them – how would a fresh breeze drive from the heads and hearts, much of the lowly, the bestial, the cruel, with which our terrible 'civilization' has infected our souls![8]
>
> (Polak 1897)

A reason connected to the foregoing for actively promoting individual autonomy is emphasized by Lindley, Taylor, Lukes and Norman, among others. They state that it would be inconsistent to give people rights on the basis of a number of unique qualities, but to be indifferent with regard to the question of whether they can also develop these qualities, whether they can also use their rights.

In Western civilization, as stated, we generally consider the capacity to make choices, to develop authentic ideas and goals, to self-determination and self-realization, to be essential for human beings. These capacities therefore have a special moral status for us, which we express by awarding rights of freedom to individuals. They have the right to express opinions, association and assembly, because they have the unique capacity to develop an opinion which is worthwhile discussing with others. However, if people really have a right to freedom of opinion, then they also have the right to the social conditions to develop a personal opinion. At least, as long as one wants to recognize the fact that for their development they are strongly dependent on their social environment, and wishes to remain consistent. After all, we know that the individual potential must be developed and that, to an important extent, this can only happen thanks to others. What then can the significance be of our respect for this potential when this respect is exclusively translated into the creation of the possibility to express oneself undisturbed by the interventions of others? Only when one assumes an abstract image of man is one satisfied with rights of negative freedom.

In short, if one really wants to take people seriously, and if therefore one also wants to take human rights seriously, then one must grant *positive* rights as well as negative ones. In the cultural–political field, it is inconsistent, therefore, even hypocritical, to believe that people have the freedom, for example, to go to the theatre or not, the concert hall, the bookshop, if they have not first been made familiar with the culture on offer in those places. A passive supply policy is insufficient in the cultural sector. One must also actively exert oneself to promote participation in cultural activities and with it individual autonomy. It is a matter of course that, in such a view, one will have to find a balance between negative and positive freedom.

A reason to actually disseminate culture, already mentioned, is that in this way one reduces the chances of people organizing their lives in a way they would not have chosen if they were aware of the alternatives. As we have seen, there is a relation between positive freedom and culture. Individual autonomy means that, on the basis of a reasonable knowledge of the possibilities of choice, one directs autonomously one's own life. This freedom is inaccessible to someone who can only imagine one way of life. Bringing individuals into contact, at a later age, with other ways in which one can look at life, is especially important because, during childhood years – a time in which our critical capacities are least developed – fundamental moral convictions are formed. The norms and values taken as natural can later form a great individual inhibition of the freedom of the individual, which can only be conquered by a familiarization with alternative visions. By disseminating culture one offers people the possibility of liberating themselves from the naturalness of their current values, ideas and attitudes.

A reason for the state to pursue an active cultural policy of not leaving the production of cultural values completely to the market, concerns the 'collective good' character of culture. The arts and letters can once again, alongside science, philosophy, politics and religion, play a stimulating role in the expansion of self-consciousness and the imagination of people. In order to make freedom meaningful, to make it possible, it is therefore desirable that artistic life, the entire cultural matrix of libraries, bookshops, orchestras, theatre groups, institutions for artistic training, museums, cinemas, daily newspapers and weeklies, publishers, etc., be promoted.

In other words, culture forms a collective good from which, when it is available, all profit even if they have not contributed to paying for it. Every citizen has an interest in this condition of individual autonomy being vital and remaining so, and even has a moral duty with regard to this, to contribute to it, for the sake of individual autonomy. After all, when people have a right to the social conditions to develop their capacity for freedom, then they also have a moral duty to create these conditions or to maintain them: the awarding of rights implies that one also assumes duties. The state has long been a suitable instrument for translating into practice this duty to contribute to the creation of a collective good.

The reasoning goes even further. Individuals, too, who thanks to their own efforts and those of others, have developed their capacities, are collective goods. Everyone can profit from the talents of Horowitz, Edward Hopper and Isaiah Berlin, even if they have not contributed to their realization. With regard to individual development, John Stuart Mill wrote correctly that even though it is possible to doubt whether someone who has developed his talents is always happier, 'there can be no doubt that it makes other people happier, and that the world in general is immensely a gainer by it' (Mill 1861: 283–40). Therefore, there is a threat that no one will be prepared to support the creation of the material and non-material conditions needed for the development of gifts, if they do not have the certainty that others will do this too. Again, it is a task for the state to create this certainty.

It was stated earlier that as a sociological concept, to a large extent, the arts can be understood as an image and critical reflection of culture. In this way, they can contribute to individual freedom. However, these functions can only be fulfilled if the arts find a response in society. Where this dialogue is lacking, artistic life is threatened with a smaller and smaller reservation of initiates, and the creation of what can be called an *art-art* is a real threat. Cultural dissemination and participation is therefore desirable to keep this dialogue going between society and art world, so fruitful for both parties, and to keep culture alive.

A motive mentioned by Raymond Williams and Richard Norman for giving everyone as much access to culture as possible, is that this access is needed if every individual can participate in the existing democratic structures. Self-management forms an essential component of individual freedom. People who do not participate in culture which is formed by the quality newspapers, journals and broadcasters, literature, the arts and sciences, are inhibited, in particular, in their participation in political decision-making, because the debate accompanying this is generally carried on in the terms, concepts and conceptions of the 'elite culture'. Dissemination of culture is therefore desirable to allow democracy to really function, to give people the possibility of influencing procedures of decision-making whose results affect them too.

Linking up with the earlier-mentioned motives, it could be said that culture is a 'welfare good': it forms a condition for being able to realize other values. Autonomy can first be achieved at the individual and social level when one has absorbed, to some extent, the existing culture. Paternalism in this area will generally be sanctioned in retrospect by the parties involved, since not possessing this 'welfare good' closes off, to a greater or lesser degree, the path to achieving more personal life-goals.

Finally, a political reason for promoting the autonomy of the individual is that this means simultaneously a dissemination of responsibility. People who are really free are also responsible for their own actions. They are therefore often reluctant to be free, they hide behind extra-individual authorities, conventions, habits and ignorance. By disseminating autonomy, this is made more difficult or even impossible. It thus prevents some hypocrisy and opportunism – and maybe even a few concentration camps. For this reason alone, it can be justified that people, to paraphrase Rousseau, are forced to be free.

In short, there are numerous reasons for trying to make people familiar and comfortable with culture, and, partly through this, to promote the development of their individual autonomy. In the final chapter, we will be looking at the ways in which this has taken shape in the government policies of several Western societies.

7   Cultural policy

INTRODUCTION

To conclude this book, we will examine the subjects of cultural politics and
cultural policy, against the background of the conceptions of freedom developed in the foregoing. Two themes are central here. In the first place, we will
support the argument that in Western countries there is a considerable, probably increasing, social inequality when it comes to participation in culture.
This implies a great social inequality in the possession of the immaterial
conditions of positive freedom. In the second place, it will emerge that in
trying, as many organizations and governments have done, to reduce this
inequality one inevitably runs up against the emancipation dilemma.
Nowadays, however, in balancing the two components of this dilemma too
much emphasis is laid on negative freedom, which is one of the explanations
of the fact that the attempts to disseminate culture are rarely, if ever,
successful.

Naturally, it is not possible to examine these subjects exhaustively here. It
is possible, however, with the help of previously developed notions on the
concepts of freedom, autonomy and paternalism, to remove a number of
obstacles, in terms of principles, to the implementing of an active cultural
policy. The other way round, the relevant theoretical notions can gain in
plausibility by confronting them with the results of empirical scientific
research.

In this chapter, we will be looking mainly at the experiences in France, the
Netherlands and Sweden, countries where the goal of disseminating culture
has been relatively high on the cultural political agenda in the last fifty years.
In addition, the situation in the United States and the United Kingdom is
studied, where this would appear to be less the case. For the empirical material, relatively copious use is made of Dutch sources. In this country, research
in the field of cultural participation has been carried out more extensively
and for longer than in most other countries. The reason for this is probably
related to the proportionally high faith found in the Netherlands in the possibility of solving social problems through policy. The greater this faith, the
more generally felt is the need to gather empirical data.

The structure of the argument is as follows. In the first place, the motives which inspired and continue to inspire the various Western organizations and governments that have been active in the field of cultural dissemination are examined. After this, we look at social inequality in, and the scale of, present-day cultural participation. Due to its importance for individual autonomy, the question also arises here of whether there is a transition in our age from a written culture to one of images. We then analyse the variables that could explain participation – or the lack of it – in cultural activities. Central to the next section is the policy as carried out in practice. From this, it will emerge that in most countries this has been chiefly a supply policy: the government has borne responsibility for a broad supply of cultural facilities and has left it up to the individual citizen to decide whether he wants to make use of it. An attempt is made to explain this one-sidedness. Of possible importance here are: the incrementalistic character in particular of policy forming, the cultural relativism which has arisen, and the current 'culture of authenticity', as Taylor calls it. Next, we take a closer look at two manifestations of the prevailing relativism and individualism and their cultural-political consequence: the contemporary concept of democracy and the 'status theory'. A critique is formulated of this theory in which cultural participation is chiefly explained as an attempt to distinguish oneself from others. Finally in this chapter, we consider how, in policy, more attention could be devoted to the stimulation of demand for culture.

CULTURAL DISSEMINATION AS POLICY OBJECTIVE

In the European countries especially, over the last two centuries numerous organizations and institutions have made efforts to disseminate culture. Naturally, in doing so, the relevant parties did not always or exclusively have in mind the goal of promoting individual autonomy. Other motives played a role. In what follows, first, a number will be mentioned which are mainly of historic importance (cf. Pick 1988; Westen 1990). After this, we will look at the most important motives behind present-day cultural policy.

Historic motives

A first important motivation behind the attempt to disseminate culture was the enlightened conviction that man was capable of improvement if only he allowed himself to be guided by virtue, religion and reason. Knowledge (of geography, history, physics and mathematics, and of the art of reading and writing) was regarded as the key to this perfection. Examples of institutions which were active with this objective are the numerous cultural associations which were founded throughout Western Europe since the Renaissance and continued to exist until this century.

A second motivation which played a role in the nineteenth century, in particular, was the integration of the population – and, above all, the lower orders – into the national state. The bourgeois authorities often regarded the formation of a broadly-based national culture as an indispensable instrument to this end.

A third motive was the sense of social justice, which was strong in socialist trade unions and political parties. People felt that the lower socio-economic classes, too, had the right to profit from the cultural achievements of Western civilization. In order to achieve this goal, they used as instrument both the government and their own specially-founded educational institutions (Boekman 1939; De Man 1933; Michielse 1980).

A fourth motivation was of a power politics nature: knowledge is power and, by spreading it among the members of one's own group, one could therefore strengthen the joint social position. Trade unions in particular were active in this field in the first half of this century.

Fear of the masses, of an approaching revolution of the hordes, was a fifth motivation. The authorities in the Netherlands immediately before and after the Second World War, for example, were afraid that the political preference of ordinary people would move towards Fascism or Bolshevism. This fear was fanned to an important extent by the rise in the interwar years of the mass media of radio and film. In general, people already felt that these exercised a corrupting influence, but this conviction was fed even more by the successful way in which the Fascist and Marxist dictators were able to use these media for propaganda and manipulation objectives. Bringing the masses into contact with the right elevated culture was supposed to counterbalance this (see, for example, Van der Leeuw 1946).

Self-interest on the part of the producers of the culture concerned was, and continues to be, a sixth motivation: dissemination of culture means more status, employment and incomes, so they too are also prepared to serve the noble goal of cultural dissemination (this is looked at again later in the chapter).

Finally, a seventh motivation, which fitted in with the ideology of the post-war welfare state, was the democratic goal of offering every citizen, in principle, the possibility of participating in cultural activities. As will become apparent, this still forms one of the most important justifications today for a cultural dissemination policy.

In brief, there have been many motives, often simultaneous, and partly still present, for disseminating culture among the population. The effect of the relevant activities, however, will have been the same in many cases: increasing the chance of individual autonomy. But this is not to deny that culture can be and is used as an instrument of repression, a means of actually preventing people having freedom. The fact that, in the past, dubious motivations sometimes lay behind cultural dissemination does not alter the insight that this effort can today exercise a stimulating influence on the development of personal freedom.

Converging policy traditions

Cultural policy has come into being in the Western democracies via various
routes. In their survey of this, the American political scientists Cummings
and Katz (1987) distinguish two patterns. The first is formed by former
absolutist monarchies such as France and Austria. State patronage of the
arts had already begun there in the second half of the seventeenth century.
This was characterized by a strong emphasis on the creation of great works
which served to glorify the nation and the ruler. Specific to these countries
is, above all, the fact that a tradition developed in which state involvement
with the arts and letters was regarded as natural and desirable.

Plutocrats, mercantilist states like England and the Netherlands, repre-
sent the second pattern. Here, there were no absolute rulers who had monu-
mental works built to the greater glory of their own person and the state.
However, thanks to the wealthy bourgeoisie there was a relatively broad
market for cheaper art forms such as painting. In the Netherlands especially,
partly for this reason, this art reached a high level. The presence of a puritan
Calvinist culture, however, prevented the growth of a very exuberant artistic
life in these countries. An important characteristic of this pattern is that the
members of the bourgeois class, who had taken power here, were generally
of the opinion that state influence in all fields, and certainly in that of culture, should be kept to the minimum. Of England, the political scientist
Ridley noted: 'The protestant-Liberal tradition sees every man as a judge of
his own good, whether in politics, religion, or leisure. As a former chairman
of the Arts Council said: "One of the most precious freedoms of the British
is freedom from culture"' (Ridley 1987: 227). Partly as a consequence of
this belief, in the United Kingdom, the state has only concerned itself with
the arts in the second half of this century, and then on a relatively modest
scale and in a restrained manner. The same applies to the USA (cf. Larson
1983) and Canada, who both have a political culture strongly influenced by
the English.

Since the 1950s, the cultural policy in the various Western countries,
despite the diverse backgrounds, have increasingly come to resemble one
another (Cummings and Katz 1987: 7–12, 357–8, 366–7). Government
involvement is increasing everywhere and with diverse accents they are
increasingly aiming at comparable goals with comparable means. There are
different reasons for the growing intervention, such as the decay of the traditional patrons of the arts, the internal dynamic of an incrementalistic policy
in a polyarchic political system (this is covered further later in the chapter),
and the relative rise in costs of the arts. (Labour productivity within the arts
sector can seldom, in contrast to other social sectors, be increased and therefore artistic expressions have become proportionally more expensive.)
However, an important reason is equally, as Cummings and Katz also
remark, the fact that in most countries the idea grew up that the state
'should play an active role in bringing the "good life" to average citizens,

providing for the working class on a collective basis what the upper and middle classes have been able to provide for themselves individually' (Cummings and Katz 1987: 8). In the welfare states developing everywhere, therefore, having access to culture was equated with having access to health care.

The official goals of cultural policy of Western governments are nowadays, on the whole, conservation of the existing cultural heritage, stimulation of cultural innovation and promotion of cultural participation.[1] For example, in 1985 the Dutch Christian Democrat minister of culture Brinkman stated that his policy was based on three fundamental pillars: preserving the existing, guaranteeing a high quality supply, and promotion of cultural participation. In short: 'preservation, innovation and dissemination of cultural values'. This principle, which, properly regarded, has characterized policy in the Netherlands since the 1950s, has since been regularly strengthened, also by ministers from other political parties (WVC 1992, 1993; Myerscough 1994).

On the foundation of the forerunner of the French Ministry of Culture in 1959, it was also laid down that the tasks of its minister were: 'To make the major works of humanity, starting with those of France, accessible to the greatest number of French people, to provide the widest possible audience for the French cultural heritage and to encourage the creation of works of art and of the mind which will enrich this heritage' (quoted by Wangermée 1991: 27). (For the objectives of French cultural policy, see also Gournay 1991: 237–8). Since then there has been great continuity in the French ministry's approach to its task. Here, too, the alternation of left and right governments has had consequences mainly for the emphasis (Wangermée 1991: 43). Social democratic ministers, such as the Frenchman Jack Lang, for example, attach particular importance to the promotion of cultural participation.

The last-mentioned goal generally has two dimensions. First, it is attempted to enlarge the absolute numbers of participants. Second, it is attempted to reduce the existing social inequality in this field by inspiring people from the lower strata in particular to participate. The latter ambition is called *social* or *vertical* cultural dissemination. Horizontal cultural dissemination refers to the attempt to spread out cultural facilities in a geographically equal manner, so that citizens of all regions have the opportunity to participate in culture. Obviously, the two policy objectives can overlap.

In the field of cultural dissemination, apart from France, great efforts have been made in Northern European states such as Sweden and the Netherlands. These are due to the great value which is attached in these countries to the ideal of equality and the correspondingly strongly developed collective sector. This can be illustrated by a resolution of the Swedish parliament from 1974, which has since then functioned as a starting-point for policy: 'The resolution rates cultural equality as no less important than economic and social equality, a democratic equality enabling everyone wishing to do so to develop his or her resources as an active creative individual, and be given opportunities for cultural experience.' In Sweden, particular emphasis is laid on the connection between being able to participate in culture, and democracy. The same policy-makers state:

> Our democracy is based on opportunities for everyone to give expression to his or her own ideas, to partake in debates and opinion-forming, and thus influence the shaping of society. A free cultural life is a condition for a living democracy. If opportunities for activities and involvement are suppressed or not given support in order to develop, that is a threat to democracy.
>
> (Swedish Ministry of Education and Cultural Affairs 1989: 72, resp. 262)

In the Netherlands, there are similar ideas on the importance of cultural participation and dissemination. For example, on her entry into the parliament in 1990, the social democratic minister D'Ancona stated that 'a reinforcement of cultural participation, in close relation to the care for the production and distribution, (must be regarded) as an essential task for cultural policy'. The minister wished to oppose emphatically the idea growing in the Netherlands that 'the pursuit of cultural participation is now out of date and perhaps can better be put away with the well-intentioned but therefore no less naive ideals of the past'. She has repeated this standpoint since then in various tones and on numerous occasions (see particularly WVC 1992: 35–53).

Though less emphatically, in the United States (see, for example, Mulcahy 1987: 327) and in Great Britain (Lewis 1990: 21) also, the government policymakers and institutions who, to a large extent, have been given responsibility for policy, name the dissemination or the 'democratization' of culture as a goal. For example, in 1945 and in 1967 it was emphatically included in the Royal Charter of the British Arts Council and it is regularly subscribed to publicly by the politicians responsible. According to Oliver Bennett (1991: 297–9), in the United Kingdom there even is a tradition in this respect which goes back at least to the nineteenth century. An institution such as the BBC is a part of this tradition too. Its first general manager, Lord Reith, declared in 1922 that the BBC would be 'a drawn sword parting the ignorance of darkness', and its function would be 'to offer the public something better than it now thinks it likes' (cited by Bennett 1991: 297). This tradition came to a head, states Bennett, in the seventies: 'Stripped of its earlier missionary overtones, [cultural participation] was represented as a kind of human right'. As is already known, after this period the political climate changed dramatically in Great Britain. The arts came to be considered more and more as a normal economic commodity.

The fact that the cultural political ambitions in the various Western democracies have come increasingly to resemble each other, does not mean that large differences cannot be observed in the level of the government budgets and in the quality of the cultural facilities present (orchestras, theatre companies, theatres, museums, libraries, etc.). For example, the expenditure of the local and national governments in the USA are relatively low in comparison to those in European countries such as the Netherlands, Germany, Italy, Sweden and France. Nor is this difference compensated for by the more extensive phenomenon of private sponsorship in the United States.[2] In Great Britain, it is true, more money is given to the arts than in the United States, but in comparison to the other Western European countries, this is not high either (Ridley 1987: 232). According to the Policy Studies Institute, the governments of France, Germany, Holland and Sweden spend two or three times more per head of the population than the government of the United Kingdom (PSI 1990:5: 74).

SOCIAL INEQUALITY IN CULTURAL PARTICIPATION

In all the Western democracies discussed here there is great social inequality in participation in culture. It is almost exclusively the higher educated, belonging to and often originating from the 'better' socio-economic classes, who visit with any regularity museums, theatres, bookshops and concert halls or, to a lesser extent, are active in amateur art activities. The attempts to introduce change into this situation through a policy of socio-cultural dissemination have largely failed in a number of important fields. The threat is rather of a growing cultural dichotomy.

For example, in his study on cultural participation, the sociologist Ganzeboom states: 'participation in cultural activities in our society is one of the most unequally divided characteristics of social groups. The correlation of cultural participation with social background variables such as professional status, training and even with characteristics dating from much earlier in life such as parents' education and the education enjoyed in the parental home is particularly high in this field' (Ganzeboom 1989: 2). According to him, there are no indications that this social inequality has changed much in the past decades. The results of the available Dutch research material are not unambiguous, but 'in so far as there are general developments, these point rather to a further exclusivisation of audience groups' (Ganzeboom 1989: 178).

Other sociologists, too, have referred to this growing exclusiveness. In his research into the postwar development of leisure time use among the Dutch, Knulst found that between 1962 and 1987 'among the regular visitors to the performing arts, elite formation rather than social dissemination had occurred' (Knulst 1989: 255). Since 1962, the average visitor to museum, theatre and concert hall also seems to have become more elderly. As there are still relatively many people with a lower education among the older public, this ageing has restrained somewhat the development towards an elite public (Knulst 1989: 25).

The great social inequality in participation in cultural activities can be observed in all the countries discussed here, as has been stated, even though in some of those countries policy is being implemented to oppose this inequality. Experts from the Council of Europe[3] write about France that it must be extremely disappointing for the policy-makers involved to have to see, after all that has been done, that 'the number of people who go to the theatre, concerts and museums is on the decline or is only increasing very slightly, and most of them still come from the same privileged background' (Wangermée 1991: 182). Research on behalf of the French Ministry of Culture by the sociologists Donnat and Cogneau revealed that in France, too, the public is increasingly becoming a social elite. Between 1973 and 1989, the number of workers in the hall dropped and the number of professionals grew at a faster rate than could have been expected on the basis of the changing composition of the French population (Donnat and Cogneau 1990: 106–7).

Socio-scientific research in Britain, too, reveals a great social inequality in participation in culture. Here, the people who profit from the supply of cultural facilities created by the government come mainly from the higher, better educated and better paid strata (Feist and Hutchison 1990: 30; Arts Council 1991: 157; Lewis 1990: 13). Research from 1986 by the British Market Research Bureau quoted by Lewis shows that people from the top two professional groups identified ('professional and managerial') visit cultural institutions like museums, theatres and concert halls four to six times more often than unskilled and semi-skilled workers. The statistics on the educational background of the visitors give the same picture (Lewis 1990: 14–5).

Finally, the situation in the United States is no different. This can be seen from, among other things, the results of the large-scale survey of the cultural activities of the American population. This was carried out in 1982 and 1985, commissioned by the US Bureau of the Census (Robinson et al. 1985, 1986). On the basis of this material, Hendon compared visitors to art museums with those staying at home. He found that these came from the highest groups in terms of education, profession and incomes, and were more active than non-visitors in almost all fields of cultural and social life (Hendon 1990: 439). It also emerged that the parents of these participants had an above-average education, cultural interest and degree of cultural participation. However, their most importance difference from non-participants, to which we will return later, was that they had had more formal art education inside and outside their education.

The foregoing refers chiefly to the social inequality in participation in cultural activities. However, the figures in this field say little about participation in the absolute sense: it is possible that both the higher and lower socio-economic classes have been participating more, with the consequence that, even though the mutual differences have not been reduced, culture has been disseminated. In addition, it is possible that the difference in cultural participation between higher and lower strata has remained the same, but that nowadays many more people belong to the middle and upper layer than before. The result of both developments should be that the participation has grown in absolute figures. Does this tally with the facts?

TRENDS IN PARTICIPATION IN CULTURAL ACTIVITIES

Before we examine the results of the research into cultural participation in a number of fields, it is a good idea to emphasize that these must be interpreted and used with the necessary reservations. On questioning, it would appear that not everyone understands the same thing by, for example, 'reading books', 'playing a musical instrument' or 'visiting a museum' and people seem to have a strong tendency to give socially desirable answers. Probably, with the generally asked questions such as 'How many books have you read in the last year?' people measure chiefly how important the reading of books is considered by the interviewee, or the people who form his frame of reference. In addition, what is socially desirable can change with country and with period. Added to the situation that researchers from different countries and periods generally use deviating research methods and definitions, this makes the international and time-related comparison of data extremely problematic. The most reliable are probably the rare time budget studies, in which people are asked to note in a diary during a particular period how they spend their time.

Despite the deficiencies or mutual incomparability of most studies, possible trends in time can, of course, be estimated and compared to each other.

Reading books, journals and newspapers

Time budget research[4] shows that in the period from 1955 to 1990, the time which the Dutch spent reading was reduced to an important extent. According to the sociologists Kraaykamp and Knulst, 'time budget data since 1955 unmistakably show a shift from a reading to a visual culture' (Kraaykamp and Knulst 1992: 22; cf. SCP 1992: 302–8). Whereas, in the autumn and winter of 1955, the Dutch population aged twelve and over spent an average of 2.4 hours per week reading books, in October 1990 this was just 1 hour, a drop therefore of 58 per cent. In 1955, people spent an average of 2 hours reading newspapers, in 1990 this was 1.1 hours, a drop of 45 per cent. In 1955, people read journals for an average of 0.7 hours, in 1990 about 0.9 hours, an increase of 29 per cent (Kraaykamp and Knulst 1992: 26; cf. Knulst 1989: 40).

The findings of the time budget studies are reflected in the sales figures of books, journals and newspapers. Between 1960 and 1970, an average of 3.5 (general) books were sold per capita in the Netherlands. Since 1970, this figure has dropped to 1.8 in 1989. The edition of national and regional dailies sold has risen in absolute figures, but related, as is usual, to the number of households, here too there is clearly a downward trend: in 1989, 0.76 newspapers were sold per household, as opposed to 1.12 in 1955 (SCP 1990: 233–5; Knulst 1989: 42–2).

The increased popularity of journals is related to the rise of the gutter press or scandal sheets, a phenomenon which was almost unknown before the middle of the 1970s. Since the beginning of the 1980s, the total paid editions of Dutch periodicals has dropped again, which seems to be at the cost of the commentary journals (SCP 1988: 268). Knulst ascribes the relative success of journals to, among other things, the fact that the contents are presented in an increasingly simple manner. According to him, reading has 'increasingly the character of looking at pictures with explanatory text' (Knulst 1989: 223).[5] Journals fit better than books into a culture in which the rapidly changing TV screen, providing a flood of stimuli, seems to set the tone – a culture which is also characterized by an increased pressure of time on the individual and a decreased possibility and, perhaps, capacity, for concentration. People, according to Knulst, are therefore inclined to choose stimuli 'which give a relatively large amount of satisfaction in a short space of time and without preparatory efforts' (Knulst 1989: 222).

Apparently contradicting the development sketched above, is the growth of library use, a development which seems not to be exclusive to the Netherlands: the numbers of registered readers and loans tripled between 1970 and 1989 (SCP 1988: 269; CBS 1992: 53). In 1989, 12 books were lent per head of the population.[6] However, these figures say little about the question of whether the borrowed books are actually read, since the price of membership is generally not related to the number of books that members take home. In this way, the tendency is first to decide at home whether one is actually going to read a particular book.[7] The extravagant borrowing is also stimulated by the libraries in the Netherlands because the borrowing figures have come to form the most important legitimization of their activities.[8]

Who are the readers nowadays in the Netherlands? From the research available, it would appear that reading has increasingly become an activity of the higher educated and the elderly, who were born before the introduction of television (SCP 1992: 307; Kraaykamp and Knulst 1992: 28). In general, it is the marginal readers in particular who have dropped out. These can mainly be found among the lower educated and among people who grew up after 1950, people who are therefore familiar with the medium of television since their youth.[9]

In general, Dutch experience hardly deviates, in so far as can be judged, from that in other Western industrialized countries. We will now look successively at the situation in the United Kingdom, France, the United States and Sweden.

A survey held in 1990 showed that 80 per cent of the English had bought a book in the preceding twelve months. However, it also emerged that a quarter of the population bought 80 per cent of the books sold (PSI 1990: 6: 14). These people come mainly from the higher, better educated and better paid strata of society (PSI 1991:10: 22). In so far as can be judged on the basis of the research material available, in the United Kingdom, too, during the last decades there has been declining interest in the written word. In addition, there is a visible gap, growing in time, between the people who read a lot and the people who read little or hardly at all. In the survey *Lesen im internationalen Vergleich*, the British sociologist Bryan Luckhan notes a growing polarization in his country with many reading less, and a few reading more. He ascribes the latter to the demands which are made on the individual in a modern society based on the communication of mainly written information. If one begins here with a deficit, it becomes steadily bigger (Luckham 1990: 159).

For that matter, in the above mentioned study, anxiety is expressed in almost all the articles (on Germany, Switzerland, France and the United States) about a growing 'information gap' between those who participate in written culture and those who do not.

In France, too, just as in the Netherlands and Great Britain, interest in books among the young and lower educated is dropping. For example, the percentage of adolescents who had already read more than 25 books the previous year declined from 39 per cent to 23 per cent between 1973 and 1988. In addition, it would appear that the young who have dropped out cannot be won back to the book at later age. The percentage of people who had read 1 to 9 books in the last year however rose from 24 per cent to 32 per cent. Although, a caveat to this is that the percentage of 'heavy readers' (more than 25 books) dropped from 22 to 17 per cent. In 1988, 26 per cent of the French said they had read no book during the last twelve months (Donnat and Cogneau 1990: 77–91).

The research carried out in the United States is unusually fragmented and often not very suitable for comparison. In the study *Literacy in the United States, Readers and Reading since 1880*, the sociologists Kaestle, Damon-Moore and others nevertheless try to locate some trends on the basis of the available material. First, the researchers analysed the data which has been assembled in the course of time by the government on the expenditure by American consumers on newspapers, journals and books. Naturally, these give no more than an indication of actual reading behaviour. If one looks at the average annual expenditure of the population, corrected for inflation, aged eighteen years and older, then between 1945 and 1974 these turn out to rise slowly between 1945 and 1974 from around $100 to $120 and after this, drop to less than $100 in 1986 (the value of the dollar in 1982 has been taken as starting-point here). Also, the expenditure on reading material, if expressed as percentage of the total expenditures and of the expenditure on leisure and mass media, turns out to lag behind that of 1929. (Between 1929 and 1986 the decline was: from 1.4 to 0.7 per cent; from 29 to 10 per cent; and from 46 to 22 per cent (Stedman et al. 1991: 157).)

Furthermore, it emerged from the available material that the total reading public has shrunk in this century. In particular, the percentage of people who regularly buy newspapers and read them has dropped from around 90 per cent at the beginning of this century to around 60 per cent in the 1980s. Relatively lowly-educated people, in particular, and the young, are to be found among the drop-outs. The percentage of people who buy newspapers dropped after the introduction of television, and in the 1980s was once again on the pre-war level of about 45 per cent. On the other hand, in this century the percentage of book buyers has easily tripled: from 15 to about 50 per cent. The percentage of active book readers nevertheless remained constant in this period: between 20 and 25 per cent of the population (Stedman et al. 1991: 163–5). The purchasers of newspapers, journals and books also belong, roughly speaking, to the same better-educated group.

These findings are largely confirmed by the results of surveys into reading habits. Damon-Moore and Kaestle found that the percentage of people who regularly read a book or journal has remained more or less constant over the last fifty years (between the 20 and 25 per cent and between the 55 and 60 per cent, respectively). The percentage of regular newspaper readers, however, has dropped from about 90 to 60 per cent, a development which they ascribe to the introduction of television news (Damon-Moore and Kaestle 1991: 203). Here, too, education and income turn out to correlate strongly to reading behaviour. For example, in 1984, 37 per cent of the people who had gone through 'college' said they read books, as opposed to 10 per cent of the people with a 'grade school' background (Damon-Moore and Kaestle 1991: 194). Together, these developments, according to the authors, led to the situation today where there are three identifiable groups of readers: a highly-educated elite who read much and read everything, a lowly-educated underclass who seldom if ever open a book, journal or newspaper, and a large middle group who read mainly newspapers and journals. This tripartite division seems to apply to most Western countries.

Finally, a clear exception to the trends discussed is Sweden. Research shows that Swedes aged nine and above in 1987 devoted an average of 2.7 hours per week to reading books, 4 hours to newspapers and 2.2 hours to journals.[10] In 1987, 4.3 books were purchased per head of the population. It is striking that reading books, journals and newspapers has become a more widespread activity in Sweden. The time which, on average, is devoted to reading grew between 1973 and 1986 by 35 per cent. Also very striking, is that people with lower educations have, on average, started to read more, and people with higher educations less. Twenty per cent of the population, however, still never reads a book (Myerscough 1989: 136–8; Swedish Ministry of Education and Cultural Affairs 1989: 276–9).

The rise of television viewing

The decline of reading has been accompanied by – but not chiefly caused by – the rise of television viewing.[11] In the Netherlands, in particular, this development has been precisely documented via the already mentioned time budget research. This shows, among other things, that television viewing (including video) grew between 1975 and 1990 from an average of 13.4 hours to 15.4 hours per week (Kraaykamp and Knulst 1992: 28). In addition, it is clear that the importance of television as a medium, in relation to the written word, has grow dramatically.[12] The young, especially children from lower classes and the lower educated, spend more time watching television and, at the same time, as has already been mentioned, read less (SCP 1992: 304; Van Lil 1989; De Jong 1987: 90–5).

The trends in the Netherlands do not deviate from the developments in other countries. It is mainly the absolute time spent watching television that differs. The Swedes watch about the same[13], the French somewhat more[14] and the English and Americans considerably more.

In the United Kingdom, the time which was spent watching television grew from an average of 15.5 hours per week in 1970 to 26.7 hours in 1992. In addition to this, however, in the last year people have spent an average of 5 hours per week looking at video recordings. An average of 1 per cent of viewing time is devoted to music and art programmes, 27 per cent to news and current affairs, the rest to entertainment, drama and sport. These proportions are about the same as those in other countries discussed here. The people in the lowest social stratum identified spend about 12 hours more per week in front of the screen than those in the highest stratum (Social Trends 1990: 24: 130–1; PSI 1990: 6: 50–7). Also, according to Barwise and Ehrenberg, about 40 per cent of the time that the television is on in the United States and England, it is watched with less than full attention: people talk to others, iron the washing, do the washing-up, etc. In the Netherlands, this is about 23 per cent (Barwise and Eherenberg 1988: 177).

In the average American household, the television nowadays is on for about 7 hours a day. Adults look at this for about 4 hours per day and children for about 4 to 5 hours on an average weekday, and even 7 to 9 hours at the weekend (these times include videos and games). American children, therefore, spend a total of about 40 hours per week in front of the television. Roughly speaking, they spend about the same amount of time on their school and homework and about ten hours less on social interactions with family members and friends (Condry 1993: 261–2). The media sociologist Van Evra states that eighteen-year-olds have spent about two years of their lives in front of the TV, and this is a longer period than that used by formal education (Van Evra 1990: xi). In the 1980s, the average television viewing time in the United States has also grown, by about 15 per cent.

The question now arises of how the rise of television viewing must be assessed.

Discussion: typographic versus electronic culture

Speaking and listening is the basis of communication between the members of every civilization. In some cases, as in the West, an oral culture was transformed into a typographic culture. Apart from the spoken word, the written word has also played an important role in the mutual exchange of information. In our age, through the rise of electronic media such as film, radio, telephone and above all television, a further transformation is taking place. The written word continues to play a significant role, but alongside this the image becomes extremely important and the spoken word is given a new impetus.

If one wants to estimate the consequences of a transition from a typographic to an electronic culture and become aware of the essential characteristics of the former culture, then there is much to be learned from the earlier transformation from an oral to a typographic culture. In what follows, first, we will briefly examine this, then the social and political consequences which a decline of the written word could bring with it are discussed, among other things.

From an oral to a typographic culture

In his *Orality and Literacy, The Technologizing of the World*, the American cultural philosopher and psychiatrist Walter Ong makes a profound analysis of the differences between civilizations based on the written and the spoken word. According to him, many of the characteristics of the present-day culture, which we regard as obvious, owe their *raison d'être* to the possibilities which the written word offered to human consciousness (Ong 1982: 8–9). This does not alter the fact, emphasizes Ong, that language is primarily oral in character. Of the many thousands of languages which exist and have existed, only about one hundred have developed a written language and have produced a literature. A language can live without being written down, but the opposite is not true.

In addition, oral cultures possess valuable characteristics which disappear as soon as the art of reading and writing expands. An example of this can be the necessity which exists in this culture of relieving memory (which is actually relatively strongly developed) by imprinting the information in an aesthetically acceptable manner. Ong writes:

> In a primary oral culture, to solve effectively the problem of retaining and retrieving carefully articulated thought, you have to do your thinking in mnemonic patterns, shaped for ready oral recurrence. Your thought must come into being in heavily rhythmic, balanced patterns, in repetitions or antitheses, in alliterations and assonances, in epithetic and other formulary expressions.
>
> (Ong 1982: 34)

The need to arrange and store the existing knowledge in this way, however, also has an important drawback: new ideas can only penetrate with difficulty the existing coercive frameworks of thought. It is therefore inherent in oral cultures that they are relatively static, conservative and traditionalist in character.

The introduction of the written word brings a change in this. It changes human consciousness to a high degree. 'Without writing', argues Ong, 'the literate mind could and would not think as it does, not only when engaged in writing but normally even when it is composing its thought in oral form. More than any other single invention, writing has transformed human consciousness' (Ong 1982: 78).

According to Ong, the written word is characterized by the fact that it, among other things, promotes consistency. As, after all, statements can be re-read, one can avoid to a greater extent contradictions and repetitions and work up earlier to a conclusion or climax. In addition, writing enforces exactness, care and lucidity. A written text must speak completely for itself as the writer can generally offer no further comment or make use of intonations and body language in order to clarify his intentions. Furthermore, it is an important difference that the vocabulary of a written culture can be many times bigger, and generally is too, than that of an oral culture. Standard English, which could only come into being due to the written word, has an estimated million and a half words. A simple, oral dialect only has a couple of thousand. Naturally, with the help of a larger vocabulary it is possible to communicate about a greater number of matters in a more accurate fashion. In addition, communication with people who live or lived in other places and times first becomes really possible with writing. Writing therefore promotes the growth of knowledge. Finally, the written word 'by separating the knower from the known', stimulates introspection and self-awareness (Ong 1982: 105).

Although, in short, writing is an unnatural, consciously formed 'technology', it is what first enables man to fully develop his potential. 'In this sense', writes Ong, 'orality needs to produce and is destined to produce writing. Literacy is absolutely necessary for the development not only of science but also of history, philosophy, explicative understanding of literature and of any art, and indeed for the explanation of language (including oral speech) itself' (Ong 1982: 14–5).

From a typographic to an electronic culture

In his now well-known book *Amusing Ourselves to Death, Public Discourse in the Age of Show Business*, the American media expert Neil Postman concentrates on the transition which, according to him, has taken place in our time in the United States, from a written to a visual culture, created mainly by television. In a powerful plea for the culture of literacy, he claims that this transition 'has dramatically and irreversibly shifted the content and meaning of public discourse. As the influence of print wanes, the content of politics, religion, education and anything else that comprises public business must change and be recast in terms that are most suitable to television.' (Postman 1985: 8) In imitation of Marshall McLuhan,[15] Postman believes that the medium defines not only the form but also, to a high degree, the content of the message. According to him, every medium implies its own epistemology and notion of truth: 'As a culture moves from orality to writing to printing to televising, its ideas of truth move with it . . . Truth, like time itself, is a product of a conversation man has with himself about and through the technique of communication he has invented' (Postman 1985: 24).

In Postman's view, for two centuries, in the eighteenth and nineteenth centuries, the written word was the dominant means of communication. This made possible a public discourse of a relatively high level. After all:

> Almost all of the characteristics we associate with mature discourse were amplified by typography, which has the strongest possible bias towards exposition: a sophisticated ability to think conceptually, deductively and sequentially; a high valuation of reason and order; an abhorrence of contradiction; a large capacity for detachment and objectivity; and a toleration for delayed response.
>
> (Postman 1985: 63)

An expression of this were the debates between political opponents which regularly lasted hours. According to Postman, in the 1850s it was not considered unusual that Abraham 'Lincoln and Stephen Douglas debated together a number of times for four to seven hours, a debate in which long complex sentences were formulated and arguments were weighed up against each other on a relatively high level of abstraction, a debate in which the texts were also prepared on paper and were read out in a written style. According to Postman, the many listeners were only able to follow this type of discussion because they were representatives of a typographical culture, a culture in which the capacity for deductive, abstract and sober reasoning was strongly developed and widespread.

From the end of the nineteenth century, the hegemony of the written culture slowly came to an end, according to Postman. An initial change en route to the contemporary television culture appears with the introduction and dissemination of the telegraph. This fundamentally changed the idea of what was to be understood by news: the news became an endless, incoherent and often also a rather random stream of messages which were sent 'in telegram style' from throughout the entire world. The recipient could generally make little of these messages as they were seldom of direct importance to him and were only sporadically placed in a particular social and intellectual context. The most important power of this electronic medium lay in its capacity 'to move information, not to collect it, explain it or analyze it'. In this, it was the counterpart of typography. 'Knowledge' of the facts received a new significance, 'for it did not imply that one understood implications, background or connections . . . To the telegraph, intelligence meant knowing a lot of things, not knowing about them' (Postman 1985: 70). The question then became what to do with all this irrelevant, incoherent information without context. The answer given to this in our television age is, according to Postman: entertainment.

Certainly with commercial television broadcasters, where the number of viewers determines the profits, the programmes must primarily amuse. In order to have the audience as big as possible, no preliminary knowledge may be demanded, the programme may not be too complicated or too tiring, and it must be possible to tune in at any moment desired – with, as a consequence, an argument or exposition can never last longer than a couple of minutes and programme makers are forced to remain at a superficial level. Whether it is about politics, religion or a new toothpaste, it always has to be 'fun'. The form becomes increasingly more important, the content increasingly subservient. According to Postman, the danger is that people believe that they are extremely well informed, while they are drowned in a sea of trivialities and banalities. The public discourse, whose quality helps to determine the viability of a democracy, becomes superficial and banal.

Postman's most important thesis is therefore not that watching television damages *cognitive capacity* (something which he does suspect but does not have to be demonstrated for the plausibility of his argument), but that the image that people have of reality, and thus of social discussion, has been fundamentally changed by the rise of television (Postman 1985: 27). According to him, the United States have increasingly come to resemble the society sketched by Aldous Huxley in *Brave New World*: a society in which the citizens have less and less of a grip on events, not as in George Orwell's *1984* the result of open repression, but by the fact that they are having such a great time that they do not realize how superficial and incoherent their view of the world has become. Postman therefore gives a sombre warning:

> When a population becomes distracted by trivia, when cultural life is redefined as a perpetual round of entertainments, when serious public conversation becomes a form of baby-talk, when in short a people becomes an audience and their public business a vaudeville act, then a nation finds itself at risk; culture-death is a clear possibility.
>
> (Postman 1985: 155–6)

Cares of the policy-makers

In the meantime representatives of various Western governments, and organizations like UNESCO and the Council of Europe, have become concerned about the decline of reading. The promotion of reading, therefore, often occupies a central position in policy on dissemination of culture. For example, in 1990 the Dutch minister responsible stated 'If tomorrow television were to disappear, then that would be an inconvenience. If the book were to disappear tomorrow, then our culture disintegrates, or, if you want, our civilization'. She emphatically linked the capacity to read with participation in culture and the ability to participate in society. 'We can see', she wrote to the parliament, 'that a gap is growing between a new class of "haves", the "knows", and a new class of "have nots", the new "know nots". And that is in a society where information has become the most important production factor and in which increasingly higher demands are made on the ability to acquire information' (Ministry of Welfare, Health and Culture 1990: 6).

This threatened cultural split also had consequences, according to the minister, for the viability of our democracy: through a lack of information, a growing number of people could no longer contribute to this. This applies equally, emphasized the minister, to literary texts. Fiction is also a form of information which helps people to get a grip upon reality. In addition, the skill acquired in reading literature strengthens the competence for dealing with other sorts of texts.

Conclusion

Postman is often accused of not basing his claims sufficiently on empirical proofs. His thesis that the world view of people has become more incoherent and superficial under the influence of television, however, is very difficult to verify scientifically. In the first place, this is because it is not simple, for example, to reconstruct the world view of people from the eighteenth century (an important reference point for Postman). Due to the lack of viable empirical research from that time, verification will soon become anecdotal. And, second, because researchers will always disagree to a great extent with each other on the answer to the question of what can be deemed a 'coherent' or 'well-considered' world view. A broad consensus on the tenability/untenability of Postman's thesis would thus seem unlikely for the time being.

Nevertheless, progress can be made in some sectors. For example, it is already broadly recognized that in recent decades people have spent less time on reading. People usually see the rise of watching television as one of the reasons for this (Knulst and Kalmijn 1988: 158; Van der Voort 1990: 5–9; Kraaykamp en Knulst 1992: 35; Koolstra 1993: 78–9; Condry 1993: 262). In addition, they refer to the increase in the number of possibilities of spending time and the pressure of time on people (Knulst and Kalmijn 1988: 59–63: 105ff.; Kraaykamp and Knulst 1992: 32–5). On a more abstract level, the decline of reading and the rise of television could also be explained on the basis of the psychic disposition which a modern industrialized society implies. It could be suggested that this is characterized by speed, tempo and haste, and demands that impressions and experiences can be immediately and simply processed. Reading a book (this applies less, as has already been stated, to magazines) requires a mental disposition in conflict with this. The growing popularity of looking at television could, from this viewpoint, be the consequence therefore and not the cause of a change in culture. The truth is probably somewhere in the middle: the two developments have probably reinforced each other.

Much research has been already carried out into various deviating possibilities offered by the typographic and electronic media for communicating information and the development of cognitive skills (cf. Van Evra 1990, ch. 3).

According to Van der Voort, among other things, this shows that reading has positive effects on our capacity for oral and written expression (Van der Voort 1990: 16; cf. Beentjes 1991: 299–300). Films contain a very incomplete language model because most is made clear from the image. In a book, on the other hand, time, place and action must also be described alongside possible dialogue, in a coherent manner. Research shows that children who watch a lot of television have a smaller vocabulary and remain more superficial in their description of events. Van der Voort says: In an analysis of essays by children the writing style turned out to be clearly related to time spent watching television. The essays by heavy lookers were less coherent, contained fewer words per sentence, and described more external, superficial elements than the essays of light viewers (Van der Voort 1990: 17).

It emerged with equal force from a panel study by Koolstra (1993) into 1050 children between eight and twelve that heavy television watching has a negative effect on the so-called 'comprehension reading' and on the scale of reading. The latter is partially explained by the fact that children who watch a lot of television come to expect that reading will offer experiences which are comparatively as pleasurable or as amusing as the average television programme. As this is seldom the case, the readiness to read declines. Another partial explanation is that watching television, through its great alternating flow of stimuli, reduces children's capacity for concentration. They can therefore concentrate less on a book. Another effect which would also appear to take place is that the difference in reading skill between weak and good readers becomes greater in the course of time. Weak readers come to watch more television and read less, the opposite happens with strong readers, with important consequences for the school achievements.

Arguments that the rise of television viewing and the decline of reading are regrettable from the cultural–political viewpoint are often opposed by the view that in former times, too, the introduction and expansion of new means of communication has always evoked concerned reactions from the cultural elite. This concern always turned out to be exaggerated, and in time even disappeared (Lowery and De Fleur 1983: x, 10–1; SCP 1988: 244–5; Knulst en Kalmijn 1988: 157–8). This happened with the introduction of the book, the newspaper, the radio, the film, the cartoon, and therefore in recent decades once more with television. However, from the empirical fact that people in the past learned to live with a particular means of communication, or even came to appreciate it in the course of time, it cannot be logically concluded that people nowadays, too, should regard as positive the introduction of a different, new instrument. Perhaps radio and film are no longer discussed because nowadays they no longer play a significant role as a means of communication.

A comparable counter-argument is that not much was read in earlier times either, and the fact that written culture is once again becoming a matter for a small elite is hardly a cause for concern (Mijnhardt 1990; Knulst 1989: 223–32). This argument is also untenable as, again, the logical gap here between fact and values is skipped. If it can be made plausible that reading promotes people's cognitive development, that the written word is indispensable to being well informed and therefore being able to participate in a democratic society, that letters are an excellent medium to bring people in contact with alternative ways of thinking and to liberate them from the limitation of their circumstances, then, normatively, it is rather irrelevant to state that eras or societies existed, or still exist, in which reading culture was, or is, even less disseminated than is the case nowadays.

Attendance for performing arts

The data available on participation in the field of a large number of performing arts show a comparable picture to that of the written word: interest in it is declining in absolute terms or is, at best, stabilizing. In addition, it is mainly the lower social classes who are participating less and the higher social classes more.

In the Netherlands, over the last four decades there is, above all, a decline to be seen in the professional and subsidized stage (there is no data on the amateur sector). The interest in subsidized concerts and operas, dance and ballet performances has, on the other hand, remained on a fairly stable level since the 1970s.[16] Although the theatre public thus dropped sharply in size, the number of performances between 1960 and 1985 doubled. The average number of people per performance also dropped spectacularly. This tendency, which is also found in other countries, confirmed the formation earlier noticed of increasingly specialized and differentiated 'art worlds'.

A comparison with the situation elsewhere shows that the declining interest in subsidized theatre is also generally discernible in other countries, too, but nowhere has it been as excessive as in the Netherlands (Myerscough, et al 1993: 89). (We will be looking at the reasons for this later on.) France is something of an exception: here the total number of theatre seats sold during the last two decades has turned out to be more or less the same. However, this is due to the fact that the people who go do so more often than they used to. The potential public has become smaller and is increasingly from the upper classes (Wangermée 1991: 156; Gournay 1991: 272; Donnat and Cogneau 1990: 101–124). Interest in classical or 'serious' music grew somewhat in France during recent years. In this field, too, however, concert-goers inevitably belong to the higher levels of the population. The average manager or businessman goes to concerts five times more often than the average skilled worker and twenty times more than someone without a school diploma (Wangermée 1991: 157).

In Sweden, visits to subsidized theatres dropped between 1975 and 1986 by 20 per cent (Swedish Ministry of Education and Cultural Affairs 1989: 285–7). In the same period, the total number of visitors to music performances had a relatively strong growth. The same is true of the percentage of people who claim to have attended a minimum of one performance during the last twelve months: from 35 per cent in 1976 to 54 per cent in 1987. This growth can partly be explained, however, by the growing significance of commercial culture and a greater acceptance of the relevant types of music as serious music: in Sweden statistics on musical performances now also include pop music, rock and folk music. In general, cultural participation in Sweden would appear to be on a greater scale than in other countries. Experts from the Council of Europe write that the percentage of the population which goes to the theatre there and visits museums and art exhibitions is, on average, a minimum of ten points higher than the percentage in the United Kingdom, the Netherlands and France. The figures for music and literature compare relatively favourably (Myerscough 1989: 115). The experts tend to ascribe this to the intensive policy of cultural dissemination of the Swedish government, but considering the large number of intervening variables, this is naturally difficult to prove.

It emerges from the available, inadequate data for the situation in the United Kingdom, that during the 1980s the number of visitors to stage performances and classical music performances remained relatively stable. The interest in opera, ballet and jazz probably grew somewhat (Arts Council 1991: 155–6; Feist and Hutchinson 1990: 29–40).

The picture given by the equally extremely limited and, in this case, not very reliable empirical data on possible trends in the United States over recent years is not very impressive. According to figures from the National Research Center of the Arts, the total number of visits to performances of classical music dropped between 1984 and 1988 by 26 per cent and that to theatrical performances by 25 per cent. Between 1988 and 1992 this trend seems to have continued, although less powerfully. During the period between 1973 and 1984 interest actually grew. The authors chiefly ascribe the fall they identified to the sharp decline in the quantity of free time which Americans have available to them: according to their calculations a decrease of 37 per cent between 1973 and 1987 (American Council for the Arts 1988: 12–5, 1992: 35–6; cf. Schor 1991).

Visiting museums

Whereas over the last thirty years attendance at performing arts has declined or at best stabilized, the museum public has grown almost everywhere, and often substantially.

For example, in the Netherlands between 1970 and 1990 the number of visits per year and per one hundred inhabitants rose from 594 to 1480 (SCP 1992: 309) The number of museums grew proportionally. This trend is also perceptible in the other countries discussed here, although it is nowhere so pronounced. A number of tentative comparisons can be made (American Council for the Arts 1988: 12; 1992: 35–6; Donnat and Cogneau 1990: 103; Gournay 1991: 280; PSI 1991:12: 73–9; Swedish Ministry of Education and Cultural Affairs 1989: 290–4).

In 1990, 35 per cent of the Dutch population claimed to have visited at least one museum in the past year. In 1987, this figure was 30 per cent for Sweden and France. The United States are the leaders.[17] In 1992, 53 per cent of the adult population declared that they had visited an art museum or gallery in the past year at least once. A problem with this sort of comparison, however, is that not everybody understands the same thing by 'museum'. This can differ from social class, country and period. In Sweden, for example, a distinction is made between 'exhibitions' which can also be seen in libraries, club houses and community centres and the like. If these visits are included in the figures, then the percentage rises from 30 to 60.

Nevertheless, it is clear that almost everywhere the museum public is growing in size. In Sweden, between 1975 and 1985, this growth amounted to 12 per cent; in the United Kingdom, between 1976 and 1990, 21 per cent; and in France, between 1961 and 1985, no less than 23 per cent. The rise in the total number of visitors seems in the meantime to have come to a halt. A reason for this is that, under the influence of a changing political climate, a large number of museums in the 1980s charged entrance fees. In the United Kingdom especially, as a consequence of this the museums have suffered a sharp drop in the numbers of visitors.

Although one runs the risk of being branded a doomsayer or cultural pessimist, the relatively rosy visiting figures to museums must be put somewhat into perspective. For example, the growth seems to have been considerably stronger in museums in the field of history, natural history and industry and technology, than in the art museums (Ganzeboom and Haanstra 1989: 17). In addition, museums worldwide are better able to attract visitors by attuning the supply to a higher degree to the taste of the great public. The former emphasis on learning has thus been shifted somewhat to entertainment.

Another explanation of the growth in museum visits is formed by the phenomenon of 'daytrippers'. Thanks to increased prosperity and mobility, tourist trips come within reach of far more people. People choose a destination which often turns out to be a museum. Knulst makes a connection between the rise in visits to museums and those to restaurants and attraction parks, and wonders whether people walk through a museum with the same attitude as they normally have sitting in a hall. He ascribes the popularity of museums to the fact that 'consumption' can be adapted to a great extent to individual needs: in contrast to a regular performance, one can come and go as one wants and determine the tempo oneself. Especially for people with children, this is an important advantage (Knulst 1989: 251).

Has there also been a social broadening with regard to museum visits? On the basis of an analysis of Dutch population research, Ganzeboom and Haanstra see no reason to give a positive answer to this question. The inequality between higher and lower educated groups has 'not declined in the course of time but rather grown' (Ganzeboom and Haanstra 1989: 25). Audience research (where not the population as a whole, but only the museum public is questioned) shows that relatively uneducated people, who in former times still went to a museum, have nowadays dropped out, a development which is in line with that of the performing arts and letters. The social psychologist Temme also concludes, on the basis of audience research, that there is little, if any, vertical spreading. Two-thirds to three-quarters of the visitors to Dutch museums nowadays have followed a third-level education (Temme 1988: 145).

Art museums chiefly, especially when contemporary art is being exhibited there, 'can expect an extremely well-educated public' (Ganzeboom and Haanstra 1989: 98). In contrast to what is generally thought, mega-exhibitions or blockbusters such as 'Vincent van Gogh' or 'Rembrandt', surrounded by publicity and – partly for this reason – heavily attended, would not appear to attract a different public. The only result of publicity is that the same well-educated professionals will travel greater distances to see a particular exhibition.

The Dutch findings are to a great extent in line with those in other Western countries. In France, the percentage of skilled and unskilled workers among museum visitors dropped from 29 to 23 per cent, a decrease which, according to Donnat and Cogneau, cannot be completely explained by the changing social composition of the French population (Donnat and Cogneau 1990: 103–9). Equally, Gournay and Wangermée express doubts about a greater flow of people from the lower classes, although they also confirm that the social composition of the museum public is more representative than that in other cultural fields (Gournay 1991: 280; cf. Wangermée 1991: 160).

In the United Kingdom, too, many studies have shown that 'museum visiting remains primarily a white/upper middle-class pastime' (PSI 1991:12: 77). A study carried out in 1991 showed that 20 per cent of the respondents from the highest social stratum identified, claimed to visit a museum at least once a year, as opposed to 4 per cent of those from the lowest stratum. If one only looks at the art museums and galleries then these figures are considerably further apart.

Finally, figures from the United States show, once again, that a rise in the absolute number of museum visits says little about the scale and the social composition of the public. Between 1984 and 1992, the percentage of American adults who claimed to have been in an art museum or gallery at least once in the preceding year dropped from 58 per cent to 53 per cent. The people who go, turned out to do this increasingly often: the average rose from 1.4 to 1.9 times per year. The absolute number of visits was therefore able to rise. It is probable that these were mainly carried out by people from the upper classes (American Council for the Arts 1988: 12; 1992: 35–6; Hendon 1990).

Receptive cultural participation at home and on the street

Visits to museums, theatres and concert halls are of course no more than an indication of cultural participation. In a certain sense what we are dealing with here is a conscious and chosen form of participation,[18] while one is constantly being confronted, less consciously and without aiming to do so, by cultural expressions. For example, someone who takes a stroll through a city, will come in contact with much art, from sculpture to architecture and from murals to posters. Numerous expressions of (industrial) design can equally be regarded as artistic expressions.

Participation can take place at home, too, with the help of radio, television, audio and video equipment. Research shows that in recent years these have really taken off. However, it also emerges that the cultural programmes on radio and television are also mainly followed by an elite. For example, an average of only 4 per cent of the Dutch population sometimes listens to classical music on the radio. The well-educated and the elderly are strongly over-represented among these people (WVC/Intomart 1989: 44). The same is true of the audience for art programmes on TV; around 60 per cent of the Dutch population never looks at such broadcasts. The young, and people with a basic education, are heavily over-represented in this group (Intomart/WVC 1989: 46; SCP 1992: 309).

These sorts of findings are confirmed by Hendon among others: the oft-heard assumption that those who do not go to museums, concerts and theatre performances will 'make up for it' at home via the television, radio or other audio-visual means, does not tally with the experiences in the United States. The people who, for example, can be considered as the museum public do watch television less than those staying at home, but if they look, they look more at art programmes (Hendon 1990: 453; cf. Wangermée 1991: 168).

The possibilities of reaching the public via television, video and the audio mediums are, nevertheless, exceptionally large. A small range in such mass media can still be many times greater than the audience of the theatres, cinemas or concert halls. For example, in 1988 in Great Britain a total of about 11 million people watched an opera performance on television, while 'only' 1.5 million attended a live performance (PSI 1990:6: 54). Researchers of the SCP note that about half of the Dutch population comes in contact with classical music via electronic media at least once a month, which is fifty times more than the percentage which attends a musical performance at least once a month (the question remains how long and intensive this 'contact' is). According to these researchers, the public for this mass media is also less elitist than that in the theatre and the concert hall (SCP 1992: 308; WVC 1993: 199).

Amateur art performance

Often, and unjustly, amateur art performance is hardly recognized as a full form of cultural participation. The attention of the policy-makers, the sponsors and the scientific researchers focuses mainly on the receptive forms of cultural participation and on the professional, generally subsidized, cultural products. As a consequence of this, in general, little empirical data has been gathered in this area.

An exception in the Netherlands is a study by Knulst and Van de Beek (1991; cf. Haanstra and Oostwoud Wijdenes 1990). They found that among the Dutch population of sixteen and older in 1979: about 65 per cent claimed to practice drawing and painting; 2 per cent sculpture, pottery, modelling and the like; 5 per cent played a keyboard instrument; 2 per cent played a stringed or wind instrument; about 5 per cent sang; 1.3 per cent were involved with the stage; 2 per cent with jazz, beat or classical ballet; about 1 per cent with folk dancing; 8.5 per cent with textile work (including waving and wall hangings); 1 per cent with writing poetry or prose; and 3 per cent with photography. A total of 26 per cent of the responses practised one or more of these disciplines (Knulst and Van Beek 1991: 23). The group of people who monthly actively participate is about 2.5 times bigger than those of the visitors to cultural institutions. The overlap between the two groups is rather large.

What are the social characteristics of the amateurs? The researchers state that 'in both active and receptive cultural participation there is an over-representation of: women, schoolchildren or students, people with a higher level of education, single people and people who are distinguished by a high degree of participation in general' (Knulst and Van Beek 1991: 47). This does not alter the fact that amateurs reflect the population as a whole, to a greater degree, than do visitors to theatres, concert halls and museums. The age and education, in particular, are of importance; income plays less of a role. As people become older, artistic activities decline sharply. This trend also continues over the age of fifty-five, when one has considerably more leisure time. Furthermore, from the research, it emerges that the chances of children participating actively in culture is considerably greater the more their parents (and above all their mothers) do this too, and that amateurs participate more receptively than the average.

Finally, it would appear that the number of participants in active forms of cultural participation, in contrast to those in receptive forms, has been reasonably stable over the last twenty-five years. The authors explain this, together with the more balanced social composition of the relevant group of participants, partly by 'the fact that the artistic citizen or his representatives in the governing bodies continue to determine the choice of style and repertoire within amateur art, while that say within the professional art circuit has been requisitioned by professional experts and advisors' (Knulst and Van Beek 1991: 99). These latter professionals have cultural preferences which increasingly deviate from (or perhaps precede) those of the average interested lay audience. The gap between audience and art is therefore bigger in the professional arts sector than in the amateur sector, with all the consequences for the scale of participation and the social compositions of the audience (we will return to this later in the chapter).

The findings in the Netherlands, in so far as can be judged on the basis of the empirical data available, are, for the most part, in accordance with those in other countries.[19] Here, we will confine ourselves to some data on Great Britain. In that country, too, it would appear that people in the upper classes participate more than people from the lower strata, but here too the social background of the amateurs is less elitist than that of the visitors to theatres, museums and concert halls (PSI 1991:12: 35).[20] Nevertheless, the chance that 'professionals, employers and managers' act, is five times bigger than those of 'skilled and semi-skilled manual workers'. Equally, the chance that they play a solo musical instrument is three times bigger, that they paint or draw about twice as great and that they write poetry, four times as great (PSI 1991:12: 3).

The percentages of people who are active in the various fields turns out to be about the same as in the Netherlands (PSI 1991: 32). In Great Britain, there is at best more acting, and more poetry written. Only the number of photographers is considerably bigger here (17 per cent instead of 3 per cent), but this difference is probably largely explained by the fact that holiday and family photos were explicitly excluded from the Dutch study. All the same, the degree of participation among the British turns out to decline strongly after the twentieth year and to not recover at a later age.

The elevation of the concept of art to 'culture'

Since the end of the 1960s a debate has been going on in practically every Western country on the tenability of the reigning concept of art. This is happening partly under the influence of the democratization movement, the rising cultural relativism and the disappointing degree of participation in culture, especially that of the lower socio-economic strata. The central idea is generally that the policy-makers and researchers are almost exclusively interested in 'traditional', 'nineteenth-century' forms of culture. These forms express, in the first place, the values and preferences of the 'bourgeois' middle classes and it is not surprising therefore that it is mainly members of these classes who participate in the relevant cultural activities. Young people and people from different social strata, however, have their own means of expression and identification. In order to evaluate this properly the traditional concept of art must be extended in the direction of the sociological or anthropological concept of culture. The starting-point here must also be that not just one culture exists, but a number, and that all these are equivalent. The thesis that large parts of the population do not participate in artistic activities is, for this reason, untenable: only that they participate in *different* artistic activities. (This way of thinking is further illustrated and criticized later in the chapter).

In this spirit, the so-called arts community movement made headway in Great Britain and, to a lesser extent, the United States during the 1960s and 70s. Lewis writes about this movement: 'It brought together in a rather muddled form a number of practices: bringing art to the community, promoting art in and by communities, and representing communities ignored by the dominant culture' (Lewis 1990: 113). Within this movement, there was particular attention to the value of active and thus not just passive participation in culture. The members furthermore oppose the dominant, elitist culture under the motto 'let a hundred flowers bloom'. According to Lewis, however, this often went off the rails: criteria of quality were abandoned and there was absolutely no interest in the answer to the question of whether there were also people who wanted to consume the 'art' produced. The goal of the production of art, however, is communication and this *implies* consumption.

The most important failures of the movement are, in Lewis's opinion, its inability to bring the arts to the great public. 'Community art' remained a marginal, harmless (and after some time even subsidized) phenomenon. The participants in community arts had an equally elitist background as the visitors to the traditional institutions; they were, at best, more left-wing in their political preference. They laid much emphasis on matters like anti-racism and sexism, and there was much attention to discriminated minorities such as gays, foreigners and the handicapped. However, this only brought into being different dividing lines rather than class and education. Lewis writes: 'Most working-class people were as alienated by the community arts as they were by the traditional' (Lewis 1990: 114).

A comparable development can be seen in the Netherlands, Sweden and France. Until the 1970s, policy-makers simply argued that everyone had the right to participate in one universal culture. An adequate infrastructure needed to be built to this end. In the 1970s this idea changed: there were different cultures and the policy had to do justice to this. In addition, the idea grew that culture cannot be communicated, but must be *experienced* by the people in their own environment. People had to be sought in their everyday existence and, to this end, other ministries and state bodies were brought in. For example, in France the Ministry of Education was supposed to reach the pupils, the Ministry of Employment the workers, and the Ministry of Public Health the handicapped. In the Netherlands, parts of the cultural policy, including the care for libraries, were accommodated in the *welfare* policy.

However, it has turned out to be difficult to give the principles named a practical translation. The size of the expenditure in this field has therefore remained extremely limited, which cannot be simply explained by unwillingness and the positions of power of the traditional institutions and their audiences. For example, in France in 1985 no more than about two million dollars were spent on special projects for people in rural communities and about a million dollars on special projects for the benefit of the workers. Not only the budget for these activities was extremely limited, but it must also be stated that the group of people who used the facilities created remained extremely small in scale and one-sided in social composition. Gournay concludes then that over the period between 1981 and 1986: 'official documents seem to indicate that achievements have been rather limited, if not extremely modest' (Gournay 1991: 290, cf. Wangermée 1991: 178).

Not only the government policy-makers were trying to reach new groups. In France and Sweden, there are committees within businesses which are concerned with the organization of socio-cultural activities. This is generally guided by trade union representatives and financed by means of a compulsory deduction from the total wage amount. Wangermée writes that the way in which the trade union members concerned (in consultation with the employees) spend the money available is an indication of the preferences of their following. A study carried out in France in 1983 shows that 3.9 per cent was spent on cultural activities in the traditional sense. This refers to libraries for books, videos and music material, lowered entrance prices for shows, and the organization of performances within the company. In addition 57 per cent was spent on trips and holidays, 25 per cent on all kinds of festivals and 9.4 per cent on sporting activities (Wangermée 1991: 171–3).

Balance

On the basis of the foregoing it can be concluded that in the countries discussed participation in most ('traditional') forms of culture has declined or, at best, stayed the same. This applies in particular to reading, possibly the most important form of cultural participation.[21]

The policy implemented in numerous countries to inspire more people to participate in cultural activities has therefore not been very successful (although the degrees of participation could of course have been much lower in the absence of policy). It is also improbable that social inequality in cultural participation has remained the same but that the middle and higher parts of the cultural stratification have expanded enormously. After all, in that case the absolute number of visitors to theatres and concert halls must have risen. However, Skok too states that absolute interest in 'traditional' culture is declining everywhere. At the same time, the significance of commercial mass culture is growing. According to him, policy will have to be more oriented to the latter culture, therefore, if it is not to lose every reality value (Skok 1991: 322).

Partly under the influence of the declining significance of the 'old' forms of culture, a tendency is indeed detectable in many countries to move the traditional concept of art in the direction of sociological or anthropological concepts of culture. This tendency is admirable in itself. It is evident that policy-makers and researchers have cleaved too often and too long to a concept of art which is too narrowly defined. There is no reason, for example, to exclude the many forms of pop music and video art. The arts are always developing: old forms drop out because they no longer have a significant message in the present day and new forms arise with which people can apparently identify. It is also naïve to exclude by definition the only popular culture we have at the moment, the commercial mass culture. A policy which seeks to be more than a facility policy for a small elite should take this culture more as a starting-point (we go into this further later in the chapter).

However, even when the concept of art is broadened in this sense, social inequality continues undiminished. Those who nowadays participate in 'traditional' cultural activities appear to be more active in *all* fields. In addition the problem of this social inequality cannot be solved by denying validity to the criteria with which it could be measured.

The experience of the arts community movement shows primarily that the little folk art or folklore which is left in modern society, is kept alive not by the 'people', but by the same elite which participates in the traditional art forms. The same is true of the means of cultural expression aimed at, among other things, minorities, which it was attempted to develop within this movement. Furthermore, the participants in the 'traditional' culture are also more active in the other imaginable forms of spending leisure time. In line with studies already mentioned, Hendon, for example, found that museum visitors not only participate more in 'traditional' cultural activities, but also show more activity with regard to reading, collecting stamps, coins and the like, visiting cinemas, amusement parks, sporting events and monuments, walking, jogging, gymnastics, camping, voluntary work and DIY on the house or the car. The only thing non-visitors do more is watch television (Hendon 1990: 449–52).

Such findings are reason enough for the American researchers DiMaggio and Useem to conclude that a large number of, in this case Americans, do not so much participate in different cultural activities, but are completely outside the culture. They write that research shows that:

> a sizable group of Americans are, in fact, cultural dropouts, individuals with no apparent artistic or cultural interests. Cultural deprivation then is not a matter of choosing performances or hobbies that diverge from upper-middle class norms; rather, it consists of having no creative or expressive pastimes, enjoying no performances, of any kind, and being equally immune to the claims of galleries, zoos, or public parks.
>
> (DiMaggio and Useem 1980: 65)

A comparable insight has been made with regard to the French, among others. A number of important forms of culture are totally ignored by the great majority of the French. Donnat and Cogneau write that 76 per cent have never attended a dance performance in their lives, 71 per cent a classical concert, 55 per cent a theatrical performance and 51 per cent an art exhibition. Twenty-eight per cent have never visited an historical monument and

26 per cent have never visited a museum, a percentage comparable to those who never read a book (Donnat and Cogneau 1990: 105). With regard to, among other things, the circus, the restaurant, the cinema or the attraction park, the degree of participation by the people who do participate in traditional forms of culture is higher (Donnat and Cogneau 1990: 115–122).

Only after one has equated, to a high degree, the concept of art with culture in the sociological sense, is it possible not to speak any more of a deficit. The British anthropologist Paul Willis (1990), for example, sees buying and wearing clothes and other fashion articles, and looking at and talking about soap operas as cultural activities (his ideas will be gone into more deeply later in the chapter). And the sociologist Owen Kelly refuses to draw a distinction between a sculptor and a maker of model ships. That only the sculptor is generally recognized as an artist is, according to him, the consequence of the position of power of the group which has embraced the relevant arbitrary art form (quoted by Lewis 1990: 6). A next step could be that eating, drinking and even sleeping are defined as artistic activities. However, it remains to be seen whether one helps people's chances of developing their talents and, in particular, their capacity for freedom with such perspectives.

This problem will be gone into further later in the chapter. The question first arises of what can explain the unequal participation in arts and letters and, related to this, why the social cultural policy implemented by some governments, especially after the Second World War, has, in a number of important fields, largely failed.

DETERMINANTS OF CULTURAL PARTICIPATION

With Ganzeboom, four variables can be distinguished which possibly influence the decision of individuals to participate in cultural activities: the available quantity of time and financial resources, the cultural competence and the desire to acquire status (Ganzeboom 1989: 31–62; cf. Knulst 1989: 99ff.; Kraaykamp 1993) These will be dealt with in succession.

Available time

The costs, in time, connected to receptive cultural participation increase when the accessibility of concert halls, theatres, museums declines. For example, this could apply to people who live outside the big cities. The research carried out in the Netherlands, however, shows that these costs do not play a significant role in the decision to participate in cultural activities (Ganzeboom 1989: 150). This finding is confirmed by research in the United States: people from smaller cities do not go appreciably less often to museums, theatre, ballet, opera, classical and jazz, than people from bigger cities. Unlike what one would probably expect, participation in the popular commercial culture is much more bound to place than that in the 'higher' culture (Horowitz et al. 1985).

The costs in time also become smaller the more leisure time people have available to them. Leisure research by the Dutch Social and Cultural Planning Bureau shows, however, that having more leisure time does not lead to more active use of that time or more participation in culture. 'The idea that people become busier simply through more free hours', write the researchers involved, 'is based on a widespread misunderstanding' (SCP 1988: 225). It is precisely the people with the least leisure time, that is those between thirty and fifty years old with a well-paid job and children, who are the most active socially, culturally and politically. Research has shown that people who do not participate in the regular work process, and should therefore have endless leisure time, often fall into apathy and lethargy. Thus, there is little empirical basis to be found for the idea that a growth in leisure time *in itself* will lead to a greater participation in culture.

Available financial resources

Second, cultural participation involves financial costs. These are smaller the more one has higher incomes and entrance prices are lower. However, research generally shows that 'having enough financial resources or not is hardly if at all related to cultural participation' (Ganzeboom 1989: 150). Some groups with extremely low incomes, such as students, can even be included among the top consumers of culture. The fact that mainly people from the higher socio-economic groups are culturally active is thus not explained by the higher incomes of the parties involved. Other characteristics of these people are determining.

Cultural competence

Third, the mental effort and the pleasure which the processing of cultural information implies, can be mentioned. According to Ganzeboom, these costs and benefits are by far the most important explanatory variable of the decision by individuals to participate culturally. A starting-point for this explanation model is that the stimuli emanated by cultural expressions can be placed on a scale of complexity and that the latter is exponentially related to feelings of appreciation: to begin with, with growing complexity, appreciation rises, boredom becomes excitement, but, after a certain optimum, over-stimulation evokes more and more feelings of unease and ultimately irritation. For example, the abstract paintings of Kandinsky or Picasso generally evoke more discomfort in unpractised eyes than the landscapes of Potter or Constable.

A second assumption is that individuals differ among themselves in their *capacity to process information*. This can be the consequence of two factors: people can differ in innate capacities for processing cultural information (for example, not everyone is equally musical), and people can distinguish themselves through their (socially determined) cultural knowledge and skills.

Someone who has already been in earlier contact with a particular cultural expression, will experience this as less complex or complicated and will sooner be bored by simple stimuli, to the extent that he has a greater cultural knowledge and skill. This *cultural competence* is the most relevant in this context: the importance of innate talent is obvious, but cannot be an explanation for the sharp over-representation of people from the higher social strata in museums, theatres, concert halls, bookshops and libraries.

This competence can be acquired in three ways: thanks to the training in the parental environment, the education enjoyed, and earlier experiences with cultural participation. Practice or habituation is therefore the midwife of art. The education received is not of only importance, in the sense that people become really familiar with various cultural expressions, also important is that the cognitive skills are developed which are needed to process complex cultural stimuli.

Ganzeboom concludes, as stated, that the capacity to process information 'is the most important mechanism responsible for differences in participation between parts of the population' (Ganzeboom 1989: 176). It has also emerged from other studies that the education enjoyed and the environment of origin are the most important determinants of cultural knowledge and skill, and thus of cultural participation (see, among others, Bourdieu 1979; Knulst 1989; Ter Bogt 1990; Wippler 1968).

According to Hendon, not following formal art education at an early age is of great importance here. On the basis of his research into museum visitors he writes: 'Clearly were we to pick among general education, arts education and parental influence, we would have to say that formal specific arts education has the strongest influence and general education the least.' Art education in the United States, as in most countries, is of little importance, and is even declining. But where it exists, 'it seems to have a powerful influence on those who undertake it, probably first by giving skill and knowledge and then by increasing and reinforcing experience' (Hendon 1990: 448).[22]

Research by Morrison and West in Canada also pointed out that *active* cultural participation at an early age exerted a much stronger influence on receptive participation in later phases of life than its receptive opposite (Morrison and West 1986). British and Dutch research confirms this finding. Furthermore, it emerges that the most important explanatory variable for the active cultural participation of children is not education or income, but the scale of the amateur art practice of the parents (PSI 1991: 36; Knulst and Van Beek 1991: 47).

It also emerges from the studies specifically focused on reading behaviour, that the acquired cultural competence is the most important explanatory variable. In particular, the status which the book enjoys within the parental environment turns out to be of great importance here. Children who have acquired in the pre-school stage a positive attitude with regard to the book, will not quickly lose this attitude. Barker and Escarpit write:

The character of reading habits has remote causes, going right back to the child's pre-school years. It is probably then that fundamental attitudes towards books are formed. The child who meets books for the first time when he goes to school tends to associate reading with the school situation, especially when no reading is done in the home. If school work is difficult or unrewarding, the child may come to dislike reading and drop it altogether once he leaves school. Ideally, therefore, books should become part of a child's life, of his play and everyday activities even before he starts school.

(Barker and Escarpit 1973: 109; cf. Brinkmann et al. 1990)

Reading aloud to extremely young children especially seems to promote this.

Acquiring status and the drive to distinction

Fourth, in the analysis of the variables influencing the decision of individuals whether or not to participate in cultural activities, it is possible to refer to 'pursuit of status'. The core of the classical sociological reasoning behind this is that various groups in society want to distinguish or distance themselves from others for reasons of status. They do this by following a specific lifestyle and characteristic cultural preferences. People announce their membership of a particular social class or grouping by conforming to the cultural norms and values applying within this. In short they 'tend to be culturally active in those areas where participation within their own social group or the reference group is laid down as the norm and accepted as a characteristic lifestyle' (Ganzeboom 1989: 60). Although his research results certainly cannot be interpreted in one single manner, Ganzeboom thinks that 'the second factor of weight in determining differences in cultural participation is that of considerations of status' (Ganzeboom 1989: 77).

People's tendency to conform to the norms and values of the group to which they belong or want to belong is often referred to in the literature to explain participation or lack of it by individuals in cultural activities. For example, the psychologist Temme claims that the source of the low participation by people from the lower socio-economic layers must be sought in their prejudices, that 'art is not for the likes of us'. He explains the tenacity of this prejudice by the striving towards a positive self-image. This becomes more of an advantage the more the values and norms of the group to which the individual concerned belongs are valued higher than those of other groups. By thus being 'rather denigrating' about the art and culture of the middle class, the lower classes reinforce their self-image. Temme regards breaking up these negative attitudes on art as a condition for a successful art policy. He sees an important role in this allotted for the mass media and education (Temme 1988: 149).

A fine illustration of the tendency of, in this case, second-level students to react against other groups, and the culture associated with these groups, is provided by an exploratory study by the Dutch anthropologist De Waal. In order to make an inventory of why teenagers participate so extremely little in cultural activities,[23] she held in-depth interviews with eighteen students aged fourteen to eighteen years. It emerged that the aversion they harboured in general against the arts was mainly due to the people they associated with them. Just like their parents, here the young people, who followed lower forms of education, distanced themselves from the arts mainly from motives of class. Young people who attend higher types of education do this in the first place for generational motives: in this way they are reacting to their parents, who usually belong to the upper socio-economic layers and the art lovers. De Waal puts it, in the words of the children involved, like this: 'A first judgement expressed about the art public is that they are arrogant: stuck-up types who can afford the luxury of concerning themselves with useless matters and exclusive types who think that other things are more important than those valued by ordinary people. Second, visiting art is associated with dull adults. Third, the art public does not fit in with the notion of manliness which is particularly held by boys from vocational schools in this study' (De Waal 1989: 68; cf. Lewis 1990: 19–20; Ter Bogt 1990: ch. 9; Willis 1990: chs. 2, 3). Certainly, boys do tend to regard things like ballet and classical music as being typically something for girls and sissies.

Temme's analysis links up partly[24] with the work of the French sociologist Pierre Bourdieu (1979) who has developed the 'status theory' most consistently in the field of cultural participation. Bourdieu's ideas are very popular among the sociologists who are concerned with cultural dissemination. They are thus regularly put forward to explain the failure of the dissemination policy.

In the interpretation of the Dutch sociologist Bevers (1988: 75ff.), Bourdieu claims that the cultural preferences and behaviours of people are rooted in the structure of society and its history over longer periods. Taste and style are used by people from different classes to distinguish and distance themselves from each other or to reflect themselves. The latter is particularly practised by the middle classes, who, in their attempt to climb the social ladder and to demonstrate that they 'belong', try to imitate the cultural behaviour of the elite. The social upper layer again wants to distinguish itself in taste and style from the rest in order to confirm and justify their superior social position. If the attempts at imitation of the social climbers unexpectedly succeed, then something else will quickly be claimed as art. The sociologist De Swaan writes in this context: 'where and when an artistic product successfully finds general acceptance, the cultural elite suddenly loses interest in it . . . as soon as a cultural item is disseminated, it is lost. It falls below the proper level' (De Swaan 1985: 47–8).[25]

The process thus formed of people and groups attracting and rejecting each other ensures, says Bevers, 'a dissemination of culture which proceeds naturally'. The dissemination which has taken place is, according to him, not so much due to the policy followed, as to the rise of the mainly middle class up the social ladder. In their quest for distinction, these social climbers have acquired great interest in bourgeois art. This self-generating cultural dissemination, writes Bevers, 'has been decisive for the possibilities of the cultural dissemination policy and only a policy that links up with it can be successful. That is why cultural dissemination has been most successful among the middle classes and has failed in so far as it was aimed at the lower classes' (Bevers 1988: 77). The boundaries of what is socially possible have, in his view, long been reached, and are happily increasingly recognized by the government. 'The state has come to realize,' says Bevers, 'that art has remained a Utopian wish for broad layers of the population and that it is better therefore to seek to link up with the circuit, in which there is already a certain degree of interest in art' (Bevers 1988: 72).

Balance

Looking at all this, it can be concluded that empirical research shows that cultural competence is the most important determinant of cultural activities of individuals. This is mainly obtained in education and the parental environment. Before people enjoy the freedom to participate in culture and, partly through this, to develop their talents and extend their horizon, they must first therefore be socialized in this culture. Without a learning process, there is no cultural competence; without cultural competence, no autonomy.

A different explanatory variable of cultural participation is formed by status-seeking. This is not very surprising as such, and also rather innocent. However, nowadays it is regularly linked to a strong cultural relativism. The perception that considerations of status play a role in the decision to participate in cultural activities is then extended into the sociologism that it is *exclusively* the drive to distinction which moves people to cultural participation. This sociologism is a threat to the development of individual autonomy. However, we go into the how and why of this in a later section.

CULTURAL POLICY IN PRACTICE

While I consider it highly unlikely, I cannot exclude the theoretical possibility that tomorrow I shall have some fabulous idea and that, within the week, I shall have written my best play yet. It is equally possible that I shall never write another play again.

When even a single author – who is not exactly a beginner and so might be expected to have at least a rough idea of his abilities and limits – cannot foresee his literary future, how can anyone foresee what the overall development of culture will be?

If there is a sphere whose very nature precludes all prognostication, it is that of culture, and especially of the arts and humanities.

(Vaclav Havel 1984: 123)

It has emerged from the foregoing, that in a number of Western countries social cultural dissemination was one of the most important objectives of post-war cultural policy. At the same time, however, it must be stated that participation in a number of important cultural activities during recent decades has actually declined. The policy has therefore not really been a success (even if it is naturally possible that cultural participation would have been even smaller without this policy). The causes of this can be found both in the policy itself and in external factors.

With regard to the latter, an example could be the technical progress and the enormously grown material prosperity which together have brought with them a large number of new possibilities for spending leisure time. Nowadays, it is not only possible to read books and visit cultural podia, but also to watch television, make day trips, maintain the car, spend holidays, visit a restaurant or fitness club, and so on. The results of these developments could be that the pressure on time has grown and this has been at the cost of the generally time-consuming participation in cultural activities.

Another possible cause is that people have increasingly come to see the pastimes mentioned as being of equal value to cultural activities. For example, Knulst seems to regard visits to theatre, concert and museum all as forms of 'leisure' or 'entertainments' that can be classified alongside visits to vaudeville and carnival. He can therefore call visitors to performing arts 'an audience of skilful and expert epicures'[26]. The cultural relativism which grew strongly in the post-war years can therefore explain the limited cultural participation. If all ways of spending leisure time are equal, then motivation for the mental effort which goes with participating in culture falls away. We will go further into this relativism and its consequences for cultural policy later in the chapter.

A different cause of the predominant failure of cultural dissemination is naturally formed by the object of the policy itself – culture. If one decides to build bridges, railway lines and roads, then the chances are that people will manage to realize the plans made. It is different with culture. Cultural developments are very difficult to direct. In this context, the sociologist Bart Tromp has accurately pointed out that the introduction and expansion of the car and the fridge have probably exercised a much bigger, and also unexpected and unintended, influence on culture than any cultural policy (Tromp 1994: 108ff.). This does not alter the fact, incidentally, that it is possible to plan more on the macro level than the micro level. In this regard, Vaclav Havel, as quoted in the opening, transfers too easily the unpredictability of his individual literary production to society as a whole. After all, for society, one can indeed plan how many orchestras, libraries, theatres and museums there are and how much attention is devoted in education to artistic training.

A different and very important reason why cultural developments, in this case participation in culture, are extremely difficult to influence, is that governments and other institutions who aim at a dissemination of culture, have little grip on the determinants of cultural participation. Rather, it turns out that it is not material but rather cultural inhibitions which prevent people from participating in culture. Considerations of time and money play hardly any role. It is a question of cultural competence which is acquired in the parental environment, in education, and by earlier participation. The state's possibilities for stimulating development of this are limited. They would have to intervene much more deeply in the existing socialization structures than happens in the current situation, which evokes resistance for understandable reasons. Here the state runs up against the emancipation dilemma.

Despite all the external factors mentioned, the lack of successes by the policy of cultural dissemination can also be due to this policy itself. In this section, therefore, it will be further analysed. Two characteristics of this policy are important here. In the first place, what is striking is the incrementalistic character of the cultural policy, and, in the second place, the one-sided emphasis laid on this policy on the supply side.

Incrementalism

> In the second half of the twentieth century, no matter where you look, politics happens to be nothing more than fiddling about, playing for time, delegation, improvisation, and its greatest ambition is to survive.
>
> (Hans Magnus Enzensberger 1990: 21)

The incrementalistic character of state policy in general, and certainly that in the field of culture, has often been pointed out. The policy with regard to museums, monuments, archives, libraries, letters, fine arts, art, media, design and architecture, theatre and mime, music and dance, amateur arts, and artistic training, has generally come into being bit by bit in a continuous process of negotiations between interested parties from the relevant art worlds, the bureaucracy, advisory councils and politics. The initiative to subsidize certain facilities was, and is, often taken here by powerful lobbies from society. Allocation is often on an *ad hoc* basis: there is seldom a weighing up of considerations within and between the various sectors (for example, symphony versus chamber orchestras, music versus theatre) and of balancing established institutions against new initiatives (symphony orchestras versus video artists). Furthermore, political discussion of this subject falls short of any substantial reasoning, with the consequence that cultural policy is not in a clear cultural–political context and is quite unsystematic and chaotic in character (Blokland 1993a; Cummings and Katz 1987: 350–67; Lewis 1990: 154; Mulcally 1987: 314, 330; Ridley 1987: 228, 234–40; Zijderveld 1988: 165–9).

However, the question is whether an incrementalistic policy model can always be seen as objectionable. For a long time, Anglo-American political scientists have argued that the incrementalistic policy model is most suitable, and in practice is generally used, for an open democratic society. Authors like Dahl, Lindblom and Wildavsky therefore regarded this policy model, inspired by political philosophers like Schumpeter, Berlin and Popper, as comparably acceptable (see, among others, Dahl 1956; Dahl and Lindblom 1953; Lindblom 1959, 1965; Popper 1945).

Incrementalistic policy is characterized, as has already become clear to some extent, by a continuous stream of marginal policy measures or adjustments, borne by various social actors or 'partners'. This is not so much an attempt to realize a well-defined long-term objective. Rather, it is an attempt to make a practical contribution to the easing of a pressing short-term problem. Decision-making is seen in this model as a product of an unremitting conflict about the instruments, values and objectives of the policy to be carried out, which explains why matters like exchange, negotiation, adjustment and compromise formation are central.

On the contrary, the synoptic model, the counterpart of incrementalism, is characterized by a fundamental consensus among the various actors on the instruments, values and objectives of the policy, and therefore by unanimity and harmony. Synoptic policy is created through an exhaustive, rational consideration of alternative instruments (and their consequences) in order to realize a rationally-planned, long-term objective. Although this form of policy plays an important role in theory, in practice it is seldom, or never, feasible.

To explain the relation between incrementalism and democracy, it is generally pointed out that the existence of many influential organizations, independent of the state and of each other, is characteristic of open democratic societies. In our Western political systems, it is not primarily the individual citizens who determine government policy through a direct form of democracy. This takes place indirectly via the so-called social midfield, consisting of a whole of more or less autonomous organizations which function as an intermediary and a buffer between the individual citizen and the state. Dahl speaks not of a democracy, therefore, but of a *polyarchy*. As a consequence of the often opposed interests and influences of these organizations, decisions are not taken by a single rational actor, from one central point, but are *disjointed*. The ultimate result is a more or less 'organically' grown compromise without any reason behind it, without a coherent and consistent plan for the realization of an extensive, well-defined goal.

To justify incrementalism, it is also emphasized that society is too complex, and the policymakers have too little information, to be able to make far-reaching and comprehensive decisions in a responsible manner. It is therefore better to implement mainly marginal alterations on the basis of the *status quo* and to gradually 'muddle on'. With smaller adjustments, less can go wrong and possible mistakes are easier to correct. In addition, marginal changes are generally accepted before radical ones. The social support which is indispensable, certainly in a democracy, for the success of government policy, is thus more easily obtained.

In short, if, in the same way, people see a democratic system as a guarantee of freedom for the individual, one makes a connection between freedom and incrementalism. In political systems guided in a synoptic manner, individual freedom would be endangered, because this would do no justice to the pluriformity of values and objectives and to the many possible definitions of 'the common interest'.

In recent years, a turnaround has, nevertheless, become perceptible in the appreciation of the incrementalistic policy model and of the polyarchic political system on which it is partly based (cf. Blokland 1993a). Precisely because they are considered among the founders of this 'pluralism' theory, it is quite remarkable that it is Lindblom and Dahl who are increasingly having doubts. The role of the interest groups especially, which is central in the theory of pluralism, is more critically regarded nowadays. For example, Dahl refers to the possibility that these organizations help to continue social inequality, to undermine the sense of public responsibility or the awareness of a common interest, distort the public agenda and keep the citizen from controlling this agenda (Dahl 1982, 1985; Lindblom 1982). Has not pluralism degenerated, goes the question, into what the political scientist Lowi called an interest group liberalism in which oligarchically organized interest groups, together with official organizations, take those decisions in an opaque process of negotiation which, in a true democracy, are reserved for politics?

Furthermore, people have started to wonder whether the mutual interpenetration or interweaving of state and society which goes with incrementalism does not lead to segregation, rigidity, immobilism and uncontrollability and, ultimately, to an undermining of the legitimacy of state and politics. A following question is whether the model offers enough space to value or substantive rationality and whether its application does not lead to technocratic instrumentalism, loss of control and direction and conservatism (see, for example, Dryzek 1990; Etzioni 1968; Goodin 1982).

The most fundamental problem seems to be that there is no more agreement on the normative criterion on the basis of which interests can be weighed up against each other or can be rejected. This leads to organized 'sector interests being unlimitedly pursued thus endangering the "common interest" ' (Lehning 1986: 6). Additional consequences include a permanent over-demand and overload on the state.

Nevertheless, it is precisely with regard to culture that an incrementalistic policy seems extremely defensible. The freedom of the individual is of exceptional importance here, and the power and influence of the organizations and authorities concerned with culture can therefore be spread as best as possible. It can also be argued that cultural diversity is the most powerful breeding ground for a vital, dynamic culture, and that this diversity can best be borne and guaranteed by a pluriform social system consisting of numerous organizations independent of each other and the state. In almost every country,[27] but especially in countries such as the United States, the United Kingdom and the Netherlands[28] a policy structure has therefore been formed in a well-considered manner with an extremely strong incrementalistic character (cf. Blokland 1993a).

In the first place, the parties involved have often consciously rejected developing any cultural–political vision. This would form a threat to the freedom of the arts (Mulcahy 1987: 328–9; Ridley 1987, 235–6). People also attempt to guarantee this freedom by placing policy implementation, as much as possible, in the hands of highly autonomous 'Arts Councils'. The politicians decide mainly on the *scale* of the budget of these councils, but they wish to involve themselves as little as possible in the spending of them. The choice of cultural–political visionlessness is characterized in both the politicians involved and the members of the arts councils. They only *react* to subsidy requests and make decisions on the basis of the quasi-objective and, for outsiders, hardly verifiable, criterion of 'quality' (cf. Ridley 1987: 240).

Furthermore, they have been able to create an incrementalistic policy structure by spreading responsibility for cultural policy over a large number of ministries, higher and lower authorities, councils, funds and institutions. What also contributes to incrementalism is that the interested parties are involved, to a high degree, in the development of the policy. For example, the members of the arts councils, which decide on the allocation of subsidies, are generally recruited from the relevant art world. For this reason, much decision-making takes place on the opaque intersection of bureaucracy and interest organizations. Finally, the relevant institutions and interest groups are often very strongly motivated and organized and have, thanks to their easy access to the media and their professional ability to manipulate the audience, a large potential power (cf. Cummings and Katz 1987: 360). Influence on policy formation therefore can also be enforced via sanctions.

We will return in a later section to the question of whether the critique of this incrementalistic model can also apply – or perhaps applies particularly – to the art and culture policy. First, a second characteristic of the existing policy will be looked at, a characteristic which is partly explained by incrementalism.

The emphasis on the supply of facilities

The second striking characteristic of cultural policy is that, properly regarded from the very beginning, it has been mainly a supply or facility policy: in practice, it boils down to the supply of cultural facilities to a small privileged group whose members were already initiated into the relevant cultural matters. This applies to an extreme extent in the United States and the United Kingdom. But it also applies to countries like the Netherlands, France and, to a lesser degree, Sweden.

Restricting oneself to providing cultural facilities is characteristic of almost all policy areas within the arts. On the basis of an analysis of Dutch policy, researchers from the Social and Cultural Planning Bureau conclude: 'Most objectives are associated with the supply side, a few with dissemination, very few with the consumer'. The policy is, in brief, 'mainly concerned with creating, conserving and making public cultural products and goods'

(SCP 1986: 164).[29] The extent to which, and by whom, use is then made of the facilities formed seems hardly relevant. Comparable analyses can be made of the cultural policy of most other Western countries.

An overview of the measures taken by twenty, mainly Western, countries to specifically promote cultural participation is offered by the contributions to the European Round Table on Cultural Research, a conference of the Council of Europe which was held in Moscow in 1991 (Wiesand et al. 1991). One of the three central subjects which national researchers were asked to examine, concerned the instruments which were used in their countries to promote cultural participation. An analysis of the resumés presented shows that, to the extent such a policy is carried out, it generally boils down to keeping entry prices low through subsidies, the promotion of dissemination of the cultural facilities in all parts of the country, and the responsibility for publicity. Skok concluded at the conference that, despite the generally recognized need to reach a greater public, cultural policy in most countries is characterized by an 'ongoing emphasis on infrastructure development, creativity, quality standards as well as mass media issues' and is still carried out within 'a supply-driven, welfare state model' (Skok 1991: 321).

In the case of Dutch policy, too, Ganzeboom states that 'the two most important measures with which the state has promoted vertical cultural dissemination, both refer to the supply side: keeping entry prices low and broadening and diversifying the supply' (Ganzeboom 1989: 160–1). Michel Schneider (1993), former policy assistant to the French Ministry of Culture, and Marc Fumaroli (1992), professor at the College de France, criticize the cultural policy of the French socialist Minister of Culture, Jack Lang, for this limitation. The return on this policy was extremely small because, in their view, it was almost solely concentrated on enlarging and improving the supply and there was hardly any investment in cultural education and cultural training. Instead of such an in-depth investment in cultural interest and competence, the demand or participation policy concentrates on spectacular media events such as the 'Fête de la Musique', which ushers in the summer, and 'Les Arts au Soleil', which enriches beach life.

For that matter, Wangermée and Ganzeboom point out that even the few measures on the demand side, which aimed to enlarge the cultural skills of the population, have probably not promoted social dissemination. Measures stimulating participation within and without education (for example, school concerts in mainly higher forms of education, music schools and artistic training) have, in practice, mainly reached the children of the better educated, with the probable result that social inequality in cultural competence has actually grown (Wangermée 1991: 181; Ganzeboom 1989: 161).

Another striking example of this are the measures taken in a number of countries to promote the purchase of artworks by private individuals, especially those with few financial resources. The parties involved are encouraged to do this by state subsidy. In the United States, especially, there are diverse tax measures with this goal in mind. However, research in the

Netherlands, among others, shows that the group of buyers and borrowers of artworks who use this sort of arrangement is extremely limited in size and very one-sided in social composition. The recipients saw the subsidy as a price reduction when they were already planning to buy an artwork.[30]

The supply policy, in short, has not led to a greater demand or social dissemination. The 'consumers' still come from the same social strata which already, in the nineteenth century, could successfully plead for state subsidy for 'bourgeois' art. It would appear that little has changed since then. In guaranteeing the cultural supply where the private sector could no longer bear the costs, Bevers then also sees the important value of state policy (Bevers 1988: 89). Through the differentiation and professionalization of the arts and of their audiences already mentioned, the tendency always present to concentrate on the supply of cultural facilities has grown even stronger. Art policy, writes Bevers, 'has become a facility policy for professionalized art forms with their sector audiences' (Bevers 1988: 91).

EXPLANATIONS OF THE ONE-SIDED EMPHASIS ON SUPPLY POLICY

Introduction

In the theoretical part of this book, the fact that positive freedom can first be acquired in, and thanks to, a society, was constantly referred to. One can only be autonomous, directing one's own life on the basis of one's own choices, if one has first become somewhat familiar with the relevant possibilities of choice. Numerous forms of artistic product are especially suitable for offering the possibility of extending one's own horizon, determined mainly by the education enjoyed, and in this way becoming free of old habits and customs. As we have already seen, the determining role of society in formal and informal education in the acquisition of culture and thus of autonomy, is confirmed by empirical research into the determinants of cultural participation: the 'capacity to process information' which is determined by education, parental, environmental and earlier cultural participation, is the most important explanatory variable for the nature and scale of participation in cultural activities. It is therefore noteworthy that in state policy aimed at promoting cultural participation by the lower socio-economic strata especially, hardly any attention is devoted to training, if at all. This policy turned out, as we saw earlier, to be mainly a supply policy: while the state ensures a high quality supply of cultural products, the degree to which they are used and by whom, seems to be of secondary importance.[31] In practice, therefore, this policy, even more than has always been the case, has turned into a facility policy for a small group of privileged experts and initiates, who together form the so-called 'Art worlds'.

How can this one-sided emphasis on the 'supply' or 'production' side of culture be explained? A number of related factors play a role.

Incrementalism: short-term thinking and the influence of interested parties

A first reason is to be found in the strongly incremental creation of the policy. This leads to short-term thinking and to a big influence by interested parties, who are seldom interested in promoting cultural participation.

In countries such as the United Kingdom, the United States and the Netherlands, state interference in the arts has generally come into being under influence of the pressure exercised on it by the middle class to subsidize certain cultural facilities, facilities which the middle class itself could not finance, or could no longer continue to finance. The historian Florian Diepenbrock, for example, outlines how, in the Netherlands, numerous cultural institutions were originally created by a 'small enterprising, visionary and daring group of prosperous citizens' and how 'rising costs and declining pioneering spirit' caused the relevant institutions to gradually end up in the sphere of the subsidizing authorities, around the time of the First World War. The notables were able to appeal successfully to the cultural conscience of the state and thus to its treasury. However, in doing so, they were mainly interested in guaranteeing the already existing cultural supply and *not* in creating new demand for it (Diepenbrock 1990 in Westen 1990: 159; cf. Bevers 1987; Eijsink 1990 in Westen 1990: 105–26; SCP 1986a: 35ff.).

The artists and the representatives of the arts world and the state, who nowadays sit on the extensive system of advisory organs, councils and committees, and who decide or advise on whether or not to award subsidies, also concentrate on the continuation or creation of a supply. This propensity is understandable as such. In this way, artists attempt, in the first place, to realize their artistic ideals and dreams and, understandably, secure their own employment. Certainly, when the state assures the parties involved of incomes, they will therefore be concerned with the product, rather than with demand for it. Here, a small consumption is often interpreted as proof that the artist involved is ahead of the common people in his understanding, and therefore imagining, of reality. Hence, a limited participation is ascribable to the people, rather than to the artist and his patron. In the course of time, the thinking often runs, the citizens will see that they were right all the same. After all, Van Gogh was not properly appreciated by his contemporaries either.

However, it is tempting for politicians and officials, too, to concern themselves chiefly with providing cultural facilities. In that case, the policy results are always tangible: a subsidized orchestra or theatre group can be heard and seen, and libraries and museums can be visited, can even be officially opened in person. The actual efforts are thus easier to legitimize politically and officially. This is much more difficult with a policy aimed at stimulating demand for, and participation in, cultural activities. The results of this are much less perceptible, and the chance of immediate success – within one government term, for example, so that it can be presented at the elections – is limited, as the determinants of cultural participation are extremely difficult to influence, and only over an extremely long period. Even just the fact that with regard to the demand side, in contrast to the supply side, there are hardly any policy instruments which produce results in the short term, means that they are inclined to concentrate on offering facilities.[32]

The tendency of policy-makers, who work within an incrementalistic mode, to concentrate on short-term problems is thus revenged here. Another characteristic of this model – the relatively large influence of interest groups – also has damaging results for the development of a demand or participation policy. In the first place, because the parties involved have, as stated, no direct interest in promoting participation. Second, because through the entanglement of state and interest groups a certain immobilism has arisen, so that it has become extremely difficult to implement a change in policy. The need now recognized in most countries to lay more emphasis on the removal of the immaterial inhibitions on cultural participation are thus hardly translated into policy measures.

Third, there is a specific problem here (cf. Blokland 1996; Cummings and Katz 1987: 16–7; Myerscough et al. 1994: 53ff.). Giving an answer to the question of whether certain producers of culture are eligible for state support is, in numerous countries, delegated by the state, as has already been stated, to committees of experts. The criterion used here is mainly 'artistic quality'. The experts, who are generally recruited from the relevant art worlds, often turn out to have a rather limited idea of this value. Dutch research (Hekkert and Van Wieringen 1993) shows that, in assessing expressions of culture, they lay far more emphasis on 'innovation' or 'originality' than the average art lover. This could be explained, in the first place, by the fact that they have an above average cultural competence and therefore require more complex stimuli, more untrodden paths, to be excited or, at any rate, not to be bored.

An additional explanation is that in the contemporary art world, innovation and avantgardism has become an almost absolute quest, and thus a cliché. According to Nobel prizewinner Octavio Paz, in this way modern art is beginning to lose its critical function: 'Its denials have for years been ritual repetitions: rebellion has become a method, critique rhetoric, transgression method. The denial is no longer creative' (quoted by De Haes 1992: 37). There is little discourse with society any more. The artists have increasingly come to debate with themselves and, in this way, according to the Belgian art critic Leo de Haes, an 'autistic' and 'hermetic' art world has come into being. Artists have therefore liberated themselves from society, but at the same time have become prisoners of themselves (De Haes 1992: 34–37).

The consequence of these two tendencies is that a supply of complex innovatory cultural products is stimulated and produced, a supply that requires ever more preliminary knowledge to be able to understand it and appreciate it. The gap between the interested layman or enthusiast, on the one hand, and the artist and initiate, on the other, has therefore become bigger and bigger. The result of this is that it has become increasingly difficult for newcomers to penetrate within a particular art world. By definition, the supply excludes a large participation. This process probably helps to explain the elite formation already mentioned within the audience for the theatre and fine arts.

Faith in spontaneous self-development

A second reason for the state's strong emphasis on the supply side in its cultural policy can be found in the widespread conviction that, certainly with rising prosperity, a supply of cultural facilities creates a demand as a matter of course. To a greater or lesser extent, the so-called 'hierarchy of values' of the American psychologist Maslov was thus implicitly assumed: people have an innate drive to spiritual self-development and to enjoy aesthetic experiences and these become stronger the more the basic needs have been met. The demand for culture would thus rise as prosperity increases; no state policy is needed for this.

Typical in this respect, is a sentence from the dissertation 'State and art in the Netherlands' by the Dutch social democrat Eduard Boekman, seen in the Netherlands as one of the founders of the idea of social cultural dissemination:

> Interest in art can exist just as little in the masses as capacity for cultural pursuits, when its level of welfare is low, its education inadequate, its working hours too long, its dwellings bad. To the extent that all this improves, its mental level also rises, its need for values which are outside the struggle for immediate existence.
>
> (Boekman 1939: 187)

A comparable standpoint was represented by the Dutch sociologist in 't Veld-Langeveld. In her influential essay of 1961, 'De sociale cultuurspreiding', she stated that the cause of the low participation in cultural activities by the working class must be sought 'in the condition that their socio-economic emancipation is not yet sufficiently consolidated. They lack the comfortable certainty of an established social and economic position, from which they can afford the 'useless' effort of cultural consumption' (in 't Veld-Langeveld 1968: 205).

Since 1961, the average level of prosperity in most Western countries has doubled, and certainly in countries like Sweden and the Netherlands every citizen is assured by an extensive system of social facilities. However, for the time being there is little extra 'unused effort' to be detected. It seems therefore more realistic to assume that human needs which transcend the elementary level do not develop independently, but chiefly in interaction with the social environment (cf. Wangermée 1991: 27, 199).

Individualization as *self*-realization

A third reason for the limited bias of the policy towards stimulating the demand for cultural products is formed by the growing individualization within Western civilization and the accompanying emphasis on negative freedom: when using the word 'self-development' the emphasis has increasingly come to rest on *self* and this has not made it easier to justify a policy in which training or enculturalization form more important elements than is currently customary. 'Self-development', the philosopher Mooij correctly writes, 'is somewhat reminiscent perhaps of the neo-humanist ideal of personality, but is nevertheless something very different. It lacks the emphasis on education, erudition and tradition' (Mooij 1987: 103). This specific idea of individualism, which Taylor calls a 'culture of authenticity', has already been examined in this book (see Chapter 3).

Cultural relativism

A last reason for the one-sided choice of a supply policy is, to a high degree, related to the last one, and has also been discussed already. It is formed by the cultural relativism which has grown sharply, certainly since the 1960s; it has become increasingly difficult to justify the dissemination of culture, which is inevitably accompanied by the making of normative choices with regard to content. In the so-called 'permissive society', driven on by a rising cultural relativism and related individualism, wellnigh all possible cultural products, values, ideas, thoughts, lifestyles and tastes became acceptable and were also considered suitable for subsidy (cf. SCP 1986a: 32). Unfortunately, this was not always an expression of a well-considered pluralism, of tolerance on the basis of a solid comprehension of the boundaries and possibilities of our understanding, but also of indifference (cf. Blokland 1988b).

CULTURAL POLITICS WITHIN THE CULTURE OF AUTHENTICITY

The two reasons mentioned last, the increased individualism and relativism, have had far-reaching consequences for the possibility of implementing a demand policy. Two important illustrations of this are developed in this section: the prevailing ideas on the meaning of the concepts of democracy and culture.

The concept of democracy

Value relativism and individualism are, as has been argued earlier in this book, closely bound up with the ideas prevailing in Western liberal states on politics and democracy, (Ideas which, in their turn, are closely bound up with ideas about policy.) These can be defined briefly as follows.

The conflicts of interests which inevitably arise in society through the scarcity which is thought unlimited are, in principle, considered irreconcilable. This is based on the assumption that no objective or generally accepted values are to be found, on the basis of which could be decided which party had right on its side in a conflict of interests. Politics is only a procedure, a system of rules, with the aid of which the inevitable conflicts of interests can be settled in a peaceable manner and prevented from resulting in social chaos and disintegration. Politics is understood, in brief, as the continuation of social conflicts by peaceful means.

This concept of democracy is founded on the principle of 'one man, one vote'. In practice, this is not only an expression of the belief in the fundamental equality of people, but also of the conviction that there are no normative truths or untruths. The deviating judgements and ideas of various individuals are therefore equally true or correct in principle, and their preferences or interests must therefore be taken completely as the starting-points in the political decision-making process. Every preference or opinion is of equal importance here. This is translated into the role ascribed to political parties: they form no sources of possible solutions to social problems, or of ideas on how society must be organized to make the 'good life' possible, but, in the first place, are conduits for the preferences articulated in society, usually through established interest groups. The stronger the value relativism within a party, the smaller the role of political ideology or theory. Ultimately, an opinion poll into the preferences of people in the country could determine their viewpoints or, directly, the government's policy.

To a greater or lesser degree, this conception of democracy is also broadly accepted, not just within liberalism, but, since the rise of the New Left, also within social democracy. This has the following cultural–political consequences. 'Policy' can be defined as 'the solving of a problem'. If the government wants to be able to implement a policy, then, in the conception of democracy sketched above, its citizens must have first perceived a particular phenomenon as a problem. This will not soon be the case with regard to culture: citizens seldom characterize their own cultural preferences as a problem and therefore press their representatives for a policy aimed at changing this. Within this concept of democracy, therefore, cultural policy can only mean a confirmation or reinforcement of the existing preferences. Government policy must after all link up completely with the current cultural preferences. Every attempt to solve the emancipation dilemma, to stimulate understanding of, and the demand for, unfamiliar cultural products, will therefore be characterized as undemocratic, elitist, or even totalitarian. Only a few politicians are prepared to take the risk of being confronted with this sort of characterization.

The concept of culture

The relativism which characterizes the contemporary concept of culture, is a second important obstacle to a policy aimed at enlarging participation in cultural activities. The popularity of the 'status theory' previously discussed is an important expression of this relativism. As was stated earlier, the French sociologist Bourdieu is an influential interpreter of this theory, which will be gone into somewhat more deeply here. According to Bevers, his theory boils down to this, 'that good taste is no personal achievement, nor does it reflect the intrinsic values of art, but is primarily a product and producer of class boundaries'. Properly regarded, according to Bevers, Bourdieu does not want to make a distinction between the *aesthetic* question of what is beautiful, and the *sociological* question of why certain people find certain things beautiful at certain places in certain times. He, writes Bevers, 'seems to occupy the radical standpoint that there is no other possible valid answer to the first question except that of the sociologist, because nothing is beautiful in itself, but is only found beautiful socially. For this reason he finds the first question meaningless and therefore exchanges it for the second' (Bevers 1989: 9).[33]

In the following, a number of examples of this status theory, whether or not inspired by Bourdieu and found in different hard and soft versions, will be discussed. These will further clarify its contents and implications. After that, a critique of this way of thinking will be formulated. The ideas related to the theory of status are not just to be found among its adherents. However, within the theory concerned they form a somewhat coherent whole, reinforcing each other, and they are formulated very explicitly. Partly for that reason, it is useful to take it as a starting-point.

A first important, widely prevalent, idea about cultural activities, an idea which is also central to status theory, is that these only serve to distance ourselves from others. An example is the Dutch literary sociologists Verdaasdonk and Rekvelt who write that Bourdieu, in *La Distinction*, 'came to the conclusion' that the use of art or taste in general 'serves to distinguish oneself from other classes . . . and is an integrating component of the entirety of strategies with which social groups try to consolidate or improve their position' (Verdaasdonk and Rekvelt 1981: 53).

In addition, a principle of status theory is that no supra-social criteria exist against which the quality of cultural products can be measured. The prevailing ideas in this field are exclusively the results of power relations. The choice of the cultural goods which are communicated to pupils in education is an example of this, according to Bourdieu, in Verdaasdonk and Rekvelt's reading: 'In *La Reproduction* (Bourdieu and Passeron 1977) education is analysed as a form of "symbolic violence": an "arbitrary" power imposes an "arbitrary" culture. Neither the power nor the culture can be derived from any universal principle and rest exclusively on the power relations between the social classes.' The same is true of the answer to the question of what the authority of literary institutions such as literary criticism and the universities is based on. Verdaasdonk and Rekveld write: 'Bourdieu's analyses lead to the answer that this authority cannot be founded on any universal principle – it is based on the power relations within the cultural force field and in consequence, in a distorted sense, on that between the various social classes' (1981: 55).

Since Bourdieu's discoveries, Verdaasdonk, now professor in the sociology of literature, has devoted himself to the empirical study of power relations within the field of letters: who determines, with what means of power, which books and which writers come to belong to the literary canon? In this he emphatically supports 'Bourdieu's insight that ideas about the nature, the quality and the attractiveness of cultural products, therefore also of books, are institutionally determined' (Verdaasdonk 1990: 4; cf. 1989). In his opinion, this insight has already been widely accepted: 'since the 1970s an awareness has generally spread that every definition of what literature is, is no more correct or incorrect than any other arbitrary definition' (Verdaasdonk 1989).

The British sociologist Justin Lewis is also inspired by Bourdieu's ideas. (He bases himself here mainly on Garnham and Williams (1980).) In line with Bourdieu he states that one must necessarily have the 'cultural capital' to be able to unravel the meaning of artistic expressions. This is acquired in the parental environment and at school. The 'higher' the art, the more complex in nature this will be and the more cultural capital is needed to be able to fathom the relevant artworks. The higher strata have more capital, can therefore understand more art, and will attempt to distinguish themselves in this way from the lower strata.

This argument is not necessarily culturally relativistic, but to this Lewis adds the thesis, actually unnecessary for his argument, that dubbing an object as 'art' has a purely ideological function. Objects do not, in fact, have a single intrinsic aesthetic quality: quality is completely ascribed. The value system on the basis of which is determined nowadays which arts are subsidized or not, is therefore also 'ultimately arbitrary'. It also legitimizes the lower classes subsidizing the chance aesthetic preferences of the upper classes. This arbitrariness, says Lewis, does not just apply to the prevailing values in the arts world: 'That is the nature of any value system: value is attributed to something, it is not part of its essence' (Lewis 1990: 20).

Lewis then goes into the question of what this value system derives its authority from. Referring to Bourdieu, he says that the current value system in the arts is maintained by the existing power relations within society, reproduced by the family and education. It derives its coherence from the logic of cultural competence and, because it is intertwined with the other power structures in society, this value system no longer seems arbitrary. Lewis summarizes his position as follows:

artistic value is an arbitrary aesthetic system. It is based upon and inscribed within social positions. It is not an 'essence' that lurks within the artistic object . . . While this system is arbitrary . . . it is both powerful and coherent. Power in our society is generally held by people who have been to university and/or who have come from 'culturally competent' backgrounds. As Bourdieu suggests, this means that this system of artistic value is maintained by the power structures that govern the society in which we live.

(Lewis 1990: 11)

In the rest of his book, Lewis turns out to abandon these principles.[34] It could not be otherwise. His central question is: 'What, of cultural value is the free market unable to provide' (and must therefore be stimulated by the state) (Lewis 1990: 1)? It is only possible to give an answer to this if one considers oneself in a position to distinguish quality, a quality which is not strictly sociologically defined.

Striking in this context is that market liberal economists like the Belgian Paul de Grauwe can completely agree with the sociological principle that people participate in cultural activities chiefly to distinguish themselves from others. This principle, which De Grauwe also ascribes to Bourdieu, enables him to conceive of the arts exclusively as economic goods, comparable to the other consumer articles such as fridges and ice creams. On the basis of this, they can then advocate allowing the production and distribution of cultural products to be determined completely by the market. Here, the generally radical social critics who adhere to the status theory, suddenly find themselves in the market liberal camp – often to their own surprise (cf. Blokland 1992a).

According to De Grauwe, the cultural elite is turning against the market because this is a neutral allocation means 'which does not recognize the superiority of the artistic taste of the elite' (De Grauwe 1990: 74). Artists who exploit the preferences of the masses, in this case the lower classes, can achieve great successes within the market system. However, this conflicts with the social role which the arts play for the higher classes. The parties involved cannot distinguish themselves with forms of art which are also consumed by the masses. They therefore choose forms which are relatively expensive, so that they remain beyond the reach of the common people. In order to pay for these, the members of the elite will turn to the state, using here the argument that their preferences are of a superior quality. As politicians and officials belong to the same intellectual elite, they will lend a willing ear to this argument. In consequence, their preferred art forms will be the most subsidized (De Grauwe 1990: 156–7).

However, in a democratic society this practice requires some legitimacy. This is obtained by subsidizing access to the arts in such a way that in principle the people from the lower classes are also financially capable of participating. However, in everyday practice this gesture is meaningless as the subsidy policy has ensured that only an 'intellectualized' art is provided which can still be appreciated only by a small group of initiates. Because of the subsidies, the incomes of the artists have become independent of the appreciation of the great public and, in consequence, they no longer need to take into account the artistic preferences of the masses (De Grauwe 1990: 158). For the elite therefore it is killing two birds with one stone: thanks to the subsidies, the cultural facilities have become cheaper and an exclusive supply is created with which they can distinguish themselves from the masses.

Another idea which is very prevalent today, certainly among the theoreticians of status, was already implicitly apparent in the foregoing. This boils down to the assumption that there is an 'authentic' culture of the lower classes, in the same way as an Indian or Japanese culture can be identified. This culture is supposed to be equal to that of the bourgeois cultural disseminators, but neglected, even suppressed, by these public educators.

A suggestion bound up with this is that advocates of cultural dissemination are guilty of elitism and cultural absolutism. For example, Ganzeboom says that the relevant efforts must be seen in the context of 'religiously inspired ideologies' rather than, as generally happens, of social-democratic ideas. Cultural dissemination, he writes, does not mean that the lifestyles of backward groups are fully recognized and are therefore also subsidized. On the contrary it is a matter of a 'civilization offensive' in which the lifestyles of social elites are forced upon the lower classes (Ganzeboom 1989: 158). However, since the 1960s, 'the idea that civilization offensives are repugnant . . . because they show a *cultural imperialism* and thus suppress *authentic lifestyles* of suppressed strata, has been gaining ground [HTB italics]' (Ganzeboom 1989: 159). However, Ganzeboom does not explain which 'authentic lifestyles' he has in mind. Also unclear is what 'inferior' means within his thinking.

Comparable assumptions are to be found in Jan Kassies, the former secretary of the Dutch Arts Council and originally one of the most influential advocates of cultural dissemination. In his view, the existing policy favours the value orientations of the bourgeois groups, who have succeeded in institutionalizing their preferences. According to him, the concepts 'art' and 'culture' must be redefined and, on the basis of these definitions, the available resources must be 'drastically' reallocated among the various cultural groupings. 'We shall', writes Kassies, 'have to strip the concept of culture of its normative implication that there is only one culture . . . in one's own country too, also among the native Dutch, many different "cultures" are to be found and by no means all of them are done justice to' (Kassies 1984: 244; cf. Kassies 1983).

A variation on the principle that the lower classes have authentic arts and letters, which quantitatively and qualitatively are equal to those of the 'middle classes', is the idea that there is a fully-fledged, original youth culture. This makes socialization into the culture of adults repugnant and superfluous. Such a standpoint is held by, among others, the Dutch pedagogue Dick van Zuilen and the British sociologist and anthropologist Paul Willis. Both consider the question of how 'the arts' can be brought to the young to be completely outdated. For example, Willis believes:

> that our best chances of encouraging an artistic democracy are not through 'democratization' of the 'arts' – opening access for new 'publics' to the established institutions and practices – but through an identification, recognition and support of existing creative experiences and activities not at present regarded as 'artistic' but which are now a part of our common culture.
>
> (Willis 1990: 10)

For him the core idea is that the narrow view of art must be broadened to *culture* or, in other words, 'the boundaries drawn between arts and non-arts need to be redrawn or declared entirely defunct' (ibid.).[35]

Willis wants to assume a 'grounded aesthetics' experienced daily by ordinary people. He distinguishes this from the 'conventional aesthetics', which are applicable to cultural expressions which in former times perhaps had a meaning which was deeply felt by many, but not today. The arts which obtained a subsidized position in institutions like museums, theatres and concert halls are an example of the latter. They give the great majority of the young no support at all in the development of an identity and frame of reference and the young therefore ignore these arts *en masse*. Instead of the arts from the nineteenth century which still control our thinking, writes Willis, 'we need twenty-first century ways of understanding cultural processes very different from the static, minority and elite notions of "culture" as the making, performance or appreciation of special or unique, artistic things' (Willis 1990: 53).

To develop a personal identity and context of interpretation, people can use numerous commodities or symbols, not necessarily artistic. Willis confirms that in our society these are mainly produced, and with great success, on the market. What the 'arts establishment' tries to promote is therefore 'already there'(Willis 1990: 52). He emphasizes that, in contrast to what is often claimed, the relevant commercial culture is not consumed passively, but actively. People must independently lend significance to it and, in Willis's view, this too is a form of cultural activity. It is therefore not possible to make a hard distinction between active and receptive participation: in everyday life everyone is a producer of culture. Thanks to the strictly individual and constantly changing attribution of meaning to, or interpretation of, the products of the commercial culture, this culture is furthermore exceptionally pluralistic and dynamic.

Willis mentions as examples of present-day artistic forms of expression, among others: playing, listening to, talking about and dancing to pop music; looking at and talking about television programmes (popular soap operas, according to Willis, especially require active participation as they compel the viewer constantly to wonder what he or she would do in the situations outlined); playing with video games; the purchase and wearing of different combinations of clothes; 'room and personal decoration'; 'the rituals of romance'; and, as ultimate proof that an aesthetic can be discovered in the most everyday activities, 'drinking and fighting'.

The consumption of alcohol creates an atmosphere of risk and uncertainty in which control has been lost and 'anything' can happen. This possibility of adventure, writes Willis, 'constitutes a kind of grounded aesthetics of risk, risk-taking and lack of (routine) determinacy' (Willis 1990: 45). This risk consists mainly of the chance of getting caught up in a spiral of challenge and being challenged, which ultimately ends in a fight. It is necessary here to constantly balance between attack and withdrawal, between acquiring or retaining respect and being humiliated. The ultimate ignition expands in a spectacular manner the consciousness of reality because the everyday conventions evaporate in the heat of battle: 'there is no past, no future, only a very consuming present' (Willis 1990: 49). An enormous uncontrolled and uncontrollable power is freed which inspires both admiration and fear and loathing, emotions which do not fit into the bourgeois culture of self-discipline. Naturally, says Willis, violence cannot be justified, but the values and identifications which accompany it:

> also concern a desperate kind of honour, a strange respect for the space around dignity and a mad courage which confronts banality with really live drama. Whether we like them or not, these are some of the contradictory living arts of survival – physical, psychic, cultural. Horrifyingly, hypnotizingly, they contain some of their own specific grounded aesthetics.
> (Willis 1990: 51)

Willis makes no concrete proposals for a different policy. This would imply the creation of new institutions, institutions which are at loggerheads with the fundamentally informal culture which young people create. According to him, institutions can be seen essentially 'as the attempt by one group with power (formerly through aristocratic patronage, now state patronage) to tell another larger group what is good for them: not to make their choices wider, but to make their choices for them' (Willis 1990: 56). As far as Willis is concerned, as much as possible must be left to the market economy, because this has turned out to be much more capable of creating symbols with which the young can create their own identity in a creative manner. This consumption must, at best, be expanded and deepened. This can take place, for example, by subsidizing the purchase of musical instruments and audio equipment.

The conclusion that 'bourgeois' arts cannot link up in any way with the world of everyday experience, does not apply to the young only, but to all non-bourgeois classes. The sociologist in 't Veld-Langeveld, formerly a very influential advocate of cultural dissemination in the Netherlands, provides an example. In 1961 she emphasized that in our age, the desire for 'public education', which was perhaps still dominant in the nineteenth century, has been increasingly replaced by the *democratic* attempt to allow people, irrespective of their origins, to share in the pleasure or happiness that cultural participation can offer. The ideal of cultural dissemination, she wrote:

> contains the desire to expand culture, without any pedagogic intention, not for moral elevation, not to directly reinforce nationalistic, democratic or socialist awareness, but mainly and above all, because it will contribute to happiness . . . Thus the desire to spread the enjoyment of culture for its own sake fits completely into the context of the welfare state, a fundamental principle of which is that all good things in life must to some extent be accessible to all.
>
> (In 't Veld-Langeveld 1961, 187–8)

Despite some annotations, however, in 1988 In 't Veld-Langeveld could broadly accept (her own interpretation of) Bourdieu's analyses. Referring to his ideas and, for the most part, the failure of postwar cultural dissemination, she writes:

> Even though understanding of art can be learned, learning is repelled by the unwillingness which arises where art is fundamentally foreign to the lifestyle of particular socio-economically defined population groups. They lack the aspirations, the interest, there is not a single motivation, on the contrary, there is defensiveness against an imposed commodity. In retrospect, I have also wondered what got into us, idealists of cultural dissemination, in the 1950s to want to unnecessarily force something on people which they clearly did not want.
>
> (In 't Veld-Langeveld 1988: 155)

It is no longer a question of creating social conditions which are necessary for being able to enjoy the cultural achievements of Western civilization, but of 'imposing'. Art is 'fundamentally foreign to the lifestyle' of lower socio-economic groups. In this context, Kassies too emphasizes the pattern character of a culture (Bourdieu would talk of a 'habitus'): the various elements of a culture are closely related to each other and 'it is not possible to pick out one element as it were in order to change just that'. As bourgeois art is more or less a foreign body in the pattern of culture of the lower social strata, post-war vertical dissemination policy had to fail (Kassies 1984: 240, 242).

The influence of ideas of the type discussed above, has not been confined to the intelligentsia. This set of ideas has also left deep traces in the policy of art and educational institutions. An article by the sociologist Prins in the professional journal of Dutch librarians can illustrate this influence in the world of libraries. Here, he looks at the question of whether the library must be guided in its purchase policy by the 'criteria of quality of a particular social grouping' or by 'the preferences of the consumer', as these are expressed in borrowing behaviour. Prins shows that, in practice, the latter has been increasingly chosen (cf. Knulst 1987; Blokland 1992c, 1996).

However, until now, this choice has remained implicit and Prins argues therefore that it should be made explicit. After all: 'The quality of the collection . . . cannot be defined by any condition . . . the standards of value with regard to literature are institutionally defined and differ from one social group to the other' (Prins 1983: 255). For 'scientific' and 'democratic' reasons therefore a 'relativistic approach to value in the forming of collections' must become the explicit principle. If figures for lending show that, in terms of business economics, too few people are interested in Kafka and Proust then these books can be removed from stock.

The Dutch philologist Jaap Goedegebuure, in his book *Too Lazy to Read?*, has described how 'democratization' took shape in educational programmes during the 1970s. According to him, during these years 'a crisis arose in literature teaching. After all, where did the standard of literary quality and the norms for designations like "classic" and "immortal" come from? Surely from the consciousness of power of the ruling class' (Goedegebuure 1989: 24)? Accordingly, an overpowering importance had to be ascribed to the pupil's needs. Kiosk books, newspapers, pornography, cartoons and political writings were mentioned here as acceptable starting-points for education, in which the unmasking of ruling ideologies was an important value. An entire generation of teachers of Dutch was trained in this spirit.

According to the philologist Robert Alter, the same happened in the United States. Under the influence of structuralism, semiotics, Marxism and other schools of thought, the critical spirit of 'a whole generation of professional students of literature' was transformed into scepticism and into a contempt for literature. Alter writes: 'In both criticism and in debates over curriculum, one encounters an insistence that daily newspapers, pulp fiction, private diaries, clinical case studies, and imaginative literature belong on one level, that any distinctions among them are dictated chiefly by ideology' (Alter 1989: 11). Partly as a consequence of the popularity of this sort of view, reading 'older' texts has increasingly become a major task for the present-day students and pupils. The necessary vocabulary and the knowledge of Western (Judeo–Christian) civilization is lacking (cf. Bloom 1987: 62–8; Goedegebuure 1989: 30–9; Hirsch 1988).

Additional critique of the status theory

> Not so much revolutionizing the arts, as unlocking to the masses the wonderful art-achievements the ruling classes until now have monopolized for themselves, is the artists' and art-lovers' obligation to the proletariat.
>
> (Karl Kautsky)

The idea of democracy discussed earlier has already been criticized in various places in this book. In this section, the discussions will be confined to some remarks on the constituent elements of status theory. These form a supplement to the critique of the culture of authenticity, which has also been formulated in numerous places.

Four related subjects will be dealt with below. Although properly regarded relativism forms the leitmotif in all sections, to begin with the cultural relativistic character of the status theory will be gone into explicitly. Second, we will examine the suggestion that cultural participation can be completely reduced to the human need to distinguish oneself. Third, the claim that 'bourgeois culture' is bourgeois and that the lower socio-economic strata have their own authentic culture, is discussed. And fourth, the thesis is briefly examined that social cultural dissemination is an instrument of control or a form of cultural imperialism.

Conservative relativism

The status theory is also an expression of relativism, this time not in the field of ethics, as in the populist concept of democracy, but in that of aesthetics. The underlying mechanism, however, is the same: one wrestles with the fact that it turns out to be impossible to find an unshakeable foundation of knowledge for value judgements and therefore tends to conclude that all judgements in this field are completely determined by the arbitrary cultural or historical context. It is not surprising that this tendency is generally more strongly developed in the field of aesthetics than in that of ethics. After all, within the world of the arts, in particular, a real explosion of styles, trends and schools has appeared in our century, and it is necessary to have a solid epistemological basis to be able to maintain a notion of quality within this enormous pluriformity.

The most important objection to the relevant sociologism or historicism is that it is a threat to the development of individual autonomy. This line of reasoning leads to the conviction that the effort to disseminate culture and distinguish quality, shows elitism, intolerance or value absolutism. The ultimate consequence of this is that the social conditions can never be shaped which are needed to offer people the possibility of deciding themselves whether or not they want to participate in particular cultural activities and, in a broader perspective, to define in which way they want to give direction to their lives.

A comparable argument can be used in the anthropological debate on the value of cultures. The starting-point that all cultures are equal and incomparable, that no civilization can be judged on the basis of another civilization, never mind condemned, is broadly accepted within contemporary anthropology. However, a problem with this attractive principle, argues the British anthropologist and philosopher Ernest Gellner (1992; cf. Taylor 1992), for example, is that its advocates have no arguments to judge abusers of human rights who appeal to the supposedly unique values and customs, beyond discussion, of their own culture. Extremely broadminded and tolerant Western anthropologists here find themselves on the side of very intolerant fundamentalists. They can only free themselves from this alliance by really taking seriously their tolerance and therefore the value of freedom. Their tolerance must necessarily end where intolerance begins and the value of freedom or autonomy will be the dividing line here. Only then can they declare their solidarity with possible victims of other cultures. In the same way, in our society, one first shows real respect for people when one offers them the opportunity of overcoming the possible limitation of their own environment and social background.

Only the drive for distinction?

That considerations of status play a role in the decision to participate in certain cultural activities is, as stated earlier, extremely probable. This ubiquitous drive for distinction has also severely damaged the arts and cultural dissemination as it has led to many cultural products being chiefly and unjustly related to an elite, to snobbery and self-satisfaction.[36] Nevertheless, there are a number of objections attached to this thesis.

In the first place, a large methodological problem for status theory can be pointed out: the motives ascribed to participants in cultural activities cannot, if at all, be researched or checked empirically. The theory is immune to falsification as one of its assumptions is that people 'in reality' or 'ultimately' have other drives than those they will tell the researcher when asked. Every concert visitor will tell you that his presence must be explained by his cultural preference or taste: he came because he finds what is offered beautiful or nice. It is rare to find someone who will explain his visit by his desire to distinguish himself from others. This desire will therefore have to be assigned to him by the researcher too.

A phenomenon which nevertheless demonstrates clearly the limitation of this theory, focused strictly on receptive art participation, is the relatively large scale of amateur art. Why should such a large group of people, often in great isolation, invest so much time and energy in mastering violin, brush and facial expression, if they are mainly or even exclusively seeking distinction and identification. With the goal of 'distinction' in mind, it is considerably simpler, and in fact more practical, to sit passively in a hall somewhere, together with many other people. There is, therefore, probably more going on here.

For the latter, we can look to an unexpected source: Pierre Bourdieu. In an interview in a Dutch quality newspaper, he distances himself clearly from a strict cultural–relativistic interpretation of his work (Bourdieu and Van Heerikhuizen 1989: 25). Bourdieu admits that enjoying art cannot be completely reduced to a drive for distinction. True art raises itself above the commercial, popular culture because it is able to postpone the satisfying of needs, that is, pleasure. In this context he approvingly quotes Emile Durkheim who once said that in all societies a high value is ascribed to asceticism, effort, self-control, postponement of pleasure instead of immediate gratification of needs. Bourdieu then argues:

> I think that asceticism, pure taste, is superior in humanity to the non-cultivated taste. I think, for example, that avant-garde painters are superior to the makers of popular pictures. And indeed, for precisely this reason: in order to get access to that art you have to make an effort, you have to know your art history, you have to see what it is a denial of, or commentary on.

(Bourdieu and Van Heerikhuizen 1989)

Bourdieu then says that this cultural knowledge, and with it access to the relevant enjoyments, is very unevenly divided among the people. He wants to draw a political conclusion from this: 'the conditions under which people have access to the universal must be universalized'.

The question now arises of why Bourdieu has not incorporated these extremely encouraging ideas in his *La Distinction*. In the interview, the author states that he has now put them down in writing but as yet has no plan to publish them. The reason for this is that it would undermine his critique of the aesthetic belief of the intellectuals. Bourdieu states:

> if I were now to say at the end of my book: there is another way out, the beautiful is really more beautiful than the ugly, great art is au fond better than secondary art, then the readers will only remember that and forget everything I wrote before. Intellectuals want so badly to hear that art is good. And then I will have written that entire book for nothing. There are things I do not want to say because I am afraid of being misunderstood.

(ibid.)

Nevertheless, he emphasizes that *La Distinction* is full of 'little signs' from which the 'really cultivated reader' could have noticed what his real intentions were. 'Imbeciles' like Alain Finkielkraut (for his critique of Bourdieu's cultural relativism see Finkielkraut 1987: Part 3), however, have failed to notice it. Equally regrettable is that at the moment the Western world is stuck with the problem of an entire generation of sociologists and 'culture critics' who apparently have not understood it either.

Bourgeois culture?

A second suggestion of the status theoreticians was that there is an authentic culture of the lower classes, which is certainly as comprehensive and valuable as the 'bourgeois' culture currently disseminated by the established cultural institutions. Nor would bourgeois expressions of culture fit into the culture pattern of the lowest socio-economic classes. The question arises of in what sense the 'bourgeois' culture is actually 'bourgeois'.

What is bourgeois culture? The Dutch art historian Mirjam Westen shows that the concept appeared at the moment when the lettered middle classes left their mark on culture in the eighteenth century. They united elements of both the elite culture of the aristocracy and the folk culture. This culture is subscribed to by *lettered city-dwellers*, rather than by a clearly demarcatable socio-economic class. Westen writes:

> If research into the bourgeois culture makes one thing clear, then it is that these concepts have no clear-cut meaning. The adjective bourgeois cannot be traced back to a homogeneous public group or a readable, unambiguous content or style of a book or artwork. The scale and composition of this public is constantly shifting, thanks to urbanization and the dissemination of prosperity and literacy among more layers of the population. The 'bourgeois' public can therefore not be traced back to a single socio-economic class or grouping.
>
> (Westen 1990: 33)

At best, it can be stated that this public consists of literate people and that these, certainly in the eighteenth century, were more often to be found in the wealthy upper classes than in the lower layers. The historian Wijnand Mijnhardt therefore states that in this context it is better to speak of a 'refined culture' (Mijnhardt 1990: 41). Also striking is that, in the course of time, the arts have become increasingly 'independent': they are increasingly less connected with and bound to particular social groupings and patrons (churches, aristocracy, bourgeois) and increasingly enter 'into debate with themselves'.

In the course of history, numerous groups have opposed 'bourgeois' culture and in doing so suggested that an alternative, non-alienated, authentic culture can be found among the non-bourgeois classes. Naturally, the rather romantic ideas about an individual 'socialist culture', which were current within the socio-democratic movement in the years between the wars, are an example of this. Despite fervent efforts to this end, this culture turned out to be impossible to find, nor capable of being formed in the short term. In practice, says the Belgian historian Blockmans, 'a large part of the educational effect of the socialist cultural organizations consisted of the provision of bourgeois products' (Blockmans 1987: 205). The philosopher Mooij also writes about the attempts, which led to nothing, to replace the bourgeois culture with a socialist one: 'There was simply no adequate, equal alternative available, or to find' (Mooij 1987: 104).

What was true of the inter-war years, certainly applies to the present age too. People who still claim to be able to distinguish an individual, authentic culture of the lower classes, completely ignore the process of modernization that has taken place within Western civilization and the accompanying 'cultural levelling'. Through, among other things, the introduction of standardized education which is compulsory for all, the rise of the mass media and the increase in scale within the culture industry people are increasingly socialized in a comparable manner. The folk cultures which once existed have been largely converted into folklore that is only kept alive for nostalgic or commercial reasons.

In order to still find an authentic culture, one can also deny every possibility of appreciating artistic expressions and lifestyles and raise the concept of art to the anthropological concept of culture. Lewis, Willis and, above all, Verdaasdonk go a long way in this direction. Verdaasdonk, for example, postulates that Dostoevsky's *The Brothers Karamazov*, Salinger's *Franny and Zooey* and Camus's *The Plague* offer us as much insight into human life, reconcile us as much with the irreconcilabilities of life and are aesthetically on the same level as pulp fiction like Brand's *Sawdust and Sixguns*, Douglas's *Nurse Chadwick's Sorrow*, and Stauffen's *Mein Leben Gehört Dir*. And everyone who says differently is a 'moralist'.

The axiom that ideas about a literary canon are completely determined by social power relations and only have an ideological function, or that a future society is imaginable where Shakespeare 'would be no more valuable than much present-day graffiti',[37] is not, however, very plausible. In the first place, it overlooks the historical fact that these ideas, despite the enormous change which political systems have undergone, have in practice turned out to be surprisingly stable. For example, writes Alter, the works of Homer, Sophocles and Virgil have had a high quality ascribed to them for two thousand years and Shakespeare has enjoyed this fate for almost four hundred years (Alter 1989: 26). In addition, the literary canon often seems to contain texts which are opposed to the values of the dominant ideology and class (Alter 1989: 31). The thesis that there are no supra-social criteria of quality, also implies that no taste development exists. After all, what could it be measured against? The personal experience of numerous people, however, does not tally with this.

What is most important is that such an ethical and aesthetic relativism shows little insight into the epistemological foundations of Western civilization. The parties involved seem to think that the impossibility of finding an unassailable epistemological foundation which is acceptable to all, implies that all statements on reality are equally true or correct and are only defined by social categories. They therefore reveal themselves as metaphysicians who have lost their faith but still continue to think in the same dichotomies: God exists or he does not exist; there is one objective truth or there are merely purely subjective opinions; the quality of an artwork is exclusively determined by the characteristics of the relevant object or merely by the powerful word of a social elite.

There are indeed no objective criteria against which the beauty of a particular artwork can be measured. But nor do we have purely objective criteria, an unassailable epistemological basis to determine the truth of a particular scientific or philosophical theory. However, it would show little understanding of our civilization if one were to conclude from this that the exercise of science or philosophy is therefore actually just a senseless activity. We can recognize that all theories or paradigms are inevitably based on a number of always disputable principles with regard to man, society and world. But we also know that some theories give us more of a grip on reality than others. One paradigm describes, explains and predicts in a more convincing manner a larger part of the reality than the other, and therefore has more 'quality'. Science and philosophy manage very well with this situation and, seen from the perspective of these fields, it is therefore curious why many here in the arts and letters are not able to do the same. Here, it would often appear to be a case of all or nothing: one demands objective, universal, eternal criteria of quality and, if it turns out that these are not available, then one concludes that the notion of 'quality' is a plot by the social elite against the common man (cf. Blokland 1988b; Doorman 1984; Williams 1961: Part 1).

The argument for more 'pluralism' and 'diversity' in cultural policy too is often an expression of value relativism and, in addition, of a misplaced belief in the 'authentic lifestyles' of the lower classes. While such proposals sound democratic and tolerant, in practice they form a justification of the existing social inequality in the capacity to participate in culture. By suggesting that the lower classes or the young already have their own authentic and fully-fledged cultural life, they can, and may, no longer be brought into contact by the state, or by other organizations, with alternative expressions of culture. Thus, they are condemned to the *status quo*, to the limitations of the current circumstances. Because the lower classes do not participate in the existing life of the arts, nor possess a full alternative, a spreading of resources will lead mainly to the shifting of cash flows from one above average 'art world' to the other (for example, from symphonic music to jazz). The lower classes will hardly notice it.

Cultural imperialism?

A third thesis of the theoreticians of status concerns the supposed cultural imperialism of the cultural disseminators. Naturally, it cannot be denied that the aim of spreading culture was *also* inspired by the desire to 'educate' the people, by the desire to integrate them into their national state or one's own group, by the fear that the masses would slip into Fascism or Bolshevism, by the fear of a rising of the masses (see the earlier section on Cultural Dissemination). But it is falsifying history to suggest that these were the only motivations, and one then gets completely derailed if one concludes from the existence of these earlier motivations that cultural dissemination is, by definition, a dubious affair. Cultural dissemination can, as I have attempted to demonstrate here, be justified on completely different grounds, grounds which are as old as humanism or democracy and which also have always played a role.

TOWARDS A POLICY OF CULTURAL DISSEMINATION OR DEMAND

Introduction

How could the existing cultural policy be adjusted in the direction of a participation policy? It is tempting to stop after the theory and leave the reader with the impression that, with a number of simple policy changes, it is possible to bring about a broad cultural participation in a short space of time. This impression would be a false one and therefore this easy path has not been chosen here. The margins are very small. Just how small, can probably best be demonstrated by formulating some policy proposals.

The development of a normative cultural political framework

A first requirement for the development of a cultural policy in which pursued objectives are argued in a somewhat coherent and consistent fashion, is the formation of a substantial–rational cultural–political framework. This has been unjustly rejected in many countries, even if unconsciously. As long as this does not happen, the policy in the countries involved, however, will continue to show the shortcomings which are unique to a strongly incrementalistic policy: it will be characterized by lack of direction, immobilism, short-term thinking, congestion and an excessive influence by interested parties.

With regard to a cultural dissemination policy, answers will have to be formulated in the desired cultural–political framework to questions which have also been raised in this book: Can qualitative judgements be justified in the field of ethics and aesthetics? What significance do the arts and the letters have for the 'Good Life' and for the 'Good Society'? Is the freedom of the individual endangered when governments or other organizations intervene in the formation and dissemination of cultural values or can individual freedom actually be promoted in this manner? And so on.

The social context: work and leisure

Every cultural policy is naturally implemented in a particular social context, a context which goes to determine the possibilities and limitations of that policy. It is precisely by not concentrating just on the arts and the letters, but by trying to change their social environment, that the possibilities for cultural activities can be extremely enlarged. Among others the relations are important between paid work, leisure and cultural activities. The constant increases in productivity within the current socio-economic constellation increasingly threaten to split society into two or three parts. A large group of people are in danger of remaining marginalized in society and another group finds itself compelled, by an ever more demanding and competitive economic system, to work longer and harder. The scale of the cultural activities of both groups is smaller than would be possible in a better division of the available quantity of work.

At the same time, economic rationalization offers enormous possibilities for freeing ourselves from what Gorz (1989) calls 'heteronomous activities' and for considerably expanding our 'autonomous activities'. Alongside political and social activities, cultural activities form an extremely important element of the last category. These possibilities, however, are not utilized as a matter of course. For this, the process of blind economic rationalization must be interrupted. This can only be done by political action. In order to inspire people to do this in a democracy they can be mobilized on the basis of a Utopia, a Utopia in which the value of freedom has a central position. It is a cultural–political task to develop this substantial–rational Utopia (cf. Blokland 1996; Glotz 1992; Gorz 1989).

Cultural education

After these two abstract proposals which, contrary to the ideas of many administrators and policy-makers, do actually belong to the category of *policy*, in what follows, we will move down to a more concrete level. This is partly based on findings of the research into the determinants of cultural participation which were discussed earlier in the chapter.

Important in a participation policy, to begin with, is formal education: if the education enjoyed is one of the most important determining factors of cultural participation, then every cultural dissemination policy can succeed only in the context of an educational policy.[38]

In the first place, it can be attempted to raise the average educational level. Participation in cultural activities can then also increase. First, this is because education develops the general cognitive skills necessary to experience culture. If more children receive longer and better education then they, too, thanks to their cognitive training, will find it easier to participate culturally. And, second, this is because more attention is devoted to cultural development within the higher forms of education than within the lower school types. Considering the relation between level of education and degree of participation, furthermore, it is evident that promoting social equality in educational careers is an important instrument in combating social inequality in cultural participation.

In the second place, the content of formal education can be improved: more attention can be devoted on all educational levels to cultural education. From the studies quoted in the section on cultural competence, it emerged that the effects of this, also in the longer term, are great. It is advisable to start this at the earliest age possible. What applies to education in general turns out to also apply to training in the arts: the formative influence of the environment is strongest at an extremely young age. In addition, children in their puberty turn out to have lost the openness to new impressions formerly characteristic of them. Nowadays, teenagers (and then mainly boys) are even very dismissive of participation cultural activities. Linked to the fact that the pressure to conform to the values of the group is enormous among these boys, efforts to work up their enthusiasm in arts and letters will be extremely laborious (De Waal 1989; Ter Bogt 1990: 153–62).

The policy conclusions drawn from this in Sweden can serve as an inspiring example. In that country, already in the crèche and infant school between 5 per cent and 10 per cent of the time available is devoted to the arts. The cultural supply is attuned to this: for example, more than 40 per cent of the total stage performances and symphonic musical performances are specially aimed at children. No single age group sees as much theatre in Sweden as the group between six and nine years old. When the young people leave second-level education, their participation in cultural activities drops sharply. Other ways of spending time (going out, relationships) become important. Nevertheless, the level remains higher than that of the parents, and it is expected that they will become more active again at a later age. The necessary basis for this, the cultural competence, has already been laid down. Because the people involved also have children themselves to whom they will pass on some of their cultural skills, there will be a cumulative effect (Swedish Ministry of Education and Cultural Affairs 1989: 304–18; Myerscough 1989: 117–20).

In education, not only more time should be spent on art education. It is also necessary to do justice to the fact that self-development, in general, and the experience of art, in particular, have an important *cognitive* element. Since the 1970s, there has been a serious misconception about this in a number of countries: in education, children in the 'expression subjects' are indeed given room to express themselves, but they are hardly given or taught any means of doing this in an aesthetically or communicatively significant manner (see Oostwoud Wijdenes 1989). However, before one ever arrives at the experience, perception and appreciation of artistic products, in a great many cases, it will first be necessary to build up a cultural competence. This also consists of knowledge of history and the social context of the relevant arts. As many artworks in the current age especially are a reaction to other works or, in other words, form an element of a *discourse*, this knowledge is indispensable.

The communication of cultural competence is, for that matter, not exclusively the task of teachers specifically employed for that. Already in 1951, the Dutch cultural socialists Banning, Vorrink and Den Uyl pointed out that 'beauty is simply not a subject that can be taught separately; it will have to permeate every lesson' (Den Uyl et al. 1951: 319). For this reason, they thought that a separate subject 'art education' in schools is insufficient: it only gives a false impression that culture and philosophy can be seen separately from the other ('useful') subjects which are offered in education, and so are unimportant matters.

Finally, art education does not just take place via formal education. For example, offering art facilities can be accompanied by training. Research into museum visiting has shown that when a museum intensively accompanies its arrangement of the exhibited objects with educational resources, the average educational level of the public is lower (Ganzeboom and Haanstra 1989: 86). However, in recent years, the museums have come to regard the education of pupils and the public from the lowest socio-economic layers, in particular, as less important. Ganzeboom and Haanstra write: 'In most (Dutch) museums there is a business attitude and a commercial approach. Visitor figures have become important and many museums aim at a further increase of those numbers. Here it is mainly aimed at more repeat visits and the playing of the tourist market' (Ganzeboom and Haanstra 1989: 97–8). This trend is apparent in almost all Western countries: whether or not under duress from the changed political environment, people are increasingly market-oriented. It is obvious that this commercialization will have to be turned back in the context of a cultural dissemination policy.

Media policy

Furthermore, art policy can be integrated, not just with education policy, but also with the broadcasting policy. Television, in particular, could make a contribution to the stimulation of cultural participation. This can be done in three ways. First, by giving information about the arts. Specific art magazines, and also current affairs, chat shows, news broadcasts, and even ads, can play a role here. Experience shows that people in the present age are only convinced of the importance of a particular event when this has been 'on television'.

Second, television itself can produce art: looking at high quality drama series, video clips, documentaries, television films and the like is also a form of cultural participation. In this way, it can bridge popular culture and the arts.

Third, the stations can broadcast recordings of concerts, operas, theatrical performances, etc. In addition, research shows (NOS 1990: 10–3) that the so-called 'sandwich formula' (alternating different programme elements so that the viewer gets a little of everything) works best for cultural dissemination. The forming of special art and culture channels such as Channel Four leads mainly to a 'reservation' for, and isolation of, the arts.

If broadcasting wants to be able to fulfil its cultural–political function, then a minimum of pluriformity in authorized broadcasting and programmes must also be guaranteed. This function goes further than promoting participation in the arts. In order to keep a democracy viable and give the citizens the opportunity of participating in the political decision-making process, a public discourse of a certain level, carried on by reasonably informed citizens, is indispensable. Certainly, in an age when people are increasingly turning away from written culture, broadcasting has an important task to fulfil here. The presence of *realistic* choice alternatives is therefore an important condition of freedom in this context.

The experience in countries such as Italy, the Netherlands and France teaches us that commercial broadcasting, now on the rise, does not enlarge the number of alternatives and, thus, pluriformity; it reduces them. The broadcasting resources, in particular, the advertising revenue, are being fragmented so that programmes must become cheaper and the target group broader, with the consequence that it is increasingly necessary to refer to the taste of the lowest common denominator and just broadcast more of the same – more sport, game shows, soap operas and so on (cf. Kuhn 1985; Lewis 1990: 52–7; Smith 1979).

In addition, current affairs, documentaries, journalistic broadcasts and art programmes, especially in small linguistic areas such as the Netherlands and Sweden, attract too little public to be able to produce them profitably. They will therefore disappear from the screen within a commercial system. For the benefit of cultural and political pluriformity, the functioning of a democracy, and the freedom of the citizen to be able to choose from real alternatives, the undermining of public broadcasting systems by commercial stations must be stopped.

Broadcasting is important, not only because of its relation to the arts and the functioning of democracy, but also because it has come to play an ever larger role in the image that people form of reality. Postman and Ong, among others, as was made clear earlier, state that in a civilization dominated by the printed word, the rational capacities of individuals are more developed and people have a more coherent image of reality than in an oral or electronic culture. If this thesis is correct, then the gradual transition from a written to an electronic culture implies that the capacity for autonomy of many people is less developed than is possible. The capacity for rational and abstract thinking and the possession of a somewhat coherent image of reality are, after all, important conditions of positive freedom.

In this context, Condry, among others, argues for a media training in the family and in education: children must be taught how to handle the medium of television, which rationality controls it, and which implicit messages it transmits. At the moment, according to him, American parents and teachers are seriously deficient in this area (Condry 1993: 270). (For the Dutch situation, see Ketzer, Swinkels and Vooijs (1989) and Van Lil and Vooijs (1989).)

For that matter, the possibilities for governments, or other organizations, to inspire children and adults to read are not large (cf. Duijx and Verdaasdonk 1989). While it is true that people learn to read in school, the 'reading climate' in the family turns out to be of great importance for the degree to which, ultimately, people pick up a book, newspaper or magazine of their own accord. Nevertheless, there are indications that nowadays too much emphasis is being placed within education on the *technical* skills of reading, with the result that children increasingly come to see this as a boring task, instead of as an activity which can bring pleasure, enrichment and comfort (Duijx and Verdaasdonk 1989: 88; Van der Voort 1989: 18).

The narrowing of the gap between professionals and laymen

In countries such as the Netherlands, the United Kingdom and the United States, the making of decisions on awarding subsidies is largely delegated, as has been stated, to professional arts councils. This organization of policy has set mechanisms going which impede participation by interested new-comers: the supply created is often of a strongly innovative or avant-garde character and demands a high cultural competence to evaluate it, as mentioned earlier.

The step to participation in cultural activities could be smaller for many if they had first made some small steps. To make this possible, there must be a permanent supply for 'beginners' which offers people the opportunity to gradually build up their cultural competence. Research shows that producers of culture who make more traditional or conventional programmes do, indeed, attract a larger and more diverse audience. Research has also shown that participation in traditional art forms generally precedes that in more modern forms. For example, there is an empirical relation between interest in classical music and interest in modern 'serious' music. This relationship is not demonstrable the other way round (Maas, Verhoeff and Ganzeboom 1990).

Another reason to disseminate traditional art forms is that much contemporary art is characterized by a certain cynicism and disdain, a certain arrogance with regard to everyday life and the ordinary man and woman. Instead of providing comfort and catharsis, many modern artists try mainly to shock, to break taboos, to disturb people. Where the supply is one-sidedly dominated by artworks made with this objective, the disseminating of art among all levels of the population will be, by definition, not only a laborious matter, but also a perilous one.

In general, what is at issue is that in cultural policy not only aesthetic, but often political, decisions must be made. This responsibility cannot be avoided by policy-makers from the arts world (cf. Cummings and Katz 1987: 16). They cannot just set themselves the goal of enabling a high quality supply; they are also responsible for the pluriformity of the whole, the possibility of participation, and the social legitimacy of the overall policy (cf. Blokland 1995a, 1996). If these last objectives are endangered by excessive influence by interested experts, then the policy-makers will have to roll back this influence. This can be done, for example, by including more representatives of the judging public in the arts councils.

Linking up with mass culture

It was observed earlier that researchers and policy-makers in many countries tend nowadays to elevate the traditional concept of art towards a broad sociological concept of culture. This was acclaimed. It is evident that they have generally adhered too long to an excessively narrowly-defined concept of art. It is also shortsighted to exclude, by definition, the extremely popular commercial mass culture. A policy that wants to be more than a facilities policy for a small upper crust, should take this culture more as a starting-point. The question is, however, how this can happen without the concept of art being so inflated that it becomes meaningless? The problems of the low participation in cultural activities and of the great social inequality in this field are not solved, however, by declaring all possible human activities to be art.

In order to be able to draw a distinction between art and culture in the sociological sense, Lewis proposes the following functional definition of art: 'Art could be defined as a cultural practice that involves the creation of a specific and definable object – a play, video, or piece of music for example. The function of that object is as a self-conscious, personal, or collective expression of something' (Lewis 1990: 5). This definition, which links up with the definition of the functions of art which were given earlier in this book (see Chapter 6), makes it possible to distinguish between bingo and ballet, tailors and fashion designers, and model-kit builders and sculptors. In addition, it does justice to the artistic character of film, pop music and fashion, among other things.

Lewis then makes a plea not to simply subsidize, as generally happens according to him, what has no chance of survival on the market, but to base the cultural policy on the market and to attempt to compensate for its deficiencies. In his opinion, these deficiencies are in the field of pluriformity, innovation, collective commodities and active cultural participation, among other things (Lewis 1990: 25–32). Lewis gives a number of examples in order to show which practical consequences his approach would have, an approach which is already being followed to a large extent in the Netherlands, Sweden and France.

The television is one of the most important examples: it cannot be denied that it occupies a prominent position in the use of leisure time by large parts of the population. At the same time, it is evident that, if television is left completely to the market, this would be to the detriment of the pluriformity, the willingness to experiment and innovate, and of the informative and opinion-giving functions which it can have in a democracy, functions which can be conceived as a collective good. For these reasons government regulation is desirable (Lewis 1990: 54–60; see also the earlier section on media policy).

In Lewis's view, the same applies to the mass magazines in, for instance, Great Britain: these are controlled by a small number of concerns and the pluriformity is very limited. It is precisely here that regulation is desirable on behàlf of the freedom of the citizen. In the field of pop music, the government, according to Lewis, can promote pluriformity and innovation by creating affordable practice spaces, stages and studio facilities – matters which receive scant attention from the music companies, which are mainly interested in profit. A last example is the video film. This has enormous potential because its production costs are low. The parties involved can make video films themselves for small target groups, such as neighbourhoods, societies and companies. Local authorities must provide production and distribution support for this (Lewis 1990: 57–64).

Amateur art performance

Organization of policy has, in a number of sectors, as stated, led to a relatively one-sided supply, which demands much competence and which excludes, in advance, a high participation.

Adjusted decision-making procedures can contribute to a solution here. There is, however, also an extremely important task for amateurs. It is known of amateur art groups that, in general, they prefer a more traditional, simpler repertoire. At this moment in time, this repertoire links up considerably better to the cultural preferences and knowledge of the average interested public (Knulst and Van Beek 1991: 98–9). This public can thus build up its cultural competence via amateur art performers.

In addition, receptive cultural participation can be promoted via amateur art practice, because those who themselves participate in courses or societies for amateur art, also reveal a higher receptive level of participation. It also appeared from the research quoted earlier in this chapter, that active cultural participation at an early age has a much stronger influence on the receptive participation in later phases of life than its receptive counterpart. Furthermore, the most important explanatory variable for active cultural participation by children turned out not to be the training or the incomes of the relevant parents, but the scale of their amateur art practice.

For these reasons, the greatest possibilities – certainly quantitative – for promoting receptive cultural participation are probably within the amateur sector. As well as this, it is obvious that active cultural participation represents a large inherent value, a value to which policy-makers have often paid too little heed. The basis of cultural life within a society is ultimately laid by the amateurs. They need the professionals as criterion of quality and as source of innovation. But the professionals cannot do without the breeding ground for talent and audience provided by the *aficionado*.

For these reasons, the government can bring the relevant associations much more into cultural policy than is now usually the case. It is possible to create more platforms on which amateurs can display their tricks more often and ask their cooperation in art education and artistic training. At the same time, the level of amateur art practice can be raised, and the pursuit of artistic fulfilment encouraged by opening up more cross connections with the professional artists. Examples could be choir guidance by professional orchestras, lessons by professional artists at centres for artistic training and music schools, and the apprenticing of students of conservatories and drama schools to their amateur colleagues.

Involving social organizations

Bringing in the 'social midfield' can also lower the threshold. Amateur art societies are naturally already examples of this. But people, who would otherwise never have come in contact with culture, can still be reached via trade unions, action, pressure and interest groups, leisure associations, church associations, neighbourhood and local associations, etc., mainly active at a local level. Dutch research shows that association activities have not suffered at all from a significantly declining number of participants in the last thirty years (SCP 1990: 239–40; SCP 1994: 582–94). Group organizations therefore are still popular despite, or perhaps because of, individualization.

Again, the situation in Sweden could serve as an example. Here, a large number of institutions (political parties, trade unions and associations, church societies, etc.) with their own educational departments or 'societies' have been successfully active in the field of cultural dissemination. The activities of these organizations include, among other things: organization of 'study circles' in the area of the arts; the formation of 'cultural groups', such as choirs, theatre and dance groups; and the organization of 'cultural programmes' such as lectures, performances, exhibitions and excursions (Myerscough 1989: 106–110; 128–32).

Evoking the drive to distinction

It can also be attempted to link up with the tendency present in every person to conform to the values and norms of the group to which they belong. The idea that 'art is not for people like us' to which Temme, Willis and De Waal refer, can perhaps be overcome therefore by showing the mass public, via the mass media, people who are considered as belonging to the same social class enjoying art. Pop idols who, in a musical programme popular among the young, tell about their great love for Liszt, Beethoven, Van Morrison, Van Gogh, Yeats and Kundera, could probably contest the idea mentioned much more effectively than teachers of musical education.

Architecture and design

Finally, something should be written here about the most democratic, and also most natural and continuous form of cultural participation: the architecture and design of the public and private space. By this, is meant the way in which cities, neighbourhoods, roads, squares and parks are designed and laid out; the way in which buildings, schools and dwellings are designed and built; monuments, statues, memorials, sculptures, fountains, murals, and so on. In his book *The Future of Socialism* the British political scientist and social democratic politician Anthony Crosland wrote:

> We need not only higher exports and old-age pensions, but more open-air cafés, brighter and gayer streets at night, later closing hours for public houses, more local repertory theatres, better and more hospitable hoteliers and restaurateurs, brighter and cleaner eating-houses, more riverside cafés, more pleasure-gardens on the Battersea model, more murals and pictures in public places, better designs for furniture and pottery and women's clothes, statues in the centre of new housing estates, better-designed street-lamps and telephone kiosks and so on *ad infinitum*.
>
> (Crosland 1985: 355)

These are perhaps banal matters, but precisely because they seem so obvious they are too easily ignored – until one has to spend one's days in one of those dismal suburbs, in one of those gloomy tower blocks or terraced houses; until one has to earn one's living in one of those depressing office monstrosities and do one's shopping in one of those depressing shopping centres, accompanied by irritating piped music. This is not a book about architecture, said Crosland of his *The Future of Socialism*. It is therefore not necessary to go into details. It is a question of a mentality which must be overcome, a mentality which in his time, too, was marked by miserliness, narrow-mindedness and indifference.

Epilogue

To realize the relative validity of one's convictions and yet stand for them unflinchingly, is what distinguishes a civilized man from a barbarian. To demand more than this is perhaps a deep and incurable metaphysical need but to allow it to determine one's practice is a symptom of an equally deep, and more dangerous, moral and political immaturity.[39]

(Isaiah Berlin 1958: 172)

A constantly recurring motif in this book has been that the range of certain ideas, attitudes and values is always limited by other ideas, attitudes and values. This standpoint is based on the metaphysical assumption that there is no knowable rational order in the cosmos which lends meaning and significance to our lives, and in which all values coincide in harmonious fashion. There are no objective universal and absolute values, but many meaningful ones, which must inevitably be balanced against each other. Nor is there any immovable foundation of knowledge in the empirical and normative field. However, this does not mean that all empirical and normative statements are equally true or correct, or that rational discussion of these statements is not possible. There are perhaps no truths, but a reasonable degree of agreement can often be reached on what is plausible or acceptable. This consensus does not come into being in a reductionist attempt to retrieve the very last foundations, an attempt that has led many only to scepticism and nihilism. In a meaningful discourse, one tries to bring together as many considerations as possible in an acceptable manner and in a single coherent model – a model in which the plausibility of each element is, to a high degree, defined by its relations to other components, and where the credibility of the whole is dependent on its empirical basis, its internal consistency, and its cohesion with ideas and moral intuitions which are already present, separate from the model. In short: 'Justification is a matter of the mutual support of many considerations, of everything fitting together into one coherent view' (Rawls 1971: 579). The possibility of carrying on a reasonable debate in such a manner also turned out to be present in the field of the subjects which were central to this book.

We have seen, for example, that freedom must be brought into relation to many notions, each one valuable in itself but also partly conflicting, and that there is no single definition of freedom which is based on just one of these notions: absence of impediments, absence of possibilities of choice, being able to identify with one's thinking and action, having a life plan and the will-power to implement it, the capacity to look for alternative values, ideas and knowledge, authenticity, etc. They all play a role, and to proclaim only one of these notions to be central is to strip the concept of freedom unnecessarily of valuable connotations. The various notions should actually balance each other in a reasonable manner. Moderation was thus always the motto.

This applies equally with regard to the emancipation dilemma and the role which paternalistic interventions could play in resolving it. A balance will have to be found between, on the one hand, the honourable and, for freedom, essential desire to have a private realm in which people can do and be what is within their capacity without hindrance, and, on the other hand, the insight that to a great extent individuals can only develop their capacity for autonomy in and thanks to society, through enculturation and socialization. In practice, taking completely as a starting-point the desires or reason of the individual degenerates into an untenable subjectivism or relativism. The theoreticians who lay down the strictest conditions for paternalistic interventions also ultimately appeal to that which is generally considered worth aspiring to in a particular society.

In the field of cultural politics, it is equally a matter of expanding knowledge of cultural products which are dubbed valuable by the society, the tradition. Ideas on this can change in the course of time, but are sufficiently stable to serve as starting-points for policy. The goal of this policy is not the compulsory dissemination of a particular aesthetic preference, but the promotion of individual autonomy. Participation in cultural activities can contribute to the development of this autonomy. Furthermore, it is only possible for people to make grounded, really free decisions to participate, or not, in these kinds of activities when they have first become familiar with the cultural products concerned. To justify a cultural policy it is not necessary therefore to be able to prove that certain cultural products are objectively beautiful or fine.

All the same, because it is not possible, even for socio-psychological reasons, to confront people with all the products of civilization, some crude choices must be made. As it is impossible to formulate definitive answers to aesthetic questions, however, many turn out to rush on to the conviction that all evaluations have an exclusively ideological or sociological basis, with all its consequences for the possibility of promoting individual autonomy through a policy of cultural dissemination. The canon in literature and the arts, however, is no different from the one we encountered in ethics, and in our treatment of the concept of paternalism – that which ordinary people, who are capable of making rational judgements where they have a reasonable knowledge of the alternatives, consider to be worthy of aspiring to or valuable. This rationale can then be aligned to plausibility within epistemology.

The attempt by various Western governments to increase participation in cultural activities by the lower classes especially, has not, up to now, been a great success. It is possible to point to many causes and reasons for this. A not unimportant one is that cultural developments can hardly be influenced. Another reason, however, is that cultural policy has been primarily a facility policy. The authorities have generally confined themselves to creating a broad spectrum of cultural facilities and keeping entry prices down by subsidies. The underlying idea was that a supply affordable and accessible to all would, in itself, create a demand for culture. However, research shows that it is not material, but non-material, inhibitions which prevent people from participating in culture. It is a matter of cultural competence, which is acquired through learning. This takes place in the parental environment, in education, and during earlier participation. In their policies, therefore, the governments based themselves too much on the negative freedom of the individual and not enough on the positive freedom. In their weighing up of the two values, which are at the basis of the emancipation dilemma, they have not managed to find sufficient balance. Naturally, the possibilities of the government or other institutions to stimulate the development of cultural competence, and with it autonomy, are limited. To intervene in a far more profound manner than is currently done in the existing structures of socialization, would provoke resistance, for understandable reasons. The problems here are no different from those in the area of social inequality in educational opportunities, an inequality which partly precedes the unequal opportunities to participate in culture. Since school aptitude – and with it children's school careers – is determined, to a high degree, by the upbringing within the family, it is only possible to reduce the existing great inequality in educational opportunities by limiting the autonomy of the family, which runs up against both ethical and practical objections. Nevertheless, it is possible that through compensation and stimulation programmes (especially pre-school), by more effective school systems and by selecting at a later stage in the school career than is now the rule, the opportunities of children from lower milieux can be improved. It can also be attempted to promote people's cultural competence by devoting more and better attention to cultural education at all levels of education and in all years in school, by attuning the media image more to the cultural policy, by creating a supply of cultural facilities which gives people more opportunity to build up their competence gradually, by bringing in the so-called social midfield, and so on.

The possibilities are limited, therefore, but they should not be made unnecessarily smaller than is already the case. The awareness that the margins are small, linked to a persistent attempt to make maximal use of these, is what makes a civilization a civilization. This is true of arguments in the field of ethics, in the field of aesthetics, science, philosophy – even that of religion.

In short, again and again an appeal has been made in the foregoing to 'rationality', to reasoned common sense, to what people in general consider to be reasonable and worthy of aspiring to. Is that all there is? Yes. But this is not negligible. It is something different from nihilism or relativism, as that is professed in broad circles nowadays, and which is seen as an expression of tolerance and forbearance, of civilization, even of socialism, but which in reality is a form of spiritual laziness. It is something other than the cheap 'postmodernist' conviction that everything is equally true, good and beautiful because the absolute validity of no single statement can be proved. It is something other than the decadent, and also irresponsible because a-political, idea that the hard reality of the people who cannot fully participate in culture, in education, in society, is only a language game, interchangeable with other representations, if necessary at right angles to this, of reality. It is something other than the conviction, nowadays widespread, that freedom only means something like 'just being yourself', 'not being involved with anyone', or 'self-development' – with all the emphasis on the self. It is something other than the misunderstanding, arising mainly from opportunism and populism, that the existing preferences are only the product of autonomous, free choices and must always be taken completely as the starting-point, as otherwise elitism, monism and totalitarianism are always waiting to immediately pounce. It is something other than the indifference, all too common in the West, as to whether people have rights to positive as well as negative freedom, whether they will really get the chance to develop their autonomy. The awareness that it is impossible to say the last word on freedom is rational. The conviction that what is actually said is, therefore, of little consequence is irrational.

Notes

1 GENERAL INTRODUCTION

1 A dilemma is, according to the Dutch dictionary *Van Dale*, 'a state in which a choice must be made between two ways, both of which produce large objections'. Because here there are two significant values, it would perhaps be better to speak of an 'antinomy', a 'contradiction between two judgements both of which appear to be true'. However, because the relevant problem can also be formulated in terms of two objectionable choices (to completely choose one of the two values is objectionable as this will inevitably be at the expense of the other), and because the concept 'dilemma' is more familiar in everyday speech and has increasingly come to include the meaning 'antinomy', it has been decided here to use the formulation 'emancipation dilemma'. The 'paradox of emancipation' used by Benton (see Chapter 5) is incidentally rejected because here there is no apparent, but a real contradiction.

2 Gray defines an essentially contested concept as: 'a concept such that any use of it in a social or political context presupposes a specific understanding of a whole range of other, contextually related concepts whose proper uses are no less disputed and which lock together so as to compose a single, identifiable conceptual framework . . . [these] concepts occur characteristically in social contexts which are recognizably those of an ideological dispute' (1977: 332–3).

3 Connolly writes that theoretical self-awareness is achieved:

> as I attain awareness of previously unexamined assumptions at the center of my theory, as I attend to its conceptual contours and to the test procedures it supports, as I probe the inner connections among these three dimensions and explore the normative implications of the entire system. Such self-consciousness is best attained through a comparison of my theory, at each of these levels, with alternative systems. In this way I begin to see how my concepts may appear limited or even defective from the vantage point of other systems; I start to probe the ways in which my test procedures protect key assumptions; I begin to explore the possibility that my commitment to those assumptions is shaped in part by my desire to sustain the normative conclusions they support. In this way I probe the depth connections among the assumptions, concepts, test procedures, and normative commitments of my theory.
>
> (Connolly 1974: 65)

4 Naturally, this method for developing a political theory is not a discovery of Rawls; in practice, political theorists have seldom done anything else. His achievement is chiefly that he has made it more explicit than others. Although Rawls considers his considerations to be primarily applicable to the normative theory, the similarity to the science theory of Thomas Kuhn is striking.

5 Here, once again, it is not the logical gap between facts and values which is bridged (it is not illogical to cherish the conception concerned as an ideal), but the so-called factual gap – a theory loses reality value when it demands things from people that they will never be able to do.

2 ISAIAH BERLIN ON POSITIVE AND NEGATIVE FREEDOM

1 An extensive bibliography of Berlin compiled by Henry Hardy can be found in Berlin (1981) (see the most recently revised impression of 1991). Berlin has recorded partly autobiographical memoirs of personalities known to him in his *Personal impressions* (1980a). During 1988, Berlin gave an extensive interview to the Franco-Iranian philosopher and journalist Ramin Jahanbegloo, which appeared in book form *Conversations with Isaiah Berlin* (1992) (it appeared in French in 1991), in which he examines his life and work. Very good, short intellectual biographies have been written by Roger Hausheer – the 'Introduction' in Berlin's *Against the Current* (1981: xiii–liii) and, partly based on this, 'Berlin and' the emergence of liberal pluralism'. The latter article appeared in 1983 on the occasion of the awarding of the Erasmus Prize to Aron, Kolakowski, Yourcenar and Berlin. It is included in Manent et al. (1983: 49–81). Festschriften have appeared in honour of Berlin in which his thoughts are closely examined. These are Ryan (1979) and Margalit (1991). Two recent intellectual biographies are Gray (1995) and Galipeau (1994). Both biographies appeared after the completion of the manuscript of *Freedom and Culture in Western Society* and, consequently, have not been assimilated in this book. I largely subscribe to the interpretation of Claude Galipeau of Berlin's liberalism, but I disagree with John Gray who states that Berlin has to be a postmodernist if he wants to stay consistent. I commented on both books in my 'Berlin and Gray on pluralism, relativism, and the foundation of the liberal society' (1997).
2 Berlin describes how in his student years he came to reject the rationalistic assumptions of Western thought through the work of Machiavelli, Vico and Herder in 'On the pursuit of the ideal' (1988); see also Hausheer (1983: 60–72).
3 Twenty-five years later, in an interview with the Belgian journalist Boenders, Berlin takes back to some extent this hard judgement. He states: 'I certainly went too far in my judgement. I regret that because I think now that I did him an injustice.' However, he still calls him 'a very irresponsible man and a slovenly thinker' (Boenders 1980: 186).
4 Wollheim's answer is affirmative. The suggestion which he elaborates upon, a suggestion that Berlin is supposed to subscribe to, is 'that the commonality of human nature is to be found in the mode of explanation to which we are all susceptible. In other words, we are all comprehensible – comprehensible to ourselves and to others – along the same lines, in the same broad terms' (Wollheim 1991: 65). Roger Hausheer makes a comparable defence of Berlin's pluralism against relativism and subjectivism (1983: 72–7).
5 Parekh writes: 'To say that whatever an individual chooses is a value, and that all such values are ultimate, is to imply that the purposes men follow and the choices they make are beyond moral evaluation, and that is simply not true. We do evaluate human purposes, and would not allow a Hitler to claim that his purposes were sacred, ultimate and beyond criticism' (Parekh 1982: 44). In order to demonstrate that absolute value relativism is logically untenable, Parekh actually uses the same argument as Berlin in 'Historical inevitability' (1953: 87, 104): the postulation that everything is relative implies that the postulation itself must also be relative and therefore forms a *reductio ad absurdum*.
6 'Pluralisme', writes Hausheer on the work of Berlin, 'does not . . . entail rela-

tivism or subjectivism. What it does entail is that there is a plurality of objective values which cannot – logically cannot – be ranked hierarchically, and that therefore the possibility of conflict between values, or between the total outlooks of different civilizations or ages, can never in principle be eliminated' (1983: 77).

7 In his essay, Berlin draws no clear distinction between the terms *concept* and *conception* of freedom. He mostly uses them interchangeably. The question of whether there is one concept and a number of conceptions of freedom (where the word 'concept' is used as a synonym for 'idea' and 'conception' as a possible interpretation of it), or two or more concepts (in the Rawlsian sense) each of which can have one or more conceptions, is examined more closely in Chapter 4.

8 In the first version of 'Two concepts of liberty', Berlin himself was a prey to this lack of precision. This has been improved in the second edition of 1960 used here (see Berlin 1969: xxxviii).

9 Compare the distinction made by Hayek between democracy and liberalism, and his plea for a 'Rule of Law' (Hayek 1944: 72).

10 Despite contradictory suggestions at the end of his essay, Berlin deliberately does not explain the growing apart and the conflict between the two concepts of liberty *logically*, but *historically*. A number of authors have unnecessarily gone to great lengths to show that the contradiction between positive and negative freedom is not natural. (This point is discussed further later in this chapter.)

11 The textbook example of this reasoning is provided by Marxist Leninism with its theory of 'false consciousness'. Within this theory democratic methods for changing society are considered ineffective, because they are based on a mistaken psychology: the belief that people's actions are based on conscious, rational motives, which could be changed by argument or persuasion. According to Berlin, in the twentieth century, Freud and Bergson (unintentionally) among others prop up this thinking with their view that the real, generally unconscious, motivations of someone's behaviour are often completely different from the reasons which are often given in good faith by the party involved (Berlin 1950: 18–20; 1979: 36–40).

12 As far as this is concerned, Berlin has been influenced by the language philosopher John Austin, who claimed that the only way in which knowledge, experiences and assumptions could be meaningfully analysed was to study the way people use language in practice (see Berlin (1969: xxiii); Jahanbegloo (1991: 151–5); and Annan (1980: xviii)).

13 Exaggerated forms of nationalism are, according to Berlin, generally a reaction to the denial, oppression or disparagement of the singularity of the relevant culture. In this context, Vico was the first to understand that culture forms a pattern of ideas, customs, expectations, values and norms, a manner of being, and Herder was the first to realize how important it is for people to belong to such a culture supported by a community (see Berlin (1972, 1978)).

14 Patterson writes that Berlin tries 'to confine (liberty) to a purely negative meaning' (1991: 3), and Lindley states: 'Berlin offers a strong warning against political leaders and writers who seek to "liberate" people – in the sense of granting them their positive liberty. True liberalism seeks to defend people's negative liberties, and leaves their positive liberty well alone' (1986: 8). See also Cohen (1960).

15 He sees values as a socio-historical product: 'A given value complex emerges as a result of a specific configuration of historical factors' (Patterson 1991: xii).

16 In a footnote to the 'Introduction' (1969: xlvii), Berlin has afterwards, in another context, proposed that the subject of his 'Two concepts' only concerned political freedom. His thesis with regard to the conflict between the two conceptions of

freedom would in that case only refer to the relation between the state and its citizens. In reality, however, Berlin is talking, as has been mentioned, about much more, and none of the authors who have examined his essay have therefore interpreted his argument in such a limited fashion.

17 Two passages in 'Two concepts' justify somewhat the interpretation of Gray and MacPherson: 'I have tried to show that it is the notion of freedom in its "positive" sense that is at the heart of the demands for rational or social self-direction which animate the most powerful and morally just public movements of our time . . . But equally it seems to me that the belief that some single formula can in principle be found whereby all the diverse ends of men can be harmoniously realized is demonstrably false' (1958: 169). 'Pluralism, with the measure of "negative" liberty that it entails, seems to me a truer and more humane ideal than the goals of those who seek in the great, disciplined, authoritarian structures the ideal of "positive" self-mastery by classes, or peoples, or the whole of mankind' (1958: 171).

18 Berlin writes among other things: 'the "positive" and "negative" notions of freedom *historically* developed in divergent directions not always by logically reputable steps . . . ' (1958: 132; cf. 152, 134); 'It seems to me that . . . in *some* cases . . . ' (1969: x); 'My thesis is that *historically* . . . ' (1969: xliv); 'The rhetoric of "positive" liberty, *at least in its distorted form* . . . continues to play its historic role . . . as a cloak for despotism in the name of a wider freedom' (1969: xlvi); 'For whatever reason or cause, the notion of "negative" liberty . . . has not *historically* been twisted by its theorists as often or as effectively into anything so darkly metaphysical or socially sinister or remote from its original meaning as its "positive" counterpart' (1969: xlvii). See also Jahanbegloo (1992: 41, 147).

3 FREEDOM OF THE INDIVIDUAL

1 Naturally the *homme révolté* is a person without morality: someone who cannot explain his actions, cannot justify them either. In this he shows a strong resemblance to the ethic developed by Sartre in *L'Etre et le Néant* as 'radical choice'. See Taylor (1976: 289–94).

2 If someone's identity is also intangible to the person involved himself, then he can never know whether he has succeeded in changing his own identity. Bergmann seems to be inconsistent here.

3 Alan Wertheimer's reaction to Bergmann's incoherent argument in this is striking: He writes: 'once Bergmann decides not to limit the "real self" to some "inner self" it is not clear what would not constitute one's "real self" and, therefore, what would qualify as an unfree act. I am not saying that such an account would not be made out. It seems that Bergmann has made some stabs at it. But I frankly do not understand just what it all means' (Wertheimer 1978: 564).

4 Sartre, on whom Bergmann relies heavily, formulates this as follows:

existence precedes essence. [This] means that, first of all, man exists, turns up, appears on the scene, and, only afterwards, defines himself. If man is indefinable, it is because at first he is nothing. Only afterwards will he be something, and he himself will have made what he will be. Thus, there is no human nature, since there is no God to conceive it. Not only is man what he conceives himself to be, but he is also only what he wills himself to be after this thrust toward existence. Man is nothing else but what he makes of himself.

(Sartre 1946: 15)

5 In 1985, twenty-two of his scattered essays on these areas were collected under the title 'Human Agency and Language, Philosophical Papers'. For a critique of Taylor's 'anti-naturalistic' hermeneutic idea of science and linguistic philosophy, written on the basis of these collections, as well as his reaction to this, see De Sousa (1988); Davis (1988) and Taylor (1988). See also the 'Critical Note' by Annette Baier on Taylor's 'sexism', 'teleological anthropology', 'socialism' and 'synthesis of Rousseau, Kant, Hegel, Foucault, Habermas, Heidegger'.

6 In contrast to Taylor, Frankfurt is of the opinion that evaluation of first-order desires, evaluations in which second-order desires are formed, are not necessarily ethical in character (Frankfurt 1971: 13n.). However, it is unclear how one can determine the desirability of a particular desire without using a normative criterion.

7 This question is particularly relevant to the problem of paternalism: may we interfere in the lives of others in the short term in order to improve their welfare in the long term? In terms of our emancipation dilemma: may we limit someone's negative freedom in the short term in order to enlarge his positive freedom in the long term (cf. Chapter 5)?

8 In Chapter 5, this will be demonstrated in the treatment of the paternalism problem: wellnigh all authors who have written on this subject, attempt (in vain) to avoid the situation in which they would have to argue that a particular manner of life is preferable to another and therefore may be enforced or secured by paternalistic interventions. In all these cases, it is attempted to develop a strict *procedural* justification of paternalism.

9 John Rawls, at whom Taylor directs his fire too, denies that the liberal idea on the priority of justice implies 'that a liberal conception of justice cannot use any ideas of the good except those that are purely instrumental; or that if it uses noninstrumental ideas of the good, they must be viewed as a matter of individual choice, in which case the political conception as a whole is arbitrarily biased in favor of individualism'. Justice and the Good are, according to him, actually complementary: 'justice draws the limit, the good shows the point'. Justice lays down limits to acceptable lifestyles, and the Good determines what they are (Rawls 1988: 251–2).

10 In this context, there is a remarkable similarity between Taylor and Rorty, the pragmatist with postmodernist features: both want to put the Good into words so that it can motivate us as strongly as possible and both see an important role in this for the arts and literature. However, in this field Taylor also sees a task and an opportunity for philosophy, Rorty no more.

11 Berlin himself has no objection to labelling negative freedom as an 'opportunity concept': 'The degree of negative liberty simply means how many doors are open to me, whether I want to go through them or not. If you call that "opportunity", that is in order' (Jahanbegloo 1992: 150).

12 The question is whether this ideal of self-realization is indeed generally cherished in modern times. For many, the ideal, political or not, is simply that people be left alone by others. What they do with this is then their affair. For Taylor, who as we have seen regards life as a *quest*, as a narrative with a point, it is difficult to imagine that people could choose to do nothing with their negative freedom.

13 Elsewhere, Taylor says that within every acceptable conception of freedom qualitative distinctions are made between different wishes (1979: 181). With a purely negative conception one also recognizes more or less important obstacles to freedom, in the knowledge that certain objectives and activities are simply more valuable in life than others. For example, we consider freedom of religion more important than stoplights in traffic. This statement is correct. The crucial

question therefore is which consequences one attaches to the qualitative distinctions of others, held to be incorrect.

14 Megone, who formulates a defence of the negative conception against Taylor, reacts to this: 'Why not say that the man who acts on his real desire, rather than one he wishes he were rid of, is a better man rather than more free? . . . It is possible that goodness and the good life are here confused with freedom' (Megone 1987: 621–2).

15 In his *Multiculturalism and the 'Politics of Recognition'* (1992) Taylor elaborates further on this book. Here, he goes chiefly into the questions of what the importance is for individuals of possessing a cultural identity and whether cultural minorities can claim special collective rights in order to protect their cultural identity against the pressure of the majority. The background to this dispute is constituted by the fundamental question of whether the state should (and can) be neutral with regard to the interpretation which citizens give to the Good Life.

16 It is a pity that Taylor provides hardly any empirical support for this here – difficult though this may be to obtain. Nowadays there are numerous authors who advance this thesis, and this is probably no coincidence, but it is not enough for a thorough extensive cultural critique when these authors refer mainly to each other by way of substantiation.

17 In a number of cases, this making of choices *as such* is regarded as the value, not the content of the choices. The idea of authenticity is here based on that of self-determination. It may be important, says Taylor, to choose on or for one's life, but such choices first become meaningful when, once again, some options are more valuable than others: if this is not the case, then the entire idea of self-determination or 'choosing' is meaningless or insignificant.

18 In his book *Strong Democracy* (1984), Barber goes into the political consequences of this mechanistic metaphor. By regarding freedom and power as each others opposites, within liberalism politics and the state are by definition suspect: 'Politics becomes the art of power and freedom becomes the art of antipolitics' (ibid.: 35). However, this does not do justice to the dialectical, dialogic and symbiotic character of social and political relations. Politics is not by definition the enemy of freedom of the individual, but also forms its precondition. Within liberalism it is unjustly assumed that freedom, equality and justice have a natural, obvious character and that our political institutions are only legitimate in so far as they are at the service of these values. According to Barber, however, it is actually the opposite: 'Natural freedom is an abstraction, whereas dependency is the concrete human reality . . . the aim of politics must therefore be not to rescue natural freedom from politics but to invent and pursue artificial freedom within and through politics' (1984: 216).

19 Barber incidentally hastens to emphasize (1984: 53) that conscious and therefore intentional action is not 'better' or 'higher' by nature than impulsive or learned behaviour and that is not being claimed that reason alone should guide human life. He therefore also dismisses possible criticism from Berlin that he divides the individual into a higher and lower self, a split which paves the way to totalitarianism. However, this standpoint seems untenable. As, according to Barber, only intentional action can be called 'free' and freedom is for him a worthy goal, this action must be more valuable to him than unconscious behaviour. In addition, he sees self-consciousness, which makes intentional and therefore free action possible, as a fundamental characteristic of man. One generally considers those things to be fundamental which are regarded as important, *valuable* in the existence of the subject concerned. He therefore considers self-consciousness, intentionality, free action to be *more valuable*, 'higher' or 'better'

than the consciousness, the impulsive response to stimuli, the unfree behaviour of what he himself calls 'animals'.
20 Sartre wrote: 'We were never so free as under the German Occupation. We had lost all our rights, in the first place the right to speak; we were insulted daily to our faces and we had to keep our mouths shut; everywhere, on every wall, in the newspapers, on the silver screen, we recognized the filthy, stupid image of ourselves that our oppressors wanted to impose on us: this made us free. Because the Nazi poison crept into our thinking, every thought which did justice to truth was a blessing; because an all-powerful police wanted to silence us, every word acquired the precious gravity of a declaration of principle' (Sartre 1949: 11).

4 FREEDOM OF THE INDIVIDUAL

1 Goodin suggests that in all this he is basing himself partly on Berlin. However, this is not possible: as we have seen, Berlin draws a hard distinction between freedom and its conditions, and he says that someone's negative freedom can also be limited by social structures and that arguments for the welfare state and even for socialism can also be based on the negative conception of freedom. Whether this thesis of Berlin's is also tenable, will be discussed later.
2 For a profound elaboration of these two distinctions see Robert Young's *Personal Autonomy* (1986). Feinberg's four categories of impediments have been taken as starting-point for the structure of this book.
3 This notion is also formally correct. However, it conflicts with what we think a reasonable normal person will generally aim at. We expect a prisoner or slave of any intelligence to want to be freed of his chains. Equally, we refuse to see the inhabitants of Huxley's *Brave New World*, who are never impeded in anything because they pursue anything to which there are obstacles, as free or autonomous people. Thus, not a single acceptable conception of freedom can exist outside a notion of the 'rational' will, being the lowest common denominator of what normal people consider reasonable to aspire to. This notion of 'rational wishes', however, does not necessarily have to be linked to a rationalistic inspired idea of a 'higher' self (see also Benn and Weinstein 1971; Taylor 1979; Gray 1984).
4 Naturally, it is confusing here that the word 'concept' is generally used (also by Berlin, and in this book) as a synonym for 'idea', and 'conception' for a possible interpretation of meaning of this (cf. Gallie and Gray on 'essentially contestable concepts' in Chapter 1). Gray thinks that Berlin, for that matter, in his 'Two concepts' is, in Rawls' terms, talking about one concept and two conceptions. However, he does not comment on what the underlying concept in Berlin would be. It is striking that Gray does recognize that there is a fundamental difference between the two questions on which, according to Berlin, the two conceptions of freedom are based (Gray 1984: 325). Berlin himself never discusses the difference between a concept and a conception and uses the two words as synonyms or as above, in the usual sense.
5 Feinberg pushes Berlin's critique to one side by characterizing the prisoner, who strives to remove his chains without knowing what he is going to do with his freedom afterwards, as an improbable, exceptional case (Feinberg 1973b: 3–4).
6 Thus, according to MacPherson, from the empirical observation that man is an active creative being who wants to use and develop his capacities, a general feeling reflected in our use of language, it can be deduced that man also has a *right* to this use and this development and to the help of others in doing so. It seems as if MacPherson is here bridging, by a detour, the logical gap between facts

and values: a normative claim is deduced from an empirical statement, which is formulated with the help of concepts already charged with norms. However, in fact there is only an appeal to those experiences, feelings and intuitions interwoven into our language, which make certain values significant for us (MacPherson 1973a: 53; cf. Berlin 1962; Taylor 1989: 53–75).

7 How this vision of man developed, which function it fulfils within market capitalism and how it relates to the vision of man in which the development of the individual is central, is discussed by MacPherson in his *The Political Theory of Possessive Individualism* (1962) and in 'Democratic Theory: Ontology and Technology' (1967b).

8 MacPherson writes: 'A man whose productive labour is out of his own control, whose work is in that sense mindless, may be expected to be somewhat mindless in the rest of his activities. He cannot even be said to retain automatically the control over whatever energies he has left over from working time, if his control centre, so to speak, is impaired by the use that is made of him during his working time' (MacPherson 1973b: 67).

9 Incidentally, MacPherson assumes this in the rest of his argument (see for example, 1973b: 117): Berlin recognizes 'only direct physical obstruction' as an intervention in someone's negative freedom, and 'domination by withholding the means of life or the means of labour . . . is put outside the province of liberty altogether'. More correct is the statement that Berlin is simply inconsistent: it is not possible to justify the welfare state or socialism on the basis of negative freedom and in his famous note (Berlin 1958: 130) he defines *positive* rather than *negative* freedom.

10 It is not for that matter directly a question here of a conscious 'conspiracy' by a specific group of people, who completely control the state. This has gained a certain degree of independence. However, according to MacPherson, it has become increasingly interwoven with the economy and in this way has also become responsible for, and dependent on its functioning. The point now is that, as a consequence of the latter, the state, despite its legitimacy from the electorate, feels compelled to defend and promote the interests of capital, the continuation of the accumulation process (MacPherson 1977: 234, 242). This theme has been particularly elaborated by neo-Marxist theoreticians like Gough, Offe and Habermas. They say that the state has reached a crisis of legitimacy through the contradictory demands of the capitalist economy and the welfare state desired by the electorate.

11 On the Utopian–voluntarist ideas of Marxism with regard to the nature of the socialist society, the Dutch political sociologist Kalma writes: 'Evil, the scarcity, the unintended consequence, they cannot be reduced to symptoms of a particular "wrong" society, which will have to disappear with that society, but must be regarded as constants in human history. The politician who does not take this into account is naïve, and in certain circumstances, dangerous; those who do take it into account, but are silent about it, are cynical and in the long term, are acting irresponsibly' (Kalma 1988: 35).

12 In order to round off his argument, Lukes also ascribes this 'capacity for negative freedom' to the human qualities worthy of our respect. However, it would appear from his definition of these that this boils down to the capacity for autonomy. Negative freedom is an expression of our respect for this latter potential and for Lukes, as for MacPherson, forms an element of the concept of freedom. It is not a capacity: it is not necessary to be able to do anything or to do it, in order to be free in this sense.

13 For an analysis of the rise of sociology, socialism and conservatism, partly in reaction to the abstract image of man, see Nisbet's *The Sociological Tradition* (1966).

14 In his *Sources of the Self* (1989), Taylor links this ontology of man more emphatically to our moral intuitions, held by him to be universal (see Chapter 3). Here he expresses the fear that when respect for people is based too strongly or exclusively on a rationalization with regard to admirable qualities (as Lukes does), this respect could be too weak with regard to people who do not possess these qualities, or hardly.

15 Here Taylor is defining *positive* rather than *negative* freedom, a conception for which the 'primacy of rights' theoreticians are, in the first place, looking. They would certainly acknowledge the value of autonomy, but the question is to what extent they are prepared to sacrifice negative freedom for this. They cannot be criticized of wrongly defining the conditions under which positive freedom is done justice to. The criticism should be that they emphasize the value of 'privacy' to such an extent that there is no room left for the realization of autonomy, and that this one-sidedness is the result of an empirically untenable image of man.

16 In his book, Bergmann confronts his ideas on freedom, obstacles and alternative choices with the educational theories of the educationalist A. S. Neill (see especially his *Summerhill* of 1962). In contrast to Neill, he would appear to see little in schools where everything is allowed and nothing is compulsory. According to him, other children, and people, need a constant interaction with, and thus impediment from, their social environment, in order to develop. Just like a baby, one only experiences an action or choice as something of one's own when one has overcome an impediment. Obstacles therefore promote the formation of an identity.

17 More readable than Marcuse's *One Dimensional Man*, but with the same tenor is Aldous Huxley's *Brave New World*. He writes:

> Government by clubs and firing squads, by artificial famine, mass imprisonment and mass deportation, is not merely inhumane . . . it is demonstrably inefficient. A really efficient totalitarian state would be one in which the all-powerful executive of political bosses and their army of managers control a population of slaves who do not have to be coerced, because they love their servitude. To make them love it is the task assigned . . . to ministries of propaganda, newspaper editors and schoolteachers.
>
> (Huxley 1932: 12)

The difference between both authors is that Huxley, who is nowhere mentioned by Marcuse in his book, has *conscious* manipulation in mind, while Marcuse considers this mainly the product of uncontrolled structures and processes.

18 For a critical description of the decay of politics over the course of time as a communal effort aimed at the general interest, as the backbone of society, into a procedure in which the promotion of private interests is central, see Sheldon Wolin's *Politics and Vision* (1960).

19 However, Berlin makes it seem that this explanation is more an exception than a rule and therefore will be offered by few. Perhaps that is why he continues to follow for the most part the traditional Anglo-Saxon liberal path: coercion is direct intervention by other people. This picture of events has extremely astonished a number of authors (G. A. Cohen 1979; M. Cohen 1960; Kaufman 1962; MacPherson 1973b; Norman 1987: 46). The majority, however, have not noticed the crucial passage in question and they thus interpret Berlin here as a traditional liberal.

20 The less a distinction is made between freedom and its conditions, the sooner one will be led to formulate a divisive theory of justice. This theory then examines the question of how the communally-produced conditions or freedoms must be divided among the participants in society. We saw this, for example, in

Norman. However, because here we are assuming that an argument about the desirability of freedom or autonomy is already actually enough to justify a social effort to promote these values, this question has only been gone into briefly.

21 Taylor also makes this appeal. He does worry about whether values which are not, or insufficiently based, on epiphanic articulations of primary moral intuitions are strong enough when it comes to the crunch (see Chapter 3). In addition he assumes that our values have a Divine, universal origin. In the practical ethical debate this principle, however, does not necessarily mean any separation of thinking.

22 Some authors have therefore taken Berlin's definition of the scale of negative freedom as a starting-point for their own definition of the size of positive freedom. See, for example, Crocker (1980).

5 EMANCIPATION AND PATERNALISM

1 One can wonder why Lukes simply equates exercise of power with *impairment* of someone's interests. After all, it can sometimes also be used in someone's interests, even if this is against the will of the parties involved.

2 See, among others, Dahl's *Who Governs?* (1961), Wolfinger's *The Politics of Progress* (1974), and Polsby's *Community Power and Political Theory* (1963). In the second expanded edition of this book (1980), Polsby evaluates the (mainly methodological) literature which has appeared since 1963 on the study of power in local communities. Incidentally, in his later work, Dahl came to add considerable nuances to the empirical and normative tenability of his original ideas; see, for example, his *Dilemmas of Pluralist Democracy* (1982) and *Democracy and its Critics* (1989).

3 Compare Vaclav Havel's description of a rationalized, bureaucratized society of which the former totalitarian states of the *Ostblok* were just one expression and where power has an 'objective' self-momentum: 'By the "self-momentum" of a power or system I mean the blind, unconscious, irresponsible, uncontrollable, and unchecked momentum that is no longer the work of people, but which drags people along with it and therefore manipulates them' (1986: 166). Havel develops this notion in his essay 'Politics and Conscience' from 1984, included in Vladislav (1986).

4 Compare Marshall Cohen's critique of Berlin's conception of negative freedom (1960). As power is limited to deliberate, direct interventions by other people, according to Cohen this conception offers no room to those freedom-restricting powers which were most feared by John Stuart Mill and Alexis de Tocqueville: the (anonymous) pressure which public opinion exerts on individuals to conform to the norms and values of the majority.

5 In a critique of Lukes, Bradshaw (1976: 121–2) states that structural power is always exercised over people, that to remove one by one all these sources of power would only create a 'ridiculously barren, asocial arena' and that there is therefore no situation imaginable in which people could determine autonomously their 'real interests'. He therefore considers Lukes' notion of 'real interests' to be not operational. In his reply, Lukes (1976: 129) points out that this critique is only tenable if Bradshaw were to assume that *all* our preferences are heteronomous, the product of some exercise of power. Lukes regards this as unrealistic. He is not concerned with absolute, but with *relative* autonomy. Naturally, it is a problem, Lukes admits, that agreement must be reached about when this is the case.

6 Compare Mill's standpoint, which is not (unjustly) quoted by Lukes and

Connolly: 'On a question which is the best worth having of two pleasures, of which of two modes of existence is the most grateful to the feelings, apart from its moral attributes and from its consequences, the judgement of those who are qualified by knowledge of both, or, if they differ, that of the majority among them must be admitted as final' (Mill 1861/71: 282; cf. Elster 1982: 220–2).

7 He approvingly quotes Barrington Moore, a quote that is too good to leave unmentioned here:

> The assumption of inertia, that cultural and social continuity do not require explanation, obliterates the fact that both have to be recreated anew in each generation, often with great pain and suffering. To maintain and transmit a value system, human beings are punched, bullied, sent to gaol, thrown into concentration camps, cajoled, bribed, made into heroes, encouraged to read newspapers, stood up against a wall and shot, and sometimes even taught sociology. To speak of cultural inertia is to overlook the concrete interests and privileges that are served by indoctrination, education and the entire complicated process of transmitting culture from one generation to the next.
>
> (Moore 1967: 486; quoted by Lukes 1976: 131)

8 Compare Gerald Dworkin (1983: 111):

> There is nothing in the idea of autonomy which precludes a person from saying: 'I want to be the kind of person who acts at the command of others. I define myself as a slave and endorse those attitudes and preferences. My autonomy consists in being a slave.' If this is coherent, and I think it is, one cannot argue against such slavery on grounds of autonomy. The argument will have to appeal to some idea of what is a fitting life for a person and, thus, be a direct attempt to impose a conception of what is 'good' on another person.

9 Compare Preston: to answer the question of whether a particular choice has been made 'freely', it will be necessary each time to make a theoretically-based study of the conditions (alternatives present) and the capacities of the individual concerned (judgement, knowledge of the alternatives). Preston writes:

> respect for individuals' freedom or autonomy is not realized by relying upon abstract notions of freedom as the absence of interference or as self-realization. We can only determine whether the choice individuals make in a particular situation is free by identifying the relevant capacities and conditions needed for deliberation in that situation and by examining whether those capacities and conditions prevail.
>
> (Preston 1983: 668)

10 That far-reaching forms of the 'contestability thesis' with regard to concepts like 'power' and 'interests' lead to an untenable nihilistic scepticism and this conflicts with the convincing *rational arguments* which Lukes himself presents for his three-dimensional conception of power, is developed in depth by John Gray (1977) (see also Chapter 1).

11 Lindley tries to justify his standpoint by refuting the critique of the 'agent-relativists'. According to him, Bernard Williams is a representative of these opponents of the neutralists. Williams points out that life must have 'substance' if anything is to have meaning and significance, and that from the moment that it does actually have this substance, the neutralistic standpoint has become untenable. If, for example, someone can only rescue one person from a burning house in which there is a stranger and a friend, then no one will later criticize the hero if he without hesitation has chosen his friend. However, Lindley argues against this that it is not possible to deduce from this experiential fact that it would

have been wrong to have chosen to save the stranger. It does not prove that the neutralist standpoint is incorrect, but only that it cannot be held against someone that cannot always maintain it in practice (Lindley 1986: 85–8).

12 Williams (1981: 209 in Lindley 1986: 88–90) states that this standpoint would seem to imply an 'external view of one's own life' and in doing so neglects that life must be given meaning and significance by the individual concerned 'from inside'. It is up to the present 'I' to determine whether and how the future 'I' will exist and not the other way round. The correct perspective on one's own life is therefore provided from the present. However, according to Lindley, this leads to the conclusion that the present 'I' does not in any way have to take into account his future 'I', as the latter would not exist at all without the former. This 'might is right' reasoning lacks credibility for him.

13 Compare the remarks by Taylor in Chapter 3 on the silencing of the debate in present-day philosophy on the *content* of the Good Life, and the tendency to produce mainly procedural theories.

14 Kleinig turns out to draw a distinction between coercion and limiting of someone's freedom of action. There is coercion when A gets B to do something by threatening sanctions. The naturalness with which Dworkin and Kleinig explain that, in the examples mentioned by them, there is no limitation of freedom or coercion, seems misplaced. It depends to what extent the relevant help or inheritance is regarded as a favour or a right. The more the latter is assumed, the sooner coercion or limitation of freedom will be spoken of (we already saw this in a different context in Chapter 4).

15 Here Mill is probably inspired by article 4 of the *Déclaration des droits de l'homme et du citoyen* from 1789: 'Freedom consists of being able to do that which does not damage the rights of another.' It is of course problematic to draw a line between individual and society, between actions which only affect the individual himself and actions which also involve others (cf. Norman 1987: 11–7 and 54–5). However, Feinberg rightly remarks that this distinction is a condition for the recognition of the problem that paternalism must be vindicated. Otherwise, after all, every intervention can be justified by referring to the welfare of others (Feinberg 1971: 111; cf. Kleinig 1983: 32–6).

16 Many of the contradictions and ambiguities in the work of Mill can be explained by his attempt to add a moral component to the naturalistic utilitarianism of Bentham and James Mill. This component turned out to be noumenalistic, a source of inspiration which by definition is at loggerheads with naturalism (cf. Bluhm 1978: 438–50).

17 'Originally', because Mill, especially when he comes to discuss concrete problems, introduces so many nuances in the course of his discourse that little is left of his original hard and unambiguous standpoint. In this context, Sabine writes:

> Without much exaggeration it might be said that his books follow a formula. On nearly every subject (Mill) was likely to begin with a general statement of principles which, taken literally and by itself, appeared to be as rigid and as abstract as anything that his father might have written. But having thus declared his allegiance to the ancestral dogmas, Mill proceeded to make concessions and restatements so far reaching that a critical reader was left in doubt whether the original statement had not been explained away.
>
> (Sabine 1973: 639)

18 According to Gray (1983) and Lindley (1986: 102–12), it is possible to give a consistent, purely utilitarian interpretation of Mill's Liberty Principle. Central to their probably correct reading is that 'happiness', for Mill, does not mean any Benthamite hedonism, but something like 'self-realization' or 'wellbeing'. In

this context, autonomy is not just a means to happiness, but here too is an essential component of it. No one who has once experienced what it means to be autonomous, according to Mill, will ever be prepared to surrender this value for another. Interfering with someone's autonomy therefore undermines his happiness. Furthermore, negative freedom is an instrumental value for positive freedom, because someone's capacity for autonomy can only develop by being able to make (correct and incorrect) choices. For a passage in Mill's work which confirms their reading, see Mill (1861: 278–83).

19 For example, Mill writes in 'On Liberty': 'To a certain extent it is admitted that our understanding should be our own: but there is not the same willingness to admit that our desires and impulses should be our own likewise . . . desires and impulses are as much a part of a perfect human being as beliefs and restraints' (Mill 1859: 188).

20 Compare the 'welfare goods' identified by Feinberg (1984: 37), being 'conditions that are generalized means to a great variety of possible goals and whose joint realization, in the absence of very special circumstances, is necessary for the achievement of more ultimate goals'.

21 Of course this is the same problem, already identified by Lukes and Connolly, that the individual is not a fixed reference point and tends to appreciate the culture which he or she has recently experienced (see the earlier section on Ted Benton).

6 FINAL BALANCE AND SYNTHESIS

1 A radio talk held in early 1956 by Chris Leeflang, chairman of the Dutch Book Association Committee. This committee, which still exists, on which mainly booksellers and publishers sit, has set itself the goal of promoting the reading of literature. (Quoted in Blokker 1990: 108.)

2 The term *Bildung* comes originally from neohumanist German thinkers such as Herder, Wolf and Von Humboldt. These authors, from the second half of the eighteenth century, continued the humanism of the Renaissance. *Bildung*, says the Dutch historian Nico Laan, must be related to 'inner growth' and 'self-development'. He defines it as a 'quest for spiritual and moral perfection, a quest aimed at bringing all the powers possessed by man into a harmonious whole'. Knowledge of letters (especially classical) was considered here the most important criterion for someone's culture (Laan 1990: 181).

3 Fyodor Dostoevsky had already written in his *Notes from Underground* (1864: 42):

> Civilization only enlarges in man the multiplicity of his feelings and for the rest absolutely nothing. And precisely through the development of this multiplicity, man perhaps also comes to enjoy bloodletting. Have you never noticed that the most refined blood spillers have almost always been the ones with the most civilization. In any case through civilization man has become bloodthirsty in a worse manner than he used to be.

4 Only for the sake of argument: every plausible definition of 'happiness' will, as we shall see, have to include a notion of 'autonomy'.

5 Just like Frankfurt, Taylor, Barber and Young, Nozick therefore mentions as plausible motives for awarding people rights, their capacity for self-consciousness, rationality (thinking in abstractions and the postponement of reactions to stimuli), the forming of a will, and the development of a morality which will lend direction to one's own life. Together these gifts make the person:

> a being able to formulate long-term plans for its life, able to consider and

decide on the basis of abstract principles or considerations it formulates to itself and hence not merely the plaything of immediate stimuli, a being that limits its own behaviour in accordance with some principles or picture it has of what an appropriate life is for itself and others, and so on.

(Nozick 1974: 49)

People's capacity to lend direction to their lives according to a life plan they themselves have designed provides them, suspects Nozick, with the possibility of lending meaning and sense to life.

6 The misunderstanding that freedom has only benefits and no costs, is well expressed in Albert Camus's *The Fall*. Grown older and wiser, the main character in this book says:

I did not know, that freedom is not the same as a reward or a knightly decoration, which you can celebrate with a bottle of champagne. Oh no, it is a difficult duty, you can compare it to a deadly fatiguing, long distance run which you have to do alone and without help. There is no glass of champagne or bunch of friends, who raise their glass to you and look at you benevolently. You are alone in a depressing hall, alone in the dock before the lawyers, hopelessly alone to decide, alone with your own judgement and that of others. At the end of every way to freedom only waits a sentence; freedom is therefore too heavy to bear.

(Camus 1956: 135–6)

7 The incomplete empirical research which has been carried out into the circumstances under which people themselves qualify their situation as 'happy' does not, incidentally, show that people with a higher education, for example, or a 'greater richness of mental life' have more chance of an unhappy life (see Veenhoven 1984: 198–205 and 287–91).

8 Henri Polak, the author of this cry from the heart, was a Dutch social democratic trade union leader, politician and journalist who was very interested in the cultural edification of the working class. Within the diamond workers' union which he led, numerous cultural activities were developed. In 1932 he received an honorary doctorate (Polak 1897; quoted by Adang 1990: 81).

7 CULTURE, POLITICS AND FREEDOM

1 In addition, naturally, in practice extremely pragmatic goals are also pursued. Nowadays, examples would be the promotion of tourism and the climate for investment, the expression of the national identity and obtaining the support of influential opinion-makers from the cultural world (see Cummings and Katz 1987: 350–2).

2 It is very difficult to make international comparisons in the context of differences of definition with regard to the sectors which fall under cultural policy (public broadcasting, monuments, the archives, the art education, etc.), the absence of reliable data (the expenditures of lower authorities, in particular, are often hardly pictured), and the fluctuations of the rates of exchange. Tentative comparisons, however, reveal very big differences which it is difficult to ascribe entirely to those factors. For example, in the United States in 1983, the National Endowment for the Arts, its state equivalents and private sponsors, spent $144 million, $126 million and $435 million respectively, in total $605 million (Mulcahy 1987: 313, 318, 323). To this, could be added subsidized institutions such as the Smithsonian ($196 million), the Historic Preservation Fund ($26 million) and the National Gallery of Art ($33 million). The total can then be estimated at $850 million (Mulcahy: 1987: 313). According to figures from the

Central Bureau of Statistics (and bearing in mind the then rate of exchange) the various authorities in the Netherlands spent $870 million in 1983 (excluding public broadcasting) (WVC 1993: 64). The expenditures on art and culture remained quite stable in both countries during the 1980s and 90s and the proportions can thus be translated into the present. Authorities and private institutions together therefore spend as much on art and culture in the United States as in the Netherlands. However, a not unimportant difference is that in 1983 there were about eighteen times more Americans than Dutch.

3 With the aim of learning from each other's findings in the 1980s, the Council of Europe started a research programme in which the cultural policy of various countries is analysed and evaluated. Up to now, reports have appeared on Sweden, France, Austria and the Netherlands – one from the national government concerned and one from an independent commission of foreign experts. These reports will be regularly drawn on in the text.

4 The Dutch Centraal Bureau voor de Statistiek in 1955, and the Sociaal en Cultureel Planbureau from 1975 on, commissioned such a study. Since 1975, every five years, a representative sample of the Dutch population is asked to record its activities in a diary every fifteen minutes for a week in October. In this study, reading time is not specified in terms of the *nature* of what is read. However, it naturally makes a big difference whether one reads Plato or Konsalik. These defects also apply to the sales and lending figures for books.

5 Considering the changing character of many periodicals, the transition from a written to a visual culture is therefore taking place quicker than can be deduced from the figures on reading times: this transition is actually taking place within the printed medium (cf. Kraaykamp and Knulst 1992: 36).

6 In West Germany, the figure was about 3 books lent per head of the population in 1986, in France 2, in Canada at least 6, in Sweden 9, in the United Kingdom 11, and in Denmark 16.5 (CBS 1992: 57; Myerscough 1989: 138). In the latter country, too, by far the most titles per head of population are published.

7 Research by Knulst supports this assumption. It would even appear that in recent years library members have fallen behind non-members in that they actually read fewer books. They borrow more, but read less (Knulst 1989: 45, 54; cf. SCP 1992: 305).

8 This is related to the 'democratization' of library work. Under the influence of the rising relativism, library staff increasingly want to draw less of a distinction between high and low literature and to help people discover 'the better sort of book'. Everything therefore which the user shows interest in is purchased and lent. It is precisely because people can, or no longer want to, refer to their former cultural–political function, that lending figures, the only measurable 'output' are becoming the most important legitimization of government subsidies for libraries (see pp. 249–56 and Blokland 1992c, 1996).

9 Between 1975 and 1990, the lower educated born after 1950 reduced their reading time from 4.5 to 3.2 hours per week, a decline of 29 per cent. For the lower educated born before 1950, this reduction amounted to 16 per cent: from 6.1 to 5.1 hours per week. Medium and highly educated who were born after 1950 reduced their reading time from 5.6 to 4.5 hours, a decline of 20 per cent. In the same group, those born before 1950, only reduced their reading time by 1.5 per cent, from 7.3 to 7.2 hours per week (Kraaykamp and Knulst 1992: 32).

10 It is unclear whether these figures are collected by a time budget or survey study; if the latter case, they are probably too high due to over-estimation of reading times.

11 The rise of television was accompanied by an enormous decline in cinema attendance. In the United Kingdom in 1956 about 22 visits were recorded per head of the population, as opposed to 1 visit in 1992. In the United States, this

number dropped in the same period from 11 to 4; in France from 9 to 2; and in the Netherlands from 6 to 1 (Social Trends 1994: 10, 135; SCP 1990: 247).

12 Kraaykamp and Knulst state that in 1990, of the time spent on the diverse media 75 per cent was taken up by television viewing, as opposed to 2 per cent in 1955. Whereas in 1955, 60 per cent of all media use went to reading, in 1990 that figure was still 21 per cent. The biggest regression here was the time devoted to reading books. In both 1955 and 1990, media use took up about 35 per cent of the total leisure time (Kraaykamp and Knulst 1992: 27; cf. SCP 1992: 303).

13 In Sweden, the time spent watching television grew between 1970 and 1987 by 36 per cent: from 11 hours to 15 hours per week (Swedish Ministry of Education and Cultural Affairs 1989: 278). However, this was not at the cost of reading. This can perhaps be explained by the fact that, in comparison to other nationalities, the Swedes have more leisure time (cf. Schor 1991: 82, 153).

14 Between 1973 and 1988, the French watched 25 per cent more television: from 16 to 20 hours per week (Donnat and Cogneau 1990: 39).

15 Incidentally, McLuhan (1964) prefers an oral to a typographic culture. Because this does justice to the entire range of our faculties and does not translate all experiences into one language, it is supposed to be less fragmenting for human consciousness. In addition, people in an oral culture are less coerced into an abstract and deterministic mental framework. According to McLuhan, primitive peoples are therefore better able to deal with the non-determinism and the chaos or uncertainty which characterize modern physics.

16 The number of visits per thousand residents to subsidized stage performances dropped from 151 to 35 between 1965 and 1990. The number of visitors to subsidized concerts swung in the same period around 90 and that to opera, operetta, ballet and dance together around 35 (SCP 1992: 309; Knulst 1989: 238). In recent years there has been a somewhat growing interest in opera, dance and ballet.

17 According to UNESCO figures in 1978, there were 1429 visits per 1000 inhabitants, at the time probably the highest numbers in the world. In 1984, this figure was 1108 for the Netherlands, 929 for West Germany and 646 for Canada (CBS 1992: 51).

18 Naturally, the greater the role played by social motives in this visit (tourism, drive to distinction, and such like), the less conscious becomes the participation.

19 Except that the French seem to write relatively more poetry (6 per cent of the population aged fifteen and older does this) and to draw in greater numbers (14 per cent). The figures from the American Council for the Arts (1988 and 1992) seem rather unreliable: when asked, at least 24 per cent of the ('overworked') Americans aged eighteen and older claimed to produce poetry or prose, 27 per cent practised painting or drawing, 30 per cent played a musical instrument, 22 per cent sang in a choir, and 51 per cent made artistic photos. These figures probably say more about the high social status enjoyed in the United States by the activities concerned, than about the actual scale of artistic involvement.

20 It emerges from the General Household Survey of 1986, for example, that 27 per cent of the audience for theatrical, ballet and opera performances consisted of 'professionals, employers and managers', a group which forms 16 per cent of the total population. The same group formed 23 per cent of the amateurs in the field of music and stage. The 'skilled and semi-skilled manual workers' on the other hand formed 43 per cent of the entire population, 20 per cent of the listeners and spectators in the halls, and 23 per cent of the amateurs (PSI 1991: 12, 32).

21 This conclusion has also been drawn by, among others, the participants in the

Congress on Cultural Participation which was held in 1991 under the auspices of the Council of Europe. Researchers from more than twenty European countries and from Canada presented in Moscow an overview of the most important developments in their countries. On the basis of this, the Canadian researcher Vladimir Skok ultimately summarized: 'While differences were apparent, and some growth was noticed in certain areas such as cultural tourism and museum attendance, the overall picture is one of declining attendance patterns for traditional cultural activities, cinema and reading' (Skok 1991: 320). The Dutch sociologist Teus Kamphorst also comes to the conclusion that over the last fifteen years such extremely diverse countries as Canada, the United States, Puerto Rico, England, France, the Netherlands, Hungary and Czechoslovakia have shown comparable development in the field of cultural participation: 'Stagnation is setting in in the performing arts in all countries, and in all countries there is a substantial rise in visits to museums. In all the countries there is a growing orientation of the population to 'home consumption'. The democratization process with regard to art seems to have succeeded nowhere, not even in communist regimes' (Kamphorst 1988: 21; Kamphorst bases himself on: Hautrais and Kamphorst 1987).

22 The importance of art education at an early age has been confirmed by Dutch research (Ranshuysen and Ganzeboom 1993) into long-term effects. In Amsterdam, since the 1950s children have received so-called 'Looking at Art Hours' and 'Listening to Music Hours' in elementary school. Under professional guidance, they are introduced to the art supply available in the city. Although it concerns no more than twenty-one lessons, these turn out to have a small but statistically significant effect on the scale of cultural participation of the parties involved, even at a later age.

23 The Dutch pedagogue Van Zuilen wrote about this: 'From the large stream of publications on the cultural behaviour of the young it emerges again and again that art is an unimportant factor in the life of young people' (1989: 98). This applies particularly to pupils in lower types of education. Cultural dissemination among them has 'failed completely' (cf. Van der Linden and Dijkman 1989; Willis 1990).

24 An important difference with Temme and De Waal is that, according to Bourdieu, the distinction policy of the upper classes has been so successful that the workers, too, are of the opinion that only the bourgeois can exercise judgement in the area of good taste.

25 According to De Swaan, the dissemination policy has failed because the cultural elite never really wanted it to succeed: this would have been in conflict with their drive to distinction.

26 An angry critique of this has been written by the Dutch poet Peter Berger. He says, among other things:

> Culture is not entertainment. Not just entertainment. Not enjoyment. Not just enjoyment . . . but also pain . . . Elevated cultural expressive cultural productions are expressions which do not avoid the pain of life, but integrate it. It is the paradox of art that it brings about a reconciliation with the irreconcilable of life by revealing this irreconcilability. The essence of high art is that it is tragic, and if there is enjoyment in the perception of art then this is a painful pleasure. To be moved is to be reconciled with suffering in suffering. That is why the term 'seasoned epicures' is so perverse. It radiates only the satisfaction of lusts or decadence.

(Berger 1990: 18–20)

27 Policy in France is more bureaucratic and centralist, but not therefore less incrementalistic in character than in most other countries. There, the arts and letters

are run by a department in a comparable manner to education for example. Incidentally, this does not appear to be to the detriment of the autonomy of the arts (Wangermée 1991: 49–56, 83–115). For an overview of the policy models used by the various national governments, which, while different, are growing towards each other, see Cummings and Katz 1987: 12–3, 354–5.

28 Partly in reaction to the shortcomings of incrementalism, in the Netherlands it is being experimented with a form of what Etzioni calls mixed-scanning policy (Blokland 1993a). The task the government sets itself here is mainly the formulation of the general policy lines. The daily policy is increasingly left to largely autonomous 'funds' and arts councils. The power of the interest groups seems only to grow in this manner. In Sweden a comparable policy model is used as in the Netherlands (Kleberg 1987: 181–4).

29 The statement applies to the policy with regard to museums (SCP 1986a: 110), letters (pp. 116–7), fine arts and architecture (p. 119), theatre and mime (p. 127), music (p. 133) and even (extra-mural) amateur art performance and artistic education (p. 135).

30 A study of the functioning of the Dutch 'Subsidy Regulation for Purchase of Artworks' (ASK) shows that 72 per cent of the users had a university or higher professional education, and that 50 per cent were freelance, director or manager. After the study, the ASK was developed and replaced by a comparable scheme; however, this time with the limited objective of widening the market for artworks. A study of the social backgrounds of the people who use art lending centres showed a comparable accumulation of subsidies in higher income groups (Welters and Eykman 1976, 1978).

31 One could also point out that although policy-makers often state that the promotion of cultural participation is an important objective, this does not at all prove that they really pursue it. The fact that generally only a small socio-economic elite uses the cultural facilities paid for by *public* resources, produces a legitimization-problem. The parties responsible can try to ameliorate this by regularly declaring that, in principle, the aim is to enable everyone to profit from the relevant facilities.

32 Eloquent in this context is the fact that in recent years a 'nearly universal preference for the massive and the attention-commanding' can be observed in the world of art policy. Policy-makers, write Cummings and Katz, have increasingly 'a preference for support of one-time blockbuster events and exhibitions, rather than less glamorous and eye-arresting arts programming' (Cummings and Katz 1987: 357; cf. Fumaroli 1992; Schneider 1993; WVC 1993: 203).

33 Bevers' interpretation is in line with that of the great majority of Bourdieu's readers. We will not be going into the question here of what is the *correct* reading of Bourdieu's ideas; what is important for our purpose is how this is explained and used in practice.

34 See for example, Lewis (1990: 112, 119–20) where he resolutely argues for the recognition of quality because otherwise much of the meaning in cultural participation is lost.

35 In this spirit, Van Zuilen writes: 'The culture of youths, that is the process of lending meaning and significance to culture, with or without analysis of that which a number of elites find important, is a better and more important starting-point for cultural education, than the constant plea for art education.' As examples of this youth culture, Van Zuilen mentions graffiti, rock, punk, reggae, rap, unconventional clothing and hairstyles (Van Zuilen 1989: 97, 100).

36 For this reason, it is necessary to handle sponsoring very carefully: the elitist, chic and snobbish image of the arts is only reinforced when elite brands like Saab, Remy Martin and American Express try to reach their sector audiences through sponsoring art (see Blokland 1992b).

37 At least this is the opinion of the British neo-Marxist critic Terry Eagleton (quoted in Alter 1989: 26).
38 Of course, in the context of freedom, education is not only relevant for its connection with cultural participation. Education also communicates different knowledge and skills essential for individual autonomy and also determines, to an important degree, the position which people will occupy in society. This position is again connected to the degree to which they can use and develop their capacity for freedom.
39 In the first part of this section Berlin quotes the Austrian–American economist and sociologist Joseph Schumpeter.

Bibliography

FREEDOM AND AUTONOMY

Annan, N. (1980) 'Introduction', in I. Berlin *Personal Impressions*, New York: Viking Press.

Arneson, R. (1985) Review of Kleinig's *Paternalism*, *Ethics* 2.

Bachrach, P. and Baratz, M. (1962) 'The two faces of power', *American Political Science Review* 56: no. 4.

—— (1963) 'Decisions and non-decisions: an analytical framework', *American Political Science Review* 57: no. 3.

Barber, B. R. (1971) 'Forced to be free: an illiberal defence of liberty', in *Freedom, Anarchy and the Revolution*, New York: Praeger.

—— (1975) *Freedom, Anarchy and the Revolution*, New York: Praeger.

—— (1984) *Strong Democracy, Participatory Politics for a New Age*, Berkeley: University of California Press.

Bay, C. (1958) *The Structure of Freedom*, Stanford CA: Stanford University Press.

Beatty, J. (1979) 'Review of Bergmann's *On Being Free*', *Harvard Educational Review* 49: no. 3.

Benn, S. I. (1975) 'Freedom, autonomy and the concept of a person', *Proceedings of the Aristotelian Society* 76.

Benn, S. I. and Weinstein, W. L. (1971) 'Being free to act, and being a free man', *Mind* LXXX.

Benson, J. (1983) 'Who is the autonomous man?', *Philosophy* 58.

Benton, T. (1981) '"Objective" interests and the sociology of power', *Sociology* 15: no. 2.

—— (1982) 'Realism, power and objective interests', in K. Graham (ed.) *Contemporary Political Philosophy, Radical Studies*, Cambridge: Cambridge University Press.

Bergmann, F. (1977) *On Being Free*, Notre Dame: University of Notre Dame Press.

Berlin, I. (1950) 'Political ideas in the twentieth century', in *Four Essays on Liberty*, Oxford: Oxford University Press, 1984.

—— (1953) 'Historical inevitability', in *Four Essays on Liberty*, Oxford: Oxford University Press, 1984.

—— (1954) 'Alexander Herzen', in *Russian Thinkers*, London: Hogarth Press, 1978.

—— (1955) 'Herzen and Bakunin on individual liberty', in *Russian Thinkers*, London: Hogarth Press, 1978.

—— (1956) 'Equality', in *Concepts and Categories, Philosophical Essays*, Oxford: Oxford University Press, 1980.

—— (1958) 'Two concepts of liberty', in *Four Essays on Liberty*, Oxford: Oxford University Press, 1984.

—— (1959) 'John Stuart Mill and the ends of life', in *Four Essays on Liberty*, Oxford: Oxford University Press, 1984.

—— (1962a) 'The purpose of philosophy', in *Concepts and Categories, Philosophical Essays*, Oxford: Oxford University Press, 1980.

—— (1962b) 'Does political theory still exist?', in *Concepts and Categories, Philosophical Essays*, Oxford: Oxford University Press, 1980.

—— (1964) 'From hope and fear set free', in *Concepts and Categories, Philosophical Essays*, Oxford: Oxford University Press, 1980.

—— (1969) 'Introduction', in *Four Essays on Liberty*, Oxford: Oxford University Press, 1984.

—— (1972) 'The bent twig on the rise of nationalism', in *The Crooked Timber of Humanity: Chapters in the History of Ideas*, London: John Murray, 1990.

—— (1973) 'The counter-enlightenment', in *Against the Current: Essays in the History of Ideas*, Oxford: Oxford University Press, 1981.

—— (1974) 'The divorce between the sciences and the humanities', in *Against the Current: Essays in the History of Ideas*, Oxford: Oxford University Press, 1981.

—— (1976) *Vico and Herder*, London: Hogarth Press.

—— (1978) 'Nationalism: past neglect and present power', in *Against the Current: Essays in the History of Ideas*, Oxford: Oxford University Press, 1981.

—— (1979) 'An introduction to philosophy', in B. Magee *Men of Ideas*, New York: Viking Press, 1979.

—— (1980a) *Personal Impressions*, New York: Viking Press.

—— (1980b) 'Wijsbegeerte, geschiedenis, vrijheid', in F. Boenders *Sprekend Gedacht*, Bussum: Het Wereldvenster.

—— (1983) 'Reply to Robert Kocis: toward a coherent theory of human development: beyond Sir Isaiah Berlin's vision of human nature', *Political Studies* XXXI.

—— (1988) 'On the pursuit of the ideal', in *The Crooked Timber of Humanity: Chapters in the History of Ideas*, London: John Murray, 1990.

—— (1990) *The Crooked Timber of Humanity: Chapters in the History of Ideas*, London: John Murray.

Bernstein, R. J. (1976) *The Reconstructuring of Social and Political Theory*, London: Methuen, 1979.

Bettelheim, B. (1960) *The Informed Heart: Autonomy in a Mass Age*, Free Press of Glencoe.

Blokker, J. (1990) *De Kwadratuur van de Kwattareep: Zestig Jaar Collectieve Propaganda voor het Nederlandse Boek*, Amsterdam: CPNB.

Blokland, H. T. (1988a) 'Review of R. Young *Personal Autonomy: Beyond Negative and Positive Liberty*', *Acta Politica* XXIII: no. 2.

—— (1991) *Vrijheid, Autonomie, Emancipatie: Een Politiekfilosofische en Cultuurpolitieke Beschouwing* (dissertation), Delft: Eburon.

—— (1992a) 'Een politieke theorie over kunst en economie in de verzorgingsstaat', in D. Diels (ed.) *Schoonheid, Smaak en Welbehagen: Opstellen over Kunst en Kulturele Politiek*, Antwerpen: Dedalus.

—— (1993a) 'Planning in Dutch cultural policy: an attempt at mixed-scanning, *Acta Politica* XXVIII: no. 2.

—— (1993b) 'Sociaaldemocratische politiek en cultuur in een marktliberaal tijdperk', in P. Kalma and H. Van Dulken (eds) *Sociaal-democratie, Kunst, Politiek: Beschouwingen over een Sociaal-democratisch Kunstbeleid*, Amsterdam: Wiardi Beckman Stichting/Boekmanstichting.

—— (1994a) 'Charles Taylor over individualisme, politiek en de onvermijdelijkheid van de moraal', *Acta Politica* XXIX: no. 4.

—— (1994b) 'De wereldbeschouwing van Isaiah Berlin: een precair evenwicht tussen relativisme en rationalisme', *Beleid en Maatschappij* XXI: no. 6.

—— (1997) 'Berlin and Gray on, pluralism, relativism, and the foundation of the liberal society', *Acta Politica* (submitted).

Bloom, A. (1987) *The Closing of the American Mind*, New York: Simon and Schuster.

Bluhm, W. T. (1978) *Theories of the Political System: Classics of Political Thought and Modern Political Analysis*, Englewood Cliffs NJ: Prentice-Hall.

Boenders, F. (1980) *Sprekend Gedacht*, Bussum: Het Wereldvenster.

Bradshaw, A. (1976) 'A critique of Steven Lukes' "Power, A radical view"', *Sociology* X.

Brodsky, J. (1989) 'Isaiah Berlin at eighty', *The New York Review of Books*, August 17, reprinted in Margalit, E. and Margalit, A. (1991) *Isaiah Berlin: A Celebration*, London: Hogarth Press.

Camus, A. (1942) *La Peste* [*The Plague*], Paris: Gallimard.

—— (1956) *La Chute* [*The Fall*], Paris: Gallimard.

Carling, A. (1988) 'Liberty, equality, community', *New Left Review* no. 171.

Carter, R. (1977) 'Justifying paternalism', *Canadian Journal of Philosophy* VII: no. 1.

Cohen, G. A. (1978) 'Robert Nozick and Wilt Chamberlain: How patterns preserve liberty', in J. Arthur and W. H. Shaw (eds) *Justice and Economic Distribution*, Englewood Cliffs NJ: Prentice-Hall.

—— (1979) 'Capitalism, freedom and the proletariat', in A. Ryan (ed.) *The Idea of Freedom, Essays in Honour of Isaiah Berlin*, Oxford: Oxford University Press.

Cohen, M. (1960) 'Berlin and the liberal tradition', *Philosophical Quarterly* 10: no. 40.

Connolly, W. E. (1972) 'On "interests" in politics', *Politics and Society* 2.

—— (1974) 'Theoretical self-consciousness', in W. E. Connolly and G. Gordon (eds) *Social Structure and Political Theory*, Lexington MA: Heath.

Cooper, D. E. (1983) 'The free man', in A. P. Griffiths (ed.) *Of Liberty*, Royal Institute of Philosophy Lecture, Series 15, Supplement to *Philosophy* 1983, Cambridge: Cambridge University Press.

Crenson, M. A. (1971) *The Un-politics of Air Polution: A Study of Non-decisionmaking in the Cities*, Baltimore/London: Johns Hopkins Press.

Crocker, L. (1980) *Positive Liberty: An Essay in Normative Political Philosophy*, The Hague: Martinus Nijhoff.

Crosland, A. (1956–63) *The Future of Socialism*, London: Jonathan Cape, 1985.

Dahl, R. A. (1956) *A Preface to Democratic Theory*, Chicago/London: University Press of Chicago.

—— (1958) 'A critique of the ruling elite model', *American Political Science Review* 53.

—— (1961) *Who Governs? Democracy and Power in an American City*, New Haven/London: Yale University Press.

—— (1982) *Dilemmas of Pluralist Democracy: Autonomy versus Control*, New Haven/London: Yale University Press.

—— (1985) *A Preface to Economic Democracy*, Berkeley/Los Angeles: University of California Press.

—— (1989) *Democracy and Its Critics*, New Haven/London: Yale University Press.

Dahl, R. A. and Lindblom, C. E. (1953) *Politics, Economics and Welfare: Planning and Politico-economic Systems Resolved into Basic Social Progresses*, Chicago: Chicago University Press.

Davis, S. (1988) 'Charles Taylor on expression and subject-related properties', *Canadian Journal of Philosophy* 10: no. 3.

Day, J. P. (1983) 'Individual liberty', in A. P. Griffiths (ed.) *On Liberty*, Royal Institute of Philosophy Lecture, Series 15, Supplement to *Philosophy* 1983, Cambridge: Cambridge University Press.

Diels, D. (ed.) (1992) *Schoonheid, Smaak en Welbehagen: Opstellen over Kunst en Culturele Politiek*, Antwerp: Dedalus.

Doorn, J. A. A. van (1988) *Rede en Macht*, The Hague: VUGA.

Dostoevski, F. (1864) *Herinneringen uit het Ondergrondse* (*Notes from Underground*), Ede: Veen, 1979.

—— (1880) *De Gebroeders Karamazow* (*The Brothers Karamazow*), Utrecht: Veen, 1988.

Dryzek, J. S. (1990) *Discursive Democracy: Politics, Policy and Political Science*, Cambridge: Cambridge University Press.

Dworkin, G. (1970) 'Acting freely', *Noûs* no. 4.

—— (1971) 'Paternalism', in R. A. Wasserstrom (ed.) *Morality and the Law*, Belmont CA: Wadsworth.

—— (1978) 'Moral autonomy', in H. T. Engelhardt Jr, and D. Callahan (eds) *Morals, Science and Sociality: The Foundations of Ethics and its Relationship to Science* (vol. III), New York: Hastings Center.

—— (1981) 'The concept of autonomy', *Grazer Philosophische Studien* 12–13.

—— (1982) 'Is more choice better than less?' in P. A. French (ed.) *Midwest Studies in Philosophy* (vol. 7), Minneapolis: University of Minnesota Press.

—— (1983) 'Paternalism: some second thoughts', in R. Sartorius (ed.) *Paternalism*, Minneapolis: University of Minnesota Press.

—— (1988) *The Theory and Practice of Autonomy*, Cambridge: Cambridge University Press.

Elster, J. (1982) 'Sour grapes – utilitarianism and the genesis of wants', in A. Sen and B. Williams (eds) *Utilitarianism and Beyond*, Cambridge: Cambridge University Press

—— (1986) *Rational Choice*, Oxford: Blackwell.

Etzioni, A. (1968) *The Active Society: A Theory of Societal and Political Processes*, New York: Free Press.

Feinberg, J. (1971) 'Legal paternalism', in *Rights, Justice, and the Bounds of Liberty: Essays in Social Philosophy*, Princeton: Princeton University Press, 1980.

—— (1973a) 'The idea of a free man', in *Rights, Justice, and the Bounds of Liberty: Essays in Social Philosophy*, Princeton: Princeton University Press, 1980.

—— (1973b) 'Harmless immoralities and offensive nuisances', in *Rights, Justice, and the Bounds of Liberty: Essays in Social Philosophy*, Princeton: Princeton University Press, 1980.

—— (1980) *Rights, Justice, and the Bounds of Liberty: Essays in Social Philosophy*, Princeton: Princeton University Press.

—— (1984) *The Moral Limits of the Criminal Law, Vol. 2: Harm to Others*, New York/Oxford: Oxford University Press.

—— (1986) *The Moral Limits of the Criminal Law, Vol. 3: Harm to Self*, New York/Oxford: Oxford University Press.

Frankfurt, H. G. (1971) 'Freedom of the will and the concept of a person', *The Journal of Philosophy* LXVIII: no. 1.

Fromm, E. (1941) *Escape from Freedom*, New York: Rhinehart.

Galipeau, C. J. (1994) *Isaiah Berlin's Liberalism*, Oxford: Clarendon Press.

Gallie, W. B. (1956) 'Essentially contested concepts', *Proceedings of the Aristotelian Society* 57.

Gellner, E. (1992) *Postmodernism, Reason and Religion*, London/New York: Routledge.

Gerth, H. H. and Wright Mills, C. (eds.) (1948) *From Max Weber: Essays in Sociology*, London: Routledge, 1991.

Goodin, R. E. (1982) *Political Theory and Public Policy*, Chicago: University of Chicago Press.

—— (1988) *Reasons for Welfare: The Political Theory of the Welfare State*, Princeton NJ: Princeton University Press.

Gorz, A. (1989) *Critique of Economic Reason,* London/New York: Verso.

Gray, J. (1977) 'On the contestability of social and political concepts', *Political Theory* 5: no. 3.

—— (1984) 'On negative and positive liberty', in Z. Pelczynski and J. Gray (eds) *Conceptions of Liberty in Political Philosophy*, London: Athlone Press.

—— (1988) 'Against Cohen on proletarian unfreedom', *Social Philosophy and Policy* 6: no. 1.

—— (1995) *Berlin*, London: Fontana Press.

Griffiths, A. P. (ed.) (1983) *Of liberty*, Royal Institute of Philosophy Lecture, Series 15, Supplement to *Philosophy* 1983, Cambridge: Cambridge University Press.

Gutmann, A. (1982) 'What's the use of going to school? The problem of education in utilitarianism and rights theories', in A. Sen and B. Williams (eds) *Utilitarianism and Beyond*, Cambridge: Cambridge University Press.

Hausheer, R. (1983) 'Berlin and the emergence of liberal pluralism', in *European Liberty: Four Essays on the Occasion of the 25th Anniversary of the Erasmus Prize Foundation*, The Hague: Martinus Nijhoff.

Hayek, F. A. (1944) *The Road to Serfdom*, Chicago: University of Chicago Press.

—— (1946) *Individualism: True and False*, Dublin: University Press .

Held, D. (1987) *Models of Democracy*, Cambridge: Polity Press.

Hodson, J. D. (1977) 'The principle of paternalism', *American Philosophical Quarterly* 14: no. 1.

Hunter, F. (1953) *Community Power Structure: A Study of Decisionmakers*, Chapel Hill: University of North Carolina Press.

Huxley, A. (1932) *Brave New World*, London: Granada, 1978.

Isaac, J. (1982) 'On Benton's "Objective interests and the sociology of power": a critique', *Sociology* 16: no. 3.

Jahanbegloo, R. (1992) *Conversations with Isaiah Berlin*, London: Peter Halban.

Kadt, J. de (1939) *Het Fascisme en de Nieuwe Vrijheid*, Amsterdam: G. A. Van Oorschot, 1980.

Kalma, P. (1982) *De Illusie van de 'Democratische Staat': Kanttekeningen bij het Sociaal-democratisch Staats- en Democratiebegrip*, Deventer: Kluwer/WBS.

—— (1988) *Het Socialisme op Sterk Water: Veertien Stellingen*, Van Loghum Slaterus/WBS.

Kaufman, A. S. (1962) 'Professor Berlin on "negative freedom"', *Political Studies* LXXI: no. 282.

Kinneging, A. A. M. (1988) *Liberalisme: Een Speurtocht naar de Filosofische Grondslagen*, The Hague: Teldersstichting.

Kleinig, J. (1983) *Paternalism*, Manchester: Manchester University Press.

Kocis, R. A. (1980) 'Reason, development, and the conflicts of human ends: Sir Isaiah Berlin's vision of politics', *American Political Science Review* 74.

—— (1983) 'Toward a coherent theory of human moral development: beyond Sir Isaiah Berlin's vision of human nature', *Political Studies* XXXI.

Kossmann, E. H. (1985) *De Functie van een Alpha*, Faculteit in Onze Maatschappij: Groningen.

Kymlicka, W. (1989) *Liberalism, Community and Culture*, Oxford: Clarendon Press.

Langerak, E. A. (1979) 'Freedom: idea and ideal', in J. Kraay and A. Tol (eds) *Hearing and Doing, Philosophical Essays dedicated to H. Evan Runner*, Toronto: Wedge Publishing Foundation.

Larmore, C. (1991) 'Review of C. Taylor's *Sources of the Self*', *Ethics* 102: no. 1.

Lehning, P. B. (1986) *Politieke Orde en Rawlsiaanse Rechtvaardigheid* (dissertation), Delft: Eburon.

Lindblom, C. E. (1959) 'The science of muddling through', *Public Administration Review* 19.

—— (1965) *The Intelligence of Democracy: Decision Making through Mutual Adjustment*, New York: Free Press.

—— (1982) 'Another state of mind', *American Political Science Review* 76.

Lindley, R. (1986) *Autonomy*, London: Macmillan.

Lively, J. (1983) 'Paternalism', in A. P. Griffiths (ed.) *Of liberty*, Royal Institute of Philosophy Lecture, Series 15, Supplement to *Philosophy* 1983, Cambridge: Cambridge University Press.

Lowe, C. (1985) 'Cohen and Lukes on Rights and Powers', *Political Studies* XXXIII.

Lukes, S. (1967) 'Alienation and anomie', in P. Laslett and W. G. Runciman (eds) *Philosophy, Politics and Society* (3rd series), Oxford: Basil Blackwell.

—— (1973) *Individualism*, Oxford: Basil Blackwell.

—— (1974a) 'Socialism and equality', in L. Kolakowski and S. Hampshire (eds) *The Socialist Idea: A Reappraisel*, London: Quartet Books, 1977.

—— (1974b) *Power: A Radical View*, London: Macmillan.

—— (1976) 'Reply to Bradshaw: A critique of 'Steven Lukes' "Power, A radical view"', *Sociology* X.

—— (1979) 'The real and ideal worlds of democracy', in A. Kontos (ed.) *Powers, Possessions and Freedom Essays in Honour of C. B. MacPherson*, Toronto: Toronto University Press.

—— (1982) 'Relativism in its place', in M. Hollis and S. Lukes (eds) *Rationality and Relativism*, Oxford: Basil Blackwell.

—— (1985) *Marxism and Morality*, Oxford: Clarendon Press.

—— (ed.) (1986) *Power: Readings in Social and Political Theory*, Oxford: Basil Blackwell.

Lukes, S. and Galnoor, I. (1985) *No Laughing Matter: A Collection of Political Jokes*, London: Routledge and Kegan Paul.

MacCallum, G. C. (1967) 'Negative and positive freedom', *Philosophical Review* 76.

MacFarlane, L. J. (1966) 'On two concepts of liberty', *Political Studies* 14.

MacPherson, C. B. (1962) *The Political Theory of Possessive Individualism, Hobbes to Locke*, Oxford: Oxford University Press, 1985.

—— (1967a) 'The maximization of democracy', in *Democratic Theory, Essays in Retrieval*, Oxford: Clarendon Press, 1973.

—— (1967b) 'Democratic theory: ontology and technology', in *Democratic Theory, Essays in Retrieval*, Oxford: Clarendon Press, 1973.

—— (1973a) 'Problems of a non-market theory of democracy', in *Democratic Theory, Essays in Retrieval*, Oxford: Clarendon Press, 1973.

—— (1973b) 'Berlin's division of liberty', in *Democratic Theory, Essays in Retrieval*, Oxford: Clarendon Press, 1973.

—— (1977) 'Do we need a theory of the state?', *European Journal of Sociology* XVIII: no. 2.

Manent, P. (ed.) (1983) *European Liberty: Four Essays on the Occasion of the 25th Anniversary of the Erasmus Prize Foundation*, The Hague: Martinus Nijhoff.

Marcuse, H. (1964) *One Dimensional Man: Studies in the Ideology of Advanced Industrial Society*, Boston: Beacon Press.

Margalit, E. and Margalit, A. (1991) *Isaiah Berlin: A Celebration*, London: Hogarth Press.

Marx, K. and Engels, F. (1845) *Die Deutsche Ideologie, Vorrede, I. Feuerbach*, Nijmegen: SUN, 1974.

—— (1857) *Einleitung (Zur Kritik der politischen Ökonomie)*, Marx/Engels Werke, Dietz Verlag Berlin, Bd. 13, 1961.

Megone, C. (1987) 'One concept of liberty', *Political Studies* XXXV: no. 4.

Mill, J. S. (1848) *Principles of Political Economy II*, New York: Collier, 1900.

—— (1859) 'On liberty', in *Utilitarianism*, London: Fontana, 1986.

—— (1861/71) 'Utilitarianism', in *Utilitarianism and other essays*, Harmondsworth: Penguin, 1987.

Mills Wright, C. (1956) *The Power Elite*, New York: Oxford University Press.

—— (1959) *The Sociological Imagination*, New York: Oxford University Press.

Nabokov V. (1961) *Laughter in the Dark*, Harmondsworth: Penguin.

Neill, A. S. (1962) *Summerhill*, Harmondsworth: Pelican, 1968.

Nisbet, R. A. (1966) *The Sociological Tradition*, London: Heinemann.

Norman, R. (1982) 'Does equality destroy liberty?', in K. Graham (ed.) *Contemporary Political Philosophy, Radical Studies*, Cambridge: Cambridge University Press.

—— (1987) *Free and Equal: a Philosophical Examination of Political Values*, Oxford: Oxford University Press.

Nozick, R. (1974) *Anarchy, State and Utopia*, Oxford: Basil Blackwell.

Parekh, B. (1982) *Contemporary Political Thinkers*, Oxford: Martin Robertson.

Parent, W.A. (1974) 'Some recent work on the concept of liberty', *American Philosophical Quarterly* 11: no. 3.

Patterson, O. (1991) *Freedom, Vol. I: Freedom in the Making of Western Culture*, London: I. B. Tauris.

Pelczynski, Z. and Gray, J. (eds) (1984) *Conceptions of Liberty in Political Philosophy*, London: Athlone Press.

Polanowska-Sygulska, B. (1989) 'One voice more on Berlin's doctrine of liberty', *Political Studies* no. 1.

Polsby N. W. (1963) *Community Power and Political Theory*, New Haven/London: Yale University Press.

Popper, K. R. (1945) *The Open Society and its Enemies* (Vols I and II, Fifth edition), London: Routledge and Kegan Paul, 1980.

Preston, L. M. (1983) 'Freedom and authority: beyond the precepts of liberalism', *American Political Science Review* 77: no. 3.

Rawls, J. (1971) *A Theory of Justice*, Cambridge MA: Belknap Press/Harvard University Press.

—— (1987) 'The idea of an overlapping consensus', *Oxford Journal of Legal Studies* 7: no. 1.

—— (1988) 'The priority of right and ideas of the Good', *Philosophy and Public Affairs* 17.

Roche, M. (1992) *Rethinking Citizenship: Welfare, Ideology and Change in Modern Society*, Cambridge: Polity Press.

Rorty, R. (1989) *Contingency, Irony, and Solidarity*, Cambridge: Cambridge University Press.

Rosenberg, M. (1990) 'Review of Taylor's *Sources of the Self*', *Society* 27: no. 3.

Rousseau, J-J. (1762) *Emile, or Education* (Émile ou de l'éducation), trans. A. Bloom, New York: Basic Books, 1979.

Ryan, A. (ed.) (1979) *The Idea of Freedom: Essays in Honour of Isaiah Berlin*, Oxford: Oxford University Press.

Sabine, G. H. and Thorson, T. L. (1973) *A History of Political Theory* (4th edition), Hinsdale IL: Dryden Press.

Sandel (1984) *Liberalism and Its Critics*, New York: New York University Press.

Sartorius, R. (ed.) (1983) *Paternalism*, Minneapolis: University of Minnesota Press.

Sartre, J-P. (1946) 'Existentialism', trans. B. Frechtman in *Existentialism and Human Emotions*, New York: Citadel, 1980.

—— (1949) *Situations III*, Paris: Gallimard.

Schumpeter, J. A. (1943) *Capitalism, Socialism and Democracy*, London: Unwin University Books, 1981.

Shklar, J. N. (1991) 'Review of C. Taylor's *Sources of the Self*', *Political Theory* 19: no. 1.

Smith, G. W. (1981) 'Must radicals be Marxists? Lukes on power, contestability and alienation', *British Journal of Political Science* 11: no. 4.

Sousa, R. de (1988) 'Seizing the hedgehog by the nail: Taylor on the self and agency', *Canadian Journal of Philosophy* 18: no. 3.

Steiner, H. (1983) 'How free: computing personal liberty', in A. P. Griffiths (ed.) *Of Liberty*, Royal Institute of Philosophy Lecture, Series 15, Supplement to *Philosophy* 1983, Cambridge: Cambridge University Press.

Storr, A. (1988) *Solitude*, London: Flamingo.

Tawney, R. H. (1931) *Equality*, London: Allen and Unwin, (4th impression) 1979.

Taylor, C. (1967) 'Neutrality in political science', in P. Laslett and W. G. Runciman, (eds) *Philosophy, politics and society* (3rd series), Oxford: Basil Blackwell.

—— (1971) 'Interpretation and the sciences of man', *Review of Metaphysics* XXV: no. 1.

—— (1974) 'Socialism and Weltanschauung', in L. Kolakowski and S. Hampshire (eds) *The Socialist Idea: A Reappraisal*, London: Quartet Books, 1977.

—— (1976) 'Responsibility for self', in A. O. Rorty (ed.) *The Identities of Persons*, Berkeley: University of California Press.

—— (1977) 'What is human agency?' in *Human Agency and Language. Philosophical Papers: I*, Cambridge: Cambridge University Press, 1985.

—— (1979a) 'What's wrong with negative liberty', in A. Ryan (ed.) *The Idea of Freedom: Essays in Honour of Isaiah Berlin*, Oxford: Oxford University Press.

—— (1979b) 'Atomism', in A. Kontos (ed.) *Powers, Possessions and Freedom; Essays in Honour of C. B. MacPherson*, Toronto: University of Toronto Press.

—— (1982a) 'Rationality', in M. Hollis and S. Lukes (eds) *Rationality and Relativism*, Oxford: Basil Blackwell.

—— (1982b) 'The diversity of goods', in A. Sen and B. Williams (eds) *Utilitarianism and Beyond*, Cambridge: Cambridge University Press.

—— (1983) 'The concept of a person', in *Human Agency and Language, Philosophical Papers* (Vol. I), Cambridge: Cambridge University Press, 1985.

—— (1985) *Human Agency and Language. Philosophical Papers: I*, Cambridge: Cambridge University Press.

—— (1988) 'Reply to De Sousa and Davis', *Canadian Journal of Philosophy* 18: no. 3.

—— (1989) *Sources of the Self: the Making of the Modern Identity*, Cambridge: Cambridge University Press.

—— (1991) *The Ethics of Authenticity*, Cambridge MA/London: Harvard University Press.

—— (1992) *Multiculturalism and 'The politics of Recognition': an Essay by Charles Taylor with Commentary by Amy Gutmann (ed.), Steven Rockefeller, Michael Walzer and Susan Wolf*, Princeton: Princeton University Press.

Ten, C. L. (1971) 'Paternalism and morality', *Ratio* 13: no. 2.

VanDeVeer, D. (1979) 'Paternalism and subsequent consent', *Canadian Journal of Philosophy* IX: no. 4.

—— (1980) 'Autonomy respecting paternalism', *Social Theory and Practice* 6: no. 2.

Wertheimer, A. (1978) 'Review of F. Bergmann's *On Being Free*', *Political Theory* no. 4.

Wolfinger, R. E. (1974) *The Politics of Progress*, Englewood Cliffs NJ: Prentice Hall.

Wolin, S. S. (1960) *Politics and Vision, Continuity and Innovation in Western Political Thought*, Boston: Little, Brown.

Wollheim, R. (1979) 'John Stuart Mill and Isaiah Berlin, the ends of life and the preliminaries of morality', in A. Ryan (ed.) *The Idea of Freedom, Essays in Honour of Isaiah Berlin*, Oxford: Oxford University Press.

—— (1991) 'The idea of a common human nature', in E. Margalit and A. Margalit *Isaiah Berlin: A Celebration*, London: Hogarth Press.

Young, R. (1986) *Personal Autonomy: Beyond Negative and Positive Liberty*, New York: St. Martin's Press.

Young, R. A. (1978) 'Review of Steven Lukes' radical view of power', *Canadian Journal of Political Science* XI: no. 3.

ARTS AND CULTURE

Adang, M. (1990) 'Over socialisme en volksopvoeding in Nederland aan het begin van de twintigste eeuw', in M. G. Westen (ed.) *Met den Tooverstaf van Ware Kunst: Cultuurspreiding en Cultuuroverdracht in Historisch Perspectief*, Leiden: Martinus Nijhoff.

Alter, R. (1989) *The Pleasure of Reading in an Ideological Age*, New York: Simon and Schuster.

American Council for the Arts (1988) *Americans and the Arts. V: Highlights from a Nationwide Survey of Public Opinion*, New York: National Research Center of the Arts.

—— (1992) *Americans and the Arts. VI: Highlights from a Nationwide Survey of Public Opinion*, New York: National Research Center of the Arts.

Arts Council of Great Britain (1991) 'The situation on audiences in Great Britain/United Kingdom', in A. Wiesand, M. Müller, A. Meuffels and J. Euler (eds) *Participation in Cultural Life: Papers Presented to the European Round Table on Cultural Research*, Bonn: Archiv für Kulturpolitik.

Barker, R. and Escarpit, R. (1973) *The Book Hunger*, London: Harrap.

Barwise, P. and Ehrenberg, A. (1988) *Television and its Audience*, London: Sage Publications.

Beentjes, J. (1991) 'Televisieverhalen versus voorgelezen en zelf gelezen verhalen', *Cominius* 43: no. 3.

Bennett, O. (1991) 'British cultural policies 1970–1990', *Boekmancahier, Kwartaalschrift over Kunst, Onderzoek en Beleid* 3: no. 9.

Berger, P. (1990) 'De wonderschoenen van Kareltje Knal', *Trefpunt Extra*, Rijswijk: Ministerie van WVC.

Bevers, A. M. (1987) 'Particulier initiatief en cultuur: over de rol van burgers en overheid bij de oprichting en consolidering van kunstinstellingen', *Sociologisch Tijdschrift* 14: no. 2.

—— (1988) 'Cultuurspreiding en publieksbereik: van volksverheffing tot marktstrategie', in H. van Dulken et al. (eds) *In ons Diaconale Land: Opstellen over Cultuurspreiding*, Amsterdam: Boekmanstichting/Van Gennep.

—— (1989) 'Kunstsociologie in Nederland', *Boekmancahier, Kwartaalschrift over Kunst, Onderzoek en Beleid* 1: no. 1.

Bird, O. A. (1976) *Cultures in Conflict: an Essay in the Philosophy of the Humanities*, Notre Dame IN: University of Notre Dame Press.

Blockmans, W. P. (1987) '"Bezield tot hoger Leven!" Sociaal-democratische cultuurpolitiek in Nederland tijdens het interbellum', in J. Berting, J. Breman and P. B. Lehning (eds) *Mensen, Macht en Maatschappij*, Meppel: Boom.

Blokland, H. T. (1988b) 'Socialistische cultuurpolitiek: onderzoek naar een fundament', *Hollands Maandblad* 29: nos. 482 (Part I), 483 (Part II).

—— (1992b) 'Tégen kunstsponsoring', *Boekmancahier, Kwartaalschrift over Kunst, Onderzoek en Beleid* 4: no. 12.

—— (1992c) 'Meer tempel en minder agora: een cultuurpolitieke opdracht voor openbare bibliotheken', *Bibliotheek and Samenleving* 20: no. 9.

—— (1994a) 'Zielvorgaben, Instrumente und Ergebnisse der niederländischen

Kulturpolitik', in C. M. Bolle and E. A. Van Trotsenburg (eds) *Neue Furchen*, Zoetermeer: Ministerie van Onderwijs, Cultuur en Wetenschappen.

—— (1994b) 'The politics of the value of culture', *Boekmancahier, Kwartaalschrift over kunst, onderzoek en beleid* 7: no. 26.

—— (1996) *Publiek Gezocht: Essays over Cultuur, Markt en Politiek*, Amsterdam: Boom.

Boekman, E. (1939) *Overheid en Kunst in Nederland* (dissertation), Amsterdam: Hertzberger.

Bogt, T. ter (1990) *Andere wereld: Jongeren en Vrije Tijd*, Amersfoort: Uitgeverij Giordano Bruno.

Bourdieu, P. (1979) *Distinction* (La Distinction: Critique sociale du jugement), trans. R. Nice, Cambridge MA: Harvard University Press, 1984.

Bourdieu, P. and Passeron, J. (1977) *Reproduction in Education, Society and Culture*, London: Sage.

Bourdieu, P. and Van Heerikhuizen, B. (1989) 'Genieten van kunst als religie van intellectuelen', *De Volkskrant*, 25 November.

Brecht, B. (1928) *Die Dreigroschenoper*, Berlin: Suhrkamp Verlag, 1986.

Brinkmann, A., Botte, A., Franzmann, B., Kreibich, H. and Zitzlsperger, R. (eds) (1990) *Lesen im internationalen Vergleich, Ein Forschungsgutachten der Stiftung Lesen für das Bundesministerium für Bildung und Wissenschaft* Teil 1, Mainz: Stiftung Lesen.

Centraal Bureau voor de Statistiek (CBS) (1989) *Negentig Jaren Statistiek in Tijdreeksen 1899–1989*, 's-Gravenhage: SDU/CBS.

—— (1992) *Jaarboek Cultuur 1992*, 's-Gravenhage: SDU/Uitgeverij.

Central Statistical Office (CSO) *Social Trends*, London: CSO.

Condry, J. (1993) 'Thief of time, unfaithful servant: television and the American child', *Daedalus, Journal of American Academy of Arts and Sciences* 122: no. 1.

Cummings, M. C. and Katz, R. S. (eds) (1987) *The Patron State: Government and the Arts in Europe, North America and Japan*, New York: Oxford University Press.

Damon-Moore, H. and Kaestle, C. F. (1991) 'Surveying American readers', in C. F. Kaestle et al. (eds) *Literacy in the United States: Readers and Reading since 1880'*, New Haven/London: Yale University Press.

Diepenbrock, F. J. (1990) 'De ontwikkeling van de culturele infrastructuur in Nederland', in M. G. Westen (ed.) *Met den Tooverstaf van Ware Kunst: Cultuurspreiding en Cultuuroverdracht in Historisch Perspectief*, Leiden: Martinus Nijhoff.

DiMaggio, P. and Useem, M. (1980) 'The arts and cultural participation', *Journal of Aesthetic Education* 14: 65.

Documentation Française, La (1990) *Nouvelle Enquête sur Les Pratiques Culturelles 'des Français en 1989*, Paris: Ministère de la Culture et de la Communication.

Donnat, O. and Cogneau, D. (1990) *Les Pratiques Culturelles des Français 1973–1989*, Paris: Ministère de la Culture et de la Communication, La Découverte/La Documentation Française.

Doorman, S. J. (1984) 'Enkele speculaties over kunst en wetenschap', in L. Casteleijn, J. van Kemenade, W. Meijer and J. Ritzen (eds) *Tekens in de Tijd, 65 Jaar Joop den Uyl*, Amsterdam: BoekmanStichting/Van Gennep.

—— (1988) 'Losse gedachten over cultuurspreiding', in H. van Dulken et al. (eds) *In ons Diaconale Land: Opstellen over Cultuurspreiding*, Amsterdam: Boekmanstichting/Van Gennep.

—— (1990) 'Over het belang van amateuristische kunstbeoefening', *Kunst en Educatie, Tijdschrift voor Theorievorming* 3: no. 1.

Duijx, T. and Verdaasdonk, H. (1989) 'Het bevorderen van het lezen van boeken', *Massacommunicatie* 17: no. 1.

Dulken, H. van, Köbben A. and Pronk, T. (eds) (1988) *In ons Diaconale Land: Opstellen over Cultuurspreiding*, Amsterdam: Boekmanstichting/Van Gennep.

Eijsink, H. (1990) 'Volksconcerten in Amsterdam', in M. G. Westen (ed.) *Met den Tooverstaf van Ware Kunst: Cultuurspreiding en Cultuuroverdracht in Historisch Perspectief*, Leiden: Martinus Nijhoff.

Elias, N. (1939) *Über den Prozess der Zivilisation: Soziogenetische und Psychogenetische Untersuchungen*, Bern/München: Francke Verlag.

Enzensberger, H. M. (1990) *Lof van de Inconsistentie (Politische Brosamen* (1982) trans. C. Offermans, Frankfurt), Amsterdam: De Bezige Bij.

Feist, A. and Hutchison, R. (eds) (1990) *Cultural Trends in the Eighties*, London: Policy Studies Institute.

Finkielkraut, A. (1987) *La Défaite de la Pensée*, Paris: Éditions Gallimard.

Fumaroli, M. (1992) *L'Etat Culturel, Essai sur une Religion Moderne*, Paris: Edition de Fallois.

Ganzeboom, H. (1989) *Cultuurdeelname in Nederland: een Empirisch-theoretisch Onderzoek naar Determinanten van Deelname aan Culturele Activiteiten*, Assen/Maastricht: Van Gorcum.

Ganzeboom, H. and Haanstra, F. (1989) *Museum en Publiek*, Rijswijk: Ministerie van WVC.

Garnham, N. and Williams, R. (1980) 'Class and culture – the work of Bourdieu', *Media, Culture and Society* 2: no. 3.

Glotz, P. (1992) *Die Linke nach dem Sieg des Westens*, Stuttgart: Deutsche Verlangs/Anstalt.

Goedegebuure, J. L. (1989) *Te Lui om te Lezen?*, Amsterdam: Van Oorschot.

Gournay, B. (1991) *Cultural Policy in France*, European Programme for the Appraisal of Cultural Policies, National Report, Strasbourg: Council of Europe.

Grauwe, de P. (1990) *De Nachtwacht in het Donker: over Kunst en Economie*, Tielt: Lannoo.

Haanstra, F. and Wijdenes, J. O. (1990) 'Buitenschoolse kunstzinnige vorming: cijfers en ontbrekende cijfers', *Kunsten and Educatie, Tijdschrift voor Theorievorming* 3: no. 1.

Haes, L. de (1992) 'Gevangene van de eigen vrijheid: elitecultuur en massacultuur', *De Nieuwe Maand,* nos 1 and 2.

Harris, L. (1992) *Americans and the Arts*, New York: American Council for the Arts.

Hautrais, L. and Kamphorst, T. (1987) (eds) *Trends in the Arts: a Multi-national Perspective*, Amersfoort: Uitgeverij Giordano Bruno.

Havel, V. (1984) 'Six asides about culture', in J. Vladislav (ed.) *Václav Havel, or Living in Truth*, Amsterdam: Meulenhoff.

—— (1986) *Disturbing the Peace: a Conversation with Karel Hvízdala*, New York: Vintage Books, 1991.

Hekkert, P. and Van Wieringen, P. (1993) *Oordeel over Kunst: Kwaliteitsbeoordelingen in de Beeldende Kunst*, Rijswijk: Rijksuniversiteit Utrecht/Ministerie van WVC.

Hendon, W. S. (1990) 'The general public's participation in art museums', *American Journal of Economics and Sociology* 49: no. 4.

Hirsch, E. D. (1988) *Cultural Literacy, What every American Needs to Know*, New York: Vintage Books.

Horowitz, H., Keegan, C. and Kempnich, B. (1985) 'Cultural participation and geographic/population schema from New York City to the rural farm', *Journal of Cultural Economics* 9.

Jong, M. J. de (1987) *Herkomst, kennis en kansen: Allochtone en autochtone leerlingen tijdens de overgang van basis-naar voortgezet onderwijs* (dissertation), Lisse: Swets and Zeitlinger.

Kamphorst, T.J. (1988) 'De onmacht van cultuurbeleid', *Kunsten en Educatie, Tijdschrift voor Theorievorming* 1: no. 3.

Kassies, J. (1983) *Notities over een Heroriëntatie van het Kunstbeleid*, Den Haag: Wetenschappelijke Raad voor het Regeringsbeleid.

—— (1984) 'Grenzen van cultuur-en kunstbeleid', in L. Casteleijn et al. (eds) *Tekens in de tijd, 65 jaar Joop den Uyl*, Amsterdam: De Arbeiderspers.

Kautsky, K. (1927) *Die Materialistische Geschichtsauffassung* Teil II.

Ketzer, J. W., Swinkels, H. and Vooijs, M. W. (1989) 'Media-educatie in de Nederlandse praktijk', *Massacommunicatie, Wetenschappelijk Kwartaalschrift voor Communicatie en Informatie* 17: no. 1.

Kleberg, C-J. (1987) 'Cultural policy in Sweden', in M. C. Cummings and R. S. Katz (eds) *The Patron State: Government and the Arts in Europe, North America and Japan*, New York: Oxford University Press.

Knulst, W. P. (1987) 'Bibliotheken in een veranderende samenleving', *Bibliotheek and Samenleving* 15: no. 9.

—— (1989) *Van Vaudeville tot Video: een Empirisch-Theoretische studie naar Verschuivingen in het Uitgaan en het Gebruik van Media Sinds de Jaren Vijftig* (dissertation), Rijswijk: Sociaal en Cultureel Planbureau, Sociale en Culturele Studies 12.

Knulst, W. P. and Kalmijn, M. (1988) *Van Woord naar Beeld? Onderzoek naar de Verschuivingen in de Tijdsbesteding aan de Media in de Periode 1975–1985* (Deel 1), Rijswijk: Sociaal en Cultureel Planbureau, Cahier no. 66.

Knulst, W. P. and Van Beek, P. (1991) *De Kunstzinnige Burger: Onderzoek naar Amateuristische Kunstbeoefening en Culturele Interesses onder de Bevolking vanaf Zes Jaar*, Rijswijk: Sociaal en Cultureel Planbureau.

Komrij, G. (1986) 'Onze cultuur wurgt ons', in W. Kuipers (ed.) *Buitenstaanders: Kopstukken over Cultuur*, Aalsmeer: De Volkskrant.

Koolstra, C. M. (1993) *Television and Children's Reading: a Three-year Panel Study* (dissertation), Leiden: Center for Child and Media Studies.

Kraaykamp, G. (1993) *Over Lezen Gesproken: een Studie naar Sociale Differentiatie in Leesgedrag* (dissertation), Amsterdam: Thesis Publishers.

Kraaykamp, G. and Knulst, W. P. (1992) 'Stijgend scholingsniveau, afnemende belezenheid: verschuivingen in het gebruik van media tussen 1955 en 1990', *Massacommunicatie, Wetenschappelijk Kwartaalschrift voor Communicatie en Informatie* 20: no. 1.

Kuhn, R. (1985) *The Politics of Broadcasting*, London: Croom Helm.

Laan, N. (1990) *Het Belang van Letterenstudie in Historisch Perspectief*, in M. G. Westen (ed.) *Met den Tooverstaf van Ware Kunst: Cultuurspreiding en Cultuuroverdracht in Historisch Perspectief*, Leiden: Martinus Nijhoff.

Larson, G. O. (1983) *The Reluctant Patron: The United States Government and the Arts, 1943–1965*, Philadelphia: University of Philadelphia Press.

Leeuw, G. van der (1947) *Nationale Cultuurtaak*, 's-Gravenhage: Daamen.

Lemaire, T. (1976) *Over de Waarde van Kulturen: een Inleiding in de Kultuurfilosofie, tussen Europacentrisme en Relativisme*, Baarn: Ambo.

Lewis, J. (1990) *Art, Culture and Enterprise: the Politics of Art and Cultural Industries*, London: Routledge.

Lil, J. E. van (1989) 'Het mediagebruik van drie-tot en met zestienjarigen: een tijdsbestedingsonderzoek', *Massacommunicatie, Wetenschappelijk Kwartaalschrift voor Communicatie en Informatie* 17: no. 1.

Lil, J. E. van and Vooijs, M. W. (1989) 'TV-opvoeding in het gezin', *Massacommunicatie, Wetenschappelijk Kwartaalschrift voor Communicatie en Informatie* 17: no. 1.

Lil, J. E. van, Vooijs, M. W. and Van der Voort, T. H. A. (1988) 'Het verband tussen televisie kijken en vrijetijds-lezen: een dwarsdoorsnedestudie', *Pedagogische Studiën* 65: no.10.

Linden, F. J. van and Dijkman, T. A. (1989) *Jong zijn en volwassen worden in*

Nederland; Een onderzoek naar het psychosociaal functioneren in alledaagse situaties van de Nederlandse jongeren tussen 12 en 21 jaar, Nijmegen: Hoogveld Instituut.

Llosa, M. Vargas (1985) *De Cultuur van de Vrijheid* (La cultura de la libertad), trans. Westra and Sabarte Belacortu, Amsterdam: Meulenhoff.

Lowery, S. and De Fleur, M. L. (1983) *Milestones in Mass Communication Research: Media Effects*, New York: Longman.

Luckham, B. (1990) 'Literalität, Lesen und die Wissenschaft in Grossbritannien', in A. Brinkmann, A. Botte, B. Franzmann, H. Kreibich and R. Zitzlsperger (eds) (1990) *Lesen im internationalen Vergleich, Ein Forschungsgutachten der Stiftung Lesen für das Bundesministerium für Bildung und Wiseenschaft* Teil 1, Mainz: Stiftung Lesen.

Maas, I., Verhoeff, R. and Ganzeboom, H. (1990) *Podiumkunsten en Publiek*, Rijswijk: Ministerie van WVC.

McLuhan, M. (1964) *Understanding Media: The Extensions of Man*, New York: McGraw-Hill.

Man, H. de (1933) *De Socialistische Idee*, Antwerp/Amsterdam: Standaard Wetenschappelijke Uitgeverij, 1975.

Michielse, H. C. M. (1980) *Socialistische Vorming: het Instituut voor Arbeidersontwikkeling (1924–1940) en het Vormings-en Scholingswerk van de Nederlandse Sociaal-demokratie Sinds 1900* (dissertation), Nijmegen: SUN.

Mijnhardt, W. W. (1990) 'Sociabiliteit en cultuurparticipatie in de achttiende en vroege negentiende eeuw', in M. G. Westen (ed.) *Met den Tooverstaf van Ware Kunst: Cultuurspreiding en Cultuuroverdracht in Historisch Perspectief*, Leiden: Martinus Nijhoff.

Mooij, J. J. A. (1987) *De Wereld der Waarden: Essays over Cultuur en Samenleving*, Amsterdam: Meulenhoff.

Morrison, W. and West, E. (1986) 'Child exposure to the performing arts: the implications for adult demand', *Journal of Cultural Economics* 10: no. 1.

Mulcahy, K. V. (1987) 'Government and the arts in the United States', in M. C. Cummings and R. S. Katz (eds) *The Patron State: Government and the Arts in Europe, North America and Japan*, New York: Oxford University Press.

Myerscough, J., Aanderaa, J., Izat, A. and Marrey, J-C. (1989) *National Cultural Policy in Sweden*, National Cultural Policy Reviews Programme, Report of a European group of experts, Strasbourg: Council of Europe.

—— (1994) *National Cultural Policy in the Netherlands*, National Cultural Policy Reviews Programme, Report of a European group of experts, Strasbourg: Council of Europe.

Nederlandse OmroepStichting (NOS) (1990) *De Televisie als Medium tot Verhoging van Cultuurparticipatie*, Hilversum.

Ong, W. J. (1982) *Orality and Literacy: the Technologizing of the World*, London/New York: Routledge.

Oostwoud Wijdenes, J. (1989) 'Onderzoek van kunstzinnige vorming in het basisonderwijs', *Kunsten and Educatie* 2: no. 3.

Pick, J. (1988) *The Arts in a State: a Study of Government Arts Policies from Ancient Greece to the Present*, Bristol: Bristol Classical Press.

Policy Studies Institute (PSI) *Cultural Trends*, London.

Postman, N. (1985) *Amusing Ourselves to Death: Public Discourse in the Age of Show Business*, Harmondsworth: Penguin Books.

Prins, H. (1983) 'De notie "kwaliteit" in cultuurbeleid en bibliotheekbeleid', *Bibliotheek en Samenleving* no. 9.

Ranshuysen, L. and Ganzeboom, H. (1993) *Cultuureducatie en Cultuurparticipatie: Opzet en Effecten van de Kunstkijkuren en de Muziekluisterlessen in het Amsterdams Primair Onderwijs*, Rijswijk: Ministerie van WVC.

Ridley, F. F. (1987) 'Tradition, change and crisis in Great Britain', in M. C. Cummings and R. S. Katz (eds) *The Patron State: Government and the Arts in Europe, North America and Japan*, New York: Oxford University Press.

Robinson, J. P., Keegan, C. A., Hanford, T. and Triplett, T. A. (1986) *Public Participation in the Arts: Final Report on the 1985 Survey* (vol. 1), Overall Project Report, Washington: National Endowment for the Arts.

Schneider, M. (1993) *La Comédie de la Culture*, Paris: Edition du Seuil.

Schor, J. B. (1991) *The Overworked American: the Unexpected Decline of Leisure*, New York: Basic Books.

Schuyt, C. J. M. (1992) *De Zittende Klasse*, Amsterdam: Uitgeverij Balans.

Skok, V. (1991) 'Summary of the discussion in Moscow', in A. J. Wiesand et al. (eds) *Participation in Cultural Life: Papers Presented to the European Round Table on Cultural Research*, Bonn: Archiv für Kulturpolitik.

Smith, A. (ed.) (1979) *Television and Political Life: Studies in Six European Countries*, London: Macmillan.

Sociaal en Cultureel Planbureau (SCP) (1986a) *Advies Cultuurwetgeving: Cultuurbeleid in Historisch, Beleidsanalytisch en Juridisch perspectief* (Study no. 5), Rijswijk: SCP.

—— (1986b) *Sociaal en Cultureel Rapport*, Rijswijk: Staatsuitgeverij.

—— (1988) *Sociaal en Cultureel Rapport*, Rijswijk: Samson.

—— (1990) *Sociaal en Cultureel Rapport*, Rijswijk: VUGA.

—— (1992) *Sociaal en Cultureel Rapport*, Rijswijk: VUGA.

—— (1994) *Sociaal en Cultureel Rapport*, Rijswijk: VUGA.

Stedman, L. C., Tinsley, K. and Kaestle, C. F. (1991) 'Literacy as a consumer activity', in C. F. Kaestle et al. (eds) *Literacy in the United States: Readers and Reading since 1880*, New Haven/London: Yale University Press.

Steiner, G. (1967) *Language and Silence: Essays 1958–1966*, London: Faber and Faber.

Swaan, A. de (1985) *Kwaliteit is Klasse: de Sociale Wording en Werking van het Cultureel Smaakverschil*, Amsterdam: Bert Bakker.

Swedish Ministry of Education and Cultural Affairs (1989) *Swedish State Cultural Policy – Objectives, Measures and Results*, National Cultural Policy Reviews Programme, National Report, Stockholm/Strasbourg: Council of Europe.

Temme, J. E. V. (1988) 'Sociaal-psychologische determinanten van het (niet) deelnemen aan culturele activiteiten', in H. van Dulken, A. Köbben and T. Pronk (eds) *In ons Diaconale Land: Opstellen over Cultuurspreiding*, Amsterdam: Boekmanstichting/Van Gennep.

Tromp, B. (1994) 'Obiter Dicta 12', *Maatstaf*, 42: no. 2.

Uyl, J. den, Vos, H., Goes van Naters, M. van de, Idenburg, Ph. J., Jong, J. F. de and K. Vorrink (1951) *De Weg naar Vrijheid een Socialistisch Perspectief; Rapport van de Plancommissie van de Partij van de Arbeid*, Amsterdam: De Arbeiderspers.

Van Evra, J. (1990) *Television and Child Development*, Hillsdale: Lawrence Erlbaum.

Veenhoven, R. (1984) *Conditions of Happiness* (dissertation), Rotterdam: Erasmus University.

Veld-Langeveld, H. M. in 't (1961) 'De sociale cultuurspreiding', in A. N. J. den Hollander, E. W. Hofstee, J. A. A. van Doorn and E. V. W. Vercruysse (eds) *Drift en Koers: een Halve Eeuw Sociale Verandering in Nederland*, Assen: Van Gorcum, 1968.

Verdaasdonk, H. (1989) *De Vluchtigheid van Literatuur: het Verwerven van Boeken als Vorm van Cultureel Gedrag*, Amsterdam: Bert Bakker.

—— (1990) 'De sociologie van het boek', *Boekmancahier, Kwartaalschrift over kunst, onderzoek en beleid* 2: no. 3.

Verdaasdonk, H. and Rekvelt, K. (1981) 'De kunstsociologie van Pierre Bourdieu', *De Revisor* no. 3.

Vinovski, M. A. (1993) 'Early childhood education then and now', *Daedalus, Journal of the American Academy of Arts and Sciences* 122: no. 1.
Voort, T. H. A. van der (1989) *Televisie en Lezen*, Amsterdam/Lisse: Swets and Zeitlinger.
—— (1990) 'Televisie en lezen', *Massacommunicatie* 1.
Voort, T. H. A. van der and Beentjes, H. (1991) 'Televisie en de neergang van het lezen', *Comenius* 43: no. 3.
Waal, M. de (1989) *Daar Ga Je Toch Niet Heen? Een Oriënterende Studie over Jongeren en de Gevestigde Kunst*, Amsterdam: Raad voor het Jeugdbeleid/Boekmanstichting.
Wangermée, R. (1991) *Cultural Policy in France*, European Programme for the Appraisal of Cultural Policies, Report by the panel of European experts, Strasbourg: Council of Europe.
Welters, L. A. and Eykman, C. (1976) *Geld voor Kunstkopers*, Amsterdam: Boekmanstichting.
—— (1978) *Huren van Kunst: het Gebruik van Uitleencentra*, Rijswijk: Ministerie van CRM.
Welzijn, Volksgezondheid en Cultuur, Ministerie van (WVC) (1985) *Notitie Cultuurbeleid*, Rijswijk/Den Haag: WVC.
—— (1988) *Plan voor het Kunstbeleid 1988–1992*, Rijswijk/Den Haag: WVC.
—— (1990) *Letterenbrief*, Rijswijk/Den Haag: WVC.
—— (1992) *Investeren in Cultuur, Nota Cultuurbeleid 1993–1996*, Den Haag: SDU Uitgeverij.
—— (1993) *Cultural Policy in the Netherlands*, European Programme for the Appraisal of Cultural Policies, National report, Rijswijk: Council of Europe.
Welzijn, Volksgezondheid en Cultuur, Ministerie van (WVC) and Intomart Qualitatief (1989) *Cultuurparticipatie: een Onderzoek naar Cultuurdeelname van de Nederlandse Bevolking*, Rijswijk.
Westen, M. G. (1990) 'Cultuurspreiding en onderscheid naar kwaliteit', in M. G. Westen (ed.) *Met den Tooverstaf van Ware Kunst: Cultuurspreiding en Cultuuroverdracht in Historisch Perspectief*, Leiden: Martinus Nijhoff.
Wiesand, A. J. and Söndermann, M. (1992) *Kultur ohne Publikum?* Bonn: Zentrum für Kulturforschung.
Wiesand, A. J., Müller, M., Meuffels, A. and Euler, J. (eds) (1991) *Participation in Cultural Life: Papers Presented to the European Round Table on Cultural Research*, Bonn: Archiv für Kulturpolitik.
Williams, R. (1961) *The Long Revolution*, Harmondsworth: Penguin, 1984.
—— (1981) *Culture*, London: Fontana, 1983.
Willis, P. (1990) *Moving Culture: an Enquiry into the Cultural Activities of Young People*, London: Calouste Gulbenkian Foundation.
Wippler, R. (1968) *Sociale Determinanten van Vrijetijdsgedrag*, Assen: Van Gorcum.
Zuilen, D. van (1989) 'Cultuurdeelname van jongeren in Nederland: een cultuurpedagogisch perspectief', *Boekmancahier, Kwartaalschrift over kunst, onderzoek en beleid*, 1: no. 2.

Index of names

Subject index

ability 89
abnormal times 144
absolutism 20
abstract conception 106–7
acceptability 173, 273
acculturation 136, 156
action 50, 61, 68, 71, 72, 81, 169, 282, 288
active theoretical rationality 76–7, 124, 157, 171, 178
aesthetics 249, 254, 268
alienation 148
alternatives 148–9, 151, 154–5, 157, 178, 274
amateur art performance 226–7, 270–1, 292
anthropology 257–8
architecture 271–2
art museums 209, 224
art/s 190–1, 200; community 228, 230; as culture 227–9; and education 233, 264–6, 293, 295; quality of 241, 261–2; and the state 205–8; and subsidies 251–2, 269; *see also* cultural dissemination; cultural participation; cultural policy
atomism 92, 107–10, 134
autarchy 75
authenticity 62–4, 65, 78, 80, 111, 247, 252, 260–2, 282
authority 32, 77, 186, 250
autonomy 11, 19, 28–7, 46–9, 63, 66, 103–4, 109, 111, 112, 114, 124, 126, 134, 142, 147, 150, 152–3, 157, 178–9, 181, 155, 188, 189–93, 195–201, 243, 257, 267, 274, 289; paternalism as guarantee of 168–70; requirements for 71–84

behaviour 15, 164
Bildung 189–90, 191, 289; *see also* civilization
bourgeois culture 189, 243, 254, 259–62
broadmindedness 75

capacities 95, 102, 114
capitalism 34, 42
categories 16
choice 18, 19, 31, 70–1, 92, 109, 117, 122, 124–5, 128, 133, 142, 147–9, 155, 157, 164, 168, 170, 181, 183–4, 187, 193, 195–6, 199, 278, 282, 287, 289; *see also* decision-making
civilization 190, 275–6, 289; *see also* *Bildung*
class 99, 101, 177
coercion 24, 28–9, 50, 67, 111, 134–5, 156, 158–9, 162, 168, 170, 172, 187, 188, 285, 288; and conscious self 69; explicit 68; and non-conscious self 69; superhuman 42–3
cognitive qualities 41, 77, 81, 82, 144, 218, 221, 265
coherence 9, 10
collective good 199
common sense 132–5, 173, 187, 275
communication 21, 219–21, 265
community 14, 46, 92, 93, 110–12, 122–3, 127, 131
conative qualities 58, 77, 81
concentration camps 74–5
concept 6–7, 11, 47–9, 87, 277, 279, 283
conception 87, 88, 283
concrete psychological-intentionalist model 68
conditions of freedom 94–103, 181–2; negative/positive 116–18; right to 130–1